Dr Paul Pearsall is Director of a Clinic at Sinai Hospital, Detroit, where he chose the couples included in this book from the thousands he has treated over the past seventeen years. He is also Director of Education at the world-famous Kinsey Institute for Research in Sex, Gender and Reproduction.

He is a lecturer at Henry Ford College, Wayne State University Medical School. He also lectures widely, making numerous TV appearances, and has been working in the new field of studying body/mind links for the past fourteen years.

D1337756

Also by Dr Paul Pearsall

SUPERIMMUNITY
Master Your Emotions and Improve Your Health

DR PAUL PEARSALL

Super Marital Sex

Loving for Life

Futura

A **Futura** Book

Copyright © Paul Pearsall, PhD 1987

First published in Great Britain in 1988
by Ebury Press

This edition published in 1989
by Futura Publications, a Division of
Macdonald & Co (Publishers) Ltd
London & Sydney

Medical Disclaimer
Sexual health cannot be separated from physical
health. The first step in any wellness program is a
visit to a trusted physician to work with you as a
partner in developing a plan for total fitness. Some
sexual problems relate to medical problems, and these
are most effectively treated at their earliest stages.
Never be afraid to discuss sexuality with your doctor.

ISBN 0 7088 4186 4

Printed and bound in Great Britain by
Collins, Glasgow

Futura Publications
A Division of
Macdonald & Co (Publishers) Ltd
66–73 Shoe Lane
London EC4P 4AB

A member of Maxwell Pergamon Publishing Corporation plc

For my wife, Celest, for a life of love

Acknowledgments

This book was made possible by the courage or the pioneers in sex research whose heresy has now become orthodoxy. Their work taught us that there can be no health without sexual health, and my clinical work and research is derived from their teaching, creativity, and documentation of the natural beauty of human sexual intimacy.

The research of Alfred Kinsey and the staff who followed him at the Kinsey Institute for Research in Sex, Gender, and Reproduction provided me with my early training in the field of sexuality. Former director of the Institute, Paul Gebhard, has been my teacher, always encouraging me to publish. June Reinisch, current director of the Institute, gave me the opportunity to join the Institute staff and has become a friend and colleague. Her scientific rigor, boundless energy, and commitment to a broad understanding of sexuality has helped me toward a more comprehensive view of sex. My colleagues and friends at the Kinsey Institute, Ruth Beasley, Stephanie Sanders, Pamela Buell, and all of the staff, demonstrate the importance of a team orientation to learning and teaching about sex.

The dignity and consistency of William Masters and Virginia Johnson and my opportunity to attend their seminars taught me the importance of verification, observation, and a systems approach to understanding human sexual response. My friend and colleague, Harold Lief, gave me guidelines for teaching my own students about the role of sexuality in health and fitness. John Money taught me years ago about the complexities of what he called individual love maps and the potential dangers of corruption of the processes that underlie human sexual development.

I heard Paul Robinson compare and contrast the trends in anti-Victorian sexology more than ten years ago at a Kinsey Summer Program, and I owe him thanks for first interesting me in the study of the assumptions underlying twentieth-century sexology. Walter Janson provided an early alternative view of sexual therapy that motivated me to consider new approaches in my own sex-therapy program.

All of these colleagues provided the basic ideas behind this book. They deserve the credit, but I assume all of the responsibility. I hope they will forgive me for any oversimplifications or errors I may have made in my attempt to provide an integration of their work with mine.

Dr. Norman Rosenzweig, chairman of the Department of Psychiatry at Sinai Hospital of Detroit, gave me the opportunity and trust to design, develop, and study new techniques for helping couples solve sexual problems. My staff in the Problems of Daily Living Clinic at Sinai Hospital have learned along with me as we worked together to help our patients discover or rediscover sexual intimacy. My secretary, Ellen Schlafer, has long been the loyal guardian of whatever sanity I have maintained.

My editor, Susan Schwartz, has provided the understanding, support, patience, courage, time, and careful multiple reviews of the manuscript that made this book a reality. She has become a valued friend in the process. My agent and friend, Susan Cohen, continues to provide encouragement, hope, trust, caring, tolerance, and a creativity that allows me to grow.

The memory of my father, Frank, gives me a love that is nurtured and made to flourish daily by my mother, Carol, my brother Dennis, my wife, Celest, and my sons, Roger and Scott. There would be no book, no me, without them.

Paul Pearsall, Ph.D.
February 1987

Contents

Chapter Seven
Why Wives Have Too Many Orgasms: Myths and Facts About Wives' Sexuality   163

Chapter Eight
Owning and Operating Your Own Sex Clinic   191

PART THREE
Living, Learning, Teaching, and Protecting Super Marital Sex

Chapter Twelve
Sexual Inheritance: Leaving Your Children
Something to Love By 323

Introduction

Their lean, firm bodies glistened as they swayed in perfect unison. She was dressed in black stockings and wore a red collar around her neck. She groaned, running her tongue over her lower lip. He grimaced, as if struggling to keep control of his building passion. They moved smoothly from posture to posture, with the effortless flow of ballet dancers. The tension showed in his muscles, her groans turned to screams, and they convulsed in perfectly timed mutual orgasm.

The married couple watched this scene on their VCR, silhouetted on the bedroom wall by the light from the television screen. The wife had summoned every ounce of courage to rent this tape, and she watched with her husband, both of them silent, passive, uninvolved observers, separately experiencing what they assumed was "the way it should be." Certainly, this movie was the standard against which this couple and thousands of others compare their own intimate relationships.

Actually, the couple could only watch and assume that the man and woman on the screen were groaning or screaming. The sound on the television had been turned off for fear the children sleeping in the next room might hear. They had learned long ago to turn their own volume off during their sexual relationships for the same reason. They had even learned a form of "restricted movement intercourse," a sexual pantomime that muted the squeaks of the bed and their own passion as well.

The couple on the screen began again. "They're going to do it one more time. Do you believe that? They're going to do it again." The wife was amazed at the couple's stamina, envious of their freedom from inhibition even in front of the camera. She wondered about her husband's reaction to all of this.

She turned to him when he failed to respond. She heard only the response that too often before had stifled her arousal. Her husband was snoring. He had been more tired than usual lately, even experiencing some slight chest pains that he planned to tell the doctor about once his schedule allowed. One of his gasps was so loud that the cat jumped from the end of the bed and fled.

Super sex is *not* what this couple saw on the screen. What they watched was an act, a pandering, a distortion, a circus exaggeration of physiological potential devised through camera tricks and deception. It was not real. Sex in marriage is real, can far exceed even the exaggeration of this pornographic farce, and can be achieved by any married couple willing to unlearn years of wrong or incomplete information to begin an entirely new way of developing sexually as a couple.

Super marital sex is the most erotic, intense, fulfilling experience any human being can have. Anonymous sex with multiple partners pales by comparison, an empty imitation of the fulfillment of a sexuality of intimacy and commitment to one person for life, a "fourth perspective" based on an entirely different model of sexual functioning, physiology, and interaction between husband and wife.

Super Marital Sex: Loving for Life will teach you about a different view of orgasm, one free of the genital limitations placed upon it by interpretations of early sex research. You will learn about the "posture of the future," an entirely new way of having intercourse that can last as long as the couple desires, requires absolutely no genital response, yet can lead to the most intense of "new" orgasms: "psychasms," related to communication between husband and wife that goes beyond words or physical maneuvers. You will learn that most men may never have realized the range of their orgasmic experience, most women are trying to have too many orgasms, and neither gender may be having "psychasms." There is an entirely new and more effective way to teach your children about this fourth perspective on sexuality, which replaces the failing current model of sex education with a new love education.

In Part One, you will learn about the ways in which the American marriage has been "desexualized" by a genital focus that emerged from the early perspectives and research on human sexuality. You will read about the sexual system and take tests that will help you understand your own marital interaction. You will learn about love maps, how they are "drawn" and can be redrawn, and how they affect your marriage. You will learn about "super love," a love that transcends romanticized, eroticized, genitalized sex for a marital experience of intimacy that far exceeds what is possible in any less committed relationship.

Part Two presents the fourth perspective of sexuality that serves as a focus for super marriage and compares this orientation with the first three perspectives that have dominated our sexual views and attitudes. I developed this fourth perspective from my work with one thousand couples, including my personal interviews with each husband and wife, the couple together, treatment sessions for sexual problems, and five-year follow-up interviews. My systems orientation to sexuality evolved through my work with these and other couples, and the new model of sexual response you will read about in Part Two is derived from the couples' subjective reports of their sexual interaction. Part Two concludes with specific recommendations for your own program for super marital sex, for setting up and operating your own super marital sex clinic.

Part Three presents the questions most often asked by the couples in treatment, and illustrates the super marital sex perspective. You will read in Part Three about the relationship between sex and problems of daily living, loving in the context of marital living, and loving and being sexual at times of illness and transitional life crises. It concludes with a sexual curriculum for intimacy, a new intimacy that offers not only sexual joy but sex for total wellness and life happiness.

Early in 1971, I started the Problems of Daily Living Clinic at Sinai Hospital of Detroit. As director of that clinic, I was able to design and research new clinical programs at a major metropolitan hospital affiliated with the Wayne State University Medical School. The thousand couples and all of the quoted material comes from my work in this clinic dedicated to preventing more serious psychiatric problems by offering professional and short-term help with transitional life crises.

As I designed the sexual-therapy dimension of the clinic, I turned to the pioneers in sexual research and treatment for guidance. I first attended training seminars at the Masters and Johnson Institute in St. Louis and at the Kinsey Institute for Research in Sex, Gender, and Reproduction at Indiana University. I later directed educational programs for the Kinsey Institute, where I am now director of professional education. The ethical, sensitive, careful, scientific orientation of both of these programs, their founders, and current staffs served as inspiration for my program based on sexual wellness.

I am primarily a clinician and educator. I had no research funds, so I decided to keep careful records of all the early treatment sessions and report these results after a thousand couples completed the entire program through five-year follow-up. There were no control groups, and this was not designed to be a scientific study or a sociological survey. The couples came from middle- to upper-middle-class backgrounds and are of course a self-selected group willing to seek help in an intimate area of their life. Their experience does not represent the variance of human sexual experience. This is a report of what happened for these two thousand husbands and wives as they learned a new way to relate sexually. It is a set of selected quotes supporting the possibility of extending the perspectives on sexuality established by the courage of Havelock Ellis, Alfred Kinsey, William Masters, and Virginia Johnson.

I was interested in how the couples felt, their interactive systems, what happened for the husbands and wives when a different view of sexual health was assumed and practiced in marriage. I started to learn, to help improve the clinic program, to monitor the effect of a systems approach to sexual problems. This book shares what I learned.

The rules with which I began my project related to my training as an educational and clinical psychologist specializing in short-term, cognitive behavioral treatment and a holistic view of wellness. As with the early three perspectives, I bring my own biases to my approach to sexuality, a fourth perspective of systems theory added to the earlier three perspectives with their respective theological, sociological, physical, and clinical emphases.

1. My report will include only information that was audio-taped. Tapes will be number-coded for protection of confidentiality. My data, then, is what couples said, not what I watched them do. It is what couples said over their five-year treatment program, three to four months of which were regular visits followed by check-in sessions up to five years. To my knowledge, this if the first thousand-couple five-year follow-up report on a systems sexual therapy model. It is not a test of the treatment technique, but a report of experiences. The tapes continue to be used by students and staff for var-

ious research projects done and published from the more traditional research formats.

2. I will report on the first thousand couples who complete treatment together to the five-year period. I will report on those couples I saw myself, not the hundreds of other couples seen by my staff. The bias is all mine, with an intentional clinical bias favoring systems theory. The selection criterion was only the first thousand to finish the whole program and all of its steps.

3. My report will include as many direct quotes as possible. It required several years to collect and organize the quotes to document the perspective I am presenting, but each point made in this report is accompanied by the actual words of the couples. Of course, it is my bias that determined their selection, and I am trying to prove my point about sexual marital systems, not do a study.

4. I will attempt to present a final report in a form that couples can use. I will include the actual tests used and write the report in a "how to do it" format. While the work of the earlier researchers was not meant to be instructional, it was used that way by a society eager to learn about sex. I intentionally organized this report into an instructional program for super marital sex, in fact, the same program I had offered the thousand couples. I have included humor, sadness, and the range of couples' emotions. I hope you will cry a little, laugh a little, and learn to share a new view of marital sex.

5. I will include reports only from marriages. I wanted to present a project for marital couples confronting pressures in an era of choice, to take a position that sex in marriage is potentially more fulfilling than any other form of sex. This is a blatant value statement and this book is about how a thousand couples and more than fifteen thousand interviews reflected this orientation.

6. I will include the new physics orientation that evolved during the later sixties and early seventies, attempting to relate my work with systems with work on the world system. The systems approach was the origin of the term "super" marital sex. Super in this context refers to transcendence, to going beyond, to relating by the laws of the universe, not just the dictates of genital and reproductive functions.

7. I will include a sexual-response model that stressed the similarity between male and female, that views penis-in-vagina intercourse as necessary only for conception, not for sexual fulfillment. I wanted to know what would happen if a degenitalized focus was

used to help people burdened by the emphasis of the early perspectives that stressed penile insertion, timing, and physical orgasm. I saw no reason why the first views of how sex was or ought to be should be the only views.

Appendix I to this book summarizes some of the characteristics of the thousand couples, but this is not a statistical report. I have no idea what most people really do in the privacy of their own sexual intimacy. I suspect nobody knows. I only hope that my report adds another way of thinking about the problems and joys of marital sex. I am a clinician and teacher, not a researcher. My time is spent talking with and learning from my patients while they experience a different way of looking at sexuality. Sometimes we must try to perceive those things that cannot be seen, to help people discover the mysteries and potentials within themselves, and then get out of their way.

I hope my colleagues will scrutinize my hypotheses, guesses, and hopes more than my method. I hope you will take the tests and try the opportunities for super marital sex to develop your own views of your own special intimacy. Science is how other people see things. Your own contemplation of new ideas relates to how you see things. Both are important, and my book focuses on the latter.

I return to the marital bedroom of the couple watching their sex videotape. Hours had passed, and the husband was awakened by what sounded like a low, quiet laugh. He raised his head from deep inside his pillow to search through the darkness for the red numbers on his bedside clock. He was disoriented and could not remember falling asleep, even going to bed. Red numbers pulsed "3:40 A.M." Who would be laughing at 3:40 A.M.?

He lowered his head again. I must be hearing things, he thought. Now he felt the bed moving ever so slightly. He looked over his shoulder and saw his wife's shoulder moving up and down beneath her covers. He reached to touch her, but she did not respond.

"Are you okay?" he asked.

She threw her covers aside, stood beside the bed, and turned on the light. His eyes hurt and would not focus clearly. He rubbed them, and saw his wife standing in garter belt, black nylon stockings, high heels, a black bra with holes for the nipples, and a red collar around her neck. As strange as she appeared to him, and as tired and shocked as he was, he seemed to recognize this costume. He had seen it recently.

Tears traced two direct paths through the same caked-on makeup that now stained her moist pillow. "Am I okay?" she cried. "You tell me if I'm okay. I've been lying here dressed just like that tramp in that porno tape. I went and stood the embarrassment of getting the tape, put it on, and you fell asleep. I feel like some terrible sad sex clown. Look, just look at what has happened to our sex life."

She reached to unfasten the collar, but was too shaken to find the clasp. She tore it from her neck, and sat again on the side of the bed. "We bought every book, watched every tape, saw every talk show, and we do everything you can think of. Just forget it. Forget it. It's hopeless."

The wife was wrong. You will meet this couple again later in this book. They found their own super marital sex, and so can you. It is not found in sociological reports, clinical observation, or the advice of "sexperts" embracing only the first three perspectives. It is found from within, within yourself and your marriage. It is the purpose of this book to help you look in instead of out, to look at sexual intimacy in marriage in a different way. Please open up and enter in.

PART ONE

Super Systems and Super Love

We often think that when we have completed our study of "one" we know all about "two," because "two" is "one and one." We forget that we still have to make a study of "and."

A. EDDINGTON

Only connect! Personal relations are the important thing for ever and ever. . . .

E. M. FORSTER

When you spend your life building walls instead of bridges, trying to find yourself instead of someone else to love with, instead of allowing yourself to be discovered, you end up very, very, lonely.

HUSBAND

If you want to read about love and marriage, you've got to buy two separate books.

ALAN KING

Alan King is wrong. The next four chapters are about a journey, a journey into super marital sex that demonstrates that love, marriage, and sex are a dynamic combination offering an opportunity for personal fulfillment and wellness. You will discover during this journey that our society has taken meaning and intimacy out of sexuality and replaced it with a mechanical, time limited orientation. You will discover, as stated by Drs. Herant Katchadourian and

Donald Lunde, that "sexuality is not a wild horse that must be tamed and then exercised periodically." You will discover that sex is the most important way to join with someone, and in so doing, become a part of the entire universe. You will learn that the rules of the universe and the stars are the same rules that have been forgotten in the sexual revolution. You will discover how you learned to love, your loving style, and that, as Dr. Sarah Cirese writes, "Love is something we create, beginning with a plausible candidate and appropriate conditions." You will learn how to create those conditions and be introduced to a super marital system, the only system that provides the appropriate conditions for super love and super sex where the "super" means beyond the mechanical and measurable and in flow with the rules of life and living. Part One is about the design and reading of love maps and ways to join two maps for a new intimate way of traveling, a treasure map for super marital sex.

CHAPTER ONE

🌺🌺🌺

The Desexualization of the American Marriage

It's funny how they say that you "get married." I mean, you really don't "get it," you have to learn to do it. And learning to do it has been the most difficult thing I have ever tried to do in my life. We never did learn the sex part.

WIFE

Super Marital Sex Rule: Sex in marriage is not something you get or do, it is how the marriage is and the shared dreams of how it will be. It is caring about and attending to each other more than caring about and attending to the lawn, the kids, the job, the car, and the leaky sink. Sex is more a matter of priorities than genitals.

Crashing Carts and Reborn Hearts: Scaring Life into a Marriage

"Hurry!" screamed the wife. "My God, can't you hurry?" They could not hear her screams, but the medical team could see her frantic gestures as they pushed the life-saving cart toward her husband's hospital room.

The husband and wife had lived together for years. They had raised children, cats, assorted rodents, developed their careers, and now did daily battle in the wars of their children's adolescence. They had faced many struggles and pressures, even tried to rekindle the failing sexual energy in their marriage, but they had never considered the possibility of a premature end to their life together.

"Oh God! Please hurry!" she yelled one more time before turning to scan the monitor at her husband's bedside for any sign of life. She was praying for their marriage, just one more chance to be with him, to love and hold him. Perhaps too late, she had been startled into the realization that her marriage was the only thing that meant anything. The cards and flowers from friends and colleagues that filled the room seemed now to be reminders of the distractions that always seemed to dominate, to rob the time this husband and wife had for one another. And now, there would be no time left.

As if to shout down the hopeless, whistling drone of the monitor, she screamed at her unconscious husband. "Carl! Carl! They're coming, darling. Hold on, damn you, hold on!"

The medical team resembled a group of urgently serious clowns trying to control their wagon of magic tricks. But now the wagon began to control them, just as this wife's life had controlled her. The wife, doctors, nurses, other patients, and visitors all stopped to watch as the cart first wobbled, then smashed on its side on the tile floor, scattering its cargo.

After the crash, the hospital was silent. The wife felt more alone than ever before, too late in her prayers for a second chance to love, really love, her husband and to love, really love, her marriage.

The stillness of despair and hopelessness was broken by a faint beeping sound. The wife's eyes caught those of one of the nurses. In an unspoken language, these two strangers shared the hope that this crisis was transforming itself into a miracle.

The wife turned slowly toward the monitor, afraid that any sudden movement might frighten away the uncertain sign of life. She watched as the monitor first showed sharp, large curves followed by the steady peaks and valleys. Even her untrained eyes knew those blips indicated that life had returned to her husband. She stood motionless, chilled, as the screen of the monitor blurred through the tears in her eyes.

The wife was startled to awareness by the medical team now crowding toward her husband. The frantic work on the doctors and nurses seemed more cultural right than necessary intervention, a formal celebration of the fact that her husband's heart and their marriage had been scared back to life by the crash of the cart. Her husband would survive in spite of, perhaps because of, this strange turn of events.

Stop. Before you read further about this couple's second chance at marriage, claim your own second chance for your marriage. Don't wait until it's too late. Go and get your spouse, call her or him at work, summon him or her from the lawn work, from cleaning the basement or repairing the faucet that will always leak anyway, and take his or her hand. Hold on now while you can, and ask each other these questions. "Why are we married? What are 'we' for anyway?" You got married, now how about really being married? Reread this little story about the couple in the hospital and talk about your own marital priority. Don't wait. Start now. Plan to read and share this book together. I have seen hundreds of couples who have waited too long, who have missed their chance for a super marriage. Please don't miss yours.

On Second Chances
Before the End of the First

> You know, if we could have raised our first child as if he were our second, things would have been much better, for him and for us. Maybe we should pretend this is our second marriage. Why don't we save the hassle and money of a divorce and just start our second marriage now? We've already met anyway, and we have a head start on our problems. Why start new ones with someone else? Okay. I declare us divorced and remarried. This is our last chance. We have to stop acting like this is some sort of stupid rehearsal that doesn't really matter. We have to stop acting like we are kids in a fire drill. Attention. Attention. This is not a test. I repeat, this is not just a test.
>
> WIFE

Super Marital Sex Rule: Super marital sex depends on remembering that there will never be a better time than now to enhance the sexuality, the intimacy, of your marriage. We behave as if we can fix things later, get to them later, do much better later when there is more time. No excuse can change the fact that now is the best time, the only time to join together for a more intimate marriage.

We watched together as the cleanup of the crash site continued. I had been called by the medical team to talk with the wife. "I'm more worried about her than I am about her husband," reported the doctor. "She's just sitting there looking off into space."

Her eyes never left the cleanup work as she talked. "Another chance. I can't believe it. Another chance." With determination and confidence more than sadness or shock, she continued. "I swear to you that I will never, ever take him, take us, for granted again. I almost lost him, lost everything. I swear to you I'll never let us forget us again. We will be first, not some afterthought, some social convenience, a pair of people who happen to be together."

Her gaze rose from the pile of clutter to my eyes. She placed a hand on each of my shoulders, looked directly at me, and seemed to appoint me clergyperson, notary public, and certified witness to her personal vow. "Listen. Do you believe me? Do you? I will devote every cell of my body to us. Do you believe me?"

She did not expect an answer, for her vow was to herself and to her husband and their marriage. Her eyes left mine to focus over my shoulder to the gurney being pushed toward us. She rose to embrace her husband, and they cried silently together. "Another chance, darling, another chance." They sobbed and held each other tightly.

Until this wonderfully terrible moment in their lives, this husband and wife had forgotten their marriage. They had forgotten to share a loving-together, not just a living-together. They had forgotten to touch one another, to nurture the sexuality and intimacy within their relationship. Don't let this happen to your marriage. Let this book serve as a starting point for a recommitment to intimacy, a second chance before your first chance expires.

Extramarital Sex vs. Super Marital Sex

> If it's candles and music instead of tuna fish and potato chips on paper plates, it probably means there will be some sex that night. We like to keep up the national average, you know. Do our share for the sex revolution and the age of enlightenment. Two and one half times per week, rain or shine. Well, a little more often when it rains, because we can't work outside.
>
> HUSBAND

Super Marital Sex Rule: Super marital sex depends on sexualizing the entire marriage, not separating sex into a category of obligatory marital duty, afterthought, or a different "part" of the marriage. The "super" in super marital sex refers to "whole," to making intimacy a way of living and being together, not something you do sometimes. There are more spouses having affairs within their marriage than outside of them, separating marital sex from marital love, resulting in a form of "extramarital" sex rather than an "intramarital intimacy."

Extramarital sex has traditionally been viewed as adultery, marriage partners having sex with a person other than their spouse. It has received good press and is statistically quite popular. More than 70 percent of husbands and 40 percent of women report sex outside their marriage. In my sample of 1,000, the number was 76 percent of the men and 47 percent of the women. Extramarital sex is variously described as forbidden, sinful, destructive, dishonest, and dangerous by some persons and by others as constructive, evolutionarily natural, energizing, fun, and somehow, if done "right," preventive of divorce and marital problems by providing "outside" stimulation.

In the thousand couples, the 760 men and 470 women who reported sex outside of their marriage were always in a marital relationship in which at least one of the partners was less than satisfied with the intimacy of the marriage. There was no evidence in my sample, and there is no evidence in anyone else's data, that extramarital sex enhances marital sex. My work with couples indicates that at the very least, extramarital sex is distracting from the effort and time necessary to develop and enjoy super marital sex.

The reasons for extramarital sex are as varied as the people who engage in it. No research has ever told us why people do it. I suggest, however, that one reason is that extramarital sex has enjoyed a sexual monopoly. It gets most of the attention and offers a cafeteria of descriptions guaranteed to meet some appetite. It is seen as so much fun that it is resisted only by control, awareness and religious punishment, self-denial, and acceptance of the myth of the more moral but less intense sexuality of marriage. Seldom do you read that sex in marriage is not only better than sex outside of marriage, but that extramarital sex falls far short of the intimacy and sexual fulfillment available within marriage. You will learn throughout this book that no form of extramarital sex can compete with super marital sex, and once this lesson is learned, spouses having affairs may begin cheating on their "lovers," and having "intramarital" sex with their husband or wife.

We live in a society in which it is much easier to look "out" than "in," to seek variety when we fail to find intensity. Super marital sex is developed not by variety, adventure, mystery, and the "affairizing" of marriage, but by learning an entirely new orientation to sexuality and its relationship to lasting love. There are many old lessons that will have to be unlearned, and a new perspective on sexuality will have to be developed. This is the purpose of this book. Follow along with each chapter and you will see that extramarital sex doesn't stand a chance against super marital sex.

Two Types of Extramarital Sex

> I have tried for years to make our marriage one long affair. Well, you know what? She had ended up having an affair all right, but not with me.
>
> HUSBAND

Super Marital Sex Rule: Never try to make your marriage an affair. Affairs are short, intense, immature imitations of love that is only possible in lasting, mature relationships. Intensity, newness, and variety are culturally learned values that cannot compete with the predictability, sameness, and comfort of super marital sex. We must unlearn the negative connotations of these last three terms.

Type I extramarital sex is sex outside of marriage. Type II extramarital sex is the attempt to make an affair out of your marriage, to use affairs as the model of true joy so that marriage must live up to the "sexpectations" of affairs. It is the attempt to put sex "outside" of day-to-day marital living, to buy the latest sex toys, sneak away on vacations, schedule candlelight dinners, and dress in the most erotic clothing. Couples trying for this extramarital sex Type II end up with "separate marital sex," a lack of closeness and trust in an effort to create a relationship within a relationship. You cannot have an affair with someone you love, but you can have super marital sex that takes place within the entire life system, not separate from it.

I offer a special invitation to single persons to join this "quest for intimacy." Legal, cultural, sociological, familial, financial commitments that accompany marriage, in our society provide a framework for formalizing the unity necessary for the super marital sex you will be reading about. There are many aspects of super marital sex, however, that apply to those persons who are not, cannot, or choose not to marry. This model offers an alternative for single, widowed and divorced persons, for anyone who desires a standard of sexual intimacy based on commitment, trust, and the potential for personal and relationship growth beyond physical closeness. I suggest that we have more to learn from prolonged intimacy evolving from within a mutually fulfilling love system than from the use of sex as a means for finding someone to love. Marrying is a healthier model for loving and sex than "mating," because it can provide for an adaptive all-inclusive style for true "living together."

I am suggesting in super marital sex a new model for intimacy, a new course objective for our culture's sex education, a new priority, a choosing of intimacy. The AIDS crisis should not frighten us into fidelity. We should celebrate the potential of fidelity, its capacity for a super sex where the super means whole, lasting, comforting, fulfilling.

The husband and wife who were given a second chance had never given their marriage a chance to grow into something very special. They had allowed their marriage to become de-eroticized. Has this happened to your marriage? Check the ways this happened to the thousand couples.

Ten Ways to Leave Your Loving: The De-Eroticization of the American Marriage

I suppose to you this will sound perverted. We have done almost everything together. We haven't missed a posture. But we never seem to experience anything together. We sleep next to each other, but not with each other. Our sex life is like masturbating, like using each other to masturbate. You might say we are the founders of the term "completing the act."

WIFE

Super Marital Sex Rule: Any part of the marriage that is ignored will disappear, and this rule is particularly true for sex. For most couples, the amount of enjoyment they derive from their sexual relationship corresponds with the amount of attention they pay to their sexual interaction. The sexual return from a marriage will usually match the intimacy investment. The following are ten areas in which the couples failed to invest appropriately or enough.

1. GENDER JUNK

Super Marital Sex Rule: Super sex depends on sex roles that evolve within the relationship and are comfortable and acceptable to both partners, not predetermined by society or limited by prior experiences, fears, and a reluctance to be and feel the way one wishes. The roles should be mutually developed, never assigned or surrendered to, and will likely change throughout the marital life cycle. Stagnant, pre-assigned sex roles will severely limit fulfillment.

> He doesn't touch. He grabs. That's men for you.
>
> WIFE

> She just cuddles. She doesn't get it on, really get down to it. She's like all women, I guess.
>
> HUSBAND

American marriage continues to struggle with the prescribed roles of man and women in our society. "I chase him until he catches me." "All women want is love, but they put up with sex." "He'll trade a little love for a lot of sex." These and other clichés were reported by the husbands and wives, and such preconceptions of role assignment severely limited the evolution of a balanced sexual interaction in marriage. It resulted in someone getting made love "to" or "for" and someone doing the "making" of love.

The original Kinsey studies of male and female sexuality indicated that marriage was often accompanied by a diminishing of orgasms for women and a turning to prostitution and affairs for men. It was as if the couples were taking part in a predestined gender dance of a sexist courtship, sexual trade-offs matched to expected roles, self-fulfilling prophecies, conceptions, maternal investment and paternal distance, inevitable decline of sexual interest, and extramarital sex primarily for the man as some form of genetic inevitabilty.

Dr. Donald Symons at the University of California at Santa Barbara suggests that women have a stronger evolutionary investment in the conceptive aspects of sexuality and that they provide the larger "mass" of procreation, the egg. Men contribute only little naked pieces of DNA with tails. He implies that men act somewhat like their sperm: quick, attacking, mobile, and low on investment. Women act out their "egg" orientation: stable, receptive, committed, and selective.

Does it have to be this way? Will men always have to contribute a little for a lot and women a lot for a little? Are we victims of some mammalian script? As one sociobiologist had suggested, are our genes wearing us? Can we break away to a more egalitarian interaction between husband and wife? If we cannot, American marriage will continue to de-eroticize, because conceptive and genetic imperatives will have been met and marriage will become a state of maintenance in the evolutionary scheme of things.

Certainly, there is little value for intimacy when human-eating animals lurked behind us as we copulated. Get together, get it on, get out, and live to copulate again. The stress of our modern world seems to create symbolic human eaters and we behave from our neurohormonal past patterns, with men as hunters and women who are kept and who raise the children. Intimacy then plays the role of providing a place for child-rearing, not for providing sexual fulfillment for the cave owners. Are we victims of this mammalian past, or do we have a choice?

There are basic biological and neurological differences between men and women. Dr. Roger Gorski, professor at the University of California at Los Angeles, has done work on the functional and structural differences between the male and female mammalian brain. Early gonadal steroids, hormones, are responsible for differences in our most important reproductive organ, our brain. But some difference does not have to mean great distance, and re-eroticizing the American marriage depends upon narrowing the gender gap, not just sociopolitically, but psycoerotically as well.

Dr. June Reinisch, Director of the Kinsey Institute for Research in Sex, Gender, and Reproduction, discusses the basic biological differences between boys and girls, but emphasizes that learning can profoundly influence the manner in which these differences are played out in daily living. Her work supports my premise that all sexuality is a system, and that, as all physicists know, everything affects everything.

Dr. Carol Nagy Jacklin studied 275 children from birth to six years of age. She visited the children and their parents repeatedly during her study and included measures of sex-steroid hormones in her work. While she found little to differentiate boys from girls early in their development, they all seemed to learn which was which quite clearly, which they were, and "how they ought to be." I maintain that we can learn to be how we want to be as well, and that we can learn roles with each other instead of in spite of each other. Super marital sex requires role creativity and adaptability, and the following chapters will teach you about changes in the sexual interaction in your marriage that will help you develop role creativity.

Dr. Carol Gilligan, in her book *In a Different Voice*, summarized the complex issue of gender roles. She suggests the same-gender caretaker experience of young girls predisposes them toward empathy through the sameness experience, an emphasis on relationship and a fear of desertion and separation. Autonomy becomes problematical for the woman who is so early, so long, and so strongly attached. The different-gender primary caretaker experience of boys results in lack of the "sameness sense," less empathy, a devaluing of relationship, and fear of commitment and loss of autonomy.

The work of Drs. Pepper Schwartz and Philip Blumstein, in their study of twelve thousand American couples of varying gender orientation, also suggests that men are eroticized and women romanticized. This pattern was present in the report of my couples as well, but the interviews revealed that men knew there was another way to be, but needed permission, help, and support in learning this "other way." Both genders needed help in stepping out of assignments and into choices.

I found a major difference in my interviews regarding eroticism and romance. It was not true that if one was less eroticized, one was more romanticized. It was also untrue that if one was less romanticized, one was more eroticized. I learned not to ask "Which are you?" in favor of "How much of each are you at what time, with whom, and why?" I found the answer depended as much on what had happened in the marriage as it did on what happened when the sperm met the egg and the genetic relay race began. Marriage provides an opportunity for role change, modification, creativity, for what I call "cross-roling," being a little of everything sometimes.

Ask yourself now how much of your marriage is dictated by "gender junk," obligatory, involuntary sex role. How much of your marriage is freedom to evolve as self with another person? One husband described his wife as "wanting only sex. She does not want to hold. She wants me on and off. She says that's how a man should want it." This wife was trapped by the gender junk that can block intimacy.

2. PATTERNED PREDICTABILITY: "IF THIS IS SATURDAY, WE'LL PROBABLY DO IT"

Super Marital Sex Rule: Super sex depends upon the development of an mutual responsibility for the erotic cycle that emerges between two persons over time. Cycles are not signs of "boredom." They evolve when persons tune in to each other. All things in life are cyclical, and super sex results from awareness of, communication about, and learning from these cycles so that changes, when necessary, can be made together and in keeping with both persons' emotional and physical needs.

> I get up. He gets up. I eat. He eats. The kids eat. He leaves. I leave. Reverse it at night. That's it. Welcome to the world of our marriage.
>
> WIFE

Our society teaches that stimulation comes from without, not within. It teaches that variety is the spice of life, and that variety is something we go "after" by seeking more and more from "out there." If we are bored, we think it is because we are not in a stimulating place. Therefore, if our marriage seems boring, if we feel bored with our partner, it must be that they have become boring or that time and overexposure have rendered them not as stimulating as someone new might be.

Until we learn that stimulation comes from within and not without, American marriage will be victim of the "sameness problem." Developmental theorists continue to preach that we must provide extensive and varied environmental stimulation for our children. Without it, they rightly assert, the brain does not develop to potential. They neglect the fact, however, that adults can generate their own stimulation by turning in, by learning to be aware of feelings, sensations, and signals. We see light with our eyes, but we perceive it with all of us that is human. What we see depends on how and who we are, on what is "in here," not what is "out there."

It is obviously counterproductive to intentionally "bore" the sexual dimension of marriage. There is such a thing as acclimation, just getting used to something and no longer reacting intensely to it. I tell my couples to pay attention to privacy, to dress and undress in private, to wear comfortable, personally pleasing clothing to bed. There is a difference between comfortable exposure and overexposure, so it is unwise to take the privilege of seeing each other nude for granted.

One of the husbands in my sample complained in a therapy session, "She just got heavy. Same old person, only a heavier version. How can I get turned on by her?"

When I responded that he was responsible for his own arousal, not merely reactive to a body image, he became angry. "Why do I need a partner, then? I can just get myself turned on."

"It's a system," I responded. "You affect her, she affects you, and so it goes. You broke the chain when you declared her the sole source of your sexual feelings. Instead of asking why she is heavier, you might ask yourself about the qualities that lead to your arousal. Are you still able to see the whole, the total person? Do you want her thinner for you, for her, or for the two of you? Are you with her in this struggle of weight, or just an appraiser of final outcome? Are you aware of her or just her body?"

"You mean like my feelings that she is the mother of my children, the person who helped me through my heart attack, the person who tolerates my immaturity, and stuff like that? Okay . . . but that's not sex," he responded, "I mean it is not really sexual or a turn-on or anything."

This husband is mistaken. Change and adaptation in marriage hinge on broadening our reactions to one another, not depending on predetermined, culturally determined standards. The stimulation comes from within the system, not from skin and bones and their respective arrangement. The question is, Does your relationship turn you on, not does someone or something turn you on. This emphasis equalizes responsibility for arousal.

If we cling to a search for newness, uniqueness, compliance by our partner to ever-changing external cultural standards of "sexiness," we miss one of the greatest opportunities that marriage provides: the familiarity of communication on levels beyond the see-and-touch world.

Take a good "look" at your marriage. Can you sense your spouse beyond the light and sound waves you receive? Does any boredom or predictability you see signal you to look within instead of without? Do you remember why you married this person in the first place? What has happened to you together, and what might happen in the future? Can you find an excitement from within the marriage itself, the combination of the two of you?

New research is showing that a marital cyclicity exists beyond the cycles of each respective partner. Dr. Phillip Sarrell at Yale University saw thirty-nine men who reported erective failure. Rather than attempting to treat their problem, he instead employed estrogen-replacement therapy with their wives and did no intervention of any type with the husbands. Thirty-one of the thirty-nine men returned to complete erective function. They reacted directly and measurably to the changes in their menopausal wives because they were intertwined with them even on a psychophysiological level. Sarrell's report is direct evidence of the system of sex within a lasting relationship, and allows speculation that psychophysiological changes in wives may equally affect their husbands.

Drs. Harold Lief and Harold Persky have done research indicating a marital hormonal cyclicity that may develop between husband and wife. We have long known that women living together begin to approximate one another's menstrual cycles, with one woman serving as the "driver," the woman to whom the other women seem to adjust their own respective cycles. Perhaps marriages, too, develop their own cyclicity, their own "marital-station," a cyclicity that can lead to becoming mutually in tune to a level not possible in less committed or shorter relationships.

Current research in the new field of psychoneuroimmunology, the study of the relationship between the brain and the immune system and our feelings, reveals that disruption of the marital bond has direct and clinically detectable impact on the immunoefficiency of each partner. It seems that immunity, like sex, is a system of interaction between people as well as cells and hormonal juices. We are well advised to look to our marriages when we look for our health.

We must not label as boredom the mutual development of sameness, the infinite ebb and flow of feelings and sexuality that takes place in marriage. Perhaps if it's Saturday and you'll probably "do it," it may be one of your mutual marital cycle days for sexuality and not a symptom of boredom at all.

3. THE PRIORITY PROBLEM: CHOICES AND LISTS

Super Marital Sex Rule: The marriage comes first. All other people and events come after the marriage. Children, parents, work, and play all benefit most by marital priority instead of marital sacrifice, because the marriage is the central unit to all other processes. The stronger the basic unit, the stronger the rest of the system. Super marital sex allows super growth of all elements related to the marriage.

I'd say we spend about ten minutes together alone per day. When we finally get in bed for the night, we are too tired to do much that takes too much time or effort. There is too much taken out of us to have anything left to put into us.

HUSBAND

If it is true that we reap what we sow, then marriages are in big trouble, for we sow very little into our relationships proportionate to what we put into our jobs and other activities. If we put as much time in our working as we allow for our loving, we would end up unemployed or bankrupt. We raise our children, go to work and work hard, help our parents, maintain our cars, paint and clean our homes, but American marriage is similar to a neglected child, a child expected somehow to take care of her- or himself. Marriage in America is underfed. We seem to be searching for intimacy, but the harvest is meager for lack of planting and nurturing.

Take the following mini-test that I gave to the thousand couples and you will see what I mean by the priority problem.

The MIMs Test (Marriage Investment Minutes)

Over a seven-day week, add the minutes you estimate you spend in the following activities:

1. Talking with your spouse with absolutely no one else around, not even the dog.   _____

2. Discussing things related only to the two of you, excluding for now the kids, your parents, work, money, or other daily activities.   _____

3. Time spent just looking at one another, not talking, doing, fixing, or fussing—just looking.   _____

4. Time spent having fun together, playing together in a non-goal-directed activity, without another couple or the kids. (Not getting ready to play, but actually in mutually enjoyable recreation.)   _____

5. Time spent during the week making love, kissing, hugging, touching in privacy without interruption. This counts for only consecutive time, not a kiss here, a hug there.   _____

6. Time spent talking about the future of the marriage. This means your future together, not retirement funds, retirement home, and insurance plans.

7. Time spent discussing world affairs, politics, issues of the day (this means actually discussing, not just one partner complaining or lecturing and the other serving as audience). _____

8. Time spent just sitting together while each of you is doing something else, such as reading, sewing, listening to music (do not count TV-watching time, which is typically mutual hypnosis, not mutual relaxation). _____

9. Time spent eating quietly together alone, with no kids or pets or phones or TV. _____

10. Time spent spiritually together, such as praying, contemplating, meditating, attending religious services as a couple. _____

TOTAL WEEKLY MIMs
MARITAL INVESTMENT MINUTES _____

To promote discussion of MIMs, I estimate that total available time for relating is a maximum of thirty hours per week, or 1,800 available MIMs. Of course, no one gets even close to that amount in our complex and "hurry illness" society, but the 1,800 available MIMs provide a starting point when time for sleep and work is subtracted from minutes in the week.

Now, a penalty subtraction. Subtract the time you spend per week, either alone or with your spouse, watching TV. This TV addiction is one of the most detrimental influences on American marriage. It is a shared addiction, which is the worst type, because it sometimes covertly robs the relationship of available time for intimacy while both partners take unknowing part in the theft.

TOTAL WEEKLY MIMs _____
MINUS TV-ADDICTION PENALTY _____

ACTUAL WEEKLY MIMs _____

I help my couples calculate a percentage so they can see what could be compared to what actually is. Watch out for the argument that "it is not how much time but quality time that counts." That argument has never been a valid one, either in raising a marriage or in raising children. Both quality and quantity are required to nurture a marriage to super marital sex.

Divide your total MIMs by the 1,800 weekly available MIMs. For example, if you estimated a total of 180 MIMs for your marriage, after subtraction of the TV penalty factor, you would divide the 180 minutes by 1,800 for a "Marital Investment Quotient" of 10 percent. By the way, if you were near 10 percent, congratulations! The average MIQ of my thousand couples was less than 1 percent!

Actually, only 732 couples provided data for their MIMs, because I did not start using this test until some months into the program. Now that I have used this test with more than 5,000 couples in the clinic, the average is still less than 1 percent.

How do you and your partner compare? Take a look at each item of the test, including the penalty factor for TV, and discuss where MIMs are lost or gained. Does your investment of time reflect your priority for this marriage, or some out-of-control obligatory life-style robbing your marriage of its potential intimacy?

One last point about MIMs. There were thirty-five couples seen in the clinic program who were having affairs with one another. That is, they came to the clinic and, while married to someone else, wanted help with a sexual problem they were having in their affair. While there are several issues to examine in such cases, it is interesting to note that the average Affair Investment Quotient was 83 percent, based on the average available time of 120 minutes together per week. When these people were together, they were together! Being together was their whole purpose. One percent vs. 83 percent. And we wonder why extramarital sex (Type I) is so popular? Of course, I am using these numbers in exaggerated fashion and the mathematics are far from statistically valid. The point is clear, however, that time put in to the American marriage may be far less than needed for fulfilling intimacy.

Bonus: You deserve credit for purchasing this book and reading this far. Add into your calculations any minutes you are spending discussing with your spouse the issues raised. Did your spouse respond when you called to discuss the couple given the second chance? Add that time in, too. Minutes spent in therapy for your marriage do not count as bonus time, but any time spent implementing the suggestions or ideas coming from your therapy sessions give you extra bonus minutes.

You will have to make choices, not just lists. You will have to choose intimacy and super marital sex, because our society places marital time at the bottom of our priority list. You will never *find* the time. You must *make* it.

4. MARITAL INVASION: IN-LAWS, OUT-LAWS, AND OTHERS

Super Marital Sex Rule: The marriage is the most important element of each partner's life. All other persons' concerns always come after the marriage, never before or instead of it. No one is more important or of equal importance to your spouse in the super marriage.

> He should have married his mother. She ran his life, runs his life, and will always try to run our marriage if he lets her. If he would have married her, it would have saved time on gas and phone bills.
>
> WIFE

American marriage is under constant bombardment by extraneous influences, as is clear from the MIM factor. Work, schools, hospitals, governmental agencies, family, and neighbors continually impinge on marriages, stretching them to provide for others what the marriage can not provide for the couple itself.

When daily living was not so anonymous, so computerized, mechanical, and fast-paced, marital and family life was free to respond more to the natural cycles of life, the changes within and among people. Now the American marriage is a socially reactive unit more than it is an intimate active relationship that governs itself.

A call from school, a computer-generated message, car phones that can even let you know if you were called while you left your car, all place us under the potential continued surveillance of others. We have become a "beeperized" culture, never really out of touch as long as a little tone reminds us that a person out there needs us more urgently than the person here with us now.

Parents live longer, so responsibilities in parenting parents as well as children have emerged. In those couples who had parents living, "parenting parents resulted in obligations, distractions," and sometimes guilt that encroached on marriage. In-laws miles away affect the marriage, with recurring themes of conflict regarding who said or did not say what to whom or who did not attend what family function or did not call enough.

It is certainly not just obligation and distraction that invades the marriage, but difficulties finding a new relationship with parents and others once we are married. Extended families require a psychological maturity that few of us attain. Sometimes it takes all of our energy to be, as one husband put it, "just civil." We may unconsciously resent the fact that our time with our spouse takes away from the expiring time available for relating to our parents. How much of what is done for whom relates to guilt, fear of loss, and split between loving now and loving for the past.

I required my thousand couples to leave a tape recorder running for ninety minutes during three randomly selected days. I played the tape back to them at fast speed, and the "noise," acoustically and psychologically, was obvious.

Even when there is a time free from invasion, a new invasion from "inner space" occurs as the couple now has time to relive issues that have built up over time. When I sent the couples away on what I call the "Real Honeymoon Assignment," (since most first honeymoons are *not* at all what we hope or expect them to be) they lapse into a "search mode," talking over conflicts and external requirements that they haven't been able to focus on due to distractions and other obligations of daily living.

One such couple, on a train ride from Detriot to Toronto (they had asked me if they could take the plane so they could get back faster for a business meeting), reported that the husband asked at about the halfway point, "Do you think the dogs have enough food for while we're gone? And by the way, the dogs, the cat, and one of the kids are due for shots."

Listen to your marital talk and you will see what I mean by invasion by the "out-laws" we allow to rob our marriage. Just for a day, count the times you use pronouns such as "he," "she," "it," "they," and "them" rather than "I" or "we." Unless we control the invasion of the American marriage, it will continue to be "occupied" by events and people rather than "us."

5. THE PROTECTIVE INSULT

Super Marital Sex Rule: The truth, and nothing but the truth, is the base of a super marriage. Lying, even to protect, prevents the total intimacy, respect, and self-responsibility necessary for intimacy.

> I don't bring my problems home. He couldn't really handle that. I come home, give him a kiss, go upstairs, take two aspirins, sigh, brace myself for the evening, or maybe call my friend to tell at least somebody how I feel. I can't just dump on him.
>
> WIFE

The central reason for being married is to enjoy and share the privilege of being vulnerable, of sharing and giving yourself to someone and inviting that person to do the same. Unfortunately, American marriage has turned away from this purpose, turning instead to a form of phoniness that, while engaged in for the sake of love, actually damages intimacy severely over time and sexuality immediately and intensely.

"Don't tell your father, you know how upset he gets," is a statement that carries with it the assumption that the father cannot represent himself. He will never be able to learn to do so if he is protected from learning.

The protective insult is one of the major blocks to super marital sex. The husband in one of the thousand couples reported, "I love to see high heels on a woman, even during intercourse. Don't tell her, though. She would think I'm a pervert." The wife reported, "I know my husband would like me to wear my heels during sex, but I don't want him to know that I know he knows I know." Each was trying to protect the other, but they were really protecting themselves from the risk, the effort of being vulnerable.

Think of one thing you could never tell your spouse. Most married people can think of more than one, but they typically have that one, crucial thing they cannot, will not tell because they are "protecting" the partner. I call this the "Senseless Secret," because it blocks the growth of intimacy, it does not protect it, and insults the partner as it detracts from his or her self-esteem.

Well-intended attempts to protect the partner are as damaging to intimacy as intentional attempts at deception, revenge, or the infliction of emotional pain. I'm not suggesting we must tell everything always. There would be no life without lies. The trouble begins when the lie is based on the assumed weakness of the spouse. If we do not choose to share something, that choice must be based on "self," not "other," on our own assessment of what we feel we can handle, not what the other can handle.

You will learn later to take major risks for super marital sex, to share what I call the "SSSH" of your sex life (the *senseless sex secret holdout*). These are secrets that we would never share outside of marital sex. It is a sad paradox that men will tell their "SSSH" to prostitutes, yet never mention them to the one person who most likely knows it already and would feel a new closeness through disclosure.

6. THE PROMISE PARADOX

Super Marital Sex Rule: The super sex marriage is based more on now than later, more on doing than intending. One of the greatest challenges of super marital sex is to attempt to live responsibly while living creatively, acting on our dreams.

> Happiness is when the dog dies and the last kid leaves.
>
> HUSBAND AND WIFE

We seem to be waiting for the major chord that ends the symphony, the finale, the conclusion, that time when the ceiling is painted, the toilet doesn't leak anymore, the kids are well behaved, and the checking account balances. Someday, somehow everything will be "ready." The problem is, that time will never come. Life is truly a way of traveling and not a station at which we arrive. We are forgetting the trip.

We promise that when the kids are in college, we will travel together, but there doesn't seem to be enough money to do it then. We promise that when we have financial security, we will buy that cottage, but inflation deflates us. We promise that when we have a little more time, we will make love, and we fail to make time or love.

Psychologist Richard Lazarus has researched "life's little hassles," and shows that they are actually life itself. We either live with them and enjoy our life, or we mistakenly assume that we can "wait them out" or "plan them away."

American marriage is in a perpetual state of foreplay, getting ready for later. Anthropologist Dr. Anthony Tofoya writes about our limited cultural orientation, bound by threes (we think that crises happen in threes, talk of the Holy Trinity, knock three times, etc.). I notice that my couples state this phenomenon in "threes," that is, we will make love when 1) the kids are asleep, 2) we are ready for bed, and 3) there is nothing left to do. Never! It is a promise that will not be kept! The triangle will never be complete.

We promise that we will love each other forever, that we will develop together and die together on the same day at the same time, knowing full well that all relationships end and it is only a matter of when and how. We must move toward super marital sex not by promises, but by action. We will come to feel as we behave, as we act. Motivation is not something we get; it follows what we do.

The "forever fallacy" causes us to miss the chance to love. We will not be together, at least in this world, forever. Life will never be that pearl, the pearl of wisdom, perfect on all sides. It is more a complex crystal, turning from side to side, showing truth and value in segments. We do not have to live as though there is no tomorrow, but we had better love as though there is only now.

7. THE MYTH OF PARALLEL DEVELOPMENT

Super Marital Sex Rule: Marital partners will never be at the same stage of development together. Super marital sex depends on learning to enjoy one another's development, both partners' valiant struggle to adjust and to grow.

> Just when I got established in my career, he wants to change his. When he first talked about women's liberation, I knew he was getting ready to quit his job. Now he wants to work, I want to work, neither of us wants to parent. When I want to do something, he does. We just don't match up right.
>
> WIFE

We assume that life's passages will be encountered by each of us in our marriages at the same time with the same ease. It just does not work out that way. There is really no such thing as a mid-life crisis, only a lifelong set of crises we are just now paying attention to. So it is with marriage. We assume that things will just "develop," but they will not. We will enter phases of life differently, putting stresses on our marriages through our lack of understanding and tolerance of individuality.

Marriage vows sometimes say "until death do us part." They should day something like "as we struggle together to renegotiate through the hundreds of changes we will each encounter together and separately." Our vows of intimacy should reflect the assumption of constant change, learning a marital dance in which leader and follower are forever changing.

I tell my couples "never divorce someone you don't know." Many couples will not listen. They see divorce as an adjustment rather than an end. Sometimes therapists teach them that. They are wrong. Divorce often relates to marital inability to work through differences in developmental challenges, changes in readiness to parent, to work, to play, to rest, to love. Until American marriage sees that it is as cyclical as individual development, reflection, directing, and responding to our changes as people, it will tend to end "too soon" too often.

All marriages struggle with the individual differences of their
partners as they go through their individual lives. You will learn
that sex can be one of the best aids to carry us through differences
in development. In fact, super marital sex can save marriage by
teaching its partners to flourish in the changes and growth of both
spouses.

We must learn to remarry a different and changing person several
times during our marriage. We can choose to divorce and seek out
dozens of transitional partners to match our changes, or use change
to sculpt the marriage as an ever-changing artwork. Good marriages depend much more on being the right person than finding
the right person. Experiencing developmental changes with someone else can be as exciting as it is difficult.

In a pre-fab, pre-developed, ready-made culture, we learn to
look for pre-developed partners, already formed to match our own
developmental stage at a given time. If our house is too small, we
move. When we get too much stuff, we look for bigger and better
places to keep it. We must also learn ways to get rid of some stuff,
particularly psychological stuff, yet stay in the same house.

8. UNMARRIAGE THERAPISTS AND
VIDEO ADVISERS

Super Marital Sex Rule: The solution to marital problems and
strategies for super marital sex are found within each marriage, not
from a prescribed set of steps, neighbor or relative advice, magazine or talk-show "easy steps" to a better marriage. Looking for
techniques is much less effective than learning a new way and place
for looking.

> I saw it on Phil Donahue. I got the book, left it by her cup of coffee.
> How direct could I be? It was right there in front of her. She never
> mentioned it once. What was I supposed to do, just tell her what I
> thought?
>
> HUSBAND

When we are maritally bankrupt, we may fall into the hands of
receivers. An entire industry is thriving that is made up of marital
therapy, marital seminars, marital encounters, marital self-help
books, sex manuals, talk shows, and even video- and audiotapes
teaching sex in marriage. In fact, most therapists themselves are
struggling in marriage or with divorce, with their own relationship

problems. At the very least, they are attempting to help marriages with no real healthy model.

The model of wellness in America is based on individuals. Those persons we see as models of enlightenment, as gurus and teachers of health, are typically unmarried or have been unable to maintain one marriage. Sex manuals have typically been separate from marriage manuals, suggesting ways to save and fix marriages. Until this book, we have not had a model of the healthy marriage beyond the cliché of good communications, good sex, tolerance, and hard work. There have been ideas for what to do, but few if any models for how to be. I suggest it is time we looked at the possibility of super, hardy marriages.

There is no research available documenting successful marital therapy. At best, researchers can identify "non-failures" in treatment programs. You will learn later how to treat your own sex and marital problems and how to select a professional helper if you need one. For now, do *not* go to a therapist who quotes "high success rates." There is really no such thing. Therapists and therapy do not cure; people must heal their own relationships.

In spite of all marital advice available on television and from books, you are the only ones who know what you want and how to get it. There is probably too much communication in marriage, not too little, as therapists like to stress. We talk too much and sense too little. Therapists may tell you to talk more, listen more, use lotions, touch each other, or prescribe an array of supposedly "tested" techniques for improving sex in marriage. Unfortunately, these models are based on an incomplete perspective of the relationship between marriage and sex.

We are told that if we can find the right technique, if we can only "do something," we can solve our problems. If I learned anything from observing these thousand "hardy" couples and the hundreds of others in my clinical experience, I have learned that marriage is first and foremost a system, the most complex of systems, and that it has been corrupted by the unquestioned acceptance of the "sexperts" and their magic techniques for satisfaction.

The answer to any marital problem rests within, not without. It rests on understanding your unique system of interacting, independent of measures of vascular change, fluid discharge, orgasmic reflex, and communicational gimmicks. You will be learning a "super sex," a way of interacting intimately that transcends the meeting of some historically imposed genital and orgasmic tradition.

Remember, if we chase a butterfly hard and fast, we will never catch it. Perhaps if we learn to receive instead of achieve, we will be open to our own natural supersystem. The butterfly will light on our shoulder.

9. THE DANGER OF MARRYING THE RIGHT PERSON

Super Marital Sex Rule: The strongest marriages, the super sex marriages, will always be the most challenged marriages, because the spouses will develop characteristics that attract interest from others. This outside interest challenges the super marriage to continued development and enhancement. The super marriage does not compete with outside temptations, but provides a growing place for both growing partners.

> She doesn't have a thing to worry about. She is married to such a dip that she will never get rid of him. Nobody in her right mind would want him. Now, Jerry, that's another matter. He is everybody's dream. I don't trust my best friend. They'd take him in a minute.
>
> WIFE

If you are married to an insensitive, mean, abusive, arrogant, unreasonable, unromantic fool, relax. At least you are not in competition with anyone for your spouse. On the other hand, if you are married to a caring, kind, responsive, warm, dedicated spouse, look around; there may be somebody out there moving in on him or her. One of the saddest paradoxes among the thousand couples was the fact that the persons you would assume to be the best of all spouses sometimes became involved outside the marriage. If not actually interacting sexually, they were at least flirting with the possibility.

Recent reports indicate that increasing numbers of single women are actively seeking relationships with married men. They have tired of the game of courtship, feeling that "the best are gone by now." They refuse what they see as leftovers, and have compromised by sharing a man with another woman.

It follows that the new professional woman may find single men who want to share her with her husband. Not only a good man, but a good woman is hard to find, and when they are found, everyone is interested. This problem puts an additional burden on an already stressed American marriage.

Until American marriage learns that familiarity can breed a sexual interest beyond that possible with new partners, it will continue to be threatened instead of enhanced by our new and less restricted gender interactions. Good partners should stimulate, not pressure good marriages.

10. MUDDLED MODELS

Super Marital Sex Rule: Your parents' marriage affects your own style of being married, but it must be a starting point, not a goal to be achieved or an end to be avoided.

> I love my parents. But I'll tell you one thing. I will never understand how they stayed together.
>
> HUSBAND

We are seldom allowed a view into the intimacy of our parents' marriage from which we can construct a model for relating in our own marriage. Few of us have the slightest idea about our parents' sexual interaction beyond some secret late-night bed squeaks and unclear murmurs. Short of pornographic distortions, we almost never see anyone else making love, and our ideas about our parents' marriages are probably badly distorted.

A basic question asked of all the thousand couples was, "How do you remember you parents' marriage?" More than half of the men and women in my sample (57 percent) had negative memories of the way in which their parents interacted. Thirty-six percent reported physical or verbal abuse in their parents' relationships. Often, couples commented that their parents tolerated one another, just ignored each other, or "survived."

When asked if they would like their marriage to be like their parents', the response (58 percent) was more typically no than yes. Even those who could find something to copy stated that they may be "seeing what I wanted to see" or "what I thought might be going on but never really knew."

How about you? What is you marital learning history? Where and how did you learn to be married?

The media marriages leave us little to go by. They are either delightfully benign "Ozzie and Harriet" or "Leave It to Beaver" styles of relating, desexualized "marrinoids" acting out life, or hot, conflicted, distressed relationships of the Archie and Edith, Ralph and Alice type, drawn together by some secret attraction that not even they understand.

You will learn in following chapters that our relating style depends to a great extent on what researcher John Money calls "love maps," early tracings of the results of our sex rehearsal during childhood. These rehearsals too often are corrupted, censored, and distorted by a society that insists on desexualizing children, preventing them from learning to unite emotion and sex. We have learned much more about what marriage is not and should not be than what it can be.

The Marital-Abuse Factor: The Kids! The Kids! The Kids!

"If God wanted sex to be fun, He wouldn't have included children as punishment."

ED BLUESTONE

Super Marital Sex Rule: The kids do *not* come first!

I don't remember how it was before we had kids. I'm sure we must have done something then, but I can't remember what it could have been. They seem to be everything now.

HUSBAND

Kids are a unique pressure and joy for marriages, so I have separated the "kid factor" from the ten items above. They deserve their own category, for they are the worst and the best thing that happens to a marriage. I maintain that kid priority has overburdened American marriage, resulting in doing for instead of with our children, applauding only them instead of each other. We fall victim to "P-M-S," parent manipulation syndrome by our children.

This child focus has an additional twist. Once the child focus dominates a marriage at the expense of the marital relationship, even the parents themselves can become infantalized, childlike in their own behavior and orientation to life. Husbands begin to buy their own toys, to expect to be mothered by their wives, cheered at softball games, tolerated in their own immaturity. Wives become princesslike, protected, cared for, and idealized. Soon everyone in the family is behaving more like a set of siblings than parents and children.

As many marriages fail because of children as children fail because of faulty marriages. Until we learn that children are not special, but equal in importance to all of us, until we learn that we must not lead our lives and our marriages for children, but with them, we sacrifice our marriages, our own development. After all, wasn't one of your greatest wishes that your own parents would be happy? Think of giving that gift to your children.

Sexual Dis-ease in American Marriage

You'd think it would be great for us in bed. But somehow we just don't mesh. It doesn't work out. It's not a Dr. Ruth problem, just that something is missing.

WIFE

As a review of this chapter and to get ready for the following lessons in super marital sex, I have provided a brief quiz for you and your spouse. Discuss each item together and score your marriage on a 0-to-10 scale. Scoring 100 points could mean two things. First, you are completely free of the pressures on American marriage I have discussed. Second, you are cheating on this test! We all have these pressures. The idea is to begin to reduce them to make way for a super marriage.

This test and others you will be taking in this book are based on a scoring system of degrees, not yes or no. All systems, particularly marital systems, change. Just the fact that you are taking a test on your marriage changes your marriage. Score and discuss each item in degrees, trends, indications, not absolutes. It will take some time for you to get used to this type of scoring, but learning to see your relationship as an adapting system is a major step in strengthening your marriage and helping it function in harmony with the rules of all world systems.

1. GENDER JUNK 0-10

Are you free from prescribed sexual roles? Do you feel, act, and do the way you want in this marriage regarding sex role, without concern for conforming to male and female expectations?

	0	1	2	3	4	5	6	7	8	9	10
not at all					somewhat						very much so

2. PATTERNED PREDICTABILITY 0-10

Are you free from the trap of "ought to's and have to's"? Are you able to accept patterns and the development of cycles in your marriage as signs of intimacy rather than boredom? _____

```
            0   1   2   3   4   5   6   7   8   9   10
not at all                  somewhat                  very much so
```

3. PRIORITY PROBLEM 0-10

Do you spend your "MIMs" talking about sex, intimacy, closeness? Is sexuality an area that you nurture and pay attention to? _____

```
            0   1   2   3   4   5   6   7   8   9   10
not at all                  somewhat                  very much so
```

4. MARITAL INVASION 0-10

Are you able to make the world go away, to go behind closed doors alone with your spouse, to make your own marriage? _____

```
            0   1   2   3   4   5   6   7   8   9   10
not at all                  somewhat                  very much so
```

5. PROTECTIVE INSULT 0-10

Do you disclose your feelings openly to your partner? Are you vulnerable and free from secrets you think he or she can't handle? _____

```
            0   1   2   3   4   5   6   7   8   9   10
not at all                  somewhat                  very much so
```

6. PROMISE PARADOX 0-10

Are you loving for now? Are you free of the "later" orientation in favor of attending to your marriage now? _____

```
            0   1   2   3   4   5   6   7   8   9   10
not at all                  somewhat                  very much so
```

7. PARALLEL DEVELOPMENT 0-10

Are you enjoying one another's developmental progress and tolerating differences in rate and style of development? _____

	0	1	2	3	4	5	6	7	8	9	10
not at all						somewhat					very much so

8. OUTSIDE INTERFERENCE 0-10

Are you free of outside distractions from pseudo-experts and advisers? Is your marriage your own? _____

	0	1	2	3	4	5	6	7	8	9	10
not at all						somewhat					very much so

9. SPECIAL SPOUSES 0-10

Are you free of the feeling that you may lose your spouse? Do you feel that you are as valuable to your partner as she or he is to you?

_____

	0	1	2	3	4	5	6	7	8	9	10
not at all						somewhat					very much so

10. MUDDLED MODELS 0-10

Are you free of myths of how other marriages are, developing your own unique marital pattern? _____

	0	1	2	3	4	5	6	7	8	9	10
not at all						somewhat					very much so

Total your points. Take the test together, score yourself and each other. The idea is to talk and share. Now add points for the kid factor.

The Kid Factor

Are you developing your marriage as well as your children? On a 0-to-20 scale (more points are possible for this factor because it is such a difficult area), with 20 representing a strong balance between marriage and kids and the absence of "marital abuse" you allow your children to cause. _____

SCORE ON FIRST 10 ITEMS _____ (0-100)

ADD KID FACTOR POINTS + _____ (0-20)

TOTAL MARITAL "IQ"
INTIMACY QUOTIENT _____ AVERAGE ABOUT 80

Think of your score as a type of marital IQ, a marital intimacy quotient. Below 80 points means that you had better pay more attention to these areas, perhaps that one key area, that cost you your points. The purpose of this test is to illustrate that sex does not take place separate from the marital system. Super sex requires a super marriage, not just a surviving marriage.

You may want to guess how your partner scored himself or herself on these items and have your partner score you in the same way. Neither one of you is right or wrong. Use these entries to begin understanding and enhancing your marital system. The thousand couples did, and they found it an important step toward super sex.

The lower your score, the more your marital system suffers "disease," or a lack of comfort in your relationship. "Ease" in your relationship results from the growth of your entire marital system. That growth is always a sexual growth, a growth of intimacy and intensity of closeness. Here is a scale to understand your intimacy system score. Remember, this test is for fun and learning, not for blame and guilt. As long as you are reading and testing, your potential for super marital sex is very strong.

Marital Intimacy Quotient Scale

110-120   SUPER MARITAL INTIMACY RANGE
          Don't take it for granted. You got here by paying attention to your relationship. Keep it up.

100-109   VERY GOOD MARITAL INTIMACY RANGE
          You are close enough to "super" to go for it now. Look at the one item that cost you points and give it some attention.

90-99   GOOD MARITAL INTIMACY RANGE
          Your marriage is better than most, so you are ready to go even further.

80-89   AVERAGE MARITAL INTIMACY RANGE
          Your marriage is surviving, but you can do much better because you have a stronger starting point than many relationships.

70-79   BELOW-AVERAGE MARITAL INTIMACY RANGE
You are in a danger zone. Continuing to neglect those factors that took away points will prevent you from discovering super marital sex and could threaten marital survival.

60-69   IMPAIRED MARITAL INTIMACY RANGE
A warning light should go on for both of you. Where did you lose most of your points? Now is the time to focus on the marriage. This book could help you solve some of the major blocks to super marriage.

59 and   CRISIS STAGE IN MARITAL INTIMACY
less   Read the coming chapters with care. Immediate attention to your marriage is required. Look carefully at Chapter Eight and consider professional help if you are unable to implement the suggestions in this book. Give yourself and your marriage credit for paying attention to your problems by reading this book.

Super Marital Sex Opportunity Number One

Couples in the clinic were asked to become reacquainted with each other, to meet as if they were meeting for the first time. Using the Marital Intimacy Quotient, as a guide, try the following activity.

Meet as a whole family, kids included. An attention span of ten minutes is all that is required. Sit down once every other day for a week for eleven periods and discuss each of the eleven items. The entire family should know that Mom and Dad are beginning a program for strengthening their marriage and that everyone's help is required, that everyone is an important part of the marital system.

The meetings are an excellent first step on the way to super marital sex and toward meaningful sex education for you children. Tape-record these brief sessions and listen to them at the end of this book. You may want to rescore yourself then, and you may be surprised to see the changes.

The couple you met at the beginning of this chapter was one of the thousand couples who went through the entire super marital sex program in my clinic. I met them again recently, and you will meet them again at the end of this book. I was visiting a patient on the cardiology unit and saw them standing hand in hand outside one of the hospital rooms.

"How have you been?" I asked.

"We've been just fine," answered the husband. "We were visiting my uncle downstairs. We came up here to look at the spot where we got our second chance."

I hope you won't wait until the type of crisis this couple experienced before you take a second chance to pay attention to your marriage and begin to enhance the intimacy of your own relationship. To help you understand this "systems" approach, Chapter Two describes the super sex model and provides another test for learning about your own marital system. I suggest you go for a walk with your spouse before you read Chapter Two. You will need all of your energy for this love quest.

Chapter Two

ⵡⵡⵡ

The Super Marital Sexual System: A Test for Sexual Wellness in Marriage

Our sex in infrequent. That is . . . I am not in frequently.

HUSBAND

Super Marital Sex Rule: Super marital sex depends upon awareness of and compatibility with the laws of the stars, the planets, and the universe. Fulfilling sex is the result of a healthy system, a system that includes every aspect of daily living. It is not limited by the rules of genital reflex or necessarily protected by the love or skills of the respective partners. Like illness, sexual dis-ease results from failure of the marital system to follow the laws of all systems.

An Explicit Sex Scene

How can I make love when I can't even make a living? Do you think I am just supposed to be able to forget everything else once we are in bed?

WIFE

''To hell with the whole damn government!'' said the husband to the anchorman for the evening news. He used the remote control as if it were a small pistol and shot off the television. ''New tax

system, my foot. Get the little guy every time. Screw 'em,'' he
finished as he turned his attention to the sports section of the newspaper that had actually been left in the family room for two days.

His wife sat alone at the dining-room table, four plates around
her empty, but hers more than half full. The family dog looked up
at her and, with a grunt and a long sigh, finally gave up his vigil
and curled in the corner to sleep. Minutes before, the woman had
been waitress, busboy, and encounter-group leader, refereeing several mini-conflicts between her three children while her husband
talked at her about his day at work.

"Yes, thank you, my sore shoulder is feeling much better,"
answered the deserted wife and mother to no one. "Oh yes, my
day was very busy. No, that tooth did not need a cap. As a matter
of fact, the dentist had sex with me three times. He drilled me,
filled me, and thrilled me."

"Did you say something, honey?" asked the husband without
looking up from his newspaper. Of course, he knew she had said
something, but he had learned that by asking this question, he would
not have to listen to her response.

"No, not really" was the answer he had expected and received.

"Bye, Mom!" she heard from one of her three children. Voice
changes accompanying adolescence made identification of the ex-
iting child almost impossible.

"Where are you going?" yelled the mother as rapidly as she
could. It was too late; the side door slammed before the words were
out of her mouth. Sometime ago, she would have run to the door
and demanded an accounting, or an apology for rudeness. This
time she remained seated. She folded her arms in front of her,
rested her head on her arms, and began to cry.

She must have fallen asleep, because she was startled to awareness by two cold hands up her sweatshirt, one cupping each breast.
"How 'bout some action, sweet cheeks. The kids out for a while?"

His erection pushed against her left arm through his jeans. She
wondered if he had become aroused by his successful shooting of
the anchorperson, the stimulation of days-old baseball scores, or
the fact that he had a few minutes before his softball game with the
guys.

"Maybe later. I've got to get this table cleared off," she bar-
gained.

"That's just what I mean. We have no spontaneity in our sex
life. You're always so inhibited. Can't you just let go? Every sex
manual in the world tells you to let go.'' The husband was angry,

frustrated, and knew that he would be too tired later for sex after a night with the guys lying about work, sports, and their sex life.

The wife had learned that, for her husband, "to let go" meant to respond to his needs whenever they arose. His needs never seemed to arise in response to her, but had a life of their own. She unzipped his fly, rubbed his penis vigorously, and looked up at him standing beside her. She knew this would not take long.

As he finished, he asked her hurriedly, "Where did you put the tissues? The kids could come home any minute."

"In the drawer by the knives," she said, wondering why she was thinking of knives at this moment.

"Now, you see? We can have a quickie. We can let go. See what I mean?" he said as he prepared to ask his wife about the location of his baseball glove.

"It's in the trunk of your car," she said, using her well-developed one-directional family mental telepathy.

"Bye!" he said. As the door slammed, she looked at the remote-control device on the family-room floor and wondered if it worked on husbands as well as anchorpersons.

This scene and its finite variations were reported by the thousand couples. It is an explicit sex scene, containing every element necessary to understand the sexual problem that brought this couple to my clinic. The husband complained that his wife was "frigid, always distracted, and not orgasmic." The wife reluctantly reported in confidence that her husband was a "premature ejaculator" and that she felt "totally asexual." They had read the sex manuals, had been to two sex therapists over the past three years, and, by the husband's report, "even tried one of those adult hotels with the mirrors, but it wasn't much."

The couple had been taught postures and techniques. They had been shown films. They were given some special cream to numb the husband's penis so he could "last longer." They had been taught to look for the wife's "G spot," in hopes that its discovery would free her for sexual bliss. They had *not* been taught that it was their system, not their sex, that was their problem.

Take the following sexual system test with your partner. Make time to discuss each issue. Sexual problems are disorders of a system, a disruption of natural flow between marital partners, and between the marriage and the rest of the world. The Chinese refer to the natural flow of life as the Tao, and there is a Tao of marital sex. When our major reproductive organ, our brain, does not function with the "sexual Tao" of the marriage, we experience sexual dis-ease. Super marital sex depends upon establishing a flow, an ease within the system that the couple I am describing has lost.

The test you are about to take is based on what we know about natural systems. Worry less about your actual score on this test and focus instead on the interaction with your partner as you examine each item. Before you put away the dishes or go to the softball game, sit down and see what is meant by "going with the flow."

A Sexual-System Exam: Finding Your Sexual Tao

First, place yourself on each axis in the direction that you feel best represents your feelings about your marriage. Next, place your partner on that same axis. Your marriage will then have four scores to discuss on the Sexual-System Exam, your score for self and partner and your partner's two scores. Remember, as with super marital sex, it's the doing, not the scoring, that counts!

It will sometimes seem that a certain score must be a better score, but systems theory, the theory behind the super sex marriage, teaches that too much of even an apparently good thing is not necessarily the healthiest status for a growing adapting system. An athlete can be very fit—scoring high on all measures of muscle, speed, and endurance—yet not be very healthy—adaptable, happy, loving, and learning. Try to break free of your assumptions of good or bad and think in terms of balance, in terms of positioning your marriage for change, growth, and responsiveness to the needs and maturation of the marital partners.

1. "IN ORDER" TO HAVE SEX

She expects me to kill all insects, catch all mice, and seek out the source of any sound in the night. Why me? I hate bugs, am afraid of mice, and would die of fright before any burglar could shoot me.

HUSBAND

Okay. But I'm the medical corps. All cuts, bruises, bangs, and bumps come to me. I hate blood. I just pour on peroxide, and squeeze tissue on all wounds. If he had a heart attack, I'd pour peroxide on him.

WIFE

ORDER:	**DISORDER:**
EASY TO UNDERSTAND,	ROLE CHANGE AND
CLEAR ROLES AND RULES	CONFLICT, RULES OF
FOR MARITAL INTERACTION	INTERACTING NOT CLEAR

```
0   1   2   3   4   5   6   7   8   9   10
```

TENDING TOWARD_____TENDING TOWARD
ORDER   DISORDER

Does your marriage have roles that are clear and of long standing, essentially unchangeable, so rigid that almost every problem is solved with marital partners filling and living up to their expected and assigned roles (order)? Or does your relationship lean more toward unclear, ever-changing roles, with each problem resulting in conflicts, readjustments, confusion, and role-reassignment (disorder)? Toward 0 is toward high order in your marriage and toward 10 is toward lack of order. There are not high scores or low scores (and 10 is not of more value or better than 0).

The woman at the deserted dinner table finds herself in a relationship of order, predictable role assignment and expectation. She prepares the dinners, calls the family for dinner, serves the dinner, and cleans up. Sexually, her role is to respond to her husband. He sees her as "broken" sexually due to what he perceives as her lack of spontaneity and passion, when in fact he is part of a highly ordered system that places both of them in their respective roles.

The wife accepts her husband's role as "fourth child," serving and cleaning up after him as much as her children.

When audiences hear the story of this couple, women get angry with the wife for her passivity and with the husband for his sexist ignorance. Men get angry at the husband for his neglect of his wife and his fitting the cliché role of "couch potato" and "boy child," and at the wife for her maternal tolerance of her husband's infantile and selfish behavior and her failure to represent herself. What these audiences are really bothered by is the "stuck system," the unbending order that traps both partners in an unfulfilling marriage. Too much order (0) or total lack of order (10) always disrupts systems in nature, for there is no adaptability.

The husband in this couple felt he was responding to his wife's sexual needs, but was in fact responding to his own misperceptions and misreadings of his wife's needs for closeness and personal attention. "If she wants it, we do it. Where and when she wants it. I never turn her down" was the report of the husband.

The wife felt totally responsible for sex. "If I don't mention it, we probably won't do it. I find myself trying so much to guess when he needs it that I can't tell if I ever need it." They were trapped by their order, not in charge of it, not planning and adapting together, not aware of and responsive to a natural rhythmic flow that characterizes all of living and the Tao of marriage.

Systems thinking is relatively new in our culture. Give yourself time to understand it and how it applies to marriage and sex. It's a new way of viewing marriage and sex, but it is the only way you will find super marital sex.

2. THE SEXUAL "CONNECTION"

We just don't connect. When I say up, she says down. If I'm horny, she's not, and if she is, I'm not. She says it's because of my "period." She says I have worse periods than she does.

HUSBAND

CONNECTION:	DISCONNECTION:
SENSE OF HUMOR, TRAGEDY, FAIRNESS, VALUES IS THE SAME FOR BOTH SPOUSES	SENSE OF HUMOR, TRAGEDY, VALUES IS COMPLETELY DIFFERENT

0   1   2   3   4   5   6   7   8   9   10

TENDING TOWARD_____TENDING TOWARD
    CONNECTION   DISCONNECTION

Do you laugh and cry with your spouse about the same things, reacting in the same fashion and intensity to life events (connection)? Or do you seem to be at different emotional levels, out of sync, with few examples of shared emotional response (disconnection)?

The dinner couple scored too far toward disconnection. Remember that some disconnection, a tolerance for different emotional levels at different times, is necessary in marriage, but this couple is out of balance, too out of sync. The wife felt a lonely sense of tragedy at her marital situation, surrender regarding the children, and compliance in sexual interactions. Her emotional reaction was unshared by her husband, who instead felt boredom, disregard, or lack of involvement with the children. He was invigorated by activities that had little to do directly with the marriage. While the wife cried alone at the dinner table and felt sad, the husband drove alone to the softball game and felt frustrated.

Disconnection was apparent in their sexual life. "I'd love it if she would do oral love more. You know. Suck on me down here. She does it, but it's not like she wants to or anything. It's kind of a gift or a trade-off. A little sucking for a little hugging." The husband hoped for but did not find in his wife a connection, a shared sexual arousal in an important part of his sexual life.

The wife felt quite differently. She performed fellatio because she perceived them as a couple of "high order," and things always seem to get done. The wife reported, "I don't mind doing it, you know. Going down on him, I guess it is. But he makes it more of a prostitute thing. I like to be stroked and touched. It's like he wants me to do it 'to him'; we don't do it together or anything. He just lies there, pushes my head down, and humps at me. I'm afraid I'll gag or throw up. Just because he likes me to do it to him, he assumes I should like it when he does it to me. Well, I don't. I can't stand it."

Our highly ordered couple is disconnected, going through the sexual motions, with both partners disappointed. Their dinner-table situation reflected the same pattern. The entire sexual system is out of balance, leaning first to too much order, then to too much disconnection.

3. GETTING INTO THE SEXUAL "SWING" OF THINGS

I'll tell you one thing. We are so in tune with each other that it gets us in trouble. If I'm really down on a given day, then he is down. We get down together in minutes. We just reflect each other perfectly, almost like one mood together. We are like one tree in the wind. The trouble is, we can't help each other if we *are* each other.

WIFE

RHYTHM:	DISCORD:
A FEEDBACK LOOP IS INTACT. PARTNERS HELP TO STABILIZE ONE ANOTHER, AND ADJUST TO AND FOR EACH OTHER	WHEN ONE PARTNER IS EMOTIONALLY HOT, THE OTHER GETS HOTTER, COLD MEANS COLDER FOR OTHER

```
    0   1   2   3   4   5   6   7   8   9   10
    TENDING TOWARD_____TENDING TOWARD
        RHYTHM              NO RHYTHM
```

Does your marriage have a "marital-stat," a type of emotional thermostat in which one partner can help the other to back off of

an argument, to cool down, and one partner can help to bring up
the other partner when emotional support is needed? The presence
of a good marital-stat is like a good sense of rhythm, a fine-tuned
thermostat in your home. When things get cooler, the thermostat
calls for more heat. When it is getting hotter, the thermostat calls
for a little cool air. Is there a lack of rhythm, with emotional heat
in one partner causing the maladjusted marital-stat to call for even
more heat from the other partner?

Scientists refer to this idea of rhythm as cybernetics, the study
of feedback, of ecological and systems maintenance through some
mechanism of automatic adjustment, heating up and cooling down,
going faster and slower in corrective responsives cycles. In a sense,
this chapter on the marital system is about sexual cybernetics. Intimacy and sexual interaction serve as the feedback instrument.
Super Marital Sex Opportunity Number Two, presented at the end
of this chapter, will show you more about how sexual cybernetics
works.

The couple at the dinner table scored toward discord. The wife
needed someone to bring her up, to help her readjust, someone
sensitive to her personal crisis. The husband only depressed her
further through his own disenchantment and his incomplete solution to their sexual problem (his own quick sexual release). The
marital system was not being adjusted, just allowed to freeze up in
the absence of emotional warmth and intimacy.

The husband required someone to cool down his hot reacting
style, but the wife was incapacitated emotionally, sensing but unable to help with her husband's overheating.

Too rapid and immediate adjustment, too much rhythm, can
result in marital instability, too many adjustments to allow for comfortable patterns to emerge. A thermostat that goes on and off too
soon and too often eventually breaks. Marriages need time to adjust
too.

In super marital sex, couples have their marital-stat working well.
They are able to maintain a comfort zone together. The frequency,
type, and intensity of their sexual relationship seems to adjust itself
automatically, just as a real thermostat is not noticed when it is
doing its job. When sex gets too hot, resulting in conflict, even
pain (dyspareunia), readjustment occurs. When sex gets too cold
(desire-phase disorders and incompatibility), readjustment takes
place, and warmth returns. Things do not have to get too hot or too
cold before the readjustment occurs. The thermostat, marital-stat,
seems very sensitive. Seldom is anyone left crying at the table or
angry as he or she drives to a softball game.

4. PAYING "ATTENTION" TO SEX

We have never really talked. When I ask her for more attention, more feeling, she takes it as a criticism or putdown. We just can't talk it over, work it out. She has no idea how I really feel inside.

HUSBAND

ATTENTION:
CLEAR READING OF EACH
OTHER ON MANY LEVELS;
WELL TUNED IN, SENSING
THE REAL FEELINGS OF THE
SPOUSE

DISATTENTION:
MISS SUBTLE MESSAGES,
MISREAD EMOTIONAL CUES,
LOW EMPATHY

```
0    1    2    3    4    5    6    7    8    9    10
  TENDING TOWARD_____TENDING TOWARD
      ATTENTION                DISATTENTION
```

Do you feel clearly understood in your marriage, sometimes even well beyond what you say or do? Do you feel "well sensed" and listened to beyond words (attention)? Or do you seem to have to expend a great deal of energy just to get your feelings stated, and even then feel misunderstood (disattention)? This attention/disattention issue is another example where it seems that attention must be much "better" than disattention. The purpose of taking this test is to learn a new view of the marital system that allows for constructive disattention, some relief from the vigilant state required for constant attention. It's the strong relationship that can tolerate misreadings and occasional low empathy because it is counterbalanced with corrective reading and sensing of one another's feelings. If you score this test by placing each item on a circle instead of a line, you see how systems theory works. Too much attention, for example, throws the circle off balance; it turns awkwardly and may steer off course. The same is true for too much disattention.

One of the husbands managed to learn this new scoring system by equating it to breathing. You need to inhale good fresh air, but you have to make time to exhale also. This "flowing" concept is at the heart of a systems view of intimacy.

Attention in this case does not just refer to talking and listening. Psychotherapy, marital therapy, and so-called sexual therapy focuses primarily on words, on talking, thinking, listening, and physically touching and being touched. Super marital sex adds "supersensory" communication. I am not referring to "extrasensory" perception, because sensing is not an "extra." We all have it, but we must learn to develop it. Supersensory marital communication can be practiced, enhanced, and strengthened. We can go beyond talk-and-touch therapy, and work toward our own forms of "marital telepathy."

Physicists know that communication takes place on levels beyond the see and touch world. Physicist Fritjof Capra writes, "Throughout history, it has been recognized that the human mind is capable of two kinds of knowledge . . . the rational and the intuitive." This part of the marital sexual system test refers to the intuitive dimension of marital interaction, a dimension too long ignored by professional therapists and health-care workers. All healing depends as much or more on intuitive communication and awareness than it does on the rules of rational, verbal communication.

Our example couple scored high toward the disattention end of the axis. Not only was the husband unaware of his wife's pain, but she, too, failed to sense his difficulties. The husband stated, "I leave the table because I just don't know what to do. If I try to help, I think she thinks I don't think she is doing a good job, sort of letting us all down." The wife responded, "He just does not give a damn. He's just lazy and self-involved. He never gives one thought to how I might feel."

When I presented a part of this report at a recent professional meeting for therapists, one of my colleagues stood up and said, "I tell my couples that the only way anyone is ever going to know how you feel is if you tell them. You must share your feelings and listen for the feelings of your spouse. Now you come along and tell us that there is some sort of 'supersensory communication' in marriage. There just is no such thing. We have to talk, listen, and do. This is a ridiculous idea . . . sensing. That's when couples get in trouble, trying to sense instead of trying to communicate."

I responded by saying, "You are making an important point, but if you will let me continue, I think I can document my ideas with case examples."

The therapist answered, "Never mind. I can just tell what you are going to be saying, and I don't want to hear it."

The audience laughed at the obvious contradiction, referring to his "sense" of what I was going to do as a means of denying that sensing goes on all the time.

Again, some "rest" from constant attention is necessary in any system. Watching and listening or being watched and listened to all of the time can be as disruptive to the marital system as no attention at all.

5. A SEXUAL "BALANCING ACT"

> I work, I wash, I clean, I cook, I parent, I give up!
>
> WIFE

> I help out around the house.
>
> HUSBAND

> Big deal! I'm used to dust.
> SUGGESTED GRAVESTONE EPITAPH BY ERMA BOMBECK

BALANCE	IMBALANCE:
50/50 APPROACH EQUAL DIVISION OF CHORES: RESPONSIBILITY SEEMS EQUAL FOR SEXUAL ENCOUNTERS	UNEQUAL DIVISION OF TASKS: RESPONSIBILITY FOR MARITAL SEX TO ONE PARTNER

```
0   1   2   3   4   5   6   7   8   9   10
   TENDING TOWARD_____TENDING TOWARD
        BALANCE              IMBALANCE
```

Do you feel that your marriage includes a shared approach to the problems of daily living, including the erotic life of your marriage (balance)? Or, does it seem that one of you is more responsible for things, that it is one partner's house, one partner's "job" to initiate sexual encounters (imbalance)?

Remember the idea of "flowing" in systems as you score your marriage on this item. All marriages must have imbalance or there could be no growth in the system. Sometimes one partner has to carry the entire burden, perhaps because of illness or work obligations on the part of the spouse. Super marriages are well enough balanced to have plenty of imbalance. As a child learning to ride a two-wheeler, eventually a safe range between imbalance and corrective balance is maintained. Some falling is needed for learning to occur.

You very seldom hear about a woman who is home "babysitting" her own children, but wives will sometimes report that their husbands are "babysitting," as if his children were not really his but instead some type of marital obligation. It is still rare to hear a woman state, "I even did the wash" or "I cleaned up his kitchen for him." Sex rules may be changing, but if my couples are any indication, not very quickly.

Our sample couple scored high toward imbalance. The wife was clearly doing almost everything, and was even responsible for sexual frequency. "I am the Hunchback of Notre House. I walk around like this, hunched over, scanning for junk, mostly other people's junk. I guess my family thinks that their dirty clothes have special magnets in them so they fly straight to the washer, rotate to the dryer, fold themselves into neat piles, and levitate to the correct drawer. Maybe they think I have magnets on me. Other people's dirty clothes sure seem to cling to me."

The husband reported, "I think I carry the major burden. If I don't provide for our security, who will? I know it sounds kind of sexist, but I really am the breadwinner, you know. What would you think is more pressure, winning the bread or cooking it?"

It does not matter who is right or how dated and sexist this disagreement may seem. Neither partner felt a balance in their marriage. Sexually, the situation was the same.

"I told you before," reported the wife. "I set the sexual frequency. I have to set it for both of us. If I am not in the mood—spontaneous, as he calls it—then I have ruined everything. He might even sulk. I guess he hopes for mercy sex, sex because he is sulking."

"I have to work, really work at sex with her," reported the husband. "She's kind of like a big cement wheel. Once I get her started, I still have to work. My hand gets tired from rubbing her nipples, then her clitoris. I always make her come before I come. Not once have I come before she comes in bed."

When this type of marital and sexual imbalance is present, both partners feel that they are the one who carries the weight. The situation resembles a scale, with both sides weighted down so heavily that the entire scale collapses. Who "starts it," how often, and when are three of the most talked-about concerns in sexual therapy.

. Remember that there are no "high" or "better" scores on this test. Too much balance, continued efforts to equalize, share, divide, assign, and assume marital or sexual responsibility robs the marriage of its spontaneous potential for a natural flow between partners, the sexual Tao. Too much attention, marital hypersensitivity, can smother the individual spouse and take away from both partners' uniqueness for the other. Too much feedback can result in over- or premature adjustments within the marriage, making it and the individual spouses hyperreactive. Too much connection can result in stagnation related to lack of new and stimulating input for the marital system. Too much order prevents change and growth.

6. UNHEALTHY SPOUSES IN "UNHEALTHY" SYSTEMS

> It's really embarrassing. My stomach seems to gurgle every time we try to make love. I mean, it's loud. He never says anything about it, but you never hear that in the movies.
>
> WIFE

> At first I thought it was coming from her vagina, this strange rumbling sound. I think it's her stomach, though. She is just in lousy shape, and she eats about four Ding Dongs or King Kongs or some junk food before bed every night. What does she expect?
>
> HUSBAND

HOMEOSTASIS:	HETEROSTASIS:
HOLISTIC HEALTH ORIENTATION, EATING, EXERCISING, ATTENDING TO WELLNESS TOGETHER	LACK OF INTEGRATION OF HEALTH RULES INTO MARITAL LIFE. SEPARATE HEALTH FOCUS AND HEALTH BEHAVIORS

```
 0   1   2   3   4   5   6   7   8   9   10
   TENDING TOWARD_____TENDING TOWARD
     HOMEOSTASIS              HETEROSTASIS
```

In terms of overall health, the rules are simple. Be moderate in caloric intake and exercise, reduce fats, minimize red meats, avoid smoking and alcohol, and learn to cope better with stress. In spite of all the research on health, these rules have long been known and many of us do our best to practice them. In your marriage, do both of you work together to integrate good health practices (homeostasis)? Or do you work separately if at all on the physical health of your marriage (heterostasis)?

The husband in our couple was a jogger and a softball player, and "demanded" that his wife buy and prepare health food. The wife had little time or made little time to attend to her own health, and was left making beds and cleaning up after dinner while her husband ran miles listening to his portable tape player.

The husband was trim, tan, firm, and energetic. My clerical staff was taken with his robust appearance, describing him as "a real hunk." The wife looked drawn and tired, and often brought sewing or other family-related work to the clinic waiting room. When I asked about her schoolwork, she said, "I get up at about five A.M. on weekends when it's quiet. I try to get it done then."

The wife complained of her own lack of sexual stamina. "I get tired easily. I'm fat, too, and I hate it, but I just cannot lose it for long. During intercourse, it almost scares me how hard he does it to me."

The husband reported, "She is so fat, so soft, so flabby. She's like a soft doll. If I am a sexual athlete, then she is Howard Cosell."

This couple, as many of the others in this report, failed to practice a system of wellness. Few wellness programs attend sufficiently to the system side of things. Doctors see individuals, not couples, for physical exams, and our wellness models are individuals, not marriages.

Super wellness depends upon a system wellness, a view that two people and their children are one, not parts. Too much homeostasis in the system, too much "oneness" can result in neglect of the individual health needs of each spouse, but a lack of homeostasis, of unit wellness, results in dis-ease for both spouses, and no amount of solo jogging will chase down total wellness.

7. "COMING" TOGETHER

We try. We try. He slows down, I try to hurry up. We just seem to miss it. We just cannot seem to come together. It was easier when I faked it. I'm sorry now that I ever told him that I faked it.

WIFE

I wish now she would just fake it. I don't think we will ever come together like everyone else.

HUSBAND

NEGUENTROPY:	ENTROPY:
MOVING MORE AND MORE TOGETHER, GETTING CLOSER AND CLOSER AS PEOPLE	MOVING APART, FEELING MORE AND MORE DISTANT, GETTING MORE SEXUALLY DISTANT

```
 0   1   2   3   4   5   6   7   8   9   10
    TENDING TOWARD_____TENDING TOWARD
        CLOSENESS                  DISTANCE
```

It is not possible to experience simultaneously any human physiological response. The complexity of genital responses, with all of the associated feelings and thoughts, makes any effort to match them in time not only a wasted effort, but counterproductive to spontaneous intimacy.

The word entropy means to become more diffuse, more distant. It comes from physics, and is referred to as the second law of thermodynamics, meaning that molecules tend to become more and more distant from each other, that the world is becoming more and more "apart." Neguentropy means the opposite, to come more and more together through a complex series of changes that look singularly as if they signal a falling apart, but really relate to a complex, infinite joining of all elements of the universe.

The world that we can see and touch is governed by the rules of thermodynamics, by entropy. The world of intuition, the world of feelings and awareness beyond see and touch, is governed by the rules of neguentropy. The word "super" in super marital sex refers to this world, to the "beyond, over, and transcendent" aspects of our life, to being at one with the universe by being at one with our marital system.

Is your own marriage getting closer and closer, seeming to merge into a "oneness" (neguentropy)? Or does it seem that you are becoming more and more distant, somehow parting (entropy)?

The couple in my example scored toward neguentropy. Their pattern of despair unfortunately was becoming solidified, almost unchangeable by the time they came for help. They were forming what I call a compensated marriage, one that gets more and more fixed through their mutually supported personal dissatisfactions. Couples who are fixed are the most difficult of all couples to work with, because they are unable to "breathe," to expand, and to grow. Attempts to help them grow result in a form of implosion, a cracking of a solidified system that has no room for expansion and contraction.

The super marriage can expand and contract, allow closeness without crowding and distance without diffuseness. A super marriage is a super system that flows between neguentropy and entropy in an intimate rhythm of life and growth for both partners, a universal dance of intimacy, a Tao of sexuality.

The husband in our example reported, "I really cannot imagine life without her. We just are like one in a strange sort of way. A dance with no song."

The wife added, "Well, he is not a part of me, I mean a part of me like my, I mean our, children are. I have become a part of him, an extension, sucked into his life. It's the way a black hole must be, a spiral, with me going down further and further into him."

This same compensated pattern was reported in the bedroom. "The more things change, the more they stay the same," said the husband. "We just repeat the same things in the same way. We could practically just call out the numbers or use hand signals. I lie on my right side, stimulate her, then we do it. That only changed once when I broke my right arm in a softball game. I was on her left side then, and it was like making it with a different woman."

"It's like a merry-go-round without the merry," added the wife. "He sort of works on me. He wants me to suck him after I come because that's the only time I can force myself to do it. Then he goes in, does it, the end."

Each time this couple makes love, the neguentropy, the merging, becomes stronger. They do not become more intimate, they become more trapped, stuck with each other and suffering together. They crash rather then merge. They have a type of marital implosion.

8. "ADAPTED" TO SEX

The crises we have had seem to have strengthened us somehow. We get better at solving things as we go along.

HUSBAND

With every setback, our marriage is set back. We just can't take much more.

WIFE

ADAPTIVE:	MALADAPTIVE:
MARRIAGE IS	CRISES WEAKEN MARRIAGE,
STRENGTHENED AT TIMES	LOSS DRAWS SPOUSES APART
OF LOSS AND OTHER CRISES	

```
0    1    2    3    4    5    6    7    8    9   10
  TENDING TOWARD_____TENDING TOWARD
     ADAPTABILITY              MALADAPTIVENESS
```

Think of the major crises your marriage has been forced to cope with. Loss of a parent, a sick or handicapped child, loss of job or other major setback. Did such events actually seem to help your marriage (adaptive)? Or did they tend to weaken it (maladaptive)?

You may find it difficult to understand how a marriage could be "too" adaptable, but the issue of room to grow explains this possibility. "Premature adaptability" excludes the newness, freshness, and challenge necessary for personal and relationship growth, much as speaking for a child can delay and sometimes permanently restrict language development for that child. All growth depends upon periods of stress within the system, times where everything seems out of whack, when adjustments must be made.

The couple in my example scored toward maladaptive. A recent work problem for the husband resulted in a severe marital argument, almost to the point of violence. "Damn it, what does she think? I have this terrible thing happen to me through no fault of my own, and she wants to go that night to visit her mother in the nursing home. Sure, I put my hand through the bedroom door, but it's only a thin door,'' said the frustrated husband.

The wife added, "He's done that before, when his Uncle Ned died. We just can't handle these kinds of things. I need help, too. My mother was all alone in that place, and all he can think about is his job. We might as well not be married. We deal with things alone.''

Their sexual problems also had drawn them even further apart. The wife reported that she was inorgasmic and had pain during intercourse. The husband had consulted sex manuals and diagnosed himself as a "premature ejaculator.'' He looked to what was wrong with him, not what might be wrong with the marital system.

The wife said, "I'm like a rubber doll to him. Sex is rare because it hurts and just verifies each time how bad the problem is, how much pain there is in our marriage.''

The husband reported, "Instead of trying to help, she actually loves it that I come too soon. It sort of saves her the time and problem of having sex too long with me.''

One of the most important questions that can be asked of a marriage is "Can you name the worst crisis your marriage has experienced and tell me how your marriage dealt with it?'' Adaptive marriages clearly are stronger for their pain, and maladaptive marriages report a weakening and a worsening of long-standing problems with each transitional life problem.

You will learn in a later chapter about strategies to help marriages, not individuals, cope with problems of daily living and the fact that none of us really has a "sex'' life but rather a full life in relationship to everything and everyone. Strong marital systems grow within their life system.

Too much adaptability and marriages can become only problem-solving units at the expense of joy and the pleasure of daily living. Again, a flow, a wide "stretchability,'' a marital elasticity makes for the healthiest, most enduring intimacy system.

The example husband added, "When my Uncle Ned died, I cried until I was dry. I cried in the corner of the basement by the workbench. I don't think anybody ever really saw me cry.''

The wife reported, "When I [notice not "we"] had to put my mother in that nursing home, it was one of the worst things I have ever had to do. I cried for hours in the tub at night. All I heard was 'Are you going to be in there all night?' I felt so alone.''

The couple I am using throughout this chapter continues to show one major characteristic: a lack of any system for mutual growth, learning, and change. Any system, and particularly marital systems, that fails to learn and change will develop dis-ease and eventually die.

9. WHAT IS SEX "FOR"?

> I can't remember what I wanted to be when I grew up. I've been too busy helping everyone else in this house grow up to pay any attention to that anymore.
>
> HUSBAND

> I notice that my husband is never in my dreams.
>
> WIFE

PURPOSE:
DO YOU SHARE A COMMON
DREAM WITH YOUR SPOUSE?
IS THERE PURPOSE TO YOUR
MARRIAGE BEYOND
SURVIVAL AND CHILD
REARING?

AIMLESS:
ARE YOU WORKING IN
DIFFERENT DIRECTIONS,
TOWARD DIFFERENT GOALS,
WITHOUT PURPOSE?

```
   0    1    2    3    4    5    6    7    8    9   10
      TENDING TOWARD_____TENDING TOWARD
      MUTUAL PURPOSE          AIMLESSNESS
```

Is there still a reason for the two of you to be married, a reason that applies and has meaning for now and for the future (purposeful)? Or, are you two people with no common dreams or purpose, just going along perhaps with separate and unshared dreams (aimless)?

One of the first questions I ask the couple is "Why are you married?" followed by "Tell me your shared marital dreams." Our society talks of individual liberty and the pursuit of happiness, and less of unity of purpose and dreams. This sample couple scored high toward the aimless axis. The wife reported, "I have always wanted to finish college. He thinks that's silly. He says I wouldn't make enough to make it matter. It matters to me, though."

The husband responded, "I have a clear dream. Living on a lake up north, fishing all day, even at night. I could even use my snow-mobile during the winter."

Two dreams, unshared, and without the appearance of the spouse in either dream. Why are you and your spouse together now? Why do you have sex and intimacy anyway?

Sexually, the couple responded to my question about their

"dream sex life" in quite different fashion. The husband reported, "That's easy. Sex every day, every night, on the floor, in the car, out in the yard, sucking me anyplace and anytime."

The wife responded, "I kind of see me walking with him on a beautiful beach, say, in Maui. The moon is behind us, the ocean in front of us, the warmth embracing us. We both feel warm, move together, kiss, and move slowly to the sand. No one is near, we are perfectly safe and alone together."

"That's no sex fantasy." The husband laughed. "Don't you think about garter belts, black panties, some real adventure?"

Sexual interaction has become goal-directed rather than dream-inspired, and the sexual system of your marriage draws its fuel from shared dreams. While too much purpose can force and drive a marriage, stressing it toward future accomplishments, too little common purpose destroys the reason for togetherness. If there is no place to go, we end up searching and lost. If we only look to the destination, our own unshared destination, we will never enjoy the journey.

10. "AUTOMATIC SEX"

Sometimes it's like a mutual trance. We just flow from one thing, one activity, to another. I guess we talk, but I don't really remember. We just seem to be one.

HUSBAND

I can have sex with him and just go through the motions. It's like washing your hands. You just do it.

WIFE

AUTOMATICITY:	CONTROL:
SMOOTH, EFFORTLESS TRANSITIONS WITHIN THE MARRIAGE, EASE OF DAILY ACTIVITY FLOW AND SEXUAL INTERACTION	AWKWARD TRANSITIONS, NO FLOW TO MARITAL ACTIVITIES OR SEXUAL INTERACTION

```
0   1   2   3   4   5   6   7   8   9   10
  TENDING TOWARD_____TENDING TOWARD
    AUTOMATICITY        EFFORT AND CONTROL
```

Is your marriage free of what I call "friction in activity flow"? Do things get done easily, simply, almost like the performance of a concert pianist who makes it look easy after years of practice (automaticity)? Or are things difficult much of the time, with much

friction, awkwardness, like dancing with two followers or two lead-
ers (control)?

Our sample couple scored high toward automaticity. Things
flowed from one to another so well that no one seemed to sense
that husband and wife were in trouble. "Life goes on," said the
wife, "I just keep it going, hand him his orange juice as he checks
the morning paper, hand him his briefcase on the move."

The husband agreed. "I have to say, we are a team. We get things
done. We're organized. I don't know if the team is winning, but
it's a team."

Sexually, this couple typifies the automaticity of the compensated marriage. The wife said, "Our sex is like a pantomime. We
are better than Marcel Marceau. We do it, don't talk, just do it. A
silent, well-rehearsed movie." The husband agreed. "We don't
miss a beat. I hate the way it is just so automatic."

Too much automaticity and there is no challenge to the system,
no reason to grow and change. Too little automatic function and
too much awkwardness fatigues the system and results in a surrendering within the system or seeking outside the system for ease to
escape this form of dis-ease.

You have now completed all ten items of the sexual system test.
Each factor is exactly the same as the factors that physicists know
influence all systems. You may have found it difficult to score yourself on this test because you are not used to the absence of good,
better, and bigger scores. Systems do not work that way. To help
you understand how your system is doing at this time in your marital
life, use the following score analysis.

Symmetrical, Complementary, and Accommodating Sexual Systems

Count up the number of items that you scored to the right of the 5
(6,7,8,9, or 10 scores that you circled). Do not add up the values,
just count the actual number of items to the right of 5. The sample
couple you have been following throughout this chapter, and whose
quotes you have been reading, had seven numbers to the right of 5
and both husband and wife scored exactly the same. You would
expect that from a couple that is compensated, stuck in a chronic
system of interaction.

Next, count up the number of items you circled to the left of the

5 (0, 1, 2, 3 or 4). Again, both spouses in our example scored identically, and they each circled three numbers to the left of the 5. Subtract the number of times you scored to the left of 5 from the number to the right of 5, and you have your sexual-system score. It is possible to have a negative score not in meaning but in the interpretation of your scores. To understand the meaning of your score in this new systems context, place it on the following line:

ACCOMMODATING MARRIAGE

SYMMETRICAL MARRIAGE>>>> <<<<COMPLEMENTARY MARRIAGE

−10 9 8 7 6 5 4 3 2 1 0 +1 2 3 4 5 6 7 8 9 10

If your score fell in the minus range, your sexual system is functioning in the symmetrical mode at this time. You tend toward an egalitarian, romaticized, nonsexist, balanced relationship. If your score fell toward the plus side of 0, you tend toward a more separated, sexist marriage that has less balance than the symmetrical marriage.

The accommodating marriage is a super sex marriage. It adapts over time. The score of this type of marriage would be near zero. This type of marriage has a high AC, or alternating capacity, going back and forth between symmetrical and complementary in response to external and internal needs in the overall marital sexual system. Like all systems, ease and balance seem healthier than disease and extremes, so a score around zero is the healthier score and a place for our focus throughout this book.

You now understand more about the systems approach and what is meant by super marital sex, a sex that goes beyond the limits of day-to-day patterns, holistically growing and changing with, for, and because of the partners' interaction. How you find someone to form such a relationship with and how you discover such a relationship for your marriage requires integrating our marital "IQ", Intimacy Quotient, from Chapter One and your sexual-system score from this chapter. I will show you in Chapter Three how the courtship ritual works in our society and how you can re-court your marital partner by a new set of super sex rules, how intimate systems are formed.

The couple we have been following managed to break their solidified pattern of male-dominated, female-compliant, distant, and misperceived patterns of sexuality and daily marital living. They did so through the steps you will learn in the following chapters. They learned about their own love experiences. They learned the

systems approach to marriage, and struggled to create new styles
of loving. Most important of all, they learned that mutual responsibility within and for an ever-changing system of intimacy was
vital to their own personal as well as their marital health. They
continue to struggle together with this learning, loving, within a
system that gives more room to grow.

Super Marital Sex Opportunity Number Two

Earlier in this chapter, I mentioned the idea of "sexual cybernetics," of getting in touch with the natural flow of your marital and
sexual system. You have made some tapes and started the process
of system enhancement in Chapter One's opportunity. Now try this
next step toward super marital sex.

Reverse everything you can in your marital system. For one week,
change sides of the bed, change who gets up in the morning first,
redistribute household chores, change who drives or who drives
what car, just change everything. Change who cooks, who makes
the beds, who watches television, who reads. Sit down together and
plan this out.

Be sure to include your children in the planning of these changes.
Get their input as to who does what in the marriage and their ideas
on how to do this "cybernetics reversal" opportunity. It is cyber-
netic because it will make you more aware, more in touch with the
other side of things in your marital system. These changes will not
be easy, but you are not working for an easy sex marriage, you are
working for a super sex marriage, one that is much wider, deeper,
richer, and adaptable than you ever imagined.

When I presented this opportunity to the couple you have just
read about, the husband responded, "Wait a minute. What does
this have to do with our sex problem? What does this have to do
with sex?" I didn't have to answer. His wife took over. "I'll tell
you what it has to do with sex," she explained. "It will give us a
chance to learn from each other, maybe experience a little of what
we each experience. I can't wait to watch you fix dinner. And I
guess I'll have to get out my old baseball glove."

CHAPTER THREE

🌷🌷🌷

Courting, Re-courting, and the Super Sex Bond

It's not like a meat market in the singles bars. At least at the meat market, you get what you went in for. You take a number and the product is government-inspected.

NEWLY DIVORCED MAN

Three Looks and a Shift

"Oh no! He's coming over here." The woman placed both hands around her glass of Perrier water, looking down as if preparing to dive into the carbonation. She had been married for nineteen years, had recently divorced, and was making her debut on the courtship carousel.

"You brought him over here, Sheila," said her friend Pam, a veteran of three marriages and several years in what she now called "meat-ing places." "You never look at one of them three times unless you want them to come over."

"I wasn't looking at him. He was looking at me," said Sheila, still afraid to look up from her drink.

"Come on," said Pam, "How did you know he was looking if you weren't looking? I don't believe you. If you look three times, he comes. Now you better go to the 'shift.' "

"What is the shift?" Sheila could feel her heart pumping, skipping beats as it had done when she first used the word "divorce" seriously.

"It's survival," said Pam. "The shift means giving him to me. I can get rid of him, but you have to shift him to me."

He arrived tableside, his glass of half-flat beer held between himself and Sheila. "I know this sounds like a line, but you look familiar."

At any other time, Sheila would have been unable to hold back a giggle. He might as well have tried "Come here often?" Now, however, Sheila was a player, not an observer safely protected within a stable relationship. There was nothing funny about this. Her heart was beating faster, and her mouth was dry. She remembered this feeling from her speech class in college. She had failed to master this eye-contact thing then, too.

"I am," she stammered, looking into his beer. "No, I mean, you think I am, but I'm not—familiar to you, that is." She felt her face glowing. Unbelievable, she thought. I'm an English teacher and I can't even talk.

"Now that I hear your voice, I guess I was mistaken." he said. She could see his undershirt beneath his shirt. It was the old-fashioned type, with shoulder bands. She had never liked that style. In fact, she had never liked undershirts at all. This style in particular usually meant the man was wearing boxer shorts, the kind that goes down both legs and comes in weird prints. She hated those. Where do they put their penis in that kind of shorts? To which side?

She was startled by her own thoughts. Why was she thinking these things now, about this stranger? Who cared anyway?

Pam took his beer glass and led him to the dance floor. She glanced back over her shoulder at Sheila with a "now look what you made me have to do" look.

Sheila looked around, hoping that no one else had seen this disaster. She wet her napkin with the bottom of her glass, lifted it, and let it drop, playing a lonely game, waiting for Pam to return.

She saw Pam coming back, putting her finger to her throat in a mock gesture of self-induced nausea. "Let's join his table," said Pam. "That's where the action is."

Sheila rose with her glass, napkin still attached. The three of them grouped around a small table already crowded with more than ten people. Someone shoved a chair into her thighs and she fell into it. She was two rows from the table, a bench player in the dating game. The man next to her offered her a pretzel.

Sheila summoned all of her courage. "You look familiar," she said, and then bit into the pretzel. It shattered into little pieces, with one big piece left dangling from her mouth. Another piece now floated in her drink with the napkin still attached.

"Have you met Al?" asked the man. Sheila had just been shifted by an expert.

If you read this passage in disbelief, then you have not been on the dating circuit for a long time. The game goes on. Courtship in America is training for divorce, a hypocritical, stressful, dishonest, and sad attempt to find someone to love. It is based on five rules that can be learned only in the field of action. No one can teach you; you must learn by experience.

Take some time now to rethink your own courtship, to recall the bonding process in your own marriage. How, why, and where did you fall in love, bond, decided to commit to and with someone else? Failure to understand that process results in the continued reliving of the same errors within your own relationship. This chapter adds the bonding dimension to the intimacy and systems concepts you have learned in the first two chapters. This bonding is not a onetime thing; it goes on forever. The thousand couples learned much from reliving their bonding process on the way to super marital sex, on the way to a stronger, more adaptive martital bond.

The Rules Of Romance Roulette

> It's hard to think back to then, but it seems like we never really dated in the formal sense. We just sort of found each other, went out, and assumed we would marry. Come to think of it, I never asked her.
>
> HUSBAND

The following five rules appeared repeatedly in the courtship stories of the thousand couples. Even those couples who had been childhood sweethearts, never dating anyone else, experienced aspects of each of the following rules. Do you remember any of this? Talk about it with your spouse. Take your own bonding history.

Rule One: You Always Lie to the One You Love

Never, but never, tell the complete truth too soon to someone who might be a possible bonding partner. Keep your emotional cards close to your vest. If things get serious, you can always modify any lies later. The idea now is to present yourself, not represent yourself.

The rule seems to mean to be careful, because if you start telling your real feelings too soon, you might develop even more real feelings without sufficient time to get ready for them. The truth is a serious thing, and no one tells the truth early in a relationship, because you should not get too serious too soon.

Rule Two: Declare Romantic Immunity

State early, often, and loudly that you are not looking for a commitment at this time. Of course, a commitment is exactly what you are looking for, but you must maintain immunity from being hurt yourself and be available just in case another, better partner comes along. If it gets out that you are looking for a serious relationship, it may weaken your position in the pursuer/pursuee game.

Rule Three: Always Be the Pursued, Not the Pursuer

Try to give your number and have the other person call you. You must create the illusion that your romantic options are endless and any person interested in you may have to wait in a long line. Never answer the phone with "Oh great, I was hoping against hope that you would be calling." Answer instead with, "Yes, I think I remember you." All of us have only a limited number of people to choose from, but we must never let that be known to each other.

Rule Four: Never Have Sex Until the Third Date

The third-date phenomenon, sex on the third date, is universally known. Due to the AIDS issue and fear of other sexually transmissible diseases, the third-date phenomenon is becoming the tenth-date phenomenon, but the timing is irrelevant. Sex is nowhere near as important as everyone says it is, and probably very important to those people who tell you it does not matter at all.

Remember, the rules are that the whole game changes after the sex act takes place. It is the turning point. For men, the conquest may be complete, and they may disappear. For women, emotional involvement may intensify now, but they must be courageous and not let the man know they take this sex thing too seriously. No research supports this sexist view, but these rules have little to do with fact.

Some people cheat on this rule flagrantly. Men and women may become close, feelings may get involved, honesty, caring, and vulnerability may follow. When this involvement happens, start discussing philosophical issues of recreational sex, short life spans, limited life pleasures, and the value of extensive sexual training prior to any real commitment. Even though there is no data to show that amount or frequency of sex relates to fulfilling sex, this argument can protect you from any real involvement related to sex.

Rule Five: Always be Ready to Get Dumped. If at All Possible, Be the Dumper, Not the Dumpee

All relationships end. It is just a matter of how and when. Those "really hot" relationships, the ones that seem very early to be the real thing, are the most likely to have high dumping potential. Getting dumped is one of the most painful of human experiences. Avoid it at all costs.

You avoid getting dumped by not getting too involved, and always watching for the slightest sign of preparatory dumping. When you see it coming, dump first and fast. It is also wise to tell the dumpees that they are being dumped for their own good. This is called the *"therapeutic dump,"* and is supposed to feel better than other forms of dump. Some of these are:

The Dirty Dump: You have found someone better, have known about it for some time, but have been staying with the dumpee as insurance against your own dumping. Once you are safe, dump.

The Dumb Dump: This occurs when someone gives you false information, probably in order to move in on your dumpee once you have done the dumping. You dump too soon, and you have been fooled into a dumb dump.

The Dangling Dump: This is a highly skilled dumping involving a built-in safety factor. You provide some hope, usually false, that you will take the person back following the dumping. This is done in case your new partner dumps you or your old partner starts to look much better compared to the new one.

The Delayed Dump: This is done when you know far ahead of time that you are going to dump someone, but delay the actual dumping until after a scheduled family event, dance, or other oc-

casion at which people might ask, ''Whatever happened to . . . ?''
Dumping is easier than explaining.

The Devious Dump: This is done when you know you are going
to dump someone right from the start of the relationship, but are
too lazy to look for a better match right now. You pre-plan the
dump for a personally convenient time, maybe when your work
schedule is easier and you have time to deal with the dumping
hassle.

As exaggerated as these rules are, you probably recognized some
of them. Beyond the described ritualistic procedures, courtship is
something that is largely ignored in our society. No one tells us
how to do it. Adults laugh at us as we struggle through dating as
adolescents, and they cry with each other as they court, suffering
the indignities of an oversexualized, stultified adult dating scene.

I asked the couples to tape their actual ''bonding time,'' just a
brief paragraph on what they felt when they started to bond. I had
them compare their stories. Whether or not the stories match or
who had the correct details was not important. The process of
sharing bonding feelings is helpful in preparation for super marital
sex. Here is one of the couples' set of paragraphs to help you get
started.

WIFE: ''I sort of remember where. We were in the drive-in, of all
places. We never really necked or anything there. It cost too much
to get in, so we thought we should watch the movie. The bucket
seats were impossible. The backseat was full of junk like hubcaps
and I think some large part of a transmission. The car always smelled
like oil.

''I remember looking over at him watching the movie. It was
some type of horror thing, and he looked ready to jump. I had to
go to the bathroom so bad it hurt, but I hated those dirty bathrooms.
Early in our courting, I sort of went to 'freshen my makeup,' usually with two or three other girls on a secret signal known only to
women. Now I just said it. I don't know why. I said I had to pee.
I surprised even myself.

''He seemed relieved at the distraction from the movie. Before,
he might have said okay and sort of let me go. This time, he climbed
out of the car. I mean climbed, because this was in the days when
boys somehow modified the car so it was about five feet off the
road. He came to my side, opened the door, reached behind my
seat, and took out a small stepstool that he had made just for me.

My own exit stool from his magic chariot. As silly as it sounds, I was moved. He seemed embarrassed, but walked me to the bathroom, waited for me, walked me back, and helped me climb back onboard. I just remember from that time on, things seemed different. Very romantic, isn't it. I still use that dumb stool to reach the top cupboard."

HUSBAND: "It was at a wedding. I remember clearly. I never thought of it until now. I was the best man, she was the maid of honor. I never saw her looking so beautiful. She looked more like a woman than ever before. It sort of struck me how very mature and beautiful she was.

"It was one of those dances when the bride and groom start out and the wedding party follows, one couple at a time. When it was our turn, I sort of felt shaky when I took her in my arms. She looked right into my eyes. Everyone was looking. It was like everyone in the room saw it happen. I fell in love right there. It seemed like we were the bride and groom."

Two different times for this couple, but each person was able, with some encouragement and questioning from me, to discover their "bonding imprint." It happened to you, even if you are having marital trouble or feel that maybe you never really fell in love. If you "paired up," you bonded, at least for a while. Try to recount your bonding imprint for your present relationship. Taping it or writing it down seems to make it more real for most couples. Add this record to your material from your first two super marital sex opportunities from Chapters One and Two.

The Sex Phases Of Courtship

> I'm not going with him. I'm going out with him. You make it sound like we're going steady. We're not. We're going steadily, but we are certainly not pre-engaged.
>
> HIGH-SCHOOL GIRL

Researchers have demonstrated that bonding takes place in phases. My work indicates a six-phase cycle identified in the thousand couples. Discuss each with your partner and see if at least some of these factors may have been present in your relationship.

Phase One: Proceptive Phase: The Announcement

> Look. He's scanning. He stands with his back to the bar, sort of leaning on it like that. He uses his glass like a type of sight on the barrel of a rifle, except that he is holding it just below his belt. Guess what type of rifle he has in mind? He'll just scan back and forth until he gets a return glance.
>
> STUDENT ANALYZING COURTSHIP TAPE

The first step in bonding is to send a message of availability through words or body language. We all do this every day of our lives, even if we are very happily bonded. We seem to be keeping in practice by sending at least mini-messages to test our "bondability." It is our mammalian background that predisposes us to this proception.

The body language of proception involves positioning, showing skin (even just a wrist), leaning toward one another, brief touches, "accidental" bumping, leaning on one another, talking closely to one another's heads because of sometimes nonexistent noise, and other "body dances." Unfortunately, we tend to abandon these bonding body dances as our marriages age. I teach the couples to "bond-dance" to recapture some of the body dance that helped make the bond in the first place. We come to feel as we behave, so if we behave "bondingly," we may learn to rediscover our bonding feelings.

We send "hot flashes" during our day. We pass one another, exchange a glance, and seem to send the message, "I could possibly relate to you. I will never talk to you, but I think we could do something together." Our eyes meet, brief fantasies may occur, and we may think about this anonymous encounter again later. These encounters may take place on an elevator, walking down the hall at work, or even at a traffic light, but they happen and happen often. "Warm flashes" occur when you have lunch with someone, talk with someone over a period of time at a party, work with someone as a colleague, or spend a little time with someone. Glances are exchanged again, and conversations may include double-meaning messages that test the bonding state of each person. These interactions may be just a form of "bonding play," but again we all do this, establish brief, mini-bonds with many people, perhaps as a way of meeting the bonding needs unmet in our primary relationship.

Phase Two: Receptive Phase: The Reception

You don't just say "Hey great, I've been hoping you would ask me out." It takes the challenge away, and without the challenge of the chase, there is no energy behind the whole thing. You still have to chase them until they catch you.

MEDICAL STUDENT

Acknowledging that a bonding invitation has been sent to you is one of the riskiest steps in the bonding process. How can you trust your senses, even your own ears? Does he really mean it? Why would she be interested in me? Maybe he's just being funny? Maybe she's teasing? I'll look like a fool if I take this seriously, but I hate to miss the chance just in case this is serious. All of these thoughts can occur almost simultaneously when a bonding invitation is perceived.

One of the thousands husbands recounted the following story. "She asked me up for a drink after the show. I have always had trouble with this 'up for a drink' thing. I sort of used to go into my 'get ready for sex' mode, but sometimes it just means up for a drink. It's hard to tell. She told me to have a seat. That's not an easy thing. Do you take a chair or the couch? She said, 'Make yourself comfortable. I'm going to get real comfortable myself.'

"Now I really went into sex mode two. How do you get yourself comfortable sitting for the first time in someone's apartment? I took off my tie, unbuttoned my shirt, kicked off my shoes, and moved to the couch. I even rolled up my sleeves. I was getting aroused.

"She returned to the room and I felt like a jerk. 'What do you think you're doing, moving in?' she said. She had changed to jeans and paint shirt. 'I'm finishing sanding my old table. Get yourself a drink and let yourself out, will you? I don't want to drag dust through the carpet.'

"I made up some cover lie. I think I said something like, 'Oh, I just can't stand that tight collar and jacket. I think I've gained a little weight and it's all too tight.' I even went into greater detail trying to save face. What a night."

Just as proception requires vulnerability and directness, reception requires a lowering of defenses, taking major risks. It requires sufficiently resilient self-esteem to endure the knocks we all receive in the bonding process. We have to be arrogant enough to assume that someone wants us and humble enough to remember that many people would choose to have nothing to do with us. Is the other person sure? Am I sure?

Do you remember taking the risk? Do you remember allowing yourself to feel that someone you wanted really wanted you?

Phase Three: Deceptive Phase: Protection by Projection

> What was she so upset about? She never forgot it. She still talks about it. So what? I told her I was Catholic when we first met. Big deal. I'm Jewish. Same thing.
>
> HUSBAND

Once the message is sent, received, and acknowledged, phase three tends to dominate the interaction. While it would seem that the two persons would be ready to open up to one another, in fact the opposite is true. Now that something important is at stake, a real possibility of a lasting bond, both persons seem to go into "projective" posture.

Persons in the deceptive phase begin to present the "they" that they would like the other person to perceive they are and each of us desperately wants to be. The projected image is not realistic, however. Deception here is as much of self as of the other. The impact on marriage is severe, for it is at this phase that many marriages occur, bonding between two projected images. Partners believe in the "magical mystical healing powers of marriage," that marriage will somehow in some way solve any problem. The more idealistic the projected images, the more denial is employed, and the more denial before marriage, the more disappointment in marriage. It takes a great amount of energy to keep denying how we really are, and "leakage" occurs. On some level, it takes recognition of what is being denied to maintain the denial, and the recognition is present in both partners. They continue, however, to trust in the illusion of the healing power of marriage without presenting the "real patients."

One clear dimension of bonding emerges so far. Marriage will only make any problem worse, and that applies most directly to any sexual problem. It probably explains in part why second marriages are almost twice as likely to divorce as first marriages. Marrying at the "deceptive phase," the time of projection of image, is a mistake. It can be corrected through techniques to be described later, but it is one of the major contributions to the high divorce rate in our country. One of my clinical rules is to tell spouses, "Never divorce someone you don't know, and be sure you start with yourself."

Phase Four: Acceptive Phase: The Settlement

> He really used to come to see my parents more than me. In fact, I think
> they came to like him more than I did. He would just sort of show up.
> No more official dates or invitations. The quality of our outings went
> down severely. We started to save money. He didn't pay for the dates
> anymore. We pooled our money and went to the Lick and Split Ice
> Cream Parlor to have small cones while we watched other people eat
> their banana splits.
>
> WIFE

At this phase of bonding, the relationship is maturing. It has made it
past the projective dimension, and the partners now start to show
their true colors. "I never in the world would have told him about
my period before. Now he knew when it was or when it should be
better than I did," reported one woman. "I told her," reported one
man, "I just can't stand her cracking her gum. I lived with that for
weeks before I told her." Now the real feelings come out.

A couple can tell when they are in the acceptive phase by the
occurrence of several breakups, patch-ups, makeups, and re-break-
ups. This phase seems to be an opportunity to test the system for
the pressures of real marital life, to learn to make up and stay with
it even at times of stress and strain. This testing is only effective,
however, if both partners are free from the myth of romance. Romance, "hot love," lasts only a few months. Researchers can trace
this pattern clearly. If one or both partners cling to the myth of
romance, that a relationship will remain hot, lustful, emotionally
and sexually intense in the fashion of early bonding, then their goal
is unrealistic. They will tend to do their "serial relating," their
breakups and makeups with several persons instead of learning to
do them with one partner as is required for an enduring marriage.

Another danger here is that one partner may learn to give in, or
to hold out for some form of later justice in marriage, letting things
go for now. This strategy is a major mistake. Later justice never
comes. The opposite of injustice is not justice, but love. Open
sharing, conflict resolution, mutual effort at problem-solving, dealing with day-to-day issues of family, religion, money, kids, and
work all must be processed during this crucial courtship phase.
Marriage before this phase is a risky proposition. It is better to
learn to divorce and remarry before you ever get married in the first
place. Perhaps then we will not have to experience "serial divorce"
in order to learn how to relate intimately forever.

Phase Five: Conceptive Phase: Creating the System

> I could see that we were going to get married. Everyone else seemed
> to know it before we did. I don't remember asking, really. The next
> thing I knew, we were talking about the hall, the band, and why her
> uncle would never come to the wedding because one of her aunts would
> be there.
>
> HUSBAND

This phase is characterized by the awareness that two must be more
than just one and one. The couple learns that career, children,
family issues, religion, and money are not individual issues combined in some form of compromise. A true bond offers the opportunity for a "gestalt," a relationship that is more than the sum of
the two people within it.

"I would have never thought of being a lawyer until I met her,"
reported the husband. "I knew I wanted to do something in government, but we talked it out a lot. It just sort of came up as
something from both of us."

"He brought out the fighter in me," reported the wife. "My
family had really asked just too much of me. He helped me find a
new independence, a new way to be with my parents."

Both of these statements illustrate the "and" factor, the birth of
a new system in which the new whole is more than the sum of the
parts, and the parts, the "partners," are more than they ever were
before.

The advantage of working with these couples for years is that I
have been able to do a modified longitudinal study, a study of couples in distress and a study of the same couple in "high-level wellness." I learned that couples which I will describe next, tended to
be the best marital problem solvers. The thousand couples who
successfully completed the therapy program were able to relive, to
discuss and re-experience their courtship patterns and apply their
lessons to their present marital system.

The super marriage for super sex became a generating marriage
in which both partners continued to become much more than they
would have been alone. Partners were able to draw from each other
and give to each other, broad strokes contributing to a completely
original artwork. What has your marriage produced that you alone
would never have produced? For many of you, the answer will go
far beyond just the biological gift of children. You yourself may
have been given a new birth through your relationship. Strong mar-

ital systems seem to offer a continuous "birthing" place for both spouses, a place where wife and husband simultaneously create and are recreated by the marriage.

Phase Six: Reflective Phase: The Reconsideration

> I'm not sure what it means. I really love her. But I wonder how it would have been with someone else.
>
> HUSBAND

It is true that we are probably not by nature monogamous. Monogamy makes little sense genetically or in strictly evolutionary terms. It makes sense in a personal, spiritual, feeling, and loving sense. It is our nature to reflect, to wonder, to imagine how others would be with us and we would be with them. Such wonder is not a symptom of marital weakness; it is a natural phase of loving. Only fear, insecurity, and denial will prevent it.

Why did we marry this person and why at this time in our life? It is much better to ask this question before reflection becomes recollection, trying to remember after the divorce. Take the time to reflect openly with your partner. Steal from other fantasy relationships ideas for the constant changing of your own relationship. Do not fear your natural curiosity and attraction to the different and unique.

"I noticed as we sat at the traffic light in our car that I was looking at him and my husband was looking at her. They were doing the same," reported the wife. It is not so much that the grass is always greener in someone else's lawn, it is just that it is a different lawn. Talk about those feelings, and your own lawn can grow greener by the mental cross-pollination. This is a way to re-court, to rediscover some of the energy behind your pairing, if only in your imagery.

A word of warning. During courtship or the re-courtship I am proposing, there will be several negatives. "I can't stand that little bit of spit that comes out when he gets excited when he talks," shared one wife. "She picks at her cuticles. It drives me nuts. I have seen her bite them and eat them," said one husband. These negatives are all a part of reflection. Share them gently and with as much tolerance as you can muster. You may want to work on correcting some of them. But remember, as the wife who bit her cuticles said, "Jeez, Sam. Everybody does something."

Courting Sexual Problems

> We just learned to do it that way. He stimulated me through my slacks.
> Now, it takes rough and long stimulation for me to come. I just got
> used to it that way.
>
> WIFE

An important part of learning about the sexual problems brought
to my clinic was to have the couples describe their typical premarital sexual pattern. It became clear that the large majority of their
problems originated during the bonding phase of their relationship.

Typically, the sexual interaction was male-instigated and female-
dictated. Men sought out the sexual encounter, and women determined when and if sex took place. This pattern seemed to be a type
of obligatory date dance that was not reflective of individual preferences. There was little verbal communication during the sex of
courtship, and the women reported rare or inconsistent orgasmic
experience. The men reported problems with ejaculatory control
and sometimes erective problems due to drinking or feelings of
pressure to perform. Sex during courtship was intense and exciting,
but characterized by the same type of sexual problems reported in
marriage.

I did not find that men or women selected future marital partners
on the basis of sexual prowess. In fact, both men and women reported that sex with someone they did not marry was better than
with the person they finally chose. It seems that people marry for
a system, not just a person, that they are actually marrying not only
a person but accepting how they themselves are with that particular
person. Good sex is never enough.

Couples fell into bad habits, rushing sex, using it for negotiation,
feeling guilty, trying to sneak to have sex at all, and sometimes
cheating on a partner for sex while staying with the courting partner
for a relationship. Since all of this was in the past, it is impossible
to verify, but two patterns emerged in the interviews.

Men tended to remember focusing on performance, on giving
their partners orgasm, or "their best time ever." All the same,
however, the men reported feeling somehow incomplete, wanting
more. "I did it an awful lot, and sometimes pretty awful. I could
do it with three different women at three different times in the same
evening. It just lost something. Finally I just felt that it was becoming like a good-night kiss, only this was good-night intercourse."
This report by one of the husbands was typical and was a fore-

warning of the "doing to or for" instead of "with" orientation that can take place in marriage. Remember, "to" and "for" are not systems words. "With" is the key word in a lasting super sex system.

Women reported a tendency to "negotiate" sex in courtship. They felt they somehow were in charge of sex, allowing it to take place in exchange for evidence of true feelings of caring or commitment. "It's not that I didn't love sex. I really think I wanted to have it more than most of the men I went out with. They seemed to do it out of a sense of duty, expectation, sort of the automatic next step or last step to a date. I just got so used to worrying about 'after' that I lost sight of the 'now.' " So reported one wife as she looked back on her courtship.

"It just seemed that things changed after we had sex," this woman continued. "Most of the men would act different, like they sort of owed me something and that frightened them. I always thought that sex in marriage would be so much more free, without the game-playing. It didn't work out that way. You still get a lot of help getting your clothes off, but not so much getting them back on again."

Sexual intercourse between men and women is constructive only within marriage. Courtship should include talking, kissing, cuddling, holding, sex play, mutual masturbation, and intense physical interaction, but not sexual intercourse. Certainly, as I will discuss in Chapter Twelve on sex and the family, our children should not be having intercourse. We should tell them so. Young adults would have to learn to energize the courtship sequence with feelings, thoughts, and touch rather than coitus. They would then select better partners for better sex that allows a total sexual system commitment.

It is pure myth to assume that practice with many different partners makes for good sex with a given partner. Sex is not like tennis. Practice does not make perfect in sex, it only leads to more practice. If we see sexual intercourse as the ultimate form of intimacy, it belongs in the ultimate committed relationship. If we see intercourse as some type of casual recreational activity, it belongs only in casual relationships and has little to do with bonding. I believe, and the thousand couples believed, that intercourse means much more than recreation, that it belongs in committed relationships. Open, more vulnerable courtship free of the "it" factor, the intercourse factor, will help us to find better partners for lasting super marriage and change courtship from a training ground for divorce to an opportunity for the learning of intimacy.

It is interesting to note that Masters and Johnson and other sex therapists almost always tell their couples in treatment to stop having intercourse, to become re-acquainted on deeper and broader personal levels before moving on to the intimacy of sexual intercourse. I suggest that we use this recommendation for our courtship patterns as well. A little preventive sex therapy couldn't hurt.

Super Marital Sex Courtship Rules

If you are courting now, or if you have accepted my invitation to re-court with your spouse by discussing the issues raised in this chapter, I suggest that the following five systems rules replace the hypocritical, distancing rules that you read at the beginning of this chapter.

Super Marital Sex Courtship Rule One: Never Lie

Right from the beginning, tell the truth, nothing but the truth, so help your present or future marriage. Give the gift of self-representation. Don't even tell little white lies; lies of any color are still lies. In courtship, in marriage, and in every religious system in the world, integrity is the key. Remember the material in Chapter One on the "protective insult" and how damaging that can be to love. Some lies may maintain some marriages, keep them surviving, but they never make for a super marriage.

My colleagues suggest that it is unwise to disclose extramarital affairs. They say this is only a "guilt dumping" on the partner, a way of clearing one's own conscience at the emotional expense of that partner. They say that the affair is irrelevant; just go to work on the marriage.

I say that such an approach is totally without support in the literature. It is opinion, and it helps a marriage survive, but not thrive. It will never work for making a super marriage, for super marital sex. It is just another form of the protective insult that can block the "psychasms" I will describe later. The question is how to deal with major problems in marriage, not how to cover them up and go on. Having sex outside of marriage is not irrelevant; it is a major obstacle to super marital sex, and that applies to extramarital sex of both Types I and II.

"There has never been anything like this in our marriage," reported the husband. "We seem to be more open than ever. The honesty seems to be arousing, sort of a stimulant. I guess truth is an aphrodisiac. I carried that burden for so long and wondered why I felt incomplete in my marriage. Now I know it was because I was not completely in my marriage. It was a risk, but it was worth it, a risk for love. I took a risk for sex, had sex outside my marriage. At least I should be willing to take this risk for love."

Super Marital Sex Courtship Rule Two: Declare Emotional and Romantic Vulnerablity

Right from the start, let partners know you are looking for love in all the right places. Do not hold back, for holding back does not stop you from getting hurt. It only stops you from falling in love. Vulnerability is another reason to save intercourse for marriage. We cannot let go if we are going to be hurt through disease, pregnancy, desertion, and loneliness. Every act of intercourse is a decision, not just an impulse. Letting go does not mean losing control. It means letting your partner know that the basic reason you are courting anyone at any time is to look for love, to find someone to bond with. We have sex within a system and with a system, not with a person. When we have sex with someone, we are being intimate with all they are or have ever been.

"I used to say, 'Look, I'm not open to getting emotionally involved right now.' How dumb. As if I had control over that anyway," reported one wife. What did she mean in the first place? Was she looking to get unemotionally involved? Or was she looking to get emotionally uninvolved? Declare yourself on the side of emotions and love, in marriage and courtship.

Super Marital Sex Courtship Rule Three: Be the Pursuer

Go after anybody you would like to try for. Forget the "league" concept. "Most of the women I wanted were not in my league," stated one of the husbands. "I decided I had two choices: Stay in the minors or go for the majors."

Waiting, seducing, tricking, maneuvering, playing coy, being wise—all will fail. "I have waited for him to call for two weeks," said the woman. "Why don't you call him now, here, from my office?" I asked. "What! Are you out of your mind? Just call him like I can't wait to talk to him? Like I am after him?"

"Aren't you?" I asked

"Well, of course, I would kill to have him. But I just have to wait it out. I don't want to be hurt," she said.

"But you are already hurt. You came to me because you feel alone, just passively waiting, ineffective. So act!"

She called, and his roommate announced that he had left town for a new job. "Thanks a hell of a lot," she said. "I told you this would happen. I feel like a complete fool."

She was angry, hurt, disappointed, and had taken a severe blow to her self-esteem. But now she could act, she could try to find him and ask what happened, or move on to someone else and try again. She really had little choice, but sitting home for two or three more weeks would have only been a waste of time and might have built her up for an even bigger letdown.

I find that the young people I see in therapy talk much more about the relationship than self, feelings, and love. They try to analyze "it," figure "it" out, come up with a new trick to work "it" out. Nothing works as well as going full tilt after someone you want and keeping on course with that person once you are married. We "go after someone" romantically by giving ourselves, by sharing, not pursuing.

Super Marital Sex Courtship Rule Four: Start Touching Now

Touch, hold, embrace, contact, but do not have intercourse. Do not use intercourse as the ultimate negotiable item, the key criterion in the relationship. Be sexual, have sex, but don't mistake coitus for intimacy and closeness, or use it as some type of substitute or shortcut.

"I swear they have a chart pinned inside their door. Each man's name is written in over this type of body chart. They mark where the man left off . . . like, Fred at the knee, Al at the breast, Steve at the nipple. They give it a little at a time." This report from a husband recalling his courtship shows clearly the immaturity of the whole situation, the bartering instead of bonding.

There are people you will want to touch right away, to hold, to be close to. There are other people with whom handholding is a major sacrifice. Let the person and your feelings be your guide, not some sex chart of cultural or gender expectations. Once we learn that sex is more decision than impulse, start teaching that in the family, in church, and at school, then we will be free to touch instead of have "foreplay," to experience sex as a process instead of a goal.

"I didn't want to be a tease. I loved making out, but I stopped at that. The boys thought I was terrible. I would love to just kiss all night, and they would complain that they could die from this, perhaps from some type of internal genital explosion. One night I told a boy to go ahead and masturbate, and that when he was finished, we could go back to kissing up a storm. He thought I was nuts. He called me one of the ultimate names of the day, a 'prick tease.' I guess he felt I was only teasing that part of him, as if it had a mind of its own. It's strange that you never hear much about a clit tease." This report from one of the wives about her early courtship shows the degree to which we have genitalized our lovemaking.

As it is in courtship, so it may be in marriage. If we cling to the "time bomb" theory of sex, that once the fuse is set, there must be an ultimate explosion, we miss out on some of the most exciting and intimate experiences of human interaction: the freedom to touch and kiss and hold just for the sake of doing only that.

One of the wives reported, "Now that our therapy is finished, do you know what we like to do? I know this sounds strange, but we go out in the car at night and neck. Just neck. We get so turned on that the windows steam over like the old days. That's all, we just do that. It's great."

Super Marital Sex Courtship Rule Five: Never Get Dumped and Never Dump Anyone Else

Once we remove the manipulation from courtship, and from marriages attempting to re-court, we are free to develop a wide range of relationships. "I don't think men and women can ever really just be friends. Once they see you as a friend, you either become their mother or their therapist, or they just vanish, to come back once in a while when someone breaks up with them." This report from one of the wives illustrates the cliché about men and women relating, that it is always sex or nothing at all between women and men.

We can develop into new relationships and modify others; we do not have to dump people. Think of the friends of both genders we would have if we did not allow our sexual immaturity to dictate that male/female relationships are either hot or cold, if our courting added to our list of friends instead of to our list of failures.

We are so genitally oriented in our society that we define infidelity by juxtaposition of the male and female genitalia. If the genitals get near one another, and particularly if an unauthorized penis enters an unauthorized vagina, cheating has occurred. If we become workaholics, ignore our families, neglect our health and the health of those who love us, if we spend most of our time outside of the family and the home, that is not infidelity. I suggest we have this backward. There is probably much more unfaithfulness to marriage because of work and play than because of extramarital sex.

Work at keeping and making friends, even if you used to have a more romantic involvement with them that changed for some reason. Men and women can play tennis without having sex. Super marital sex depends on maintaining attractiveness to others, experiences with others that enrich the marriage. The same goes for courtship. Don't dump people, save them. Keep their name and number. Keep them as friends. It may sound impossible, but it works. If you view courtship as collecting a wide range of friends, one of whom will become that one special lover for life, then courtship will lose its defensive orientation, its manipulation and pain. It will become a process of personal and social growth.

Super Marital Sex Opportunity Number Three

In Chapter One, you shared your reactions with your partner and family about the reasons for marital failure. In Chapter Two, you took the sexual system exam with your partner, scheduled time to discuss the results, and have now gone through a form of marital re-courtship.

Take out your marital log, a tape recorder, and the records you have kept on your opportunities in Chapters One and Two. Record you reactions to the points made in this chapter. Record your "bonding imprint" and courtship sequence in discussion with your partner. Collect some old pictures of your courtship days, not just with your spouse but with anyone. Discuss your courtship of others with your spouse, the good and bad times.

Remember Sheila? We left her sitting there with the pretzel half broken and hanging from her mouth. She was treated in my clinic for loneliness and depression. She felt that she would never love or be loved again. During her therapy, she reported another trip to another bar. By her report, this particular bar was one of the darkest she had ever been in. It seems that most bars are quite dark, perhaps another way of promoting deception in the courtship ritual?

"I went this time just to hear the band. I got a soft drink and sat far enough from the speakers to hear quality instead of volume. Well, I really got into the music. This man came and sat beside me. We didn't talk, but I could tell he was really into the music, too. We listened to the whole set, about forty minutes, I'd say." Sheila continued to describe a meeting that would begin an entirely new relationship.

"I spoke first," Sheila continued. "Not really to him, just sharing how I felt. I didn't even look at him. I told him that the last song made me want to cry because it reminded me of my ex-husband. He answered, "Me, too. And by the way, you look familiar.""

"Well, I know you won't believe this, but I was familiar. It was my ex-husband," continued Shelia. "He had seen me sitting here and come over to talk. He didn't want to bother me when I was so engrossed in the music and was kind of embarrassed about the whole scene. We laughed, but I think we were crying. You know what? I'm going out with him this Friday night. I hope we do it right this time."

I hope you and your spouse will do it right this time, too, that you will recourt with the intimacy you learned about in Chapter One, the awareness of the rules of systems from Chapter Two, and the rules of bonding from this chapter. If you really try, you might make the next major step, a step toward super love, the topic of the next chapter.

Chapter Four

⊌⋀⊌

Finding Someone to Fly With: Super Love for Super Sex

I'm not actually "in love" with him. I love him, but I'm not in love with him.

WIFE

Leo Buscaglia lectures that we are all one-winged angels who live to our fullest human potential only when we join intimately with another person. Poets, artists, musicians tell us that love is the most important element of all human experience. To paraphrase George Bernard Shaw, love is a good idea, someone ought to try it. In spite of our fixation with the concept of love, we continue either to be falling into or out of it, getting stuck with it, doing something dangerous or illegal in the name of it, killing each other over it, eating or purging because of its absence, or spending considerable time trying to make it. We seem to love to make a mess of whatever love is. If we listen to composers of popular songs, love is akin to a terribly debilitating viral condition rendering its victim emotionally hypnotized, in a type of "love seizure." Somehow, in some way, we are taught eight basic "love lies" that get in the way of the super love that I will describe later in this chapter, the super love necessary for super sex. We need the joy of love before we can find the joy of sex, but the following distortions about loving create a serious obstacle to finding people to embrace.

Love Lie Number One

"Love is an emotion."

> It's the deepest feeling, the most intense of all feelings. You can't describe it, but you'll know it when it happens. Love just knocks you out. It's an emotional powerhouse.
>
> HUSBAND

Ask anyone and that person will tell you that love is an emotion, some type of euphoric bliss with which you are smitten. We tell our teenagers that the love they feel is not "real," and that they will know the real thing later. We tell them that their hormones are deceiving them. We tell them that love it an adult emotion, and they must wait until their hormones are out of the way before they can feel the true power of emotional love.

Actually, love is not what we are describing to these young people, but "limerence," a term coined by Dorothy Tennov. Limerence is a vacillation between elation at a partner's perceived reciprocity of feelings and melancholic jealousy when the partner is seen as not returning this feeling. It is intense mood change because of another person, not stable and meaningful feeling for someone else. In real love, there is little vacillation, for real love is not just a feeling at all, but a complex interaction between thinking, feeling, intentionally behaving, and believing in a "bonding manner." Love is not exclusively a feeling, it is a multidimensional combination and balance between what researcher Robert J. Sternberg identifies as commitment, intimacy, and passion. Commitment is volitional, intellectual, and intentional. Intimacy is a feeling of bondedness evolved between two people over time. Passion is the combination of intense feelings and physical longing resulting in the strong desire to be a part of someone else, to join together physically.

The following mini-quiz may help you understand the difference between limerence, the one-dimensional and unstable feeling state similar to drug addiction, and love, the complex, more stable and controlled state of bonding. Without too much thought and a lot of feeling, answer yes or no to the following questions:

A Limerence Mini-Quiz

1. Does your feeling state depend upon your partner's feeling state?

2. Do you experience intense jealousy regarding your partner?

3. Do you feel palpitations. digestive and eating problems, or other metabolic upset when you are in the presence of your partner or even when you just think about your partner?

4. Do you feel "swept away," dizzy, light-headed, out of control when near your partner?

5. Are you in an altered state of consciousness, disconnected from the world, when near your partner or even when just thinking about your partner?

6. Do you have constant genital stirrings, erotic feelings about your partner?

7. Do you "long" or pine for your partner in his or her absence?

8. Do you feel lucky that your partner accepts you, almost not believing your luck?

9. Does everything else in life diminish in significance compared to being with your partner?

10. Do you feel that, without your partner, life would be barely worth living?

If you answer yes to more than two of these questions, you are leaning more toward limerence than love, experiencing a one-dimensional feeling that you can be sure will not last. Data indicate that this state is a lust state that lasts only a few months. Sit down and this "love seizure" is likely to pass.

When I talk with adolescents about sex and love, they ask many different questions, but the question they ask most often is, How do you know if you are in love? I answer the question this way: If you think you're in love, you are certainly in something. It could be love and it could be lust. Lust is distracting, worrisome, takes away your attention at school, at home, takes time away from your friends. Love will cause you to be more involved in many people and find energy for your school, religious, and family life in general. If you're in lust, it will never last because you are hooked on some "quick high" brain chemicals. If you allow time for love, which can follow lust sometimes, you are in for a treat, for the chemicals of love are the heavy-duty, long-acting type.

So limerence is a feeling. Love is only partly feeling, and much more behavior, thought, commitment, and belief. Most of the love songs you hear are really limerence songs, and when you hear them, remember, they may not be playing your song, a song of super love.

Love Lie Number Two

"Love is separate from sex."

> She is just not able to separate love from sex. She thinks they're exactly the same thing. If she's turned on, she says she wants to "make love." She really means that she wants to make sex, but she just has to make them the same in her mind.

HUSBAND

If the nineteenth century attempted a sexless love, then the twentieth century tried for loveless sex. Both efforts failed. Freud taught that love and sex could not be separated, and this view was incorrectly translated to the idea that love was sex or that sex was love. As the clouds and sky cannot be separated, they also are not the same thing. One would not exist without the other, they are part of a system, and so it is with sex and love.

The couples spent hours on their tapes debating the issue of who wanted sex, who wanted love, who needed more love for better sex or better sex for more love. The division is completely artificial. As psychoanalyst Reuben Fine states, "Both love and sex are essential for a full life."

Love is the feeling and behavior of bonding. Sex is one of the bonding behaviors, the physical merging part of love. A problem is created when we equate that merging exclusively with a genital merging. Touching a shoulder, exchanging a glance, cuddling a child or parent, all are sexual acts and all are part of bonding.

Bonding is a mature, intentional, behavior as well as a feeling. Attachment, on the other hand, is an immature, childlike relationship pattern. I learned early in my work that the couples who had bonded experienced an easier remediation of any sexual difficulty. The couples who had "attached," dependently and immaturely "linked to" one another, had considerably more difficulty solving sexual problems. They had not been able to integrate sex and love in their own minds, hearts, and relationships.

Ask yourself about your own relationship. Is it a "bond" or an "attachment"?

BOND	ATTACHMENT
Mature, interdependent	Immature, dependent
Intentional	Spontaneous
Mutualized touching and holding	One partner does most of the touching and holding
Balance of sexual needs	One partner experiences more sexual needs
Intimacy in all areas of marriage	Intimacy only in sexual area

Here's an example of a bonding relationship, of a couple integrating sex and love:

> We worked on it. It didn't just come. At first I never thought we would necessarily end up together. I mean, we hit it off, but it wasn't near as intense as some of my other relationships, particularly not what it was with my first longtime boyfriend. But it changed over time. We just seemed to move closer, talked it out. He had to be coached into hand-holding, but he loves it now, too. We really are together. I couldn't tell you who starts each sexual encounter. It just happens. We don't take each other for granted, but we are relaxed about us.
>
> WIFE

> I know what she means, but then, I always seem to know what she means and she knows what I mean, and that is what I mean by how our relationship is.
>
> HUSBAND

Here is an example of an "attachment" relationship:

> I support her in her career and she essentially takes care of me. I know just how to please her, to take care of her in everything, including sex. I need her and she needs me. It's more like she is the provider and I take care of the house. I can tell when she needs sex and she is never disappointed. I can tell you that she would never be able to have her life this way without me. I am really perfect for her. . . . I meet her every need. Her wish is my command. It's just how our relationship works.
>
> HUSBAND

> He is my life, my support, my everything. He is just what I need
> sexually, too.
>
> WIFE

In the second example, it is clear that an automatic, strongly patterned, dependent relationship exists, with sex tending to be one-
sided and separate from marital life, almost one item on a list of
chores, divided out from total intimacy. The husband's description
does not refer to his own sexual needs, or any of his own needs for
the matter. The wife accepts this role, attached both to her husband
and to the pattern of their marriage. Attachment works and can
keep spouses together, but not together for a super sex marriage,
the bond of a growing and adapting love system.

Love Lie Number Three

"Love is an involuntary emotional reflex."

> Love is an emotional experience, a deep feeling. It just happens. You
> don't have to do anything about it, it sort of does everything to you.
> You have to let it happen.
>
> HUSBAND

I referred earlier to the "smitten" aspect of the mythology of love.
We expect love to happen to us, that we are somehow full of pre-
planted love seeds that sprout spontaneously in response to a person
who stimulates them. We feel that we ourselves have little to do
with love, because it overwhelms us. Cartoon characters develop a
silly grin, their eyes gloss over, and their heart may grow inside
their chest, throbbing to the breaking point. We assume that we are
stationary targets for love arrows, targets more than archers.

"I know he was probably the worst thing that could ever have
happened to me, but I just could not help myself. Love is blind,
and so was I. He turned me inside out." This report from one of
the wives illustrates the assumption of love as an involuntary reflex.

Psychiatrist Scott Peck states, "Of all the misconceptions about
love, the most powerful and pervasive is the belief that 'falling in
love' is love." We do fall in "limerence," but love itself, loving,
is not a reflex, it is a volitional act. We decide to love. All love is
a conscious decision, not a helpless mammalian legacy.

One of the key steps in helping couples discover super marital
sex was to re-teach them about the voluntary nature of love. If they
clung to the assumption of love as a helpless, "willing victim"
state, then they were trapped into the conclusion that once the reflex

mysteriously "went away," it was gone for good. At best they had to wait for it to return again, to be rekindled by some mysterious evolutionary biochemical spark. You "do" love, you do not get it, for "it" is not a thing. Love is a dynamic, volitional process that takes place within a system.

"I lost it, and I don't remember really when. Love just went out of our life," stated one of the wives.

"Yes," said the husband, "We sort of became brother and sister one day. It was probably gradual, but the light went out."

Our "love light" is not automatic. We light the match, and you will learn techniques for doing so later in this chapter.

Love Lie Number Four

"Love is the natural human state."

> Love is the most basic, natural of all feelings. If the world would only give love a chance, return to its natural love state, we could save the world from this mad dash into global disaster.
>
> HUSBAND

During the major blackout in New York City some years ago, people shined flashlights down from their apartments to help those below find their way. At the same time, looters and muggers were on the loose to an extent never before imagined, even in New York. Which is the "natural state," the aggressive capitalizing on human misfortune or the caring, helping motivation of the apartment dwellers? The answer is that both states are natural.

Nobel laureate Konrad Lorenz suggested that aggression is basic to human nature. Anthropologist Ashley Montagu speculated that human cooperation and caring have an evolutionary base. Dr. Reuben Fine describes what he calls "love cultures": harmonious, sexually open, contented, and happy places where aggression, if present at all, is directed to outside forces and spirits. Freud felt that love and aggression were both characteristic of human nature.

Theorists and researchers have been unable to support the conclusion that any one human characteristic or experience is more natural than any other. To assume that "love will out" is to be unrealistic. The effort must be to maximize our efforts to teach, encourage, and nurture love, not trust in its evolutionary advantage.

"So help me, I could just kiss you," said the wife. "So kiss me.

I'll help you," said the husband. Love needs all the help it can get. It will never make it on its own.

"If he doesn't love me anymore, there's nothing I can do or he can do about it," the wife reported. "You either love someone or you don't. It's a basically natural feeling, like hunger or sex."

"At least give me a chance to make it happen again," replied the husband.

"I don't see how," she replied. "You have exploded at me for years, and I have seen nothing but anger in your eyes. There's no room for love there."

The wife had taken the either/or orientation to love, that it is natural and that the presence of any other emotion means that the natural love either was never really there or is crowded out by less "unnatural" emotions of anger or distrust. All emotions are human, and the systems orientation to loving I have been describing does not exclude or favor any one aspect of our humanness.

Love Lie Number Five

"Love is an all-or-none proposition."

> Look. You love me or you don't. There is no halfway in this thing.
> HUSBAND

One of the most common confrontation moments in the therapy program for couples came in the form illustrated by one wife: "This is it. Just say it. Yes or no. You either love me or you hate me. I want to know which it is."

For this wife and many of the persons in my sample, there was the assumption that love, anger, resentment, joy, and other emotions were somehow exclusive, that it was possible to feel only one emotion at a time. This is not true. We are capable of the simultaneous experience of a range of emotions. The language of love does not contain prepositions, on/off, in/out, beside/away from. The system of love is one of simultaneity, of the balance and flow, the Tao of loving I described in Chapter Two.

There is an important exception here. Research indicates that while we may be able to attach to many people at one time, we can bond with only one person at a time. It is not that we cannot bond with several people, just that the actual bonding I referred to earlier—the mature, intentional bonding—can only take place on one-to-one basis, one interaction at a time. This concept is called "monotropy," the technical word for bonding relationship by relationship. It became an important concept in treatment, and I required couples to suspend any other bonding processes for the few weeks they worked on their marital bond. Therapy would not begin until this could be done. Extramarital sex, "Type I, sex outside marriage," is debilitating to marriages because energy spent on bonding is an invested energy. If you are spending it in one bond, it is not available for forming another.

Love, however, is not monotropic. You can love many people and feel many other feelings while you are loving. When you are bonding, establishing or re-establishing love, it is a one-at-a-time event. But isn't there a "one and only" for everyone? This assumption underlies the next love lie.

Love Lie Number Six

"There is one love-match partner for everyone, a one and only."

> I think my one and only, the person for me, must have relocated to the tundra region of Russia. He sure doesn't seem to be housed anywhere around here.
>
> WIFE

Monotropy, bonding with one person at a time, requires an enormous amount of emotional and even physical energy, especially because we can feel several emotions at one time while we are doing this bonding. If we add to this problem the myth that we must also search for the singular right person meant for us, we overstress the entire love system. The "one and only" concept is a myth that limits loving.

It is possible to live with and love almost anybody. I have said that love is volitional, not just emotional. It is inextricably tied to sex, and we have sexual attraction for many people. Love is something you do, and you can do it with an infinite number of people. As one wife stated, "So many men, so little time."

Persons struggling with bonding are often limited because of their uncompromising stance regarding a partner. One of the rules of super marital sex mentioned earlier is that super marriages depend much more on *being* the right partner than on *finding* the right partner. Efforts to look for Mr. or Ms. Right will always fail, for it is your reputation with yourself that matters. Would you fall in love with you? That is the key question, and it puzzles many of my patients. We are more used to looking "for" than looking "in," looking for lovers instead of discovering our own loving.

"Would I fall in love with me?" responded the wife. "Are you kidding? I have taste."

It is true, as Martin Buber stated, that love is when we "happen to one another," but we do not have to happen to one particular person pre-assigned to us by some universal dating service. We cannot happen to or with one another until we happen to ourselves. Susan Campbell, in her book *The Couple's Journey*, a study of 150 couples, writes about "co-creative" relationships. Just as we can recreate and procreate with a large number of potential partners, we can also co-create with a large range of possible lovers if we look to how *we* choose to be, how we "happen" with someone, rather than spend our time looking for someone to "happen" to us.

Love Lie Number Seven

"Real love is forever."

> Then promise me you will love me forever.
>
> WIFE

The myth of forever was discussed in Chapter One. As with all events in life, love changes. I mentioned earlier that every love eventually is broken by illness, separation, or death. It is the *process* of loving that constitutes our wellness, our ability to achieve super marital sex. The process of loving is infinite even if people aren't.

Marion Richards, in her book *Centering*, writes, "The product is not what binds the artist to his craft. Nor the actor to the theater. Nor the person to his being. It is the transformations." We should commit to process, not people, to a process of vulnerability and the sharing of self, not the struggle to keep love alive as somehow separate from us.

Remember, love is a decision and a decision is necessary to end it. Even in grieving, there comes a time when the decision to "un-bond," must come. Unbonding does not cancel the memory, the love trace, but it requires a change in the relationship because of the loss of the physical presence of the loved person. Ending is as much a part of loving as beginning.

The love decision is never mutual. Author Zick Rubin points out that the decision to separate comes when one partner feels that the costs of being in a relationship exceed the perceived benefits *and* one partner is willing to take a chance, to try for another bonding. As I discussed in Chapter Three, we all "dump" and "get dumped." It is part of the process of loving and being loved. To believe that any relationship or bond is forever is self-deception. To remember that loving is forever is the ultimate human hope.

A bond's end is one of the most painful of human experiences, but as writer Shirley Luthman writes, "I don't believe people put themselves through very painful situations unless that is the only way they can learn what they need to know." Researcher Clark Moustakas states that the very power of the loving process is its continued jeopardy of changing and ending. This is a universal truth for all living systems.

"I never thought I would hurt like this. I feel it everywhere, in every inch of my body. I'm sick, heartsick," reported the wife. "I'm sorry I ever loved, and I would have never loved if I knew I was going to pay this price." She should have known. It is the very nature of love to contain in its intensity its own destruction, as a star explodes from its own heat. The decision to end will never be mutual; we all end up hurt. Understanding this will not lessen the pain, but it may free us for a focus on the joy of the process, for it is the process, not the product, that is forever.

Love Lie Number Eight

"Love is never having to say you're sorry."

> I have a very clear definition of love. It is simply—well, not so simply—putting someone else's needs above your own.
>
> HUSBAND

"Come on now, answer truthfully," questioned the husband. "If we were in a sinking lifeboat, and you could save yourself or me, who would it be?"

The wife attempted to laugh away this interrogation, but the husband pushed on. "Really, who would it be? This is the best love test in the world. Who would it be?"

"Okay." she answered, smiling. "Try this. I would save me, so I would be able to live on with your memory, so I could stand the grief instead of you, sort of take the pain for you. I would save me for you, for our love."

The final love lie, that love is self-sacrifice, self-deprecation, even self-suicide on behalf of someone else, only diminishes the purpose of love: to love and to grow and to be. We are sorry for our partner more than we are ever sorry for ourselves. We live for our lover. It all sounds so romantic, so dramatic, so beautiful. It just doesn't work that way.

Abraham Maslow wrote of the psychology of being. He felt that loving required attention to self, to taking care of our own physiological needs, to protecting ourselves before we could be strong enough to protect anyone else. If we put someone else before our "self," and they do the same, there will be no selves to do the loving, only struggles to care for the other.

"I could eat if you want to eat, but if you don't want to, I don't want to. Are you hungry?" said the wife on the tape.

"It's up to you. Are you hungry? I'll eat if you want to eat. How hungry are you?" responded the husband.

"It's too late. We just passed the restaurant," said the wife. "You drive me crazy. We can't even get a decent meal without a therapy session."

This couple had to be taught that the constant effort to please, to guess at and attempt to match the needs of someone else belongs only in the realm of parenting the very, very young. Even then, such pleasing has its limits, for it may "spoil" the child as we spoil a relationship.

We can *neglect* a love by philosophically ignoring it, not attending to someone's needs at all, not helping someone to help himself. We can *deprive* a relationship by isolating ourselves from it, focusing only on a narcisistic orientation to life. We can *abuse* a relationship either physically or mentally by intentionally blocking our partner's attempts to meet her own needs. We can *exploit* a relationship by allowing a partner to be a "love slave," ever vigilant for any need we have, even attempting to anticipate our needs. These four patterns destroy love. We can also *smother* love, rob it of its freedom to grow and change with its lovers, by engaging in a self-sacrifice competition to prove who loves whom the most by giving up the self.

A balance between nurturance and succorance is the essential component to balanced love. Taking care and being taken care of must be in balance over time for a relationship to survive and grow. Lack of balance on this dimension is one of the major barriers to growth in a relationship and to personal growth as well.

It is not a question of loving self or other more or less, it is an issue of attending to both at once, to maintaining the system more than self. This is the ultimate struggle and reward of the process of love, to merge with, not for, someone else.

Twenty Love-Map Landmarks

I discussed earlier the concept of love maps, guides for our loving determined in our early development that predispose us to select certain partners to love and determine our own unique ways of loving. To study super marital sex, I designed and administered a twenty-item questionnaire about the ways in which the husbands and wives "drew" their love maps. I found that their responses to these questions were important for understanding their marriage and their sex, for understanding why sexual problems developed, and for learning how to chart new courses for love.

Think of your own love map as a transparent sheet with light trails and dark highways marked on the sheet, each mark placed there by the experiences of childhood and adolescence. Think of your love map placed over the map of your spouse, both held to the light. Look for the roads and paths that overlap, comparisons between the dark and light trails, the more and less frequently traveled roads, the detours and roads under construction or in need of repair. Conceptualizing loving in this way provides a mental set for learning to love together, for traveling down new and familiar roads, major and minor byways.

Remember that the term "sexual preference" is not an accurate way of understanding the final arrival point on your love map. There is more we do not know about our sexual living and loving style, what John Money calls our sexual status or orientation, than we actually do know, and to use the word "preferences" implies a decision that we never really make about our loving style. Our loving style is no more a preference than a mountain "prefers" to be by the sea.

The prenatal determinants of our sexual style are sometimes seen as primarily biological, and what happens postnatally as learned or sociological. You will be better able to understand your own love map and make intentional changes in that map if you remember that learning and socialization have biological implications, too. Again the lesson of love as a system, an infinitely complex socio-biological "dance" among the brain, the body, and the world, is clear. Your love map is always changing, because all systems are constantly changing. There is as much biology in learning as there is learning in biology, so to look for the psychological, sociological, or neurohormonal answer to our sexual orientation, our love system, is to attempt to read and interpret our love map in the dark. The question is not what causes us to love as we do, but how we are loving and how that loving is changing. Everything you do and experience makes marks on your love map, and when you are married, those maps change together. It is impossible to mark one map without marking the other.

To help you understand the evolution of your loving system, answer each of these questions about your own love map before reading what a husband or wife had to say. Unless you understand love-mapping, you may find, as suggested by Gertrude Stein, that when you do get there, there will be no there there.

1. DESCRIBE THE FIRST EXPLICIT SEX SCENE YOU EVER ACTUALLY WITNESSED IN PERSON

Love maps begin to develop very early and are written in some very dark ink. The husbands and wives often had to be prodded into remembering a sex scene they witnessed, but each of them could. It does not matter that it is really the first, or that it ever really happened at all. It is the memory, the image, that gets itself placed on the map.

> I still get nervous talking about it, even thinking about it. I was sleeping in the loft with my cousin. We giggled away half the night together. Then, we got tired. It must have been 3 A.M. Her parents were sleeping in sleeping bags on the main floor just beneath the loft. They must have waited for hours for us to shut up and fall asleep. When we quieted and were just lying there exhausted from laughter, we could hear a sound like someone rubbing something back and forth. I heard it and looked at my cousin. We were twelve and we had talked about sex, but this was amazing. We seemed to know what the rubbing was. I still remember that sound, and I am aware of it when my husband and I make love. Rubbing, back and forth. We looked out over the railing and saw them. His sleeping bag was going up and down, up and down. He would make a little noise and she would tell him to ''be quiet, they'll hear.'' She seemed so disinterested. She looked up at the railing and we pulled back. I will never know if she saw us. All I remember is that the rubbing stopped, I heard the toilet flush, and when we looked again, they were in their own sleeping bags.
>
> WIFE

Further questioning revealed that the passivity of the wife, the mystery of why the toilet flushed after sex, and the rubbing had remained key parts of this woman's love map. She continued to be easily aroused by rubbing sounds and was alert to any escape of "sex sounds" during her own lovemaking. As you re-create your own first witnessed sex scene, check it for such "imprints," as they may affect your sexual life.

The way in which love maps are formed, why we see and remember or do not see or forget various sexual happenings in our lives remains a mystery. The answers to this mystery probably rest somewhere between prenatal influences and neurohormonal predispositions and the influence of learning. Your own relationship will be enhanced, however, if you take the time to re-examine some of the influences that make you love whom you love and how you love.

2. HOW SEXUAL DO YOU THINK YOUR PARENTS WERE?

Few of us really know much about the sex life of our parents, but we all have formed an opinion, a "sex theory" about it. Even if we find it impossible to believe that our parents are sexual now, we know they have been sexual. What do you remember about your parents' sexuality as you grew up? What is your sexual theory about your parents' sexual interaction pattern?

"I would guess maybe they did it when my father was drunk. I could hear it, I think, although I'm not sure. They would fight so much that I was too little to tell if they were fighting or actually doing it, having sex. They never hugged, never kissed. We kids were hugged all the time, but they never hugged each other. I would guess their sex was a biological release, mostly for my father."

This husband's report contained several "leftovers" in his own sexual life that related to his memories. He now feared what he thought was too much drinking on his wife's part. He was so alert to his wife's sexual needs and the danger that she, too, would accommodate him as his mother might have accommodated his father that he now had sexual problems of his own within his sexual system. He was unable to ejaculate, stating, "I think so much about what's happening for her, I just can't let go for me."

3. HOW WOULD YOU BRIEFLY DESCRIBE THE MALE SEX ROLE?

Sex roles are very complicated in most societies. This third point is less a sociological or anthropological question than it is a clinical question about expectations of maleness in your own relationship. Warren Farrell, in his book *Why Men Are How They Are*, and Carol

Gilligan's book *In a Different Voice* provide interesting insights about this issue. How do you see men?

Dr. Farrell reports that male fantasies emphasize variety of sexual partner and the challenge of the hunt, of finding new and better sexual objects. He writes that women value sameness of partner, commitment to and from one man. Dr. Gilligan suggests that all interactions with the primary caretaker, in almost all cases the mother, determine the gender-role behaviors of men and women. Both researchers know that the brain-experience connection is a mutually influential one.

"I know this will date me, but I see men as providers, caretakers, and sexually active. They are aggressive and less emotional than women. I know that sounds stupid, but it is how I see them." This report from one of the wives was not atypical. Stereotypes die hard and continue to influence the sexual interaction within the marriage, regardless of intellectual protests of "nonsexist" views.

"Men just have to do it all, and I think they want to do it all. It is in the nature of things and in their nature to be the doers, the responsible ones," reported one husband. You can see the love maps of both these spouses. Can you imagine how each of these people came to feel and behave as they do?

A word of warning. It is not always the case that the spouse's actual behavior matches his or her report. How we feel is the real love map. How we behave is only a rough approximation of that map and is filtered and changed by social constraints that may mask the real map itself.

4. HOW WOULD YOU BRIEFLY DESCRIBE THE FEMALE SEX ROLE?

The female sex role is just as stereotyped as the male's among the people interviewed in this sample. How about you? How do you view the female sex role, personally view it, not intellectually think it should be?

"Simply stated, I'd say women are emotional, essentially the caretakers of the family. They are stronger psychologically, more mature, and have to sort of nurture men along," reported one wife.

"Well, women are really inferior copies of men. They have their own strengths, but they are not up to men in most things. They are really just a little short of men in most things except having and raising kids," reported one husband.

Both male and female sex-role expectations influence the love maps of both genders profoundly. Talk these roles over with your partner. Your sex role is how you behave sexually in our society and your sex or gender identity is how you feel, your sexual self-concept. Both are the result of love-mapping, and the gender identity is the capital city, the control center on the map.

5. DESCRIBE A "SEX REHEARSAL": SEX PLAY YOU ENGAGED IN WITH SOME-ONE OF YOUR OWN GENDER

Same-gender sex play is common, and most spouses could remember a specific time when they engaged in such behavior. Think back to your own sex play with a same-gender person, perhaps a sibling, a cousin, a neighborhood friend?

"That's easy," one wife reported. "We had a breast-comparison contest. My best friend and I. I must have been about fourteen or so, and so was she. It started out with looking, then she touched mine and I touched hers. It wasn't like sex excitement like it is an adult, but a tingling sensation. I imagined she was a boy. Somehow we kissed. She stuck her tongue in my mouth, and I started to spit. I spat until I was dry."

This wife had mentioned a concern that she might be homosexual, not an atypical concern of the wives. She felt guilty even now, and added that "I'm still curious about other women's breasts." She was converting natural curiosity and arousal to fear and misunderstanding. Love maps can take wrong turns when we compare what happened to us in our natural learning with what we fear might happen to us.

"We just unzipped each other's pants and reached in. I touched his penis and he touched mine. Then we watched each other pee," reported one husband. "I think he is probably a fag now as an adult, because he was the instigator."

There are societies in which the absence of homosexuality activity during sexual development is viewed as abnormal. One such society is the Sambia tribe of New Guinea, where all young boys are expected to live temporarily with males, ingesting semen as a counterbalance to their drinking of mother's milk. Only after this act takes place can they truly become men. We must look far beyond our own ethnocentrism if we are to begin to learn about the evolution of gender orientation. Certainly, sex play with the same gender is almost universal in our own society, and fears about it only block further healthy love mapping.

6. DESCRIBE A "SEX REHEARSAL": SEX PLAY YOU ENGAGED IN WITH SOMEONE OF THE OPPOSITE GENDER

It was difficult for some of the husbands to remember childhood sex play with a girl. Our society allows more sex play of the same-gender type than of opposite gender. At least, it is easier for two boys or two girls to get together in private. Think back to your first childhood sex play with the other gender and discuss it with your partner. These are not easy things to discuss, but open exploration of these love-map landmarks is a prerequisite to the super marital sex program you will be learning. The openness and vulnerability between partners that I have discussed in the first section of this book is for super sex. Merely good sex requires much less disclosure and yields much less fulfillment.

One woman reported, "I can think back to it, sort of vaguely in my mind. This boy was about ten, I think, and I was about the same age. He said he wanted to ride me. I thought he was nuts. I bent over, like to let him ride on my shoulders horsey-back. He rode me, sort of humping on my shoulders. We fell down and he got between my legs and started to hump. I giggled and he told me not to laugh, that nobody laughed at times like this. My mother came in, pulled him off me, and didn't say a word. Later, she asked what else we did. I sort of knew something was very, very wrong about all of this, but I wasn't sure what."

The not so subtle guilt that accumulates in our early sex play, as well as the confusion it causes, is clear in this example. No sex education followed, only a mysterious unspoken censorship of daughter by mother which became another turn in this person's love map.

A husband reported two experiences. His same-sex and opposite-sex play experiences were combined. "This boy and girl, about fifteen, I think, were teasing me. I was about eight, and I was in my younger brother's wading pool. They came over and took me to the garage. I was scared, I remember that. The boy pulled down my swimming trunks, unzipped his pants, and rubbed his penis against mine. I said I was going to tell. He said if I didn't tell, he had a surprise for me. He told the girl to suck on my penis. I had no idea what she was doing, and the whole time she was doing it I kept wondering what the great surprise was going to be so I wouldn't tell. Our dog started to bark, so the boy and girl took off."

The fear, the negotiation aspects, and the confusion remained with this man. He added, "I try to talk my wife into a threesome. She asks why I want that. I'll bet that kid is one of the reasons. I was never more surprised, turned on, and frightened at the same time. I would do anything for my wife if she would try a three-way thing."

There is no way to tell if the early experience of this man accounts for his interest in three-person sex. The number of partners is less significant than the feelings that stayed with him, for these are the true marks on the love map. He equates surprise and fear with sexual arousal instead of the comfort and predictability that characterizes super marital sex.

7. DESCRIBE YOUR BEST CHILDHOOD SAME-SEX FRIEND

Whom you choose to bond with depends not only on early experience of adult sex scenes, perceived parental sexual behavior, male/female sex-role interpretations, and sex play with boys and girls, it also relates to friendship patterns. Most of us had one special friend of the same gender, that one special playmate or school chum who shared our developmental joys and griefs. We often spent time talking, listening to one another's lies, discussing one another's life philosophies. This friend became a major point on our love map, a major determinant of some of the characteristics we would later look for in a marital partner. Do you remember such a friend?

One man reported, "Yes, it was Dennis. He was with me from early elementary school. We played together for hours. We formed a club, built a clubhouse, and were the only two members. We didn't talk much about sex or anything like that. We just sort of shared the same terrors and hopes. One time we actually held hands. I'll never forget it. We must have been about eight years old or so, and they were going to take blood tests, something about civil defense procedures. We were scared to death. We just held hands in line. I'll never forget it."

The special support from his boyhood friend became a key part of this man's love map, and one that directly affected his later choice of a wife. His wife reported a similar incident, perhaps explaining in part the overlapping of love maps that I mentioned earlier and the impact of this overlapping on the sexual system.

"I never forget her. I just cannot think of her name, but she was always with me for about three years in school. She saved me many times. I remember not being able to jump rope worth anything.

The other girls laughed at me. She told them to stop, that I could do it if I wanted to, but that I was in training for ballet school and was not allowed to jump rope. Of course, this was a lie, but I would never have been fast enough or devious enough to think of it. She could always save me."

This woman had selected a husband who did much the same thing in their marriage, supported her and covered for her. "He gets me out of any social event I really don't want to go to. He is a good strategic liar," she reported.

Her husband's report supported this overlap theory. "She is always there for me. She even held my hand once in the waiting room at the dentist's office. She did it beautifully. She held a magazine on her lap and put one on mine and we held hands under the magazines. I was scared to death, but she really helped me, and nobody ever knew about it." A love-system bond is evident here, a map match that helped this couple find super marital sex.

8. DESCRIBE YOUR BEST CHILDHOOD OPPOSITE-SEX FRIEND

All of us can recall one girl or boy who became a friend, our first encounter with "one of *them*." It was not a sexual encounter, it was a boy/girl relationship that taught us a little about the person-hood of the other gender. Perhaps then we were just immature enough to see people as persons first, gender second, and the lessons we learned became a part of our life and our loving.

One wife reported, "He was really cute. If I met him now, I'd find him irresistible. We talked, rode bikes, just hung around together. It was not a boy-and-girl thing, just two kids. My parents called him 'my little friend,' and next to an imaginary friend I made up for a while, he was one of the closest persons to me at that time of my life."

A husband stated, "She was a real friend. She could play football better than any boy in the neighborhood. I learned to throw a spiral from her. We would sit and drink pop together. A real friend. I'd love to find a woman friend like that now."

I often ask a question of audiences to whom I lecture. I ask first how many women were "tomboys." Usually several hands go up. Then I ask, "How many men were "sissies?" Not a hand goes up. Love maps are very influential, not only now and for the future, but even when we look back. Somehow, we learn to fear that combination of maleness and femaleness within all of us. Perhaps we lose our ability to de-genderize or fail to work hard enough to maintain it. We lose that innocent, open exchange between children, and it leaves a barricade somewhere within us and between us.

9. DESCRIBE YOUR MOST THREATENING SAME-SEX CHILDHOOD FOE

Do you remember a bully, a "meany," some child who just seemed to have it in for you? There seemed to be something about you that resulted in a monstrous reaction on the part of this one particular child. You might have sprinted with terror past his house, snuck down the alley on the way home from school, done anything to avoid direct confrontation with this one child.

One husband reported, "His name was Carl. This kid hated my looks, my name, my clothes, my walk, my parents, even my dog. I have never been so afraid in my life, not even in the war, as I was afraid of Carl."

"She was the meanest girl. She gave the word 'bitch' a bad name. She put me down to everybody. I hated her. I wished she would die. I'll bet she became a gossip columnist." This wife frowned, reliving her anger as she described this love-map imprint.

The same-gender conflict and fear gets on our love map, a danger zone that is reflected in our choice of a partner and in our day-to-day working and loving. Think about conflicts with people at work, about conflicts with certain family members, and try to relate these relationships to your love map. You will see that these maps influence all living.

10. DESCRIBE YOUR MOST THREATENING OPPOSITE-SEX CHILDHOOD FOE

It may be difficult to recall, but try to think of that one girl or boy of the opposite gender who seemed to clash with you. This most likely would have taken place around later elementary school, when the genders are trying to mix in a society that blocks that mixture with a set of double messages. It is strange that boys who "hang around with" or "play too much" with little girls in elementary school are seen as "queers," as being strange, and that later, too much playing with the boys is labeled the same way, unless of course there is aggressiveness involved. Girls who play too much with boys are tomboys, somehow not appropriately feminine. Too much contact with boys later, and they may be seen as "loose." Not enough, and they may be seen as "gay." Listen to children playing at a very young age, and you will hear what they consider to be the ultimate insult: "You're gay!"

Do you remember that one opposite-sex child with whom every boy/girl, male/female issue in the world seemed to be acted out? One wife reported, "he just would not leave me alone. He'd take my hat, knock my books from my hand, wash my face with snow, just was on me all the time." One husband reported, "She was a little snitch. She would tell on me anytime, making up things as if I didn't do enough bad things already." This aggressive male/female interaction, most likely following some "you always hurt the one you love" pattern, also became a part of how you love later.

11. DESCRIBE A SEXUAL-ABUSE EXPERIENCE

The frequency of sexual abuse in our country is frightening. Its scars cover our potential for intimacy unlike any other influence in our life. Think back to this experience, as painful as it may be. Remember that professional help may be needed to explore the memories of this abuse, but as you will learn in Chapter Eight, specific help is available and you are not alone. Thousands of persons have been sexually abused and are able to establish loving bonds and fulfilling sex lives. Confrontation with the problem and seeking support from professionals and those who love you can do much to negate the damage. Sexual abuse does not have to be a permanent blemish on your love map.

"It's a nightmare," the wife reported. "I can't really remember much of it. He would just touch me. Every night, my father would touch me." The wife continued in more detail to describe her experience. Her therapist was able to help her free herself from feelings of guilt, even responsibility for her own abuse.

"They all grabbed me," reported the husband. "They pulled my pants down and took turns hitting my penis. I cried, and they said that until I stopped crying, they would not stop hitting. I couldn't stop. The coach came in, and I told him I just fell. I never told anyone this."

Men and women in the couples sample all reported some instance of sexual abuse. This becomes the dark part of our love map, a part that leads us away from love, leads us to seek out compensation or sanctuary from the threat of a corrupted intimacy.

12. DESCRIBE YOUR OWN "SEX IMPRINT," YOUR OWN PRIVATE "FETISH"

The term "fetish" has specific clinical meanings, but for the purpose of this interview, it was defined as an object that can lead to sexual arousal. Think of your own sexual turn-ons. Does soft, hard, cool, warm, rough, rigid, or some other characteristic seem to hold erotic stimulation for you? Mild, even strong preferences for certain clothing, colors, shoes, and fashions are natural. When these things become necessary adjuncts, even substitutes, then the love map develops roadblocks for mature love.

Dr. John Money, in his book *Love and Love Sickness*, describes "paraphilias," sexual responsiveness to unusual or socially unacceptable stimuli. More frequent in men than women, paraphilia literally means "aside from love." One husband reported, "I just love hair. Long, full hair. Just the hair can turn me on." He came to the clinic because his wife felt that he was a "pervert" (she actually said he was a "pervert") because he had "this hair thing." Through counseling, the couple learned together to move "this hair thing" from necessity adjunct in their sexual interaction to a strong preference, with the wife able to enjoy with her husband different hairstyles during some of their sexual interactions.

"I would have never believed it. I even put on wigs. It's fun, but it's not all the time," reported his wife.

"It really gets me that she will share in this thing. I get turned on with her and she gets turned on that I am turned on, just so long as the whole thing does not replace my feelings for her," reported the husband.

Think of objects that have some erotic value to you. Try to think of three such objects, even if it at first seems impossible. The spouses were able to come up with such objects after some prodding. Place these at some point along the "arousal line" below and have your partner do the same. Discuss these objects, your feelings about them, and how and why you think these objects came to have erotic value. This is a helpful step to the sexual disclosure necessary for super sex.

(slight turn-on. . . . .real turn-on. . . . .necessary for turn-on)

Here is one example from one of the men: "I would put a soft and silky nightie, like a robe, at the slight turn-on level. Real strong perfume, I mean like the dime-store type, is a real turn-on. I guess that's because I had a babysitter who wore that stuff when I was getting sexual. Necessary for a turn-on would be, let's see, that's more difficult. Oh yes, I would say smooth legs. I hate stubble.''

His wife reported the following: "I get slightly turned on to the most gentle hint of aftershave. Now, tight colored underwear is a real turn-on. I hate boxer shorts. They remind me of my father. Necessary turn-on? Well, I can't make love with anyone, anyone at all, unless they have nicely manicured fingernails. I remember my uncle always had dirty or broken nails, and that still turns my love button to past off.''

As these spouses reported another sex imprint, their fetish imprint, you can see the impact of early childhood experiences in both examples. Stubble, dirty fingernails, and boxer shorts are on the love maps, whether these people wanted them there or not.

13. DESCRIBE YOUR FIRST DATE

Remember that each of these questions was followed by long taped discussions. They are presented here in outline form to serve as stimuli for the intimate sharing of your marriage's love maps. Couples enjoyed discussing their first date, often laughing at the memories most of us share. You will be reading about one such example in detail in Chapter Twelve. Here are two examples from the love-map histories.

"He opened the door right on his own face," she said, laughing. "He came around the car in tuxedo and all, opened the car door, and almost knocked himself out."

"I can beat that," added the husband. "I got up after the movie, and my leg was asleep. I mean, really out, like it had been amputated. I dragged it up the aisle with me. She never looked back. I tried to stomp it back to life, and she looked away. I was dying of embarrassment."

14. RE-INTRODUCE YOUR BODY TO YOURSELF

Body image is like home base on the love map. Take a good, long look in the mirror, naked if you have the courage, and describe out loud how your body looks and feels. If you really have courage, try this with your partner standing by your side.

"There we stood," said the wife. "It was surprising. We didn't get past the hair on our heads. We looked at our own, each other's, and talked about it. Maybe it was just safer to talk about that, but I never realized he felt his was too thin. I have always felt mine was too thin. It has bothered me for years."

How we think we look is a key in our love map, a type of legend and scale for interpreting the map and for reading other persons' maps, for we tend to pick partners that we perceive as maybe just a few steps up from our own place on the body market. Even children rapidly develop good or poor body images, which sometimes sentence them to the sidelines at dances and to a loneliness that is based on a hypercritical, usually unrealistic self-appraisal.

I have three hundred slides of the work of major artists. These are all nude paintings, and I have my patients pick the one painting they feel most resembles them. This assignment is usually fun and sometimes most enlightening, especially when I also have them select a slide that most resembles their partner. Looking at and discussing these pictures usually helps defuse the anxiety over the body-image issue and teaches about the wide range of human appearance and the perceptions of that appearance.

I help my patients discuss feelings about their genitals and other erotic zones. Most men seem to feel that penises come in one size, too small. Women seldom talk much about genital appearance, but describe their breasts in two sizes, too big or too small. It is helpful to break down the barriers that exist between the body generally and the erotic zones specifically, integrating both into a sensuous gestalt.

When I lectured on this concept of the sensuous gestalt, one woman told me after the lecture that she thought "sensuous hole" might be a better term. She added, "After all, I think I have what I call a 'grand opening.' Let me tell you, women do not have penis envy; men might have vaginal awe." Even in her humor, you can see the anxiety we have about perhaps the least important element of the sexual system, the genitalia.

15. DESCRIBE YOUR OVERALL SELF-ESTEEM

What is your reputation with yourself? What you think of yourself determines in large measure what you will think of others.

"I sort of feel okay about me. Not good, not bad. Just okay," said one husband.

"Well, then," answered the wife. "What does that make me? Why did I marry just okay? I think I deserve A-plus."

My interviews of sex offenders and persons debilitated by paraphilias, when sex is separated from love, indicate that one common thread unites all of these persons: They all have extremely low self-esteem. Sex becomes more important than people. They seem to treat others sexually as they feel about themselves. They become driven by a sexual compulsion for "it" rather than him or her. How you feel about yourself will predict to a great extent how you feel about your marriage and how your partner will feel about himself or herself.

16. WHAT ONE PERSONALITY CHARACTERISTIC DO YOU FEEL YOU LACK?

It has not been shown that we marry to make up for a personal deficit, or that we pick partners who balance for some personally perceived deficiency. It is true, however, that our most remarkable (at least in our own eyes) personality deficit influences our bonding.

"I've never seen myself as particularly smart, I guess. Just about average," said a husband. "I'd steer away from real bright people, people with book knowledge. I know my wife is much smarter than I am, but I offer her other things, like steadiness, reliability."

Our selection of partner may not be determined by our perceived deficits, but you can see in this man's description that specific areas of experienced inferiority can act themselves out within our relationships.

"I'm not beautiful, but I am smart," reported one wife. "My husband is beautiful but not too bright. Together, we make a beautifully intelligent marriage."

Think about your own deficit area on your love map and consider how this may influence your interaction with your spouse.

17. DESCRIBE YOUR FEELINGS ABOUT AUTOEROTIC BEHAVIOR

Masturbation is one of the most difficult of all topics for couples to discuss. If your own religious orientation forbids it, it is still an area in which you most likely have strong feelings. I will discuss this further in Chapter Twelve, but for now, discuss it with your partner. You do not have to share what you do, just how you feel.

Remember, autoeroticism is not limited to self-stimulation of the genitals. Taking a long, sensuous bath or shower is a form of autoeroticism. Feeling the wind in your hair (no matter how thin it is) can be erotic. Do not let the genital orientation of our society trap you into the same limited view of you enjoying you, of giving you permission to stimulate yourself.

"I think it is disgusting, unnatural, and a complete waste of time," said the wife. "I don't know why anybody does it, and certainly people don't do it if they have someone."

Her husband said in his private interview, "Sure I do it. Three or four times a week. It has nothing to do with her or our sex. I just like to look at a few pictures and get off."

The impact of such different views, totally unshared, is clearly important to marital sex. "At least it's a cheap date," said one man during the interviews. "No risk of disease, and you don't have to get up and get dressed afterward. In fact, you don't have to get undressed at all." Humor, comfort, fear, shame, and other emotions are evoked when the topic of self-stimulation is raised. Our love maps are influenced strongly by such feelings about our right to self-pleasure. Don't let fear prevent you from discussing this issue with the one person with whom you should be able to share anything.

18. WHAT IS YOUR PRIMARY MODE OF EXPRESSION?

Are you a talker, a toucher, a shower, a feeler, a senser, a listener? How do you best express yourself?

One husband said, "I'm a man of few words. My wife has all the rest."

The wife responded, "Oh really? Your few words are worth hundreds of mine, because you never listen anyway. I have to send ten for one to be heard."

Styles of communication are as different as the people who use them. Try now to identify your basic style: quiet, reflective, passive, active—how do you send your signals?

"I don't talk about love," said the man. "I show it, I give it, I demonstrate it."

"Then I must be blind," answered the wife. "So try talking a little more. I listen better then I see."

When you really want to be heard and understood, how do you send your message? How do you communicate, show the road signs along your love map?

19. ARE YOU "OUTSIDE"- OR "INSIDE"- DIRECTED?

Psychologists refer to the concept of "locus of control." Some of us are strongly influenced by our inner feelings and sensations. Others are more reactive to outside cues. Which seems to be your style?

"He doesn't spend much time with feelings," reported the wife. "He's a realist. See it, do it, and that's it."

"Yes," agreed the husband. "And she is all feelings. There is not a bone of practicality in her."

This "locus of control" issue becomes important in sexual interaction. Some partners respond to sexual stimulation coming from within, from feelings and sensations that seem to originate from the psyche. Others react to visual or touch stimulation almost exclusively, are more haptic, sensation-oriented. How would you characterize yourself and your partner on this branch of the love map, reactive to the outside or active from the inside?

20. DESCRIBE YOUR SEXUAL-INTERCOURSE DEBUT

Every person asked this question had a very specific answer. Intercourse is not something we take lightly, even though we talk very crudely about it sometimes. Share your first intercourse experience with your partner. It will be difficult, but again a necessary step for super marital sex. Being happily married does not require the level of disclosure required on this test, but this book is a program for super marital sex, and for this, such vulnerability is necessary.

"I'll tell you, it was crazy and quick," reported the husband. "A bunch of the guys got together, got drunk, and went to this place. This woman was there. We all took a turn. What a wild time. I don't know how I got it done."

"Mine was after the prom," said his wife. "I only remember my hoopskirt up in the air like some stupid tent. I couldn't see anything. To tell the truth, I don't know if he ever really got in me. It might have been between the seat and my butt. I worried for weeks until I got my period."

Clearly, these initiations to intercourse become "main roads" on our love map, and unless we study and learn from them, no detours to better routes are possible.

Super Love for Super Marriage: The Joy of Marital Sex

Super sex requires super love, a love that is possible only in a relationship that lasts; a nurtured love that is "raised," much as a child is raised. We focus so much on independence that we have fogotten the value of interdependence. We have searched for the joy of sex, forgetting that there is no joy in just "doing." The joy of marital sex is discovered through a super love, the total, voluntary merging with someone else over time. This love contains no secrets, protects the individuality of each partner while resulting in a combination that exceeds the individual capacities of both partners. It changes and grows in response to both partners. It includes a sexual interaction based on an entirely new view of orgasm and intercourse. It provides an opportunity for growth and feedback about each partner's own behavior. It is as challenging as it is supportive. It is a love system, and we are at the same time able to experience it and be it.

Shapiro and Shapiro examine the "super healthy" relationship in their article "Well-Being and Relationship." They point out that is is sometimes easier to love humanity in the collective, abstract sense than in a committed, interpersonal sense. They describe the super love I am suggesting as a relationship that "one cannot take credit for, but to which one must contribute to the utmost of one's ability, which one marvels at and is privileged to be part of." I hope Part One of this book has helped you get ready to take part in what the Shapiros have called "a type of miracle."

This miracle is possible not through spontaneous, romanticized, intense, "hot" love, but through considered, realistic, steady, "warm" loving, a process of being one with someone else while still being "one" for yourself. By paying attention to what can happen to desexualize a marital relationship, understanding the rules of how systems grow and flourish, bonding and rebonding with your spouse, you are able to move beyond the eight love lies at the beginning of this chapter to a true loving allowing the merger of two love maps for a new and exciting journey to super marital sex.

Super Marital Sex Opportunity Number Four

Write your own love book as a couple. Select artwork, pictures, poems, articles, anything that expresses your feelings about your love maps and your loving. Include notes from your answers to the questions in this chapter. Make sure it is "your" book, not a copy of what the experts tell you love is or should be. Have your picture taken together (this time no kids, just the two of you). Make that picture the cover of your book. Add to it whenever some interesting poem or words to a song come to your attention. Keep the book in a private place, because this is a marital diary, a love diary, a collection of things and words that relate to elements of your love maps. This book is an atlas of your ever-changing super love, a love that makes possible the sexuality of the fourth perspective described in Part Two.

PART TWO

A Different Perspective for Super Sex

The meeting of two personalities is like the contact of two chemical substances; if there is any reaction, both are transformed.

CARL JUNG

This whole thing is not like anything else we have ever experienced. It's a whole new way of looking at our sex together. We actually feel each other, and it seems to go way beyond the genitals. This is super!

WIFE

This section explores four perspectives on human sexuality. You will learn about the history of our views of how we have sex, that there is another way to understand sexual response that has not typically been included in studies of marital intimacy. You will learn that most men may not really enjoy their sexual experience to its fullest potential, and that most women may in fact be having too many orgasms. You will learn a whole new way of being sexual together that is not limited by prior perspectives on our sexuality. You will learn about psychasms, the posture of the future, new F and R areas in the husband and G and C areas in the wife. You will learn a super marital sex program that helps you change and enhance not only your sexual style, but your living and loving style. You will learn how to find super marital sex.

CHAPTER FIVE

🙟🙠

Sexuality from Another Perspective

We bought and read every single book on sex there was. We underlined the best parts, tried the postures, even bought a sex board game. We learned what the experts thought, but we forgot what we thought. It's almost like it's not even our own sex anymore.

WIFE

There have been major contributions to our understanding of human sexuality over the last six decades. Thanks to the courage of a small number of men and women, we have been able to learn about the most human of all responses, the sexual response. It is not possible to understand the view of sexuality that underlies the super marital sex model without first understanding the earlier and in most cases still dominant models of sexuality, the first three perspectives of sex that have served as the core of clinical sex therapy. I began my work with a different set of assumptions about human sexuality, one based on the systems, bonding, intimacy model you learned about in Part One, but as you will see, the first three perspectives contained their own and quite different assumptions about the purpose and nature of sex.

The First Perspective: Ellisonian Sexuality

Many people believe that Sigmund Freud is the "father of twentieth-century sex." His influence has been profound, but the work of one of his contemporaries, Henry Havelock Ellis, has been much more influential on our sexual ethos, the way we have become and are sexually. Author Paul Robinson writes, "I would even go so far as to state that Havelock Ellis stands in the same relation to modern sexual theory as Max Weber to modern sociology, or Albert Einstein to modern physics." The later work of Alfred Kinsey and William Masters and Virginia Johnson was strongly influenced by Ellis, and his assumptions became in large measure the assumptions of the first three perspectives of sexuality.

Ellis was an English physician who later turned to the study of psychology and literature. His work was in the form of case histories, parallels from animal to human sexuality, cross-cultural comparisons, and theoretical speculation. He was a "reasoner," a "speculator," more than a researcher or clinician. He valued touch, closeness, intimacy, and was tolerant in his approach to masturbation, homosexuality, and what he came to view as a natural interest in sexual variety.

His "model" of human sexual response was based on the assumption that the male penis was the primary focus of sexual excitement in the male. While touch and intimacy were viewed as important for the male, Ellis believed that it was the female who experienced a trilogy of sexual response: the clitoris accompanied by responsiveness of the vagina and the uterus.

He saw the female as an "instrument" to be played during sexuality and from whom sexual response was elicited. She was seen as essentially "receptive," responding in much more generalized fashion than did men. Men were "propulsive," discharging their more rapidly occurring buildup of sexual arousal through penile contraction. The female vagina was thought to "suck in" the penis.

Ellis was one of the early writers to describe the "buildup and discharge" model of sexual response, and it became the model for future researchers. He wrote, "Tumescence is the piling on of the fuel; detumescence is the leaping out of the devouring flame." This energy buildup and energy discharge model was related essentially to the genitalia, although Ellis was also one of the first to describe erogenous or erogenic zones responsive to touch.

Ellis thought that male sexuality was "predominantly open and aggressive," while female sexual response was "elusive," slower, and much more elaborate. While men responded to touch, the penis was the focus for them. Even the scrotum was seen as without much sensitivity.

Ellis saw the nongenital areas as sexually responsive in the female. He felt that the breasts were particularly sexually responsive. Women were viewed as sexual "all over their body," and much more "total" in their sexual response, more mentally and emotionally involved. He wrote, "In a certain sense, their brains are in their wombs." By this unfortunate phrase, he meant that women were not the asexual beings of Victorian doctrine, that they were in fact highly sexual. The misrepresentation of this view became "women are preoccupied with sex," are more emotionally involved in it. Women came to be seen as sex objects, sexually driven by some innate procreative and unique feminine drive.

Ellis changed his views of marriage throughout his career. He continued to view it, however, as a natural state, "the most natural expression of an impulse which cannot, as a rule, be so adequately realized in full fruition under conditions involving a less prolonged period of mutual communion and liberty." He added, "The needs of the emotional life . . . demand that such unions based on mutual attraction should be so far as possible permanent."

He would later add that some form of erotic variety was necessary, even within marriage, but that such variety should be in the form of sensitive affairs, "liaisons" of love that protected, even enhanced marriage. Like most researchers, he felt that marriage could not compete with variety, his own theories paralleling the change from exclusivity to a search for variety characteristic of many marriages.

Ellis did not think much of traditional Western marriage. He felt that Western marriage deromanticized the marital relationship, making a contract out of a natural state of relating, changing the substantive joining of two people to a formal agreement between two partners. He repeated that marriage was "not a contract, but a fact." As with all of the theorists of the first three perspectives, Ellis struggled with the conflict between the erotic and hedonistic on one hand and the romantic and intimate on the other.

Richard von Krafft-Ebing, Karl Heinrich Ulrichs, Albert Moll, Edward Carpenter, Auguste Forel, Iwan Block, Magnus Hirschfeld, and certainly Sigmund Freud were all influential in the period of sexual transition beginning in the 1890s with Ellis's work. Masters and Johnson's recent book *On Sex and Human Loving* traces many of these influences on what philosopher Paul Robinson calls this "modernization of sex."

Ellisonian sex, then, is a male-driven, female-responsive sex of intense and rapid sexual energy buildup in the male and slower, more generalized, somewhat less urgent response in the female. Orgasm was the ultimate goal, but touching, particularly for women, was enjoyable if not necessary. The penis and its spontaneous erection was the center of male sexual response, and the clitoris with its connections to the vagina and the uterus was the center of female response. Marriage was a natural manifestation of the desire for prolonged companionship, but might have to be augmented by some type of sexual variety to keep it alive. Men acted and entered, women reacted and received. In spite of this mechanical-sounding emphasis, Ellis was a new romantic who valued closeness and tolerated deviation from "the normal." Paul Robinson states, "Havelock Ellis is the most unambiguously Romantic of the great modernists . . . at the heart of his sexual writings stands the same union of physical and emotional energies that one finds in Keats and Schlegel."

Ellis's work confronted a guilt and fear about sex that permeated daily living. To save ourselves from what he saw as our innate sexual sickness, the Reverend Doctor Sylvester Graham suggested that we rid our diets of meat, animal products, and all spicy foods. Graham suggested that these caloric corrupters be replaced with, of course, nutritious Graham bread and Graham crackers. He was joined in his concern for the digestive sexual degeneration of American by Dr. John Kellogg, who invented corn flakes to save us from too much snap, crackle, or pop in our sex drive. The first modern perspective on human sexuality and its relationship to intimacy offered a freedom from this type of restrictive, fear-inducing approach to sex. At the same time, however, Ellis's views about sexual energy, male and female differences in sexual response, and the power of sexual variety are still present today, and they strongly influenced the work of Alfred Kinsey, the pioneer of a second perspective on sexuality.

The Second Perspective:
Kinseyan Sex

Alfred Kinsey stated, "This is first of all a report on what people do, which raises no question of what they should do." This statement became translated quickly by others to, "This is an outline of what you ought to or could be doing." The second perspective was now beginning.

The Kinsey reports on male (1948) and female (1953) sexual behavior remain the most complete and reliable references on human sexuality. There has never been and likely will never be another work like them.

Kinsey's background was in the study of insects. He spent more than twenty years classifying tiny gall wasps. He was a taxonomist who valued size and distribution of sample. He classified more than four million insects throughout the United States and Mexico. If Ellis thought in terms of process, Kinsey thought in terms of classification, or categories. The perspective on sex was changing. We thought now not only about what we did, but where we "fit" compared to other people and new sexual categories.

In the male study, he identified six categories of sexual behavior—"outlets," he called them—that related to factors that influenced outlet. The energy orientation of the first perspective is clearly present, and "energy-outlet style" was the focus. The six categories were masturbation, nocturnal emission, heterosexual petting, heterosexual intercourse, homosexual behavior, and sex with animals or other species. A second-perspective vocabulary was evolving. Words such as "leaping" and "devouring" were replaced with "petting," "mounting," and the "seeking of outlets." In some ways, animal sexual behavior became the model for human sex. If animals did it, then we ought to be able to do it. The focus changed from the romantic to the rural.

How are you doing in your category-four behavior? We had started to think in a partialistic, not holistic, fashion about sex. Kinsey studied orgasms as his exclusive measure of a completed sexual experience. Orgasms provided a category; either you had one or you didn't, so it could be classified. The second perspective brought with it an "all or none" orientation to sexual expression, a less romantic view, a Sergeant Fridayism of "just the facts, ma'am."

The Kinsey sexual-response model was based on three phases:

buildup, orgasm, and aftereffects of orgasm. Rhythmic muscular contractions accompanied orgasms in the Kinsey view, and this was the same for both sexes. Kinsey focused less on the male penis than did Ellis, describing more general stimulation to both the male and female as characteristic of human sexual interaction.

The female was described as less sexually responsive than the male, but by this Kinsey meant that her frequency of orgasms was less. Men reported more than 1,500 orgasms before marriage, women reported approximately 250. There was no category for "almosts" and "super." Kinsey described the female as more physically responsive, requiring touch and direct contact for arousal and orgasm. Males were more psychologically responsive, reacting to images, pictures, and objects.

It was implied that marriage was a "convenient state," providing a ready opportunity for sexual outlet. The more than 11,200 two-hour interviews yielded statistics that came to be prescriptive. Ninety-five percent of men had some sexual experience before age fifteen; men reported having 4 orgasms per week; 70 percent of men reported contact with a prostitute; 50 percent of men reported having sex outside their marriage before age forty; 30 percent of unmarried women reported not being virgins at age twenty-three; women reported 233 orgasms before marriage, with a significant decline in orgasmic frequency after marriage; 25 percent of girls reported having some sexual experience before age twelve, and 52 percent of these experiences were with a stranger. A lot of people were doing a lot of things sexually, and an unintended invitation to join a category was issued.

If Ellis focused on what was "normal," Kinsey examined what he considered "natural." If mammals could to it, it was natural, and Kinsey attempted to avoid the confrontation of what was right or wrong in favor of describing what "was." The only unnatural sex act was one that could not be done. Several response came from the individual, not from within a relationship.

Kinsey saw nothing particularly special about our humanness. He wrote, "The elements that are involved in sexual contacts between the human and animals of other species are at no point basically different from those that are involved in erotic responses to human situations." In fact, Kinsey felt that it was our arrogance about being human, our attempt to distance ourselves from our mammalian ancestors, that caused us to take sex out if its "natural" context.

The Kinsey perspective, then, saw orgasm as essentially pelvic muscle contraction in both genders, but women tended to be less responsive and slower to respond than men. There were several categories of sex from which to choose. Marriage saved time in searching for outlets, but women tended to diminish in sexual responsiveness once married and men tended to seek out variety, were by nature sexually promiscuous. Love was not a category or a factor, it was not something that could, even should, be studied if it existed at all. "Tell me what you did, not how you felt" was the second-perspective question.

The emphasis on energy buildup and discharge, on doing it instead of experiencing it, and an implied drive for variety of the first two perspectives interfere with the super marital sex that stresses flow instead of discharge, an intimate comfort, not variety.

The Third Perspective: Masters and Johnsonian Sex

William Masters and Virginia Johnson observed the sexual behavior of 382 women and 312 men for a total of 10,000 individual sexual-response cycles. Their courageous and pioneering work not only provided long-needed medical knowledge about sexuality, but allowed the public and medical acknowledgment that sexual problems were a part of many, if not most, sexual relationships. More important, their work provided hope for solving these problems.

The sexual-response model of Masters and Johnson maintains the "energy buildup and release" orientation of the first and second perspectivces, but divides energy buildup into excitement and plateau, and energy release into orgasm and resolution. Sex researchers have questioned this four-phase cycle, suggesting that it is far from accurate in the male response and misleading regarding the female response.

The four-phase model suggests that the refractory period, a phase during which continued genital stimulation is ineffective, even uncomfortable, applies only to men and is somehow separate from the four phases. It suggests that excitement and plateau are separate phases, an assertion that does not bear out in subjective experience. The four phases do not identify such issues as desire, interest, or satisfaction, yet problems with desire are the most frequent of sexual problems.

Masters and Johnson indicate that male and female sexual response is essentially the same. They identify the orgasmic platform, or contractions of the outer third of the vaginal barrel, and vaginal lubrication as generally equivalent to the erection of the male penis. In fact, the third perspective of sex contains a "new feminism" that seems to use the female cycle as a model or standard for the male response.

Masters and Johnson presented a sexual problem-solving book that quickly became the spark for an entirely new form of couples therapy. In *Human Sexual Inadequacy* and in *The Pleasure Bond,* they suggest techniques for slowing men down and speeding women up in their sexual response. They present sensate focus, a technique for learning to touch and be touched, and describe the "tease technique" and the "squeeze technique" to help with impotence and premature ejaculation respectively. Their diagnostic categories are based on time, on coming too soon, taking too long, or not spending enough time. Women may have problems having orgasm, but men are always orgasmic if they ejaculate, preferably "on time" for the female. For the first time, we had individual diagnosis based on two people; men were premature, but women were never postmature. Sex clinics proliferated following their work, as Masters and Johnson gave unwilling birth to the Arthur Murray "sex" studios of the seventies. While Masters and Johnson trained only a few teams, their educational programs were offered to hundreds who in turn felt themselves to be "Masters and Johnson" qualified, franchised sexperts. Unlike the first and second perspectives, this third perspective was being directly interpreted for us on talk shows and in popular magazines, each preaching the same "time-frame sex" of this third view of sexuality. Perhaps a society that now had more time to recreate and less need to procreate was more than ready for a perspective on sex that stressed efficient, effective use of our sex time.

There is no question that Masters and Johnson made a significant and lasting contribution to "democratizing" sex. Their treatment program was for couples, and even though their sexual-response model was based on the individual, they treated couples with treatment teams, and saw marriage as much more than a natural state or convenience. They saw it as a challenge, a potential for pleasure and sexual satisfaction as well as companionship, a place where time could be better controlled. In my view, the most significant contribution of Masters and Johnson was not their flawed sexual-response model, which modified the original Ellis model. Their contribution was to focus on a system, an interaction. They were a team, a man-and-woman team, and that allowed the feminist balance so lacking in the first two perspectives. They started the systems approach to sex that I emphasize in the super marital sex perspective.

The Fourth Perspective: Super Sex for the Twenty-first Century

The first perspective was a new sexual theology. Ellis was a moralist, and much of his work grew from his attempts to free us from the fear of the consequences of our "unnatural sex." He was a romanticist, helping free us from a fear of punishment and insensitive religiosity, replacing that fear with understanding of the basic humanness of our sexual needs. He would have agreed with the idea of love maps.

The second perspective was of the "contraceptive" period, when a new freedom was emerging that allowed sex without inevitable consequences. Kinsey taught us what could and was being done, and the romantic emphasis evolved to a naturalistic focus, the categorization of behaviors that fit a time when people wanted to know if they were doing what everyone else seemed to be doing, to be free to enjoy what they were doing anyway.

The third perspective was a time-focus perspective, following the direction of a society that was moving faster and faster, developing a type-A sexual pattern, enjoying their "natural" sex. Masters and Johnson added a medical emphasis to the romantic and naturalistic focus of the first two perspectives, a fix-it, more egalitarian sexuality that fit the emerging feminism of their time. They attempted to replace dysfunction with sexual functioning.

Each of these perspectives emerged from a time, an ecology, as much as it emerged from the creativity of each of these scientists. Now, I suggest, we are responding to a new time, a time that requires a worldview, a systems view of sex, one that heals the disconnection that has taken place, the loss of intimacy in this era of choice.

We have gone full cycle. We are back to fear, the fear of sexually transmissible disease. AIDS has changed everything, and it, too, is a product of our time. We must learn not to think of the "AIDS virus that is transmitted through sexual intimacy." There is a human immunodeficiency virus, an AIDS-related virus (ARV) that is transmitted through some forms of sexual interaction and through other and some as yet unknown means of transmission. We do not

	ELLISONIAN SEX
SOCIOSEXUAL ATMOSPHERE	Strict religiosity and moral sanctions
"DOMINANT" SCIENCE	Physiology
SCIENTIFIC "PHILOSOPHY"	Theological
	Romanticized
SCIENTIST	Speculator
METHODOLOGY	Animal and cultural comparisons, theory
	Speculating and theorizing
MOTIVATING "OLD" FEAR OF THE PERIOD	Fear of divine retribution, moral punishment
MOTIVATING "NEW" HOPE OF THE PERIOD	To combine morality and sexual freedom
SOCIOSEXUAL IMPACT OF THIS ORIENTATION TO SEXUALITY	Opened topic of sex to discussion and study, more tolerance
"PSYCHO- SOCIO- SEXUAL" RESULT	Made possible and necessary a descriptive study, what people "were and are" doing, not just what we "thought" they were doing

KINSEYAN SEX	MASTERS and JOHNSONIAN SEX	SUPER MARITAL SEX
Sexual curiosity combined with hypocrisy →	→ Pressure to perform live up to "norms" →	→ Unstable relationships
Biology	Medicine	Psychology
Naturalistic ——— Mechanistic	Medical ——— Physiological	Transpersonal psychology ——— Holistic health
← Asker ——————	→ Watcher/Helper ——	→ Reflector/Integrator
Survey of large numbers of individual sex histories	Observation, physiological recording of sexual response	Reports from and analysis of "couples" systems
→ Asking and counting →	→ Watching and directing ——	→ Experiencing and learning
Fear of being "atypical," abnormal	Fear of failure, of "missing out" on pleasure potential	Fear of disease (AIDS) fear of loss of self
Free of conception worry, sex without consequences	Potential to overcome sexual problem	Sexuality beyond genitals, a new intimacy
Developed "norms," comparisons and categories	"Competence" motive control, skill emphasis	Discovery of sexual potential of long-term relationships
By providing "documentation" of sexual activity, provides a focus for observation of sexual response, verification of the theory and the count	Made possible a "treatment" of sex, correcting problems, rearranging the numbers. Denial of role of sex in living could no longer be denied. So someone had actually "seen it."	Focus on intimacy, systems and lasting relationships. Allowed evolution a more, generalized, holistic sexuality

know how or why some people who are exposed to the virus experience disease of their immune systems when and how they do, but it is likely that overall mental and physical health are as important to this process as the virus itself.

The virus is not the disease. To blame a virus or a specific group of "carriers" is to return to a Victorian fear orientation, that is, the fear of punishment for our sexuality. We must learn that AIDS and all sexually transmissible diseases are diseases of a world system, related to how we all interact and live, to our holistic health. We must learn to cure a system, not a disease, and this is the lesson of the fourth perspective. It is a lesson of hope, not a return to fear and punishment and alienation to avoid divine retribution. It is a hope that we will be able to connect now more than ever and move toward an elective intimacy, an intimacy of faith in loving, not an intimacy of default to disease. Super marital sex is a hope, not a surrender, and the fourth perspective that underlies this form of relating is based on the rules of new physics, of rules that govern all living systems, the rules that come from all four perspectives: Sex is not immoral, sex is natural, sexual problems can be solved, and prolonged and enduring intimacy is the most important of all health-maintenance systems.

The accompanying chart summarizes and compares these four perspectives of human sexuality. It compares the social atmosphere from which each perspective emerged, the worldview of each perspective, the new freedom each perspective provided, the basic orientation of the scientist or theorist representing each perspective, the basic fear that resulted in the evolution of each perspective, the consequences of sexual behavior that determined the orientation of each perspective, the scientific orientation and sociosexual impact of each perspective. The fourth perspective emphasizes the value of long-term intimacy because it is in keeping with what we have learned about health, that all healing and wellness depends upon a system of intimacy, acceptance, and loving. It may be that even AIDS cannot wreak its havoc unless it encounters a weakened system, both social and personal. The hope of the super marital sex perspective is that loving systems will provide a strong defense against any attack.

Biologist Clause Bernard has stated, "Illnesses hover constantly about us. They are seeds blown by the wind. But they do not set in the terrain unless the terrain is ready to receive them." We can not harness the wind, but we are able to cultivate a healthier, hardier terrain.

Here are fourteen of the assumptions regarding human sexuality that emerged from the first three perspectives. In each case, I have altered the assumption from the fourth perspective to illustrate this orientation to sexuality.

1. Intercourse is the ultimate sexual act between a man and woman, and intercourse means insertion of the penis into the vagina. Anything less than penetration is not really intercourse.

   FOURTH PERSPECTIVE: Intercourse with the penis inside the vagina is not the ultimate intimate sexual act, but one option among many intimate choices. When it becomes the ultimate act, we miss opportunities for forms of intimacy that involve equally intense pleasure and sharing and we become goal-directed and one-dimensional in our sexuality.

2. Men are the "inserters" and women are "receivers" in sexual intercourse.

   FOURTH PERSPECTIVE: A more productive orientation to sexual intercourse and all sexual interaction is one of "merging" rather than "penetration," of doing with and together rather than to or for.

3. Genital contractions are orgasm.

   FOURTH PERSPECTIVE: Genital contractions following sexual stimulation are pleasurable reflexes. The total experience of physical, emotional, and cognitive merging with someone we love is called a "psychasm," and may or may not be accompanied by genital or pelvic contractions.

4. Orgasm is the measure of sexual fulfillment.

   FOURTH PERSPECTIVE: The number of orgasms is related to the number of neuromuscular responses to genital stimulation. Sexual fulfillment is a more complex interpersonal process involving all levels of human responsiveness.

5. Women have more trouble having orgasm than men.

   FOURTH PERSPECTIVE: There is no evidence that pelvic reflex is related to gender, but expectations can influence physiological responsiveness.

6. Women respond sexually more slowly than do men.

   FOURTH PERSPECTIVE: "Speed" and "time" are not the key variables in sexual response, and mental, emotional, and cognitive factors are person-, not gender-, related.

7. Men have a refractory period and a period during which they must rest before continuing. Women can go on forever.

FOURTH PERSPECTIVE: All neurological responses are followed by some period of refraction or rest. Gender is not predictive of the length of this rest period.

8. Men are turned on erotically by a wider range of stimuli than women.

FOURTH PERSPECTIVE: People are erotically responsive to wide and changing ranges of sexual stimuli, and love maps, not gender, determine such responsiveness.

9. Men cannot control their ejaculation for long periods of time. They must ejaculate to be "complete."

FOURTH PERSPECTIVE: Ejaculation is a reflex, but it can be influenced through practice, awareness of body response, communication, and separation of ejaculation from the idea of release, completeness, or outlet.

10. Intimate body contact is necessary for sex.

FOURTH PERSPECTIVE: Sexual communication can take place on many different levels, including levels that are not always measurable by our present instruments.

11. Variety in sex partners is one of the strongest of sexual aphrodisiacs.

FOURTH PERSPECTIVE: Sameness, familiarity, predictability, knowing, and comfort are more important to sexual intensity and fulfillment than newness and variety.

12. Erection of the clitoris and penis is necessary for sex.

FOURTH PERSPECTIVE: There is no need for erection of the clitoris or penis in order to achieve sexual fulfillment. Such erections are reflexive and not necessarily indicators of arousal.

13. Sexual response is a cycle, one phase following and building upon the other, followed by a complete reversal of this cycle.

FOURTH PERSPECTIVE: Sexual response is a system, and does not have to follow a step-by-step, orderly process. Changing back and forth to various phases of response and experience is possible.

14. Sex energy builds up and then it must be released, followed by rest.

FOURTH PERSPECTIVE: The energy of sexual intimacy is as much mental and spiritual as it is physical. It does not have to build, but can be maintained at a chosen level. Rest is not necessary after sexual intimacy. In fact, sexual interaction may be invigorating.

The erect penis in a receptive vagina for a long time, but not too long, continues to be the sexual standard. Erection, lubrication, reception, insertion, contraction is the cycle. As I looked at these factors, I learned that absolutely none of them were based on anything but assumption and that if we change our assumptions, a new model of sexual response results. Chapters Six and Seven will detail the sexual response of men and women. I present here the "Fourth-perspective sexual response model" that results when we change our assumptions about sex to include a systems, intimacy view.

The Super Sex Response Model

DESIRE: This term refers to frequency of sexual interaction. It does not mean "wanting" sex, only how many times you and your spouse are sexually intimate. With this use of the word "desire," a systems orientation is necessary because it refers to interaction, not a drive state. "Low" desire and "high" desire are relative terms indicating a couple's report of how often they are sexual together. You will understand more about this way of using the word "desire" by learning about the other nine phases of sexual response.

"You have absolutely no desire," said the wife. "You have sex but you don't really want it."

"Well, you want it, you have desire," responded the husband, "but you don't really have it, you don't enjoy it."

You can see the danger in "assigning" sexual motives. I have found it helpful to use desire simply and directly as a number, a count that means nothing but number and certainly is not a symptom of the presence or absence of sexual interest or arousal.

INTEREST: This term is the "thinking" dimension of sex. It can take place in the total absence of any genital response. We all think about sex, some times more than other times. I found that when I asked about interest, not physical arousal or "wanting to do it," just interest, couples had difficulty answering. They had been taught by the first three perspectives that interest had to be "shown" or it did not count, and that if we showed it then we must be interested.

I found that understanding and identifying differences in this cognitive area were important steps to solving sexual problems of the couples, and once they understood that interest carried with it no requirement for defense regarding what happens after interest, they talked openly about their concerns in this area of sexual response.

Of course, animals do not have interest, only reflex, so the early perspectives seldom spoke of interest. The couples did. "You look at every dirty magazine you can find," said the wife. "If there is a half-naked woman, you'll find her. You have some type of breast or genital radar."

"Maybe," responded the husband. "But you could pass a naked man on the street and comment on his bad posture." Clearly, the couple is having a debate over interest differences, at least perceived interest differences. There were an equal number of opposite examples. Interest is not gender-determined.

AROUSAL: This term refers to the emotional component of sexual response, the emotional reaction to interest. It does not have to be accompanied by any genital change. It is what some people call "HQ," the Horniness Quotient.

This factor was also neglected in the early perspectives. Masters and Johnson described sexual response in terms of body cues (contractions, pulsations, emissions). Subjective experience teaches that "emotional arousal" does not have to lead to "evidence" of genital arousal, yet early in treatment, couples argued over the "fact" of arousal.

"You couldn't be aroused," said one wife. "You were as flaccid as a day-old noodle."

"Neither were you aroused," replied the husband. "You were as dry as a desert." Both partners had been well indoctrinated in the early perspective of "you can't feel it if you don't show it."

Both couples in the above two examples had not talked at all about the body to this point. They were talking about thoughts and feelings, two key aspects of the super sex paradigm.

READINESS: Readiness is the one phase of the ten-phase super sex model that was focused upon by the first three perspectives. Readiness refers to the body's response to interest and arousal. It is the physiological reaction that accompanies interest and arousal, the tumescence stage, when blood rushes to erotic areas of the body, including the genitals, preparing for body-to-body interaction. Readiness is an entire body response, not just a genital response. Remember, lack of readiness does not mean lack of interest or arousal. Research does not support such a relationship. Readiness is a reflex, and can take place with little arousal and be absent even when there is a great deal of both interest and arousal.

Your own experience teaches you that you have been aroused, but not ready. Sometimes you have awakened ready, but not aroused. You have been interested and ready, but not aroused. You have been ready, but not interested, and your desire, your frequency might or might not have reflected any of these changes in the sexual system, because sex is really not an automatic cycle, it is a system of interactions of different mind and body states. The cycle orientation of the first three perspectives mislead us. Use your own experience as the couples did and you will see that sexuality is not some type of automatic slide, but a complex mind/body interaction. This fourth perspective emphasizes the subjective experiences of the couples rather than the observational orientation of earlier perspectives.

"I know you think I'm ready," reported the husband. "You think I'm always ready. Well, I'm not. My penis does not speak for me."

"If I can't tell by your penis, how am I supposed to know if you are ready?" asked the wife.

The orientation of the first perspectives is clear in this exchange. Both partners have confused what the body does with how the person feels.

EXCITEMENT: This term refers to the emotional and cognitive reaction to the readiness. The changes of readiness are pronounced, as you will learn in Chapters Six and Seven. But the system does not stop there. We can react to our body as much as our body reacts to our mind and emotions. Again, we are talking about a miraculous intimacy system, not a hedonistic hydraulic system.

"I just get so aroused when I see what happens to my body when I am ready to do it," reported the husband. "I get red-like, full, eager-looking, like a real hunk, you might say. I never look better than at that time. I wish she could see me, but she never looks."

"I'm not sure what you mean by how do I feel or think when my body gets ready. It just is ready to do it, to receive him. Do you think I should jump up, run to the mirror, turn on the light and look?" asked the wife.

"Sure, just as long as you run to the mirror with your spouse. Better yet, have a mirror and soft light nearby. See what it looks like when the two of you happen with each other,'' was the way I answered her.

The terms desire, interest, arousal, readiness, and excitement have been used so interchangeably that most of the couples found it useful to discuss their definitions. Try it in your own relationship; your communication will become not only wider, but deeper and more connected.

PHYSIOLOGICAL ORGASM: This dimension of the super sex model refers to the contractions of the muscles in the pelvic area followed by a detumescence. In males and in some females, physiological orgasm is accompanied by emission of fluid. Whipple and Perry report that females experience a buildup and discharge of muscle tension in the pubococcygeal muscles and in the orgasmic platform (the area that can contract in the outer third of the vagina in response to sexual stimulation). They add that the buildup and disharge of myotonia in the deeper muscles of the vagina results in the uterus contracting and pushing down, causing the orgasmic platform to open, resulting in what they call an ''A-frame'' effect in the vagina. The former response, called the ''tenting response,'' is not typically involved with emissions in the female. The A-frame response can be involved in such emission, probably related to the Skene's glands (glands around the urethra) and stimulation of the Grafenberg area (Whipple and Perry called this the G spot.)

Men in my interviews reported different types of physiological orgasms as well. Some felt more of an ''opening'' sensation similar to that of the A-frame orgasm, while others felt the contractive response of the tenting type. I will return to a discussion of male physiological orgasm in Chapter Six and female physiological orgasms in chapter Seven. I will elaborate then on such issues as female ejaculation and G and C areas and the male F and R areas.

''I definitely know when I come. I feel this tensing, then a series of pulsations,'' reported the wife.

''I feel like that, too,'' said the husband. ''It's like I'm going to come, then I come. It is just like strong pulses in the groin.''

The physiological orgasm was the emphasis of the first three perspectives, with a focus on the body response rather than ''psychasms.''

PSYCHOLOGICAL ORGASM: I first became aware of the occurrence of ''psychasms'' in my work with physically impaired persons. Even in those persons with complete severing of any connection between genital stimulation and the brain, orgasms and sometimes more intense orgasms than prior to injury were reported.

"I feel it. Well, I don't actually 'feel' as much as I 'experience it.' It may be an 'eargasm,' or 'neckasm' or related to just a 'cuddleasm,' but is clearly an intense orgasm. I really think I never had orgasm, at least not anything but physical orgasms, before I broke my neck." This report came from a young skier who had injured herself in a fall several years ago. As I worked with her and her uninjured husband, they both reported a clear and distinct difference between physiological and psychological orgasms.

"I learned from her what it meant to really have orgasms, to really come. It wasn't like just in one place . . . it was an overwhelming event. It sort of came over me instead of me coming." Her husband had been freed to experience the difference between physiological reflex in reaction to genital stimulation and psychological experience through a shared body/mind experience.

Psychasm has been one of the most difficult of concepts for me to present at professional programs. "Orgasm is orgasm" is usually the argument, even though basic neurophysiolgy teaches that ejaculation and contractions are not the same as the full orgasmic experience. Discuss the issue with your partner. You will see that you are able to divide the physical from the psychological aspects of orgasm, and be able to take the "organ" out of orgasm.

REFRACTORY PERIOD: All neurological reactions in the human body are followed by a "rest period," a period during which another neurological response is diminished or impossible. Such refractory periods range from milliseconds to minutes.

When you enter someone's home, you may notice a unique odor. After some time you do not detect it (at least in most homes) because of the olfactory refractory period. The principle is the same in sexual response.

Sexually, refractory periods occur for both men and women. They are not the "beached whale" phenomenon of a man collapsing from sexual fatigue. They are periods of varying duration occurring in both genders during which time direct stimulation to a specific part or area of the body is ineffective, bothersome, or uncomfortable.

Emotionally, there is also a refractory period. We cannot maintain any emotional state indefinitely. In fact, most emotions last only a few seconds. We must change gears or burn out. The same is true for sex. We need to pause, to rest, to take what I call a PON, or post-orgasmic nap; a POR, a post-orgasmic rest, or even a POS, post-orgasmic sleep.

The husband said, "I used to think I had no control over it. I just knew that after I ejaculated, I would be immobilized. I learned that feelings changed in my penis after I ejaculated, but that the refractory thing is the same in my wife and not just in the genitals either. I used to think she could go on forever until she finally told me she felt like I did."

"Sure," responded the wife. "I don't know why men think women are some type of sex machine that once turned on becomes a perpetual-motion instrument that sort of putters out because the man goes to sleep. There are times when to touch my clitoris just hurts. It depends on when, how, and certainly by whom."

Talk this issue over with your spouse and you can validate it for your own relationship. Refraction is not just physical, not just male, and not always the same. The early perspectives on human sexuality viewed refraction as a response only in the male. It, as with all of the dimensions of sexual response that I have discussed, does not have to follow a predetermined order. Physical and/or emotional refraction can happen anytime in the sexual interaction, depending on emotional state and area of stimulation. If we are bound by the "cycle" concept, we begin to anticipate refraction as the inevitable aftermath of the goal of orgasm, similar to the exhaustion of the long-distance runner. We can touch, hold, talk, and hold, wait and resume sex later. Super sex depends on learning this concept. It will require considerable unlearning, but the rewards for this effort are new levels of intimacy and sexual fulfillment free from psychologically determined physiological limitations.

AFTERGLOW: The old term for this phase was resolution. One wife referred to it as "restitution." Prior sexual perspectives saw this phase as essentially a complete reversal of the whole process of the sexual response. Masters and Johnson saw this as "phase-specific," a retreat of all prior physiological changes occurring only at the end of the cycle.

The thousand couples did not substantiate this phase. Sometimes the "sex flush," the reddening of the skin in the facial cheeks and upper chest, would go away quickly and sometimes it would linger on. Instead of a feeling of settling down, some spouses reported a "glowing," almost a "suspension in time" preceding a readiness for another experience. If we expect "resolution," a resolving of all of this energy buildup that was talked about so much in the first perspectives, we will probably experience it. If we expect to "glow," to enjoy, to share, following a physical or psychological orgasm or at any time in our interaction, then we will be free to do so.

"I never thought of sharing too much after we came. It was a whole new thing. We would lie together and glow. It was like E.T., but the light was not just a heart light. It was all over. We learned to really enjoy this period instead of lying there waiting for it to pass so we could go to sleep," reported one of the husbands at five-year follow-up. His comments illustrate the importance of not being "phase-specific," of turning in instead of out for our sexual reference points. Enjoying the full-body response of our partner during intimate relationships does not have to be preparatory; it can happen at any time.

CONTEMPLATION: Seldom were early research subjects asked much about what happened "after." I found this to be a very special time, as the couples learned to free themselves from the "separation phenomenon," the tendency either to just cuddle and sleep or to start thinking about the kids, the car, the dog, or the cat. As pointed out earlier, leaving one another quickly, getting our minds on other things, might have helped in prehistoric times. Lingering too long in a sexual experience would make a couple a double-course dinner for a predatory animal. We now have the luxury of pausing awhile, for quite a while if we choose. Once we are aware of the role of contemplation, of sending and receiving signals to our spouse even in silence following physical intimacy, we add an entirely new dimension to our sexual interaction; we find super sex.

"We would look into each other's eyes. It was strange. I could almost hear him, receive something from his, but we didn't talk at all. It was like the sex set us up for a whole type of being together that we could never have at other times." This report from one of the wives illustrates the "contemplative" phase.

"X-rated films always end each scene with ejaculation. You never see them together much after that. It's a whole different thing to sort of stay with her. I don't mean to get ready again or anything, I mean to almost relive the sex, even your marriage just by being quiet together." This husband at five-year follow-up had discovered the importance of "being" instead of "doing" in his sexual experiences with his wife.

Super Marital Sex Opportunity Number Five

To review the concepts presented in this chapter, make some time to talk with your spouse about the ten-phase model of super sex response. Each of you write down the ten phases on ten separate index cards. Now, based on your last sexual encounter together, write a brief paragraph about how you experienced each of the ten phases. Write the description on the back of each card. Exchange your set of cards with the description side facing up and try to arrange each other's responses in the order I presented in this chapter.

Of course, there is no real "order," because we have not described a "sexual cycle." When you look on the other side of each card, you may find that the phases do not match, that your experiences as a couple and as individuals are unique to you.

The next step is to set up your own marital super sex response model. Write up ten new cards combining your responses and establishing an order you find interesting. Just play "sex cards," and don't take the whole thing too seriously. This super sex opportunity, as the first four, is for fun and learning, not diagnosis and problem-solving.

The next two chapters include mini-tests to illustrate a new way of looking at male and female sexual response. Give yourself time to think about and discuss the new perspective presented in this chapter. Play the sex-card game, relisten to the tapes you have made as a part of the earlier super sex opportunities. Reread and add to your marital love book. Take your time, a marital time, before moving on to the next two chapters, because they should be read as a pair, both chapters together by both partners together. Remember, as a popular song once pointed out, you can't hurry love.

CHAPTER SIX

Why Husbands Don't Have Orgasm: Myths and Facts About Husbands' Sexuality

> I wish it could feel as good as it does when I am going to come, after I come, but the better it is, the shorter it is. By the time I get to feeling really good, there's not much time to enjoy it.
>
> HUSBAND

Coming To False Conclusions

"I know when he says he's coming, that's about the time he'll be going." The wife frowned as she expressed her marriage-long frustration with her sexual relationship. Her husband busied himself straightening the books on the table next to his chair, as if looking for some quick retort to save his self-esteem.

The wife continued, gaining momentum from her newfound freedom to express her concerns openly. "He seems to be trying to get something accomplished. I call him pelvically hyperactive. When they talk about going all the way, I'd really love to, but it's just that I don't think he can last long enough to go even halfway."

The husband laughed at his wife's sarcasm, but his smile masked the pain evident in his clenched fist. He shuffled his feet on the floor, much as a little boy caught stealing cookies once too often. He smiled at me awkwardly, as if appealing for some form of universal male empathy for our failure to explain to the opposite gender the nature of our sexual enigma. Why does it seem that the better it feels, the sooner it's over? If we are not coming too soon, we are having trouble coming at all. Why does it seem that we enjoy so little of what we talk about so much? When we come, it sometimes feels that we haven't been very far at all, not really been anywhere.

The Number-One Male Sexual Problem

You'd think that something I think about so much and do so much would be more fun, be more fulfilling. It seems to have lost its zing. I do it just the same, but something is missing.

HUSBAND

I can say without fear of contradiction from any sex researcher that the number-one male sexual problem is not erective failure or ejaculatory control, but the failure to enjoy sex, the failure to really enjoy sexual interaction with a woman. My clinical experience teaches that the male genital focus, the phallocentrism of the American husband, has seriously jeopardized and compromised his potential for true sexual happiness. Men are not orgasmic, they are ejaculatory. Climax for too many of them is an end to an activity, the accomplishment of a challenge, the extra point after the touchdown, the completion of a project rather than the beginning or renewal of feelings of closeness, intimacy, and warmth.

"When my husband finishes—shoots his load, as he likes to say—he is really shot. I feel like I should ask him if I can get him anything else. I feel like a waitress instead of a sex partner."

Her husband responded, "Sure. Remember the time you said 'wait until the girls hear about this.' Really made me feel great. I'll bet I am the feature story for your coffee klatch."

And so it goes, a perpetual sexual sparring, with both partners getting hurt. Such difficulties might be expected outside of marriage, for seldom do shorter-lasting, more anonymous sexual relationships provide the opportunity for learning, communication, mutual growth, understanding, total life-sharing, and intimacy that is available over time within marriage. Unfortunately, more than half of married people report dissatisfaction with their sexual lives. One reason is that men may be doing it more but enjoying it less.

Men feel valued for what they do, not who they are. They feel like success objects rather than sex objects. As a result, their sexual behavior is characterized by emphasis on skills, foreplay, technique, timing, and love-making prowess. Accused of being selfish, men are not really selfish enough, for they are too busy trying to do instead of be and experience. Love becomes a product they try to "make." They feel they have to "get it on" and "get off." They feel a burden of culminating the sexual interaction with expulsion of fluid. "You know if a man comes, but you can't tell if a woman comes," was the report of one husband. This is not true. The presence of ejaculate tells only that there was a contractive reflex similar to the vaginal contractions of the woman. Contractions are not the only criterion of orgasm. If they were, other animals would have orgasm. They don't. With the possible exception of some higher primates, orgasm and its subjective dimension is uniquely human.

Men have learned to release muscle tension, to achieve a pelvic settledness, but they have failed to achieve a settledness of the spirit. Men may have orgasm if by that term we mean organ reflex to sexual stimulation, but they fail to have psychasms. Psychasms require an alteration of consciousness, but men are seldom aware of what they are experiencing at the time of ejaculation. As long as this reflex orientation continues, men will go on trying to "get some" but fail to give or take anything.

The husbands completing the super marital sex program in my clinic report being stunned at the difference between orgasm and psychasm. They discover after forty or more years of "coming" what it is like to experience "being." "I never imagined it could be like this," commented one husband. "I thought you were nuts when you talked about this psychasm thing. It's a whole other thing. There is no language to describe it."

The Male "F" and "R" Areas: "G Spots" for Men

Men have two "areas" that are particularly responsive to sexual stimulation. Take time now to find these areas for yourself.

In the privacy of your bedroom, with the door locked, lie side by side naked as a couple. With the husband's and the wife's hand, find the little piece of skin that is on the underside of the penis running from the coronal ridge, the edge of the mushroomlike top of the penis, to the penile shaft. In uncircumcised men, it will be necessary to pull the foreskin out of the way gently to find this piece of skin. This is the frenulum, or F area, one of the most erotic of sexual areas for men. During intercourse, this area is typically deeply within the moist and warm vagina resulting in intense stimulation and eventual pelvic muscle contraction in men and little stimulation to women. The positioning of the F area for intense stimulation results in timing problems for many men, for they feel a loss of control when the F area is stimulated while their partner receives much less stimulation. Her C area (or clitoral area) is usually not stimulated to the same degree as the male's F area, so her orgasmic contractions are relatively delayed if not nonexistent.

A new posture, a posture of the future, allows a positioning of the F and C areas together. This posture allows for long and intense stimulation that promotes both the organ part of orgasm and psychasm as well. Described in Chapter Eight, this posture allows for a juxtaposing of the F and C areas.

One technique I have taught my patients for discovering the F area is as follows. The wife places her fingers just behind the scrotum, gently touching the fingertips to the perineal area or area behind the testicles. With her fingers in this position, the length of the fingers and palm will be in contact with scrotum and the shaft of the penis. With some adjustment of the hand, the lower wrist at the base of the thumb should be in contact with the frenulum or F area. Some men are able to feel their wife's pulse in this position. It takes practice to develop this level of sensitivity, but all men can learn this. Unlearning is necessary, too, for most men think that movement is sex, and pelvic thrusting is almost automatic in response to genital contact. Men can learn to lie still and feel. This technique is particularly helpful in learning psychasm. The man can practice this technique himself unless religious beliefs preclude self-stimulation.

The R area relates to the raphe, the line along the scrotum that you can see and feel. The skin on the scrotum is unique on the male body, and it can be sensitive as the labia, or lips, around the vagina. The wife can gently rub her fingertips back and forth along the center of the scrotum, along the raphe line, and the husband will feel a pleasurable sensation. Again, he must learn to be still instead of active, to receive instead of do. The scrotal skin will seem to wrinkle and shrink as the testicles rise. Another suggestion is for the wife to run the top of her middle fingernail gently along this line from behind the scrotum to the front and up the penis. This kind of stimulation will help the man to integrate the scrotum and penis in a total-unit response, replacing the "end of the penis" focus most men have developed.

The Friction Fallacy

Just put your first two fingers against your thumb and move your hand up and down and everyone will know what you mean. That is how men come.

TEENAGER

The early perspectives of sexuality asserted that men experience orgasm by thrusting, resulting in friction to the outer third of the penile shaft, which in turn resulted in "orgasm" and an "organ" emphasis. Men grow up believing and learning that there is one way to "come" and that is to have friction applied to the penis in a steady rhythm. This belief is one of the reasons that men learn to be the "do-it-to-ers" rather than receivers. For men, movement is sex.

A key to learning super marital sex is for men to learn to be still. While women were liberated when "even nice women moved their hips during sex," men will be liberated when they learn that they can be still, that orgasm and psychasm can be received, not just achieved.

One of the most difficult assignments for husbands in the super marital sex program was to try to hold their pelvis still, not by effort but by surrender, while their wife stimulated their genitals. It took a while, but when the husbands learned this technique, they were amazed at the range of sensations that resulted. "I have never in my life felt anything like it. It actually happened to me without me trying to make it happen. What a trip!" This husband was like many others who reported a new freedom of choice in sexual interactions when they discovered the F and R areas and choices beyond friction and movement.

Masters and Johnson state that male sexual response is exclusively in the glans or end of the penis and the shaft of the penis. This is not the case. *The Hite Report* in 1980 and my own data indicate that men also masturbate by gently stroking their scrotum and that the penis is the "main place" only if that is the lesson that is repeated throughout life and the design of the love map.

Testosterone Poisoning: Eve's Rib

Starting at approximately three weeks of development in the uterus, if there is an X/broken-X (Y) chromosome pattern with one of the X chromosomes missing its lower right leg, a male will develop in relationship to the presence of testosterone. Overstating the case, we could say that the clitoris grows out to a penis, the ovaries become testicles and drop down into a sac created when the labia grow together. You have discovered the line where the scrotum grew together, the line called the penoscrotal raphe, the R area of sensitivity along the scrotum up the penis to the frenulum.

This theory of "male from female" is called "inductor" theory in that the male is induced by androgens and MIS, Mullerian Inhibiting Substance, which causes certain female formations to disappear in utero. Early female development is not dependent on hormones; it is autonomous. Mary Jane Sherfey proposed this idea in her book *The Nature and Evolution of Female Sexuality*. While not totally accurate and in many ways incomplete, the earlier Freudian notion of male superiority or "penis envy" is further from neurophysiological accuracy than inductor theory.

Of course, masculinity and femininity are not mutually exclusive developmental axes. You can be less feminine in terms of society's criteria without being more masculine, and you can be more feminine without being less masculine. I had the husbands and wives point to areas on the following lines to show how they felt about their own gender orientation and share these feelings with one another.

        MALENESS_____ a little_____very much_____
        FEMALENESS_____ a little_____very much_____

Throughout life, even throughout the day, people vary on both axes. It is a mistake to ascribe a natural superiority in sexual function to either gender's sexual response.

The Tao of Super Marital Sex: The Yin and Yang Sex Problems

> We just don't seem to be together. We are out of step, not flowing together. We can't get together on anything, especially our sex life.
>
> HUSBAND

I used another test in my work with the thousand couples that led to much discussion between partners on the issue of being a man or woman in today's world. This test is based on the Chinese model of yin and yang. Our Western world has distorted this paradigm by equating male with yang and female with yin. Actually, the Chinese believed that all of life and all of us had elements of yin and yang in everything we do or experience. Sometimes we lean more to the yin, the feminine orientation to life, and sometimes we lean, even the world leans, to the masculine side, the yang. The idea is to get into the flow, what the Chinese called the Tao, of life and not to be trapped into a static yin or yang orientation to living.

Many philosophers feel that the yang or masculine orientation has dominated for thousands of years and that unless we, as a world of men and women, are able to flow more easily with yin and yang, the masculine and feminine, there may not be a world at all, for the yang tends toward a hot, competitive, aggressive orientation that can "Yang" us right out of existence.

Try this Yin and Yang of Masculinity and Femininity Test and discuss it with your spouse. Circle the score on each axis that indicates your tendency on that factor at this time.

1. FEMININE 0 1 2 3 4 5 6 7 8 9 10 VERY FEMININE

Do you possess traits society typically characterizes as more feminine, such as tenderness, sensitivity, caring, nurturing, and do you possess them to a lesser (feminine) or greater (very feminine) degree?

2. MASCULINE 0 1 2 3 4 5 6 7 8 9 10 VERY MASCULINE

Do you possess traits society characterizes as more masculine, such as aggressiveness, distance from feelings, nonexpressiveness, hostility, and do you possess them to a lesser (masculine) or greater (very masculine) degree? Again note that you can be less or more masculine or feminine without affecting your score on either axis.

3. CONTRACTIVE 0 1 2 3 4 5 6 7 8 9 10 EXPANSIVE

Are you a person who leans toward the understatement, tending to stay within yourself, reserved, held back (contractive), or are you more open, demonstrative, outgoing (expansive)?

4. RESPONSIVE   0 1 2 3 4 5 6 7 8 9 10   ACTIVE

Are you a person who reacts rather than acts, tends to watch for signals rather than send them (responsive), or are you more likely to be the sender, the starter, the initiator (active)?

5. COOPERATIVE   0 1 2 3 4 5 6 7 8 9 10   COMPETITIVE

Are you more of a team member, going along, fitting in, trying to make things go smoothly (cooperative), or are you more likely focused on trying to do your individual best, trying to stand out, be unique, different, better (competitive)?

6. INTUITIVE   0 1 2 3 4 5 6 7 8 9 10   RATIONAL

Do you go by feelings, senses, even your own form of extrasensory perception (intuitive), or do you emphasize cold, hard logic, facts, the see/touch world (rational)?

7. SYNTHESIZING   0 1 2 3 4 5 6 7 8 9 10   ANALYTIC

Are you an arranger, organizer, a "putter-together" type of person, trying to coordinate and integrate (synthesizing), or do you tend to break things down, look for the parts that make the whole, outline and divide things (analytic)?

8. COLD   0 1 2 3 4 5 6 7 8 9 10   HOT

In my book *Superimmunity: Mastering Your Emotions and Improving Your Health,* I identified cycles of withdrawal, helplessness, hopelessness, the more passive orientation of life (cold) and the excitable, hyper-aroused, agitated orientation (hot). Which do you lean to?

9. CONSERVATIVE   0 1 2 3 4 5 6 7 8 9 10   DEMANDING

Are you reluctant to express needs, holding back, even buying few things for yourself and more for others (conservative), or are you more self-enhancing, buying for self, taking care of your things, blaming others for failing you more than trying to make others happy (demanding)?

10. ECO-ACTION   0 1 2 3 4 5 6 7 8 9 10   EGO-ACTION

Physicist Fritjof Capra writes clearly of the yin/yang archetypal poles as dimensions of the rhythm of life. He and other writers differentiate between the "world," "us" orientation to life (eco-action) and the more selfish "I" orientation to life (ego-action). Which way to you lean?

Add up the total number of items that you circled on the scale above that are to the right of 5. Now, subtract from that number the total number of items that you circled to the left of 5. Ignore any 5 responses. The closer your score to zero, the more balance, the more in flow with the "Tao of super marital sex" you can be. If you lean strongly toward yin or yang, you are more likely to experience problems sexually.

Those persons leaning strongly to the yang orientation tended to have what I called the "hot" sex problems. For men, these were ejaculatory control problems, erection problems, and what some sex researchers are calling "sexual addiction," "sexual compulsion," "hypersexuality," or "hyperphilia." The yang sex problems for women were insufficient lubrication, painful coitus, vaginismus (anticipatory spasm of the muscles around the vagina preventing intercourse), and sexual addiction.

The yin problems for men tended to be inability to ejaculate, problems with orgasm and psychasm, and low interest and arousal. For women, the yin problems were low interest and arousal, problems with orgasm and psychasm, and diminished vaginal contractions.

Scores on the couples' tests predicted some of these sexual problems. When our neurohormonal system is in a state of stress, hyper-aroused, the "hot" sexual problems may occur. When our neurohormonal system is deactivated and appropriate arousal blocked, the "cold" sexual problems result. The lesson is that balance, both physiological and psychological, is a prerequisite for mutually pleasing sexuality.

Take this Yin and Yang of Sexual Problems Test as a couple. Talk over each of the ten items and place your relationship on each scale.

Is your marriage balanced, in flow, or is it leaning hot (yang) or cold (yin)? Are you yin or yang and the marriage characterized by a different pattern? The concepts of balance and adaptability are important in understanding the yin and yang of sexual relationships.

The next test is one of the most controversial tests taken by the couples, the Husbands' Orgasmic Inventory. As you take this test and read this chapter, remember that Chapters Six and Seven are a pair and are best read and discussed *as* a unit *by* a unit, your marriage. Keeping this in mind will help you find the Tao of sex.

The Husbands' Orgasmic Inventory

SCORING: 3—ALWAYS
                     2—USUALLY
                     1—SELDOM
                     0—NEVER

1. I feel responsible for the sexual experience. Whether the interaction is good or bad depends on me. _____

2. Once I ejaculate, I have to rest. I feel less energetic and have to recuperate. _____

3. When I begin to feel very good sexually, I know I am getting very close to ''coming'' or ''climaxing.'' The better it feels, the sooner I know I will come. _____

4. It is better if my wife is relatively still during the act of intercourse. If she moves too vigorously, it tends to make me come sooner. _____

5. When I ejaculate, I feel a few strong throbs in my penis at the time of ejaculation. _____

6. I seem to come much sooner when I have not had sex for a long time. _____

7. I feel a numbness or insensitivity in most of my body just after I come. This is particularly true in my genitals. _____

8. I need to take a PON (post-orgasmic nap) or even a POS (post-orgasmic sleep) after I come. _____

9. I notice that my wife really seems to get much more intensely involved in her orgasms than I do in mine. She seems to almost be ''gone''. _____

10. I feel that ejaculation is essentially the same thing as orgasm. If I don't ejaculate, then I know I haven't come. _____

11. My orgasms are essentially the same no matter what type of sex I am having (coitus, oral sex, masturbation). Whatever the source of stimulation, I essentially come the same way. _____

12. I have noticed as I get older that my orgasms are less intense than they used to be. The throbbing is less intense and there are fewer of them. _____

13. I have sex mostly at night. It sort of allows me to release the tension so I can sleep. _____

14. My sexual patterns with my wife are essentially ''turn-taking.'' I try to help her have an orgasm before I try to have mine. _____

15. Before I come, I feel as if I would have loved to have sex all night. After I come, I seem to lose interest. _____

16. I usually get to the point that no matter what happens, there is nothing I can do to stop my ejaculation. Even if all stimulation is stopped, I ejaculate anyway. _____

17. I try so hard to time my ejaculation that I cannot ejaculate at all during intercourse. _____

18. I am a quiet person during sex. I might moan or groan, but I do not intentionally say much. _____

19. If I have masturbated, I tend not to want to have intercourse several hours after I have masturbated. _____

20. When I am having sex, everything seems to be focused in my genitals. I notice very little about any stimulation to any other part of my body. _____

TOTAL POINTS_____

If you score thirty-five or more points on this test, it is very likely that you are experiencing the physiological reflex of orgasm emphasized by the first three perspectives of sexuality but are not experiencing psychasm, the ability to enjoy a full emotional and cognitive dimension to the sexual experience. The idea is not to replace the quest for orgasm with a quest for psychasm. The idea instead is to open up new options for sexual interaction free of the artificially imposed limits of a mechanical, gender-assigned model of sexual intimacy.

Reread each item and you will see that each depends on a reflex orientation to sex, the energy buildup and genital discharge model. This model is based on myths, wrong assumptions about male sexuality that have never really been seriously questioned by the first three orientations described in Chapter Five.

Ten Mr. Myths

Without giving each item too much thought, answer true or false to each of the items below. If possible, take this test with your partner and discuss each answer. The process of super marital sex depends more on this open exchange than on learning new techniques.

	True	False
1. Orgasm and ejaculation are the same thing.	____	____
2. Men cannot be multiply orgasmic.	____	____
3. Men must learn to control themselves sexually, so that they are able to fulfill their partner through an appropriately timed sexual response.	____	____
4. The best time for sex as a man is when you are completely rested.	____	____
5. The penis is the most sensitive part of the body for sexual interaction.	____	____
6. Intercourse is the ultimate form of sexual fulfillment.	____	____
7. The fewer sexual outlets you have, the more aroused you become. By having less sex you can become sexier and want sex more.	____	____
8. Firm erections are necessary for fulfilling sex for yourself and your partner.	____	____
9. Excessive masturbation can interfere with sexual interactions with your partner.	____	____
10. Whether we like it nor not, new and different partners are more arousing than the same partner.	____	____

You probably knew by the title of this test that all of the answers are false. I will examine each myth in detail to explore the new model of sexual response. If possible, turn back and forth between this test and the female version of this test in Chapter Seven and discuss points of interest. Even though books are written in separate chapters, super marital sex does not happen in sections. Turning back and forth between Chapters Six and Seven and reading them together as a couple will help you learn the ideas of change, balance, and rhythm discussed in Chapter Two.

Mr. Myth One

The Ejaculation-as-Orgasm myth

> You can't tell me that ejaculation isn't orgasm. This is just a bunch of crap, some type of psychobabble. You come or you don't. I don't want to hear any more about this stuff. It is just crap.
>
> HUSBAND AT SESSION ONE

I never would have thought it. It seems so obvious now. How could I ever have thought that ejaculating was the same as really enjoying sex? This is remarkable. I can see that psychasm is not a gimmick. It's real. You have orgasms and psychasms, it's just obvious. But I can't convince my friends. Now they think I'm crazy, like I bought some new sexual mantra.

SAME HUSBAND AT FIVE-YEAR FOLLOW-UP

The danger in discussing the difference between ejaculation and orgasm is that the earlier perspectives on sexuality are so firmly established in our society. The mere suggestion of psychasm sounds like the worst of pop psychology, like some strange throwback to a psychology of the past. The Masters and Johnson position is clear and dominates our thinking. They write, "Orgasm refers specifically to the sudden rhythmic muscular contractions in the pelvic region and elsewhere in the body that effectively release accumulated sexual tension." Kinsey reported orgasms without ejaculation, but was referring to the same contraction concept, and he reported it only in young boys, sexually immature persons. Masters and Johnson state, "Ejaculation without orgasm . . . can occur in certain cases of neurological illness." They clearly feel that ejaculation is orgasm in the male.

I suggest that ejaculation and pelvic muscular contractions are "orgasm," organ-based, and that more generalized emotional, cognitive, and body response is "psychasm." Men are capable of both, separately and simultaneously, and understanding this capacity in men is important not only for super marital sex but for other health-related issues.

Women can emit a fluid during sexual response that may come from the Skene's glands along the urethra. Women do not typically define their orgasmic experience by this fluid release, but for men, "the fluid is the fun." Fear, anxiety, and joy can all result in ejaculation, so it is a response that is typically but not exclusively related to sexual stimulation.

ORGASM	PSYCHASM
TYPE I	
F-Area stimulation penile contractions and contractions of bulbar area	Generalized body, emotional, thinking experience
TYPE II	
Scrotum and R- Raphe-area stimulation	Imagery, altered state of consciousness
TYPE III (MERGE-GASM)	
F and R areas stimulated General pelvic sensations	Body, mind, emotion experience, sense of merging with partner

The husbands in my couples initially reported that they were orgasmic in intercourse. There were times when they were unable to ejaculate—in their view, to be orgasmic—but usually they felt that they "came." Once they learned what psychasms were, that is, this more general, less genital orientation to orgasm, most (936) reported never having experienced one in intercourse. At the five-year follow-up, 833 men reported psychasms. The chart above illustrates the orgasm and psychasm possibilities for men.

To illustrate the complex possibilities of the above combinations, I asked the couples to point to places on the following triad of axes and discuss their feeling about each.

NONE_____MILD_____STRONG_____INTENSE
TYPE I—F-AREA ORGASM

NONE_____MILD_____STRONG_____INTENSE
TYPE II—SCROTUM AND R-AREA ORGASM

NONE_____MILD_____STRONG_____INTENSE
MERGE-GASM—TYPE III—R- AND S-AREA STIMULATED
ORGASM

NONE_____MILD_____STRONG_____INTENSE
TYPE I—GENERALIZED BODY AND EMOTION PSYCHASM

NONE_____MILD_____STRONG_____INTENSE
TYPE II—IMAGERY AND ALTERED-CONSCIOUSNESS PSYCHASM

NONE_____MILD_____STRONG_____INTENSE
MERGE-GASM—TYPE III—EMOTIONAL, PHYSICAL, IMAGERY,
COGNITIVE PSYCHASM

Here is a good place to compare Chapters Six and Seven and
discuss this material with your spouse. You will note strong similarities between male and female sexual response. The frame of
reference above is provided only for discussion and for widening
the experiences within your own sexual relationship, not for labeling and adding only more pressure to have "types" of orgasm or
psychasm. It is much more important to use this material to discover "your-gasm" together. Here are five findings from the interviews of two thousand people about their orgasms and psychasms.

1. Orgasm and psychasm can happen to men and women.

2. Orgasm is more "organ"-related. Moving beyond that limiting orientation
   frees men and women for pyschasm.

3. Type I, Type II, and blended orgasms and psychasms are all matters of
   degree, with varying combinations and experiences possible over time
   within a committed relationship. Without time and prolonged, enduring
   commitment, the full range of sexual experience is not available.

4. The energy buildup and discharge model applies only to orgasm. Psychasm
   does not have to involve tension but may involve relaxation.

5. Psychasm is the holistic response to mental, emotional, and physical intimacy over time with one partner and is not limited to neurological response
   initiated at the genital level. (This is an important point for health issues
   later.) Paraplegic partners most easily learned psychasm because they were
   no longer "addicted" to the neurological/genital link.

Mr. Myth Two

The Once-Is-Enough Myth

> I've heard it said that men can be multiply orgasmic, but I never met
> one. Some of them are not only not multiple, they don't even seem to
> be fractional.
>
> WIFE

Masters and Johnson state, "Men are not able to have multiple
orgasm." They report this because in their view orgasm is a phys-

iological response accompanied by feelings associated to these responses. They see the body as directing the mind. It is a fact, however, that the mind also directs the body, and while men cannot continue to ejaculate indefinitely, they can have multiple experiences of pelvic contractions. "It was something unique. I almost thought I was broken," reported one husband. "I couldn't ejaculate, but I kept on being able to contract, to have spasms down there, like when I was a kid."

Before men find female partners, they are taught to "get off quick" to avoid being caught while masturbating. After they find female partners, they struggle to last longer for fear of being seen as inadequate. Masters and Johnson report that the "quickest" time between ejaculations was about eight minutes in one of their male subjects. No one thought to ask the subject how he felt about each ejaculation.

Almost all pornographic films exploit not only women but men as well. Each scene ends with the mandatory ejaculatory episode, the indisputable evidence of male enjoyment. One producer of such films includes a hidden pump that shoots cream high into the air in large amounts. His men really enjoy sex! Men clustered around a projector or videotape player are being conditioned clearly to the fluid orientation.

Once free of this myth, men are not only able to be multiply orgasmic (not multiply ejaculatory), but they can also be multiply psychasmic. The men in my study cared less about numbers than they did about the experience of intimacy and fulfillment with their partner.

Mr. Myth Three

The "Hold On, I'm Coming" Myth

> I have tried holding back, gritting my teeth, thinking terrible thoughts, even biting my own cheek. Nothing works. I cannot control it. I just come too quick for her, probably for anybody.
>
> HUSBAND

One of the major paradoxes of clinical sex therapy is that the more men try to control themselves, the less control they have. There is absolutely no reason to control ejaculation, to time the sex act, to work toward simultaneous fulfillment and punctual penile performance.

Masters and Johnson originally defined "premature ejaculation" as a situation in which a man ejaculated too soon for his partner to be orgasmic. A corollary to this definition is "If you finish your meal before me, you are a premature eater." Men do not ejaculate for women. There is no such thing as a "mature ejaculation" any more than there can be tardy female orgasm. Like sneezes, ejaculations happen as a natural human reflex. We respond as a system. We cannot be late for each other because we are happening with each other.

Sex manuals and clinics have focused considerable attention on techniques to control ejaculation. The well-publicized "squeeze technique" through which the partner grabs the end of the penis and squeezes hard before the man ejaculates, has been used to "train" men to last longer. This approach has been around for decades, and we now have quick-treatment programs for quick ejaculators.

One of the couples in my clinic described their sexual encounters as similar to a fire drill. The wife reported, "As soon as I sense he is getting ready to ejaculate, we hurry up and change postures." The husband added, "Yeah, and when I sense it, too, I start to yell or scream to distract myself. We have to do something to hold back the floodgates."

To illustrate the absurdity of this couple's sex life, I asked then to put their favorite piece of music on the tape player. I told them to hold back any emotional reaction, not to tap their fingers or toes, not to enjoy the music. "That's ridiculous," reported the wife. "It's automatic." This automatic nature of the ejaculation is just the point. Ejaculation is a procreative reflex. It feels good, but it is not one and the same with male response and has little to do with female response.

Another mini-myth is that men are not multiply orgasmic because they have a refractory period. Men, not women, are viewed as being unable to continue sexual response beyond the contraction phase. They may be able to struggle to hold back ejaculation, but once they come, they go. You have already learned in Chapter Five that men and women both have neurological limits to physical response, but emotions and thoughts are not determined by the body. Sexual response is not a one-directional cycle, but a reverberating system.

Super marital sex depends on reassessment of the early sex perspectives. If men or women are in training to learn control, then they will never learn surrender, a surrender to a more natural mind/body interaction allowing for equality of sexual response beyond nonexistent gender-dependent limitations.

Mr. Myth Four

The Sex-Is-the-Last-Act Myth

> We don't have sex very often. You have to be rested when you have sex, and I can't remember the last time we were rested. By the time we have time, there won't be much more time. We'll be too old for sex. We have sex on vacations. That's the only time we have time or energy.
>
> HUSBAND

Most couples have sex at night, after the house is straightened up, the cat let in, the kids asleep, and everything else is out of the way. Neurohormonally, the best time for sexual interaction is sometime in the late-morning hours when the sex hormones are at their peak. Of course, there is much more to sex than the hormones, but we are more rested and energized in the morning hours.

The argument for having sex at night is difficult to accept. Turning in for a night's sleep is hardly the time when we are the most rested anyway. Sometimes sex can be energizing, something to share when you are tired, and this would be a good reason to have sex in the morning. Many people have fallen into a pattern of sleeping after sex, resulting in a conditioning process of kiss, hold, have intercourse, go to sleep. After a time, sex means sleep. Wouldn't it be nice if awakening meant sexuality rather than the obligation to go to work? Wouldn't it be nice if we could replace the alarm clock with a sexual clock signaling us to intimacy rather than calling us to the day's starting line?

One man in the clinic stated, "I never like to have sex in the morning. It gets me tired, and anyway, you never know who else you might meet during the day." Although he laughed as he shared this idea, it was apparent that he felt sex was de-energizing, a discharge of energy, and he did not want to waste his vital fluids. He also assumed that new or different partners demand more energy than familiar partners. If we view sexual interaction as dependent upon some predetermined amount of available sex energy, our intimacy is determined by a sense of strength and weakness rather than awareness and responsiveness.

The couples who visited the Masters and Johnson Clinic in St. Louis reported an invigoration of their sex life. They stayed in a hotel room, were not working or parenting, and made love at various times of the day. They communicated about sex almost continually. It became, at least for two weeks, a major part of their life-style. I have found that just changing "when" couples relate sexually has major impact on their IQ, their Intimacy Quotient. One wife reported, "I don't know what it would be like to make love when the sun is out." Sex may have come out of the dark ages, but still has a long way to go before it comes out of dark bedrooms.

Mr. Myth Five

The Penis-Is-the-Thing Myth

> Every time I try to touch my husband anywhere else than his penis when we are having sex, he directs me back to his penis. It's like a magnetic rod.
>
> WIFE

The penis is not the most sensitive part of the body for psychasm. It is the most important part of the body for ejaculation, and you have already learned the difference.

One of my paraplegic patients reported, "I know now that I never really came, not like this. I have a neckasm now. She licks the side of my neck and it's rocket city!"

This patient's report is on videoptape, and when I show it during my lectures to medical students, I notice some of the males moving their hands to their necks in disbelief. The women nod in agreement. Usually, a physician will say, "This is impossible." When I ask in turn if it is not true that orgasm is neurologically different from ejaculation, they agree, but the psychological factors of sex are not taught in most medical schools' curricula.

I receive hundreds of letters following my lectures. While most are positive, some husbands write with anger. One man wrote, "You have ruined everything. I had a good thing going. Now she asks how I feel, what is happening, all kinds of questions. She wants me to have a fingergasm or something. Let me tell you something, Dr. Pearsall, I was in the navy and ten thousand sailors can't be wrong." The point is that ten thousand sailors *can* be wrong, very wrong. It was not long ago that army and navy training films taught that sexually transmissible disease was carried by immoral women to victimized men. It seems that men are either victims of women, totally responsible for sex with them, miserable failures when compared to female response capacity, or generally oversexed. We fail to be real benefactors in mutual intimacy when we embrace the phallocentrism of the early perspectives of human sexuality.

Men still go to massage parlors for "local massage." One man reported, "I couldn't believe I could get taken like that. I went in to get a massage, you know, and that is what I got. A damned massage. She didn't touch my cock once. All I got was this hour-long touching all over me. She didn't even speak English. I asked her once if she touched genitals. She said yes, but she had been massaging mostly Jews lately. What a rip-off." Men rip themselves off when they believe that sexual feelings focus or even originate in vascular and muscular genital response.

Mr. Myth Six

The Getting-In-to-Get-Off Myth

> You keep asking us to touch and talk. When do we get to do it?
> HUSBAND AT FIFTH VISIT TO CLINIC

> It's funny. Intercourse has a whole new meaning now. It's like it is a part, not an end, of our sex.
> SAME HUSBAND AT TWELFTH VISIT TO CLINIC

Insertion of the penis into the vagina is necessary only for conception. Even then, full insertion may not always be necessary. Another major super marital sex lesson is that penis-in-vagina intercourse is totally unnecessary for sexual fulfillment.

Intercourse has had excellent P.R. We are taught early and repeatedly that anything short of intercourse is foreplay, preliminary to the main event. Actually, intercourse is reported as unsatisfying for more than half of sexually active people in the United States. Men and women report more intense sexual response to masturbation, at least from a physical point of view.

Our language of sex contains words such as "mounting," "humping," and other mammalian concepts from our agrarian history. The industrial revolution brought such terms as "screwing," "drilling," and "balling." The space age may bring terms such as "blasting," "orbiting," "re-entry," and "burn." The future may hold robotic sex, even remote-control intimacy. We have many more terms for intercourse than for intimacy in sex.

I have treated hundreds of couples with fertility problems. In their efforts to conceive, they have nearly destroyed their sex lives. They have been treated mechanically, from medicines that affect sexual interest to sperm samples and other medical maneuvers that take sexual intimacy totally out of its loving context. Fertility experts are becoming aware of this problem and referring couples to my clinic to balance the medical intervention for conception.

Super marital sex's posture of the future involves an entirely new view of what intercourse can be, one free from the mechanical dimensions emphasized in the earlier sex perspectives.

Mr. Myth Seven

The Sexual-Deprivation Myth

> I try to deprive myself. I don't masturbate and I stop even asking for sex. I thought that maybe a few weeks of celibacy would prime the pump. Maybe I need a new pump.
>
> HUSBAND

The energy concept of sexuality continues to dominate sex in marriage. It is simply not true that by holding back your sexual expression, you will build up a "sex-drive bank." As a matter of fact, the less sex you have, the less sexual you tend to feel and think.

One of my medical students was very critical of this material as I presented it. "I'm sure that the less sex I have, the more I want it." He came back three months later to report, "You're right. I got so busy in this medical school curriculum that I forgot all about sex. Then I had sex with my girlfriend last night. Now I can't get it off my mind."

Sexual activity leading to more sexual interest is why it is important to schedule sex, even though you have been taught that sex ought to be spontaneous. Super marital sex requires making time for sex, not counting on some inner drive to perpetuate sexual interest. Nothing about our health is automatic. Diet, exercise, dental care must be scheduled. Sex is no different. Spontaneity is more likely if regular sex is taking place, because the opportunity for spontaneity is created.

Not all sex can be mutual. If we over-romanticize our sexuality, see it exclusively as a mutually pleasing interaction in every instance, we burden our relationship. The emphasis on doing everything right, putting everything together, completing the shift, is another mechanistic approach to sex left over from the first three perspectives. Sexual frequency and style is a matter under our control. All motivation is preceded by behavior. You will feel sexier if you behave sexily. Saving it up, trying to create a sexual savings account, trying to make sure all account holders are pleased every time only results in loss of interest.

Mr. Myth Eight

The Firm-Rule-of-Sex Myth

> I used to be so stiff, like a stick. Now I'm sort of stiff and sort of limp, too. I'm not hard like I used to be.
>
> HUSBAND

If there is one Mr. Myth that has caused more trouble for men and women than any other, it may be the myth that an immediate, long-lasting erection is the key to sexual fulfillment. Men have lied about their erections, worried about them, exaggerated about them, made jokes about them, mocked other men about them, celebrated and magnified them in all forms of art, and given them all types of names.

The medical establishment has accepted this orientation. New implants are now available. There is now an injection that causes temporary erection. Firm penises are becoming a major industry. Urologists who once ignored or dismissed the sexual concerns of their male patients now find it financially wise to keep up to date on keeping men up.

The penis is more sensitive when it is flaccid. Erections were designed in our evolution to allow for quick and easy insertion of the penis for conception, not for pleasure. The blood that engorges the penis to firm it also renders it somewhat less generally sensitive except in certain specific areas. Erections are actually only neuro-logical reflexes that have little to do with complete sexual fulfill-ment. They have little to do with fertility, with psychasm, or even with all types of orgasm. Our attitudes about erection have become more rigid than the organ itself can ever be.

Erections do not signal arousal or interest and can be present when there is no sexual interest at all. Erections are reflexes, not only to our thoughts and feelings, but also to aggression and even bladder pressure. Just as Chapter Seven will teach that female lu-brication does not mean arousal, so the erect penis has received too much credit and blame for our sexual situation.

Men who fail to have "erections" are sometimes called "im-potent." A diabetic man came to me, stating, "I have absolutely no erection. Well, maybe just a little, but nothing to write home about. My doctor wants me to have special tubes put in or maybe a harness-type thing to hold it up." Following several weeks of counseling with his wife present (the wife had never been consulted by the physician), he stated, "Now I don't know why I was so fixated on that. I'm having more fun than ever." The wife added, "Me, too. And you know what? You are more erect now."

"Really?" questioned the husband. "I never really noticed."

Physicians have believed for years that diabetes, blood pressure medications, and other situations can "destroy sexual response." This is not true. Many things affect circulation to the penis, but firmness is only one and a relatively insignificant dimension of sexual interaction. It certainly does not deserve its own form of sexual orthodontia, and the posture of the future discussed in Chapter Eight does not require penile rigidity at all.

Mr. Myth Nine

The Masturbation Myth

> I knew I would pay for it. I masturbated when I was a kid and I continued it into marriage. Now I just don't enjoy sex. This is my punishment, I guess.
>
> HUSBAND

This man guesses wrong. Masturbation cannot cause any trouble for anyone unless it is engaged in against one's own moral sanctions. It is an excellent educational opportunity, can lead to intense orgasms and a degree of psychasms through imagery, and is one way to develop sexual comfort and sexual self-esteem.

One problem, though, is that men tend to masturbate incorrectly. They try to get it done quickly, and their posture, technique, process, timing, and stimulation are all wrong. It does not train them for interaction with a partner but rather to "get off" or to "get rid of tension." For men and women, masturbation offers an excellent opportunity for learning about the body, but may end up teaching a lesson of guilt, hurriedness, and secretiveness about sex.

The fact is that masturbation is separate from other forms of sexual behavior. It is not something that is done because you don't have a partner, because you can't find a partner, or because it must be done to be "good at sex." It is not something that means that sex with your partner is not as good as it should be. Masturbation is one form of sexual stimulation, and if it is an option chosen with comfort and a sense of self-enhancement, it is generally helpful to sexuality in all areas of life. If you don't masturbate, it means one thing: You don't masturbate. It is not a sign of a hang-up or deficiency. It is no big deal unless we make it so. It probably gets too much good press and too much bad press, and it needs much more truth in advertising. It is a human sexual option.

Masturbation, or at least pleasurable self-exploration, can teach much about the F and R areas (and the G and C areas in women). It can teach about the types of orgasm, about psychasms. But it teaches nothing but negative lessons if you feel badly about yourself for doing it.

Mr. Myth Ten

The Variety-Is-the-Spice-of-Sex Myth

> I don't mind my sex with my wife. I know it can't be as good as sex with a new partner. Variety is the spice of life, but I can settle for a spice-free diet.
>
> HUSBAND

Gay Talese writes in his book *Thy Neighbor's Wife*, "Instead of loving him less after sleeping with another man, she was sure that she loved him more." Variety in sex has been seen in early sexual perspectives as an almost irresistible attraction, and it has been assumed that sameness of partner cannot compete with newness of partner. In a society that values newness and change over sameness and predictability, an entire industry has emerged to provide men with anonymous partners. Look in the Yellow Pages in any major city under "Escort Service." Pick any number and call it. Women will be sent by home delivery, made to order. Our double standard has, of course, not made such services widely available to women.

Emphasis on variety neglects one fact. Practice still makes perfect, and the best practice is with one partner. One rule of sexual practice is that it does not generalize. Making love well with one partner is no guarantee of making love well with someone else. The tests and opportunities in this book are of most help to a man and woman committed to being together over time. It is simply not possible to have fulfilling sex with a variety of partners in short, anonymous meetings. It is possible to have ejaculation and tension release, but seldom psychasms and never super sex. Some of our most treasured moments in life relate to sameness, repetition, tradition. As Tevye sings in *Fiddler on the Roof*, there is nothing quite like "tradition!" Sexual traditions are important, too.

Ask people you know about their view of sexual variety. Most people, following a divorce, go through a period of sexual freedom with new partners. After several weeks of this activity, they begin to look for one partner. Sex manuals that encourage marriages to "compete" with anonymous sex by creating mystery, or even wearing costumes and wigs, miss the key value of one partner over time, the value of knowing someone totally. As a popular song pointed out, freedom can come to mean nothing left to lose.

So there you have it. Ten myths about male sexuality. You can probably think of many more yourself. By now, if you have discussed this material with your spouse, you have done much to open new possibilities for a sexual style of your own design.

Twelve Types of "Sexual" Husband

Based on my interviews with the thousand men, their wives, and thousands of other interviews by myself and my staff, I offer twelve types of sexual husband. These are presented for fun, for discussion, for comparison to the twelve types of sexual wives in Chapter Seven. Compare that list with this one as you look over the types. Remember, we all have elements of all these types, because they are not types at all but really behaviors, ways of being sexual sometimes. There is no need for more labels in the field of sexuality, so place the emphasis on the "fun" of these categories.

1. The Helper

Nobody gives her what I give her. I make her a princess.

HUSBAND

This is the husband who feels that he must assist his wife to sexual fulfillment. His daily activities, gifts he provides, things he does for his wife, and his behavior in bed are "help" rather than "share"-oriented. This husband attempts to live up to his perceptions of his wife's expectations, which perceptions, by the way, are usually not accurate.

2. The Hounder

If I keep it on her mind, focused, bring it to her attention, we will have sex. I have to keep the ball rolling.

HUSBAND

This is a husband who oversexualizes everything. He comments about sex on television, in books, in the newspaper, purchases every source of erotica he can find. He has an extensive collection of pornography and may bring home X-rated videotapes or films to "turn her on." There may be a secret pornography collection that the wife knows little about. Wives might want to look in the tool area of the basement under the wrenches. They may be surprised at what they find.

3. The Heel

She's not passionate. She tries, but she is of the fifties and I am of the eighties. That's why I have to have a little modern sex on the side.

HUSBAND

This is a male who criticizes his wife sexually, while at the same time seeking his sexual fulfillment outside his marriage. He may defend his extramarital sex by blaming the wife for failing him sexually, when actually he has neglected the intimate dimension of his marriage for some time. Men and women who look outside the marriage have usually not looked long or deep enough inside the marriage or themselves.

4. The Hermit

I just don't think much about it. I run every day in the morning and sometimes at night. I am in training for the marathon. Sex isn't everything. We're partners. She doesn't mind. She keeps me in carbohydrates and Coke. You know how running is. It takes your full attention.

HUSBAND

This husband has withdrawn from sex with his wife completely. While the wife may blame herself for this, actually the husband has neglected intimacy in the marriage and may be having an affair, not with another woman but with work, golf, or the television. Sex is very low on this man's priority list, and so is the marriage. The wife may feel that she is just living in the same house with this man, not sharing a life with him.

5. The Hero

I give her anything she wants. I really set her up. She wants for nothing. I kill all bugs, paint all ceilings, and am able to leap all of her problems in a single bound.

HUSBAND

F. Scott Fitzgerald once stated, "Show me a hero and I will write you a tragedy." This is the man who seeks to establish sexual IOUs by contributing a house, child care, money, status, a car, or anything else he feels will earn him his sexual due.

6. *The Humpty-Dumpty*

> I am really the one she counts on. Just ask her.
>
> HUSBAND

> He needs to think I count on him.
>
> WIFE

This is the fragile male, the man whose wife reports a private displeasure with sex in the marriage but protects her husband from that knowledge. For years, she has created a role for him to fill that enhances his self-image. Long-standing sexual problems are sometimes present in this situation, but the wife has been reluctant to disclose this trouble in order to protect what she sees as her husband's low self-esteem.

7. *The Hypocrite*

> I fake it. I'll admit it. I fake it. I really turn it on. She expects it.
>
> HUSBAND

This is the husband who is faking his sexual satisfaction. While it is assumed by some clinicians that more women fake sexual fulfillment, my interviews indicate that men fake it at least as often as women. They may groan and moan and mock a sexual delight, but they privately disclose a sense of incompleteness. It seems easier to this man to fake than to open up with his wife and learn approaches to a new intimacy.

8. *The Hesitator*

> I can go on forever. I can hold back until she has her full cycle.
>
> HUSBAND

This is the husband who attempts to control his ejaculation and in the process ends up controlling the entire sexual act. He tries to take turns, fulfilling his wife and then trying to fulfill himself. The wife may sense this control and would actually enjoy more freedom and spontaneity. Sex seems somehow a project, with the wife grading the final product.

9. The Hunk

> I hate to brag, but my wife is one lucky lady. If I were a woman, I would give anything to make love with me.
>
> HUSBAND

This is the sexual athlete husband. Typically one or more gold necklaces adorn his neck, and gold bracelets are on each wrist. Actually, there is much fragility to this man, but he hides behind a mask of super stud. Sex for him becomes an event or performance rather than a mutually intimate sharing. The wife may feel more like a sexual teammate than a partner, sharing a form of aerobic intercourse.

One wife of a "hunk" reported, "The other night he hit himself in his front tooth with that damn necklace he wears. It banged him and I know it must have knocked a piece of his tooth out. He didn't miss a thrust, though. The game must go on."

10. The Hurt

> I really deserve more. I have put up with so much. My childhood was a wreck. And now I can't even get my wife to really want me.
>
> HUSBAND

This is the "poor me" husband who feels sexually unappreciated, misunderstood, and deprived. He seems to look for mercy sex, a sex born of sympathy, a marital gift, rather than a vulnerable and mutual give-and-take.

"He has the Eeyore Complex like Eeyore in *Winnie the Pooh*," said the wife of a "hurt" husband. "He tries to mope me into sex. It just turns me off more."

11. The Humper

> I don't know what she complains about. I give her a great ride. When I am in the saddle, she knows she has been on a real trip.
>
> HUSBAND

This is the "wham, bam, thank you, ma'am" husband who may even have sex with his wife while she is sleeping (or perhaps while she pretends she is sleeping). Immediately upon contact, he begins to hump, to thrust his pelvis. This male may experience ejaculatory problems due to the muscle tension he creates in the pelvic area. He creates similar problems for his wife, who feels done to instead of with.

12. The Super Husband

> I love her, I love touching her, I love holding and being held. I guess it's really us I love.
>
> HUSBAND

This is the husband in the super sex marriage. He is free of concern for erection, for timing, and is keenly aware of his own style. He knows how his love map was made, and how it looks now. He reports psychasms, orgasms, but more important he also reports that his marriage is the most crucial part of his life. His daily living style reflects that fact.

Super Marital Sex Opportunity Number Six

This is a very private opportunity. Never, but never share the results of this exercise with anyone other than your partner. Write down the twelve types of sexual husband on index cards, twelve by each spouse. Now, on the other side, write the name of someone you know or some movie star or entertainer that you think might fit the category. Share your answers to you partner. Discuss why and what behaviors you both see in daily living that might reflect sexual style, and then discuss what changes each man could make to improve his situation.

The idea is to relate daily living to sexual living and to extend the marriage's view of intimacy outside the marital context. There is something very special about controlled marital gossip and the feeling of "us," the sharing of a common view of the outside world that may develop. Remember, this is not intended as a criticism exercise, because you never can really know how someone else relates in their marriage. Have fun with this opportunity and enjoy the luxury of talking together about others without the worry of being discovered or betrayed. Super marriage is super trust. Be careful. Make sure the kids aren't around, and unlike the first five opportunities, be sure to destroy the evidence.

I hope you have been reading back and forth between this chapter and Chapter Seven, the chapter on the female sexual response. If you have, make twelve cards each for the women's "types," too, and discuss change strategies for these types in the same way you did with the men. If you haven't been reading these two chapters as a pair, turn back to this chapter often as you read next about the woman's role in super marital sex.

CHAPTER SEVEN

❦

Why Wives Have Too Many Orgasms: Myths and Facts About Wives' Sexuality

> It's energizing for her. I don't understand it, but I'm left exhausted and ready for a few months' sleep while she is ready to jump my bones again.
>
> HUSBAND

The "Sexual Witch" Fallacy

He gestured with his hand as if he were erasing a chalkboard. "On and on and on. I work on her until she comes. She has two, maybe even three or four orgasms, then it's my turn." The husband described his typical patterned sexual process of pleasing as if it were an indelible code of sexual marital conduct.

"I know, and I feel worked on," said the wife as she grabbed his hand from its circular path, took it in her own, and held it in her lap. "It's like I have to come, usually a couple of times, for him to feel that he has done his job. Then he does it. I feel like a prerequisite instead of a partner."

"Name one time, just one time we have ever had sex when you were not completed," demanded the husband as he pulled his hand from hers and rested it in his own lap. "You are satisfied every damned time. I make sure of it. I know how it is with women. I know that they, I mean you, can go on and on and need a lot to get going but then you keep going." His hand returned to its circular motion in the air. "I just use this technique and you know it takes

163

work. I can't believe after all of these years you don't appreciate the fact that I take your feelings into account. Some men just don't care. At least I'm not the 'I don't care as long as I'm happy' type.''

"No, you're not that type," answered the wife, again grabbing his hand, this time stopping it in mid-air. "You're the 'make 'em come, then you get some' type. You seem to think I'm some sexual object that needs preparing for your pleasure, some bagful of orgasms that you withdraw from until you deposit yours, ejaculation, I mean." She held his hand firmly to her chest as she began to cry. "Why can't we just make love? I'm sick of orgasm, orgasm, orgasm."

The first three perspectives freed women, at least theoretically, to be sexual persons, to respond, to enjoy, to be orgasmic, to be multiply orgasmic, to have sexual choices. Women were viewed as not only the erotic "equals" of men, but as somehow sexually superior, mystical persons with sexual capacities far exceeding those of men. In fact, their sexual-response model was seen not only as different, but as a goal, the standard against which the male sexual capacity fell woefully short. They became "sexual witches" with almost magical sexual powers.

As many as nine million women were murdered in the 1500s and 1600s, burned, hanged, and tortured as possessed with erotic demons. *The Malleus Maleficarum* (The Witches' Hammer) was written in 1486 by Heinrich Kramer and James Sprenger. They wrote that "all witchcraft comes from carnal lust which is in women insatiable." Early sex researchers unknowingly gave indirect physiological and alleged psychological credence to the idea that women were much different, much more erotic, much more sexually responsive than men. The evil ascribed to women was related to their mysterious sexual prowess, the "evil woman" syndrome.

Orgasmic denial was replaced with orgasmic obligation, and capacity was mistaken for requirement. Women were no longer to be made love "to" but to be made love "for." As I suggested in Chapter Five, the female sexual-response cycle was seen as separate in many ways from the male's, totally devoid of a refractory period, and dependent on much more general, romantic stimulation than the male's. Women were now seen as intensely responsive, multiply orgasmic sexual athletes who, once appropriately and rigorously stimulated, lost all control, succumbing to their unlimited "carnal lust." Men had to learn, according to the third perspective, to harness this infinite lust through clever stimulation, self-control, timing, endurance, and the patience to wait for the emergence of this special sexual capacity. While they were no longer sexual objects to be used and abused, women were now to be "handled with care," erotic puzzles to be solved by liberated men.

Women were never seen as prematurely orgasmic. Indeed, there was no limit to their sexual capacity. Only men "came too soon." Women were seen as having "orgasmic dysfunction," as not having orgasms or not having enough or intense-enough orgasms. Men, of course, were always easily orgasmic. In fact, they were seen as too easily orgasmic in comparison to these sexual women whose orgasmic threshold was high and required intense, generalized, and prolonged stimulation in order for "the force" to be released.

For men, the female orgasm became a goal. For women, it became an assignment, a signal of the effectiveness of their male partner. Even though many women talked privately of the fact that orgasms were highly subjective and that sometimes they were totally irrelevant to sexual fulfillment, they knew they had better have them if sexual relationships were to flourish. Group therapy for women was offered, "orgasm groups" helping women to find the way to their inner sexual potential. If men had their orgasms too soon, women tended to take too long. While men put desensitizing creams on their penises to numb themselves, women sought "sexual inventions" for easy orgasmic release. They discovered a magical spot that could help with all of this. After all, we were now living in a pushbutton culture, so why not look for the female sex button? Men didn't need one, because they were turned on all the time anyway, but it seemed important to look for the female "on switch."

"G" . . . I Don't Seem to Have One: Putting Women on the Spot

> I don't know. I've looked and looked. Either my G spot got erased, or I never had one, or there was never such a thing.
>
> WIFE

There is no G spot. There is no debate in the research literature on this issue. The authors of the book *The G-Spot* themselves did not mean that such a "spot" existed, but that there was an area, a region in the anterior outer third of the vagina related to innervation that Dr. Grafenberg had described years earlier. Some women find this general area very sensitive, sometimes too sensitive. Others have very little sensitivity in that region.

One of two "sexual inventions," then, was a magical spot that led to quick, more intense orgasms. It is easy to understand this issue by finding the G area for yourselves. In a relaxing environment, alone, quiet, and just for the learning of it, lie naked with your partner face to face. Guide the husband's index finger into the vagina using saliva, K-Y Jelly or other nonallergenic lotion as necessary. With the husband's palm facing up toward you, have him push gently around in the area of the outer third of the vagina's top region. Don't expect sparks, orgasms, thrills, or anything at all. Just experience the tender exploration of the top part of the outer third of the vagina. Whatever you feel, from nothing to something, is still the G area. The wife may feel this area as pleasurable, very distinguishable, not distinguishable at all, or even somewhat uncomfortable. Try this at different times and you will find that the sensations change. You may even feel the urge to urinate when the husband pushes firmly up with his index finger about two knuckles into the vagina. Publicity for a G spot far exceeds the actual "product" performance.

To make this point more strongly with the couples in my program, I ask them to discover their "P spot," the palm spot. I ask husband and wife to open their left hands to one another and with slight pressure, slide their right index fingers across the spouse's palm. I ask them to report one particular spot that seems more sensitive than another. The couples always report a spot, and the same would be true for any other area of the body. The spots will be different for each person, and they will be different at different times. There is nothing about being human that relates to any one spot anywhere. We only put ourselves on the spot sexually if we continue to look for one.

The C area, the region around the clitoris including the clitoris itself, the prepuce or foreskin that partially covers the clitoris and surrounding tissue, is much more richly and surface-innervated than the G area. It corresponds to the F area I described in men in Chapter Six. Juxtaposing the F and C areas in a comfortable posture is the idea behind the posture of the future described in more detail in Chapter Eight. The clitoris and G area are no more "spots" than the penis is a "spot." They are erotic areas, and the body has as many of those as we each care to create for ourselves.

In intercourse, the F area is typically caressed and stimulated by warmth and moisture. The C area receives little direct stimulation. The posture of the future suggests contacting the F and C areas for a more balanced and prolonged stimulation that can, as I have suggested, take the "organ" out of orgasm and allow for psychasms.

Vibrating to Orgasm: Electrical Thrills

I love it, really love it. It's fast, easy, efficient. No mess, no fuss. I always come. Plug it in, turn it on, and it turns you on. The vibrator set me free.

WIFE

I hate the damn thing. Sometimes she wants me to use it on her. I can hear her using it sometimes. Buzz, buzz, buzz. What does she need me for anyway? She says she has better orgasms with her vibrator than with me. The damn thing has three speeds. It probably has an overdrive. I just hope she doesn't use it near water. If she does, when she comes, she'll go.

HUSBAND

Invention number two in the quest for quick, convenient female orgasms was the vibrator, an electrical or battery-operated device used to apply direct stimulation to the C area. One sex therapist called it the greatest discovery for women, perhaps as important for sex as the discovery of Pompeii was to world history.

The concept of "vibratory orgasm" grew from the myth of the first perspectives of sexuality that men come by friction and women come by vibration. Men seldom report using vibrators on their penis, and, as the man above, sometimes report a form of "gadget envy" regarding this device.

Research indicates that many women find the vibrator enjoyable. Some women report that they find the vibrator painful, annoying, and distracting to their sexual response. It is not likely that there will be a successful invention for making men come quicker. The male inventions have more to do with making genitals bigger and less sensitive.

As an occasional source of fun, variety, and different stimulation, the vibrator seems to be enjoyable for the women in my group of couples. When it, like anything else, becomes a focus, a replacement, even an expediter to save erotic time, problems result.

"He knows the vibrator always works," reported one wife.

"Now he just tells me to get it out and start it up. It gets me more than ready, saves us time. We always use it now. I can't remember a time when we just made love the two of us, without the vibrator. It has gotten so I hate the sound of it. I associate it with orgasm, but not with lovemaking. It's group sex, and one of us is a sex robot. The thing used to be mine; now it seems to be his, some type of sexual power buffer."

As you consider the husband's and wife's sexual response systems in Chapters Six and Seven, you will see the orgasmic focus for women and ejaculatory focus for men that was so strongly emphasized in the early sexual perspectives. This focus resulted in the destructive effort by men to "hold back" and by women to "hurry up." Men mislearned that pelvic contractions and emission of fluid were synonymous with sexual fulfillment, while women experienced an obligation to have intense, rapid, and multiple orgasms as a sign not only of their own sexual fulfillment but of the sexual skill of their male partner.

The Wives' Orgasmic Inventory

In Chapter Six, you took and discussed the Husband's Orgasmic Inventory used with the couples in my clinic. You might have looked ahead then to this next inventory, the Wives' Orgasmic Inventory. Take time again to read, score, and discuss each of the following items.

SCORING: 3—ALWAYS
            2—USUALLY
            1—SELDOM
            0—NEVER

1. I feel I must respond sexually to my spouse's advances.

2. I try to match my response to my husband's, faking if I have to.

3. When I start to feel very good sexually, start to really get involved in the sexual experience, I get distracted by my spouse's response.

4. I find that if I am too active in my sexual motions, it tends to cause my spouse to lose control of his sexual response, sometimes making him come too soon.

5. My orgasms are characterized by a throbbing in the vaginal area.

6. When I have not had sex in a long time, I tend to be more easily aroused.

7. I experience some physical discomfort when I have sexual intercourse.

8. I try to "match" my response to my spouse's, and if he is tired or wants to suspend sexual interaction, I go along.

9. I have trouble letting go and getting lost in my orgasms, usually trying to "come" like my husband "comes."

10. If I don't feel contractions in my vagina, I don't feel as if I have had a really complete sexual experience.

11. My orgasms are essentially the same no matter what type of sex I am having (coitus, oral sex, masturbation). Whatever the source of stimulation, I essentially climax the same way.

12. As I get older, I notice that my orgasms are less intense than they used to be. The throbbing is less intense and there are fewer throbs.

13. I notice that my lubrication is less and less reliable than it used to be.

14. I feel a "turn-taking" in our sex, so I must have orgasm first and then he takes his turn.

15. Before orgasm, I feel warm and close in our lovemaking, but after orgasm, there seems to be a distance between us.

16. I have trouble "getting over the edge." I seem to get right to the point where I could come and then it is difficult for me to go the rest of the way.

17. I hold back during sex. I might want to talk, groan, or say loving things, but I have trouble expressing myself during sex.

18. If I have masturbated, I feel some guilt, and this can even extend to my sex with my husband.

19. I feel that sex is focused on my breasts and in my genitals. I feel reacted to in parts, not "me."

20. I feel "worked on" during sex, rubbed and stimulated to get ready or to get "there."

Thirty-five or more points on this test, and it is likely that you are not experiencing psychasms but orgasms, working toward physiological reflex in response to genital or breast stimulation.

As in Chapter Six, remember that the object of this test is to promote discussion with your partner, not replace one set of expectations with another. Super marital sex depends on being open to the gift of complete erotic response with someone else, not on living up to the new goal of psychasms instead of orgasms. Orgasms are reflexes. Psychasms are emotional and conscious experiences related to a freedom from "organ reflex."

A high score on the Wives' Orgasm Inventory indicates that you have probably been well indoctrinated in the early perspectives of sexuality and that these perspectives continue to dominate your marital sex. To break free of this sexual "myth-information," take the Ten Ms. Myths Test, again with your spouse. Remember to look back to Chapter Six as you read this material.

Ten Ms. Myths

	True	False
1. Women do not ejaculate.	___	___
2. Most women have orgasm in intercourse.	___	___
3. Women take a longer time to respond than men.	___	___
4. Women have sexual fantasies less often than men.	___	___
5. Women are less turned on by visual stimulation than men.	___	___
6. The more lubrication of the vagina, the more aroused the woman is.	___	___
7. Women can go on and on. They do not have a refractory period.	___	___
8. Women relate sex and love together while men tend to be able to separate the two.	___	___
9. Women prefer one partner and are not interested in variety.	___	___
10. Women do not like oral love but might do it if their partner really wants it.	___	___

You already know that all of the above statements are false. As I did in Chapter Six, I will examine each of the above myths to describe in more detail the fourth-perspective sexual-response model I am proposing. All of the answers to this quiz are false because each myth is based on the premise that men and women respond completely differently, and this is not necessarily true.

Ms. Myth 1
The Dry-Orgasm Myth

> I get this warm, full feeling. And then, when I come, I almost wet the bed. I used to think it was urine, but it isn't. I feel it come out differently, sort of squeezing out in little spurts.
>
> WIFE

Some women lose urine during sexual response. When you suspect this is the case, a complete urological examination is in order. Be sure to tell the doctor the exact circumstances under which you experience this loss of urine. If you cannot talk candidly with your doctor, you have the wrong doctor. Ask for a referral from your local medical school. If you masturbate, notice if urine seems to escape under that circumstance. If there is a medical reason for this loss of urine, a specific physiological cause, it is possible to correct it. Sometimes surgery will be required.

Remember, feelings of urinary urgency are related to emotional states as often as they are related to anything physical. Excitement, fear, anticipation, and anxiety can all cause urinary loss. Some loss of urine with orgasmic contraction is not unusual in women, for their orgasmic physiological contractions do not prevent loss of urine as happens in men.

In some cases, women do experience an emission of fluid through the urinary meatus, the opening to the urethra which transports the urine outside of the body. Data indicates that a very small number of women report this fluid during orgasm. The fluid is not ejaculate, urine, or vaginal lubrication, but seems to come from the Skene's glands along the urethra, as mentioned in Chapter Five.

Of the 1,000 women in the 1,000 marriages, 106 reported that they felt and saw some fluid released with orgasmic contractions. So, while women do not really ejaculate in the sense of forcefully emitting a fluid, some women do report what they feel to be an ejaculatory type feeling at orgasm. This seems particularly true in what I call Type II orgasms, the concern of myth number two.

Ms. Myth 2

The Intercourse Myth

> We tried for the first seven years. I just could not come when he was in me. I loved our sex, I loved him holding me, but I could not come in intercourse. I came every other way, but the feeling to get to orgasm wasn't there.
>
> WIFE

I have already mentioned the difference between orgasm and psychasm. Orgasms are organ-based, physiological reflexes characterized by rhythmic muscular contractions in the pelvic region that are associated with the release of accumulated physiological tension. In women, the uterus, the outer third of the vagina, and the anal sphincter contract. There may be three or four contractions in some of these orgasms to as many as fifteen with other orgasms. This is the Type I orgasm brought on primarily by the stimulation of the C area.

Type II orgasm includes an opening or gaping of the outer third of the vagina. The uterus pulls down, and some researchers say that an "A-frame" shape of the vagina results (unlike the "tenting" of the Type I orgasm, in which there is contraction instead of opening of the outer third of the vagina). Stimulation of the G area seems involved in the Type II orgasm.

Both Type I and Type II or a blend of the two can take place in intercourse or in masturbation. Some researchers call these vulval, uterine, and blended respectively. The women in the couples group seldom experienced orgasm of either type in intercourse. Of the 1,000 wives, 86 reported Type I (56), Type II (20), or blended (3) orgasms in intercourse. Seven wives reported orgasms, but could not differentiate as to type. Their reports are purely subjective, without observational verification. The husbands substantiated the reports either by repeating what their wives had told them or describing sensations they detected in their wives. The remainder of the women (914), at five-year follow-up, reported no orgasm in intercourse.

Researcher Helen Singer Kaplan writes that lack of orgasm during intercourse "may represent a normal variant of female sexuality." If focus is exclusively on orgasm rather than psychasm, one would be hard pressed to understand why intercourse is so popular with women other than for closeness and intimacy. Of the 1,000 women, 823 reported psychasms in intercourse at five-year follow-up. "Once I learned the difference and stopped working for just something in my genitals, I started to really have orgasms, I mean psychasms." This wife's report was typical of those women who learned, as did their husbands, that orgasm and psychasm are different. Brain-wave patterns change during psychasm, and even Masters and Johnson, the third-perspective researchers, state that "the mind turns inward to enjoy the personal experience."

The early perspectives of sex research mistook physiology for psychology. Masters and Johnson write, "The subjective experience of orgasm in men starts quite consistently with the sensation of deep warmth or pressure that corresponds to ejaculatory inevitability." In women, Masters and Johnson report the subjective aspects of "orgasm" as a "pleasurable feeling that usually begins in the clitoris and rapidly spreads throughout the pelvis." The women in the thousand marriages reported such sensations as "an altered state of consciousness," "being free from everything," "sort of merging, actually being my husband," and being "lost, tripped out, gone but more here than ever."

Contractions in the pelvic area accompany orgasm in both genders. Both male and female experience the anal sphincter contractions. There is a physiological phase of being "on the brink," of being about to experience pelvic contractions. Masters and Johnson saw women as not experiencing a sexual "brink." They write, "Women do not have a consistently identifiable point of orgasmic inevitability." The women in my couples group did in fact report the sensation of a "brink," and inevitability of physical orgasm. Four hundred twenty-two of them reported this phenomenon "always," and a total of 644 wives reported this brink sometimes.

Here is a chart comparing the orgasm and psychasm possibilities from a Type I and Type II and blended orientation. Compare this chart with the Male Orgasm Chart on page 134 and discuss the possibilities together. Remember, the idea is not to label but to open up options and couple discussion.

ORGASM	PSYCHASM
TYPE I	
C-area Stimulation Outer third of vagina contracts, tenting response of vagina	Generalized body, emotional, thinking experience
TYPE II	
G-area stimulation Upper third of vagina contracts, A-frame contraction of vagina	Imagery, altered state of consciousness
TYPE III (MERGE-GASM)	
C and G-area stimulation, combined pelvic contractions	Body, mind, emotion experience, sense of merging with partner

To illustrate the complexity and possibilities of sexual response, orgasmic, and psychasmic response, I asked the couples to point to places on the following axes and then discuss their response.

NONE_____MILD_____STRONG_____INTENSE
TYPE I—C-AREA ORGASM

NONE_____MILD_____STRONG_____INTENSE
TYPE II—G-AREA ORGASM

NONE_____MILD_____STRONG_____INTENSE
MERGE-GASM—TYPE III—C- AND G-AREA STIMULATED ORGASM

NONE_____MILD_____STRONG_____INTENSE
TYPE I—GENERALIZED BODY AND EMOTION PSYCHASM

NONE_____MILD_____STRONG_____INTENSE
TYPE II—IMAGERY AND ALTERED-CONSCIOUSNESS PSYCHASM

NONE_____MILD_____STRONG_____INTENSE
MERGE-GASM—TYPE III—EMOTIONAL, PHYSICAL, IMAGERY,
COGNITIVE PSYCHASM

By pointing to various places on the above lines and the lines in Chapter Six for men, the couples were able to broaden their view of the emotional, cognitive, and physical dimensions of sexual response. The idea is not to debate about achievement of new or better orgasms or psychological experiences of sexual response, but to learn to see an infinite range of sharing sexuality. The following five points evolved from my interviews of women about their sexual response.

1. The issue of orgasm is not an either/or issue, but a complex combination of mind, body, and interactional factors.

2. Orgasm in intercourse can be of many types and degrees, so those spouses who felt they would never be orgasmic in coitus could learn to have a range of options to replace feelings of obligation, pressure, or abnormality.

3. Men and women did not experience "totally different" sexual response, but very similar response, including orgasmic and psychasmic opportunities.

4. Talking about sexual response from this perspective had an immediate effect on marital sex, opening communication verbally, emotionally, and physically.

5. Orgasm and psychasm are not individual experiences, but strongly affected not just by the "what" and "how," but by the "with whom" as well.

Ms. Myth 3

The Waiting-Game Myth

> I feel like I am just too much work, so I try to hurry. If I try to hurry, I just can't come. Then I end up faking it. Sometimes I try so hard that my muscles hurt.
>
> WIFE

I have discussed the fact that the first perspectives of sexuality saw women as sexually sluggish, capable of intense response only after intense, prolonged stimulation. It was an accepted fact that women take longer than men. This view was not upheld in the wives in my group.

In cases where the wife was seen as "slow" to respond, it was clear that there is no such thing as a slow sexual response. Just as we would not speak of a slow sneeze, we cannot view sexual response as anything but natural and reactive to the specific situation, partner, and type of stimulation.

"I rub right on her clitoris for what seems like hours," reported one husband. "I know it's probably only minutes, but it does seem

a long time. She will usually finally come, but by then I can have
a sore forearm and I am not excited. She's just real slow to respond."

This report illustrates the blaming of female response for couple
ignorance about sexuality. Later in my work with this couple, it
turned out that C-area stimulation for this wife was not effective.
G-area stimulation combined with simultaneous talking about fantasy led to intense and what the couple reported as "really quick
coming." They eventually became less interested in the quick part
and learned to enjoy the journey more than the destination.

Sexual response cannot be wrong, too fast, too slow, "too"
anything, because it is a natural human response, unique to all of
us and each of us. Once we learn this, we are free to become sexual
together, for there can be no right or wrong in what is natural and
beautiful.

Ms. Myth 4

The Closed-Mind Myth

> I don't fantasize. I'm sure I don't. Everyone talks about that, but I can't
> do it and I never have. I just think about holding, being close, warm,
> intensely in love with my husband, just alone together, becoming more
> together, more in love, more turned on with each other. I think about
> that a lot, but I don't fantasize.
>
> WIFE

The early sexual perspectives saw fantasy related specifically to
physical and genital imagery. Questions in the research protocols
were about "physical turn-ons," typically leading questions from
the point of view of the male researcher. It is a fact that everyone
fantasizes. Women fantasize, men fantasize, children fantasize.
Sexual fantasy is the mental rehearsal of the love map, including
some new paths that I described earlier, and relates much more to
the individual experience of that love map than it does to gender.
Here are two fantasies from the couples. See if you can tell which
is a husband and which is a wife.

"I can see it in my mind even while we are doing it. My partner
goes down on me while somebody is kissing me and somebody
else is rubbing me all over. Then all three do everything to me.
Then I do it to each one of them alone."

"I see an image of the two of us embraced, close, kissing deeply.
A candle is nearby, and our shadow is on the wall. The kiss becomes more and more intimate, and I come just by kissing."

The first fantasy is that of a wife, the second was reported by a husband. You have already learned about the sexual similarities between men and women, so you probably expected the unexpected in this example, but most spouses reported the first as male, the second as female and were surprised to learn that personal and relationship development had more to do with sexual imagery than gender.

I discovered that it was more meaningful to ask about "sexual images" than fantasy. Some spouses were raised to censor the fantasy process but would readily discuss a set of mental images. It was as if the image was something to be "viewed" from a safe distance, while fantasy was something one participated in and therefore wrong. I explored not only individual imagery but "marital imagery," asking couples to create and continually modify their collective sexual images. Here is one example.

"My wife is naked with me on a tropical island," reported the husband. The wife is then asked to provide the next image. "We walk hand and hand in the warm sun and gentle breeze," she reported. "We stop to shower in a warm, refreshing waterfall, and the water hitting us seems to arouse us," reported the husband. "I notice his erection and touch it, begin to kiss it," shares the wife. "I caress her breasts and run my hands through her hair," shares the husband. The imagery assignment continued until the husband stated, "That's about all we want to say in this session." The wife added, "Good-bye, and we will leave you to finish this up with your own images." Perhaps you and your spouse can take their imagery from here and develop your own scenes. Remember, images have no gender. You together are the producers, directors, and cast of this I-rated (intimacy-rated) movie.

Ms. Myth 5

The Female-Fantasy Myth

> I hate those X-rated videotapes. They are disgusting. A bunch of naked bodies humping each other. I like the parts where you can see some feeling, but that almost never happens.
>
> WIFE WITH HUSBAND PRESENT

> I get turned on a lot with those tapes. I feel guilty, but I got one out to look at while he was at work and I masturbated. I know it's filth, but some parts turn me on.
>
> WIFE IN PRIVATE INTERVIEW

The early perspectives assumed that men looked and women felt. I did not find this assumption to be the case with the couples I interviewed. Women were aroused by visual stimulation, and sometimes were quite specific in their report. "I love the turn in the shoulders by a man's neck, sort of the neck and shoulder area. I love to sort of smooth out his suit coat or jacket by running both my hands out from that turn on both sides of his neck to his outer shoulders. I love to look at men in the theater from behind and look at their shoulders." This wife's report illustrates a strong visual reaction, and other examples were similar.

The individual love maps of men and women, not their gender, determine what stimuli will elicit a sexual response at any given time. If we tell women that they do not respond visually, then they are likely to report that they do not. If we ask open questions without gender bias, we get the same range of responses in husbands and wives.

Talk together about your reactions to erotica and you will discover that both of you are turned on and off to various visual cues. Asking whether or not a woman is turned on to X-rated material is like asking if someone is turned on to books. It depends! And remember, the sexual-response system is not a closed energy system with an on-and-off switch. It is a flowing, ever-changing system. We do not really get turned on or off, we respond to varying degrees.

When we free our relationship from the mechanical orientation of the early sex perspectives, we learn that we are always "on," and in control of our response through our selection, sharing, and awareness of our love maps and the variables that determined it.

Ms. Myth 6

The Moisture Myth

> It worries me that I get dry. Sometimes I think I am so turned on and my husband tells me I am dry. Sometimes just when I really want to do it, it burns when he tries to go in me. I think I might be having menopause or something. I'm only thirty-two years old and I'm drying out.
>
> WIFE

If men have been pressured by the focus on erection of the penis as a tangible sign of emotional state, then women have been pressured by a form of "sexual dipsticking," checking for vaginal "fluid levels" as a sign of arousal. Both indicators are invalid because erection of penis, clitoris, and lubrication are merely reflexes that do not accurately reflect our emotional or arousal state. Men can be intensely aroused without erection and intensely erect without arousal, and women can be intensely aroused and not lubricated and abundantly lubricated and not aroused.

The sexist orientation of a well-lubricated opening for a rigid male organ neglected the fact of female clitoral erection. This orientation saw women as being made ready by men to receive men, and is unlike the new perspective, which sees couples getting ready together to merge and share. The early perspectives tried to make sexual response totally different from all other human physiological response. Our bodies just do not work that way. We are a system, and the sexual part of that system does not enjoy or suffer from exclusivity. If you are sweating heavily, you would not necessarily report that you are vigorously exercising. Sweating is determined by many factors, including temperature, humidity, general metabolism, diet, feelings, thoughts, and activity level. This concept is true for lubrication (actually transudation or a sweating of the vaginal walls).

We cannot look to our genitals to tell us whether or not we are turned on or aroused, because they are only a part of a complex interactional system that can arouse us as much as signal arousal. The phallocentric, vaginalcentric orientation limits our potential for sexual development by assuming a one-directional, stimulus/response mechanism that does not exist in human experience. Learning this key point is another important step toward super marital sex.

Ms. Myth 7

The Perpetual-Woman Myth

> He thinks I am some kind of sexual perpetual-motion machine. He even tells people that once he turns me on he can't turn me off. Absurd. I get to a point where stimulation actually hurts. Maybe all those other women can go on forever. I can't.
>
> WIFE

I have already discussed the "sexual witch" mythology, and myth seven perpetuates this view of women. Chapter Five pointed out that women have a refractory period, a time when sexual stimulation is ineffective or even painful. Men and women are not different on this issue.

Masters and Johnson state that "there is a major difference between male and female sexual response immediately following orgasm." They go on to state that only men have a refractory period, but that "all females have the physical capability of being multiorgasmic." They add, "Men, on the other hand, cannot have multiple orgasm." This idea is based on the erroneous assumption that, as Masters and Johnson state, "An orgasm is an orgasm is an orgasm." The couples, and your own subjective experience, teach otherwise. Orgasms and psychasms exist in varying degrees at varying times. We do not "climax." Eric Berne writes, "Climax started off as a decent enough word, but it has been so overworked on the newsstands that it now sounds like the moment when two toasted marshmallows finally get stuck to each other." We have been taught that women can "take a licking and keep on ticking." They can't, men can't, because sexual response is like any other human response. It is cyclical, not phase-specific, unidirectional or gender-determined.

Masters and Johnson state, "From the viewpoint of physical capability, females have an almost unlimited orgasmic potential." It would seem, then, that until absolute physical exhaustion results, women can experience a machine-gun-like series of orgasms but men have one and then go into "refraction." Apparently it is men who must pause in sexuality. The women in my group were well aware of this idea, but felt that it was just not true for them. "I guess I could go on and on," reported one wife. "But I don't, never have, I can't imagine how or why, and I guess my husband could, too. But why? You could take a bath forever, too, but for what purpose?"

If one purpose of marriage is to share a range of activities, of transitional life events, then sex is only one of the many dimensions of life that spouses can experience together, physically, mentally, and spiritually.

Ms. Myth 8

The Romantic Myth

> I love it, I love sex. Sometimes I want sex, and sometimes I want love, and sometimes I want both, and sometimes I'd sooner ride my bike.
>
> WIFE

Women trade sex for love and men trade love for sex. This myth has enjoyed a long and invasive reign in male/female interactions.

Although cultural factors may teach such lessons to children, causing some young girls to think they must be in love if they have had sex with some boy, there is no truth to this view. Love is not the sole prerogative of either gender. Love is a system word, a process for a unit of two.

Husbands and wives did not differ in their reports of needs for love and loving, and it is not possible to divide sex and love. Touching, feeling, holding, being, trusting, talking, stimulating, and an infinite range of human experiences is involved in all sexual interaction, but when "sexperts" perpetuate the myth of romanticized women and eroticized men, they corrupt the natural interaction between the genders.

A dangerous "sub-myth" has evolved in this association of love with women and sex with men. You may have heard the line that "rape has nothing to do with sex. It is a violent, aggressive act, a crime, and is in no way related to sex." This statement is absurd and dangerous. While rape is a violent, aggressive crime against women and sometimes men and against all human dignity, it nonetheless involves sex and is related to corrupted love maps and the sexual maldevelopment of the rapist. To say otherwise is to fail to address the crisis of rape directly. The sexual motives and impact of rape are profound. The motives for rape relate in part to a societal view of women as covertly wanting or allowing sex only in exchange for or surrender to the work, deception, force, coercion, or effort of the male. It is as if women, from the male viewpoint, are seen as in charge, and rape is a terrible male way of circumventing the system, "taking" sex and "taking" women without the exchange of love. The motives for rape are many and always unique to the rapist and his distorted love map, but the cultural view of women as having something that men must earn or take contributes to the tragedy of rape. Until we confront and destroy this myth of women seeking only love while they parcel out sexual favors or succumb to male sexual aggression, until we teach our little boys that love and sex are one, the tragedy of rape will continue. None of us is served by separating rape from sex. We only delude ourselves about the sexual immaturity of a society that continues to abuse its men, women, and children. Sexual child abuse and rape are not crimes separate from sex, they are sex crimes, and we all suffer.

Ms. Myth 9

The Bored-Woman Myth

> I never told anyone this, but I always wondered what it would be like
> with two men. I even wonder what it would be like to do it with the
> washer repairman. He bent over to fix the thing and I could see his
> butt. When he stood up, I could see his penis in his pants. I've devel-
> oped what I call PCV, peripheral cock vision. I can look straight ahead
> but I can still check out the man next to me to see which side of his
> pants is holding his penis, to see if he is dressed left or right.
>
> WIFE

Myth nine is an extension of myth eight and assumes not only that
women are lovers who will trade love for sex but that women are
not interested in variety, excitement, different partners, affairs,
cheating, newness, and other "male" things. It may be that men
find it easier or more acceptable to report their extramarital sex
than women do. Our sexist society has allowed the male more
freedom and anonymity than the female, in effect more time and
opportunity for sex outside of marriage.

"When in the hell do you think I could do it? I don't travel, my
day is under constant child surveillance. I don't have time. I am
never anonymous, as my husband is. How many massage parlors
do you think there are for women anyway? Even if I wanted to, and
sometimes I think about it, I don't know if I could or how I could."
This wife's report is an example of the limits set on women, the
assumption that they don't because they don't want to instead of
that they may not be allowed to, at least overtly.

Data indicate that as women travel more and have more freedom,
they, too, may seek out variety. Not all women will do this, for not
all men do it. The scarlet letter "A" originally designated a woman,
but gender does not predict proclivity for extramarital sex (Type I
or II). Again, the love map determines such things, not genital
insignia.

Ms. Myth 10

The Orality Myth

> I don't know about oral love. I did it once, and my husband sort of
> humped up at me and I almost gagged. I don't like the idea of it, the
> taste of it, and I'm afraid he will come in my mouth. I just don't do it
> anymore, but I think it is probably his favorite thing. I think he wants
> my mouth more than he wants me.
>
> WIFE

Of all the arguments and differences in the couples' program, the issue of fellatio and cunnilingus was one of the most frequent sources of disagreement regarding actual sexual interaction. Husbands wanted it, were reluctant to give it, wives wanted it less and were very reluctant to give it. Of the 1,000 women, 266 reported that they enjoyed fellatio. The rest reported never doing it or doing it reluctantly. Nine hundred twenty-seven husbands reported that they enjoyed or very much enjoyed fellatio, and 88 husbands reported seeking out partners outside the marriage specifically for fellatio.

Three hundred forty-four husbands reported enjoyment of cunnilingus, while 233 wives reported enjoying or very much enjoying cunnilingus. Generally, oral love was a male-oriented preference in these couples. However, following education regarding posturing, a new perspective on the ejaculatory reflex, hygiene, and changing conceptions of oral love as "dirty," couples learned to discuss oral love as an option. The use of approximations of oral love, kissing of thighs and abdomen, was also helpful. The five-year follow-up showed that oral love was mutually incorporated into the sexual pattern of 743 of the couples.

Men discussed attitudes that women were "dirty down there," reporting odors or tastes that were negative. The husbands apparently were unaware that they, too, have odors and tastes. Once open discussion took place, oral love was demystified, and became another opportunity rather than a forbidden act performed by perverted people. The issue was not a woman's issue, it was a couples' communicational and educational issue. There was much more blame than fact to the myth that women dislike oral love, but nobody likes one type of loving all the time. What oral love means to each partner is more important than how it is done.

More Sexual Yin and Yang: The "Person" Sexual-Response System

The purpose of this next test is to illustrate the similarities between men and women, the fact that we all vary from time to time in our orientation to being male and female, that we are not on mutually exclusive gender-response scales. Sexual response is a person phenomenon, not a measure of gender division. This "oneness" lesson is another key aspect of super marital sex, for it allows us to avoid the "gender traps" that provide quick shortcuts for quick sex.

Here is another version of a yin/yang test, one emphasizing sexual response. This time, it is based on the twenty male and female myths from Chapters Six and Seven. See how you do now in understanding your own super marital sexual response.

The Personal Sexual-Response System

Place yourself on each of the following scales and discuss the results with your spouse. For fun, place your spouse on each scale and discuss this result. Remember, you are not "scoring," you are learning. As soon as you are done with this test, your score will have changed, just as your sexual-response system is always changing.

GENERALIZED MIND/BODY SEXUAL RESPONSE TO STIMULATION	GENITAL RESPONSE TO SEXUAL STIMULATION
0 1 2 3 4 5 6 7 8 9 10	

R- OR G-AREA SENSITIVITY	C- OR F-AREA SENSITIVITY
0 1 2 3 4 5 6 7 8 9 10	

PSYCHASM FOCUS	ORGASM FOCUS
0 1 2 3 4 5 6 7 8 9 10	

MINIMAL REFRACTORY PERIOD	DISTINCT REFRACTORY PERIOD
0 1 2 3 4 5 6 7 8 9 10	

HIGH AROUSAL, EMOTIONAL SEXUAL INTERACTION	PHYSICAL FOCUS IN INVOLVEMENT
0 1 2 3 4 5 6 7 8 9 10	

EXCITEMENT TO OWN SEXUAL BODY REACTION	EXCITEMENT TO BODY STIMULATION BY PARTNER
0 1 2 3 4 5 6 7 8 9 10	

AFTERGLOW INTENSE						SHORT AFTERGLOW				
0	1	2	3	4	5	6	7	8	9	10

ALTERED STATE OF CONSCIOUSNESS DURING SEXUAL-RESPONSE CYCLE						HIGH AWARENESS OF SELF DURING SEXUAL RESPONSE				
0	1	2	3	4	5	6	7	8	9	10

REFLECTION ON SEXUAL INTERACTION DURING AND FOLLOWING SEX						IMMEDIATE RETURN TO "OTHER" THOUGHTS FOLLOWING ENCOUNTER				
0	1	2	3	4	5	6	7	8	9	10

FEELING OF SELF- AND PARTNER-ENHANCEMENT FOLLOWING SEX						FEELING OF TENSION RELEASE FOLLOWING SEX				
0	1	2	3	4	5	6	7	8	9	10

Now, add up the total number of items that you circled in the scale above that are to the right of 5. Subtract from that number the total number of items you circled to the left of 5. As before, ignore any 5 responses. There is no "good" score, only an indication of how you are responding sexually at this time, with yang being in the positive scores and a yin orientation to sexual response in the negative scores. Compare your score to the score on your Yin and Yang Test in Chapter Six and you will have much to discuss with your partner about the range of sexual opportunities in your marriage. And remember also that yin or yang is not good or bad, right or wrong; they are just variations of living. Getting "stuck" on the above scale, trapped in one type of reaction, is more detrimental to marital sexuality than any positive or negative score. Marriage provides the opportunity to experience all aspects of living sexually, the Tao, a flow of sexual energy beyond a mechanical, gender-specific orientation, a movement of life and sex far beyond the pelvic movements and genital stirrings that have dominated the sexuality of earlier sex perspectives.

Twelve Types of "Sexual" Wife

At the end of Chapter Six, I offered twelve types of husbands derived from the interviews. These were provided for discussion and for the fun of reviewing stereotypes that can emerge from a limited view of sex. Compare these twelve wife categories with the twelve husband categories. As I suggested in super marital sex opportunity number six, try to "match them up," try to see those times when you and your spouse might have been acting out roles assigned by "sexpectations" rather than enjoying the opportunity for "share-gasms."

1. The Helpee

> I know that if I'm happy, he's happy. God knows, I try to be happy. I try to respond in the way he wants, but I have to work on my groans a little more.
>
> WIFE

This is the wife who feels that her role is to be the responder, to react in the sex-manual-predicted ways to the husband's sexual ministrations. It seems from my work with couples that ministration is far more dangerous to sexual fulfillment than masturbation. She feels that her sexual response is a measure of her husband's effectiveness rather than her own self-representation.

2. The Hounded

> I love to hug and hug him hard, but when I do, he always gets harder than my hug. If I don't want sex, I just don't hug.
>
> WIFE

This is the wife who feels that any sign of tenderness may be the overture to sex rather than an expression of love. Some wives felt that they had to monitor their expressions of feelings and touching for fear they would set off a chain reaction.

3. The Faker

> I've never had an orgasm, but I'll bet I fake it better than it actually is. It could never be as good as I make it look.
>
> WIFE

This is the wife who has learned to pretend. Feeling that her husband will not be fulfilled until she is fulfilled, she has learned to act rather than experience, to try rather than be. While there is nothing wrong with a little drama and acting in sexual encounters, faking it to "get it done" ultimately destroys any hope of intimate sexual communication.

4. The Hurrier

> Someday, someday, I hope we can really take some time with this. I can get off quick, but it seems that I am trying to get off more than trying to enjoy us making love.
>
> WIFE

This wife who is capable of extensive and fulfilling sexual response but rushes herself for the sake of time. She may feel that her husband is tiring, is struggling to control his ejaculation, which he has defined as his orgasm, or is becoming bored or anxious to get on with it. As a result she pushes herself to early and abbreviated sexual response.

5. The Piece

> I feel like a piece of ass, just a piece. It's funny how men are hunks, large hunks, and we are pieces, small pieces. We are diminished even in size.
>
> WIFE

This wife feels that her husband is making love to someone, but not necessarily her. She feels that she represents "a woman" more than her "self." She does not feel valued as a person but needed as a sexual outlet.

6. The Misunderstood

> If I say faster, he goes so fast it burns. If I say slower, it's like no movement at all. If I say stop, he keeps going too long or stops too fast. If I say go, he goes wrong. I don't know. I'm just too fussy I guess.
>
> WIFE

This is the wife who seldom feels understood in her expressions of sexual need. If she wants to be touched faster, she ends up being touched slower. If she wants soft, she gets hard. She feels that "if he really loved me he would know what to do" instead of "if I really love him I will teach and teach until he learns." It sometimes surprised me how patient couples would be with their children and how impatient they would be with each other. All learning takes time, and sexual learning takes about seventy-five years. Even then, you are just beginning.

7. The Target

> I feel like one of those blow-up dolls. He moves me around like a pillow, does it to me. Next time he wants to do it doggy style, I'll just bark. Maybe I'll sit up and beg. Maybe that will please him.
>
> WIFE

This is the wife who feels that her husband's pelvic thrusts are "aimed" at her rather than "shared" with her. Wives in this category reported being trapped under their husbands, propped up on top of them, or "attacked" from behind. They did not feel that intercourse was a dance, but more of a sparring match with her being the sparring partner. There was little sense of identity, even in the limited sense of "The Piece" who felt she was just "any woman." "The Target" feels a loss of personhood.

8. The Madonna

> I was raised to be special, I mean that sex was special. If he wanted a tramp, he should have married one.
>
> WIFE

This wife assumes her husband's projected image of her and becomes the pure, motherly, sisterly person in her husband's life rather than his equal partner. This wife feels elevated to a pedestal, lonely and on display. She senses that her husband sees other women as more sexual and sees her as a "nice woman." She adjusts by either filling the madonna role even more or tries, usually in vain, to compete with the vague image of a "loose" woman. Both attempts fail because she is neither. She struggles unsuccessfully to find her lost sexual identity because she is looking for it through her husband's eyes rather than her own. Her love map is being drawn for her. The madonna/whore and lover/playboy dichotomies play themselves out in male/female sexual interaction. They are extreme routes on the love maps formed in a punitive, hypocritical society. They are labels that hamper the development of adult sexual maturity.

9. The Caretaker

> I'm the dorm mother—three kids, one husband, two dogs, one gerbil.
> I like the gerbil best. He puts out less crap than all the rest put together,
> literally.
>
> WIFE

This wife has abandoned her sexual role and identity in favor of
providing what she perceives to be "the rest" of her husband's
needs. She picks up after him, cleans for him, takes his messages,
and sees to it that he enjoys his life. She may attempt to provide
him with sex as just another of his daily living needs, but primarily
she has infantilized her husband to such an extent that she feels she
is parenting an adult child.

10. The Figurine

> I'm just not as strong as he is. I need him. He takes care of me like no
> one ever could.
>
> WIFE

This is the fragile wife. The husband feels he is protecting her, and
she assumes this role by acting weak, even physically sick or emotionally insecure. Sexually, she conveys an image of breakability,
holding back her own assertive and expressive tendencies for fear
of "blowing her cover," for fear of letting her husband see that she
is not as fragile as he thinks or perhaps needs her to be.

11. The Searcher

> I have watched every time a talk show has anybody on about sex. I have
> tried everything. My women's support group says my husband is just a
> sexist pig. Maybe they're right, but I'm not going to tell him. I'm used
> to him that way. I call him Mr. Piggy.
>
> WIFE

This wife has sensed that something is not well sexually and has
turned to talk shows and sex manuals for direction. She talks more
with friends about her sexual problems than she does with her husband. Most of her sexual knowledge is derived from friends, books,
romantic novels. She assumes the role of Scarlett from *Gone with
the Wind*, provoking, teasing, trying new techniques to encourage
her husband to be Rhett and sweep her off her feet, up the stairs,

and into bed. Unfortunately, some of these husbands continue not to "give a damn."

12. The Super Wife

> I never knew how strong I was as a person until I learned how strong we were as a couple.
>
> WIFE

This is the model of the wife in a super sex marriage. She is aware of her sexual physiology, the forms and formation of her love map, understands the fourth perspective of sex, and integrates sex, love, and loving into her own unique and ever-changing role as a self-representing love partner.

You have probably found yourself in all of the above types. We all do. If you are open enough to see this, then you are open enough to start the process of super marital sex, to start your own private sex clinic servicing one special couple, your own marriage.

Super Marital Sex Opportunity Number Seven

Now it's your turn to be creative. Up to this point, you have been taking tests and responding to my questions. Integrating this pair of Chapters Six and Seven, design your own sexual-response system. Write it down. Make up names for each phase if you want to, but set up your own model that the two of you feel describes your sexual interaction. Stress the positive, the good parts of your relationship, and focus on your relationship, not one partner's strengths or problems.

After you both write this brief description together, talk it over and decide what parts you would like to change or improve. Would you like to change the places, the ways in which the whole process seems to get started in the first place? Is there a phase that one or the other of you feels you have not been fully involved in and would to share even more? You are writing the only model of sexual response that has any meaning at all, your own sexual interaction, the interaction you will be studying in your own sex-therapy clinic in the next chapter.

CHAPTER EIGHT

✿✿✿

Owning and Operating Your Own Sex Clinic

Here are the twelve steps for discovering super marital sex, for owning and operating your own perpetual sex clinic. It will be under the direction of the persons most qualified to enhance the sexuality of your marriage: the two of you.

Your own sex clinic can be designed specifically for your unique relationship and can be based on the new perspective on sexual intimacy. All sexual therapy depends on the patient's assumption of self- and relationship responsibility. By attempting to correct sex problems and enhance your sexual relationship in the context of your everyday living, you avoid the artificiality of once-a-week therapy visits and sporadic assignments removed from the day-to-day reality of modern marriage.

Step One: Building the Clinic and Remodeling the "Bored" Room

> Our house isn't made for us; it's an institution for kids, pets, relatives, neighbors, and repairmen. Even if we could have sex, there isn't any-place to do it.
>
> WIFE

191

The reported success of the Masters and Johnson treatment program had as much to do with the fact that the couples had a private place to have sex anytime they wanted to as anything else experienced during the program. Couples stayed at local motels during their therapy, always returning at night to be alone together to carry out sexual assignments. No matter what else you learn about super marital sex, real progress depends on having a place to be intimate.

The American marriage must reclaim its rightful territory. Your home belongs to you, is for you, and should reflect you.

To have super marital sex, you have to have one place in your home where nobody else can go but you and your spouse. This rule can never be violated. You will learn in the last chapter that the best form of sex education is to let your children know, let anybody know, that you make love. How, when, and what kind are private, but the act itself cannot be a secret, and the public setting aside of a place for the two of you to make love is one of the healthiest of family sex-education lessons.

Put a lock on the bedroom door. Paint a sign if you have to that reads PARENTS ONLY! or QUIET! PARENT LOVING GOING ON IN HERE. The bedroom will probably be the room that becomes your "clinic" because it is most often the most easily separated from the activities of the day, not because that is where the bed is or because sex must occur before sleep.

Once declaring the place, you must outfit it. The bedrooms of the couples I treated contained televisions, books, medicine for colds and flu, sewing machines, desks, computers, and assorted other items that had little to do with intimacy. One couple reported that "we keep the dog cage in there because he yelps at night and we can hit the cage from the bed with a slipper." For super marital sex, some drastic and difficult changes are necessary. Here is the construction blueprint for your super marital sex clinic.

Turning on Your Sex Lights

> I don't know why we fell into the habit of making love in the dark. We aren't shy or anything. Maybe we're too lazy to turn the lights on and off.
>
> HUSBAND

You will not be reading in bed in this new program, so candles or soft, full-spectrum lighting is recommended. James Ott, in his book *Health and Light*, states, "We have finally learned that light is a nutrient much like food, and, like food, the wrong kind can make us ill and the right kind can help keep us well.'' The reason for healthy lighting in your place for intimacy is not just so you can see the beauty of your sexual interaction. Making love exclusively in the dark or with artificial incandescent lighting deprives us a natural sexual stimulant to the brain, to the pineal and pituitary glands. Try to create natural, soft full-spectrum lighting for your room. Let your sexual life see the light.

Sexual Soundproofing

> The only soundproofing that would work in our house would be a gag for each of us and lots of oil for the squeaky bed.
>
> HUSBAND

Just as we suffer from lack of natural lighting, so we suffer from the constant pollution of noise. Listen now as you read this paragraph and you will detect constant humming, clicking, rattling house noises and outside noises of traffic and day-to-day living. Ask any parents and they will tell you that the one thing they want more than anything else in their house is quiet.

It is as important to keep noise out of your private place as it is to keep your intimate communication private. The only approach that seemed to meet both of these needs was to suggest to my couples a music system. Pick a system that is of sufficient quality to reproduce the full range of sounds from your favorite music. The couples reported that music free of a strong theme, vocals, and changes in beat or rhythm was the most pleasing. Your own tapes are much better than the radio, because they are free of commercials and tailored exactly to your tastes. Make your own set of super sex tapes together.

Some couples added extra sound insulation for the bedroom and others tried ''white noise,'' a system that creates a background that masks noise. A little creativity and effort can help you to keep your own natural sex sounds in and distracting noises out. Super sex requires sound nutrition to match your natural lighting nutrition.

The Sexual Atmosphere: Sex in the Air

> I don't know. Sometimes it's not me or her that doesn't feel sexy. It's more like ''it,'' the environment, just doesn't seem right.
>
> HUSBAND

Albert Krueger and David Sobel write that "there are ions in the air around us all the time, but changes in their concentration, or in the ratio of positively to negatively charged molecules, can have marked biological effects on plants and animals." I have stressed the fact that super marital sex depends on viewing sexual response as a system, an interactional flow between partners within their environment. We are living in an ocean of air, breathing at least ten thousand liters of air every twenty-four hours. To believe that this does not affect our health and therefore our sexual response is to ignore the fact that how we feel affects whatever we do.

That fresh, invigorating smell and feeling you sense after a rainstorm relates to the negative air ions that occur. It is invigorating because the ratio of positive to negative air ions has been distorted in our cement and steel world, and the rain hitting cement or stone restores a temporary healthy balance. Tropical islands and oceanfront areas are so popular because they usually have a natural healthy ion ratio.

Purchasing an air ionizer may improve your overall feeling in your private place. Inhalation of negative air ions actually alters our brain chemistry, possibly relating to secretion of pleasurable chemicals called endorphins. The increase in respiration during sex can result in either more "bad" air or more "good" air going in. For your own sex clinic, I suggest you place a tested, high-quality air ionizer in your room. Be careful. There are many fraudulent claims about these ionizers. Buy from a trusted dealer. Opening a window and letting in some fresh air for sex can help, too.

The Furniture: What to Get on When You Are Getting It On

> Man, I'm telling you, I think I almost threw my back out. We tried it on one of those water beds. We never got into the swing of the thing. The thing took control of us. It was like making love on a bucking bronco.
>
> HUSBAND

In outfitting your clinic, pick a bed that is large, firm, and quiet while in motion. Test it out, at least a little, before you buy. Considering how much time you spend in bed, it is worth a major investment. If possible, dispense with a stand and place the mattress and springs directly on the floor. Doing so will add firmness and soundproofing. Forget water beds. Contrary to mythology, and except for variety, they are not the best environment for sex and certainly not for the posture of the future.

You will also need about ten large, firm pillows. Some wedge-shaped pillows will come in handy for the posture of the future. Bedding should be mutually appealing to both partners, but satin sheets, again contrary to popular myth, are not the best for sex. "I slip, he slips, the bed slips, the pillows disappear, and I almost get shot right out from underneath him. When I'm on top, I can't get any traction," reported one wife in the couples' sample.

Make sure the colors in the room appeal to both of you. Both partners must be involved in the design and decorating of this clinic. It will take some time, but make this private place the best place for both of you to be free. Make sure the phone unplugs and anything distracting is removed. If you want mirrors, put them up. Nobody will see them if you keep this room locked.

If you have followed along to this point, stand back now and do an inspection of the construction. Any artwork should be mutually chosen, preferably enlarged pictures of both of you. No pictures of the kids, the dog, parents, or friends. This one private place should reflect a celebration of your marriage, your intimacy, and your sexuality. Add any last-minute details such as incense, candles, a new soft rug, space heater if it gets too cold, and air conditioner if it gets too hot. Make sure you have removed any and all excuses for why this room is not totally yours. Once you have done that, once you have prevented your bedroom from being a "bored" room, your clinic is ready for staffing.

Step Two: Staffing the Clinic

> We never realized it until now, but we never took time to choose our sexual life-style. It just happened to us.
>
> HUSBAND

You will need two "sexperts" for this sex clinic—you and your partner, the experts on your sexuality. The expert on your spouse *is* your spouse. And the expert on you is you. Each of you must take full responsibility for "your" patient in this clinic. Your patient is you.

You have already taken major steps toward the training of your staff. You have studied the history of sexuality, analyzed your sexual system, and learned a new model of human sexual response. As training continues, add to the records you have kept for the opportunities at the end of each chapter. Make up your own audio "sex tapes" in your private place. Listen to them altogether as a follow-up to your clinic program.

Training the staff depends on getting the staff in shape. If you have not had a recent physical exam, schedule one now with a doctor you trust. Tell the doctor that you both want a physical and want him or her to do it with both of you present. All health is a system, so there is no reason to go for medical checkups alone. Make sure the doctor schedules a feedback session to tell you both about the physical exam results and to plan healthy changes that may be needed, changes you can make together. Doctors complain that patients often fail to comply with their recommendations for healthy living. One reason for low compliance is the medical establishment's insistence on an individual focus when changes can be made only within a system.

Two more steps are needed to train the staff. First, you must get some mutual exercise. From now on, every day of your life, rain, snow, or sun, walk together for twenty minutes holding hands. This one simple step was one of the most popular activities for the couples in the clinic. "I found out that we just never made time to be together. That simple walk has become a part of us." Be sure to leave the dog and kids at home. This is a marital walk, not a family parade.

Lastly, not only are you what you eat but you also may have sex related in part to what and how you eat. Of all physical functions, eating is one human function that seems to be related closely to sexuality. Researchers are learning that problems with sex can result in eating problems and the reverse also seems to be true. Both sex and eating have to do with timing, taste, feelings, self- and body esteem, pleasure, and general physical, emotional, and interactional health.

Caffeine, cigarettes, and sugar are not good for sex. All of these alter the metabolism in the direction of disruption and/or depression and all have impact on the neurohormonal system. Eating a low-fat, low-preservative, high-fiber diet is not only good health, but it positively affects sexual response. Kenneth Pelletier, in his book *Longevity*, presents evidence relating good health to longevity and continued sexual activity. The patients in the clinic who neglected sound health practices, particularly if they abused alcohol or other substances, had the most difficulty correcting their sex problems. Actually, there is no such thing as "sexual health," for health is an all-inclusive term for the way we live and love.

Step Three: Conducting the Evaluation

You have taken several tests already. Review those tests as a couple. Remember that the scores are not the issue. The process of learning and discussion is the key point.

Six Sex Drawings

Add to your tests, tapes, medical examination results, and the seven super marital sex opportunities a couples' drawing test. Doing and sharing the drawings was fun for the couples and led them to interesting insights. Each of you should buy a small pack of crayons. Draw, in color, yourself and your partner separately and then draw one picture of yourself and your partner together. Claims of lack of artistic ability are not accepted because this is not an art test. Anything you draw will give you some ideas about how you see yourselves, each other, and the relationship. Here are some questions to help you learn from your six drawings.

1. Look at the size of the figures. Who's bigger, smaller, fatter, skinnier?

2. What details were focused upon in the drawings? (Head, genitals, breasts, legs, arms, stomach?) Who focused on what and why?

3. What colors were chosen for which drawings and why? What do they mean to you? (Red=hot? Blue=cool? There are no correct answers; just discuss what a color meant to you.)

4. What was each figure doing?

5. What was the couple doing in the couples drawings?

6. How do the figures seem to "feel" as they appear in each drawing?

7. Write down one sentence that each figure is saying, and don't forget the two sentences for the couples drawings.

8. On the back of one of the drawings, complete each of the following sentences:
   1. To me, sex is . . .
   2. What I like best about our sex is . . .
   3. The characteristic of my spouse that turns me on most is . . .
   4. My favorite thing to do sexually is . . .
   5. The characteristic about me that I think turns my partner on most is . . .
   6. What I think my spouse likes most about our sex is . . .

If you can laugh and share as you go over these drawings and your answers to the questions, you have made considerable progress already. You are now ready to focus on any problems you may want to correct in your sexual interaction.

Step Four: Finding Out Who's the Matter with Us

One of the most important steps in the super marital sex treatment program was to help the couples understand their marital system in measurable, behavioral terms. This is difficult, because we tend to speak in the terminology of pseudopsychology, using such words as "defensive," "aggressive," "regressive," "passive-aggressive," "neurotic," "masochistic," and "infantile." We have become what Martin Gross calls "psychologically directed," seeing normal reactions to daily life as "sick." Anger, despair, and frustration are viewed as "problems."

Our sexual diagnostic terms reflect this same psychology orientation. A NIMH study reported that virtually no family in the nation is free of mental disorders, and that up to sixty million Americans exhibit deviant mental behavior related to schizophrenia. The same thing that has happened to our sexual health has happened to our mental health. We have been declared statistically sexually ill. Masters and Johnson indicate that over half the couples in the United States have sexual problems, and they provided the terms that, with slight modifications by the American Psychiatric Association, are the new sexual-babble of our time.

Here is a system for formulating your own "diagnostic system" from the fourth perspective. "Talking it over" is much more important than "labeling it."

Fourth-Perspective Sexual Problem Terms

When asked about their feelings rather than their bodies, the couples taught me a diagnostic system based on the systems nature of sexual response. They taught that everyone in every marriage has sexual problems sometimes, and realizing this dynamic nature of human sexual response helped me to learn with the couples to view problems in a wellness rather than a pathology mode. There could be no "good" sex if there was no "bad" sex, just as health has no meaning without illness.

The couples also taught me that sexuality was related to all of their life, not just their sexual interaction or coitus. You will note that every one of the early-perspective sex terms was based on a coital model, penetration of vagina and energy release without pain in an appropriate time frame. The following chart is based on the lessons of the spouses in the super marital sex program. Look for the area that you might like to focus on in your own therapy program.

Sexual Problems at Hot Times in Your Life

At those times when we are running "hot," when we are feeling hostile, impatient, competitive, and suffering from "hurry illness," we are in a phase of what I call maladaptive hyperarousal. My interviews indicated that asking about how people were "running" in this regard led to more information than asking how their genitals were working. In "diagnosing" your sexual relationship, ask first if the two of you seem on a "hot" cycle of personal and marital pressure: excessive responsibilities, and feelings of too much to do in too little time, of hyperreaction and agitation.

If you are running hot, your neurohormonal system runs hot too, and the biochemistry of your sexual system interferes with your natural sexual reflex system. These are the hot problems that might result:

MALE	FEMALE
Seminal seepage (losing ejaculate without contractions)	Skene's glands or urinary emission without contractions
Hyperarousal	Hyperarousal
Ejaculatory urgency (feelings of not being able to control pelvic contractions)	"Emission" urgency (feeling of not being able to control pelvic contractions)
Shortening of refractory period	Shortening of refractory period
Absence of psychasms	Absence of psychasms
Diminished afterglow	Diminished afterglow
Hypersensitivity of F- and/or and R-area response	Hypersensitivity of G- and/or C-area response
Diminished contemplation	Diminished contemplation
Pelvic reflex addiction or maladaptive hypersexuality (loss of intimacy)	Pelvic reflex addiction or maladaptive hypersexuality (loss of intimacy)

All of these "hot" problems are natural responses to daily living styles. There is no reference to lack of orgasm or psychasm in intercourse because the couples reported that coital orgasm was not a major concern. They learned to focus on their feelings and interactions in the general sexual relationship and the interaction between sex and living. They were trying to learn "who," not "what" was the matter with their sexual life.

Sexual Problems at Cold Times in Your Life

At those times when we are running cold, feeling defeated, inadequate, and passive, our sexual response reflects this life-style. We all run hot and cold at different times, and when we are cold, we experience a "learned helplessness," a feeling that there is little hope, that the world does not live up to our expectations and that our efforts to do much about it are ineffective.

The neuroendocrine system reflects this life orientation and influences sexual response. Here is a list of the cold sexual problems, and remember, the person is not cold, but his or her life-style at this particular time is.

MALE	FEMALE
Diminished pre-ejaculatory fluid	Diminished lubrication
Abbreviated orgasmic contractions	Abbreviated orgasmic contractions
Absence of orgasmic contractions	Absence of orgasmic contractions
Diminished F- and/or R-area sensitivity	Diminished G- and/or C-area sensitivity
Prolonged contemplation	Prolonged contemplation
Decreased arousal	Decreased arousal
Absence of psychasms	Absence of psychasms
Diminished sexual interest	Diminished sexual interest
Lengthening of refractory period	Lengthening of refractory period

If you have forgotten some of the meanings of the terms in the list, check back to Chapter Five to the Super Sex Response Model. Talk with your spouse about the problems you are having or might like to avoid. Remember that you are trying to provide a working diagnosis, not a verdict. Talk as much about how you are living as how you are loving, for they are really one and the same.

Here are the actual reports of spouses as they subjectively reported their sexual problem from the fourth perspective.

Hot Sexual Problems

ABSENCE OF PSYCHASMS: I came, but it was no big deal, really. I felt the pulsing down there and everything, but I just didn't feel like I was finished, I mean complete.

I had everything the books say, but I didn't feel it like you would think. It's a little like being numb. I went through the whole self-help thing, but it's like I still had something more in me.

I did not indicate which of the above reports was from a husband or wife so that you could try to guess for yourself. Can you tell? The first was a husband, the second the wife. Early in the treatment program, 881 men and 492 women reported this problem. More men reported this only because the whole idea of a psychasm was new to them. Once I started asking, they knew just what I meant. The women related more easily to the problem as a concept, but tended to be more holistic in their orientation and more capable of psychasms in some form of their sexual activity.

SEMINAL SEEPAGE: It was a strange sensation, almost like I was peeing. It felt warm, and there wasn't a thing I could do about it. She didn't even touch me—touch my penis, I mean—and it all came out. I lost my erection and felt like I just didn't want to go on, but I never really felt the throbbing I get. It just all came out, almost all at once.

HUSBAND

Nineteen men of the thousand reported similar experiences. Each was associated with anxiety, a performance orientation to the sexual encounter, resulting in excessive and early discharge of the excitation part of the neurohormonal system (the sympathetic nervous system).

URINARY OR SKENE'S GLANDS EMISSION WITHOUT CONTRACTIONS: I felt like I was peeing, like something was coming out down there. It was embarrassing because I have had no control over it, it just happened. I tried to pretend nothing was happening, but I know he knew, too. He never said anything, but sometimes it happens and I can't control it. It's not coming or anything. It just comes out.

WIFE

Thirty-eight women of the thousand reported this phenomenon. Since my report is purely subjective, with no visual laboratory investigation, I cannot interpret these reports to support the conclusion that women emit an ejaculate. This fluid may be related to the Skene's glands, some mixture of Skene's glands fluid and urine, or emission of urine related to stress incontinence. Nonetheless, the subjective experience was similar to the male reports of seminal seepage and related to sympathetic (hot) orientations to the sexual encounter.

Since sex research does not focus on "hot or cold" life orientations in favor of a genital focus, it may be yielding inconsistent findings regarding the controversy of female ejaculation.

> **HYPERAROUSAL:** I get all sweaty. My heart beats, my hands are wet, but I feel kind of cold. I get over-ready, overanxious. I'm so turned on that I can't even feel anything really. I just seem carried away, like I have to do it now or I'll explode. My wife keeps saying "Slow down, slow down, take it easy," but I just want to take it fast. I really can't control it.
>
> HUSBAND

> I have an "on" switch, I swear. I even start kind of a nervous laugh and get dizzy. I don't know what's happening, but it's like running as fast as I can down a steep hill and not being able to stop. It's frightening, really.
>
> WIFE

Three hundred forty-nine men and 284 women classified themselves as experiencing this hyperarousal state in what they felt was "most" of their sexual experiences. Remember, we all experience this state sometimes in our sexual lives, and we can all experience more than one sexual problem at a time. In fact, hyperarousal and seminal seepage or early Skene's glands emissions in the absence of contractions commonly occur together.

Hot times in our lives typically result in this "out of control" orientation, and it extends to our sex life. When we are running hot, when we are hostile, impatient, and competitive, we are in a state of maladaptive hyperarousal. Sex can be so intense, so fast-paced, that we almost miss it entirely. Our sexual intensity, our sexual speed seems to break the intimacy barrier instead of the sound barrier, but little real intimacy results as we go right past it.

This category of problem contains erective difficulties. The failure of the penis or clitoris to erect or a lessening of intensity of erective experience is simply a natural reflex to the accompanying emotional state of anxiety, of running hot. It makes little sense to treat the symptom instead of the cause or to blame the penis or clitoris for failing to erect while we are sending direct neurohormonal orders for them not to do so.

> **EJACULATORY URGENCY:** It gets like a fire drill. I can just feel like I am going to come and a bulldozer couldn't stop it. I don't care what I say or do, I am going to come.
>
> HUSBAND

The ejaculation reflex is under much more control than men have learned, but running hot results in neurohormonal changes that diminish or prevent that control. Six hundred twenty-three of the thousand men reported the ejaculatory-urgency problem as characteristic of their sexual encounters, and again hyperarousal often accompanied this difficulty.

> **CONTRACTIVE URGENCY:** I thought only men did this, I mean had this happen, or whatever. I just start to come. I get strong squeezing in my vagina. This happens mostly when he does oral love to me. I can't hold back.
>
> WIFE

Forty-six women reported this problem as typical of their sexual experience. Since the early perspectives of sexuality considered immediate, even out-of-control, sexual response in the woman to be desirable and a time and effort saver for the man, this problem has not been explored in prior sexual programs. I found in the couples now being treated that questions about such a problem lead to a higher percentage of reports than the 4.6 percent rate in the thousand couples included for this report.

> **SHORTENING OF REFRACTORY PERIOD:** I think I could go again and again. We don't, but I can have sex and then go into the bathroom and masturbate and then come back and have sex.
>
> I just stop because we stop. I can get ready in a matter of a few minutes, no, seconds. I could do it over and over if I had to, no, I mean, if I wanted to.

Can you tell which is the husband and which is the wife? The first is the wife. Both partners are experiencing shortened refractory periods in part because of hyperarousal and in part because of their "hot running, keep on going" style of living. There is less of a refractory period following a hurried, less intense sexual experience than following a mutually involving, prolonged, emotionally intense sexual interaction. One hundred eleven men and 44 women reported this type of problem as occurring often in their sexual relationships. Remember that the problems mentioned here are reported at a higher frequency when the question is changed to "Have you ever experienced this problem?" instead of "Is this problem characteristic of your sexual relationship?" When the first question is asked, all of us have some or many of these problems sometimes, and discussing them even before they are experienced can be good preventive sexual therapy.

> **DIMINISHED AFTERGLOW:** I don't glow after sex, I just sort of smolder. I think it's the origin of the word "burnout." I feel spent.
>
> HUSBAND

Absence of afterglow was reported in 907 of the husbands. They could not understand the idea of feeling invigorated after sex, instead feeling that sex had exhausted their energy supply, at least temporarily.

> I feel a sense of relief, or completion, but I sure wouldn't say a "glow." It's like a job well done. It's getting off.
>
> WIFE

Five hundred fifty-one women reported the lack of or diminished afterglow. More often than the men, they knew about afterglow, might have felt it following some of their sexual experiences, including masturbation, but reported a connection between partner and the afterglow phenomenon. It is difficult to glow alone after being sexual with someone.

> **HYPERSENSITIVITY OF F AND/OR R AREA:** I feel like a big stick of dynamite and my penis is the fuse. It is so sensitive that it can hurt.
>
> HUSBAND

Virtually all of the men reported some hypersensitivity of the F and/or R area sometimes during their sexual experiences. Two hundred twenty-one of the men reported it as frequently problematic. Some of them (62) reported "strange" sensations in the penis or scrotum during sex that they felt interfered with their enjoyment.

> **HYPERSENSITIVITY OF G AND/OR C AREA:** It's like it's hot or gets hot. It actually stings. It burns right up to the inside.
>
> WIFE

Seventy-three women reported this problem. As I have reported, it is a mistake to indicate that there is a G "spot." However, all of the women in the thousand were able to discover, according to their subjective report, a region of sensitivity in the anterior vaginal wall. For some women, this region extended throughout the entire anterior and posterior parts of the vagina.

> **DIMINISHED CONTEMPLATION:** I just tune out after it's over. I don't feel like moving, thinking, talking, or doing anything but sleeping. I drift away.
>
> HUSBAND

Four hundred fifty-three men reported the absence of or no understanding of reflection or contemplation following the sexual experience. The "energy release" model of early sexual research probably conditions many men to feel that an athletic event has ended when sex is over. It was new for most of the men to ask themselves about satisfaction, to reflect on the sexual experience rather than to forget it.

> I've learned to tune out after sex. I used to laugh sometimes, cry other times, or sometimes get real philosophical. It was like I was on a drug after sex, like it was with some good pot. Now I don't have the time or the interest. I just turn over and go to sleep.
>
> WIFE

One hundred twenty women reported this problem, and the majority of the wives in the sample reported that the reflective phase of the sexual system diminished with length of marriage. Our culture's linear view of time, the start/stop orientation we bring to sex, does not help us reflect. We tend to be prospective in our sexuality; foreplay is much more popular than after- or replay. Hot-running life-styles allow little time for looking back or prolonging experiences through reflection. We barely have time to enjoy the moment once, and seldom twice or thrice.

> **PELVIC-REFLEX ADDICTION** (maladaptive hypersexuality): I can't get enough. I can sit in my car in the shopping mall and see a good-looking woman. My hips will hump a little and I might move my hand down and rub my penis. I would screw every good-looking woman in the world if I could. I think I do in my own mind. One partner would never be enough for me. Maybe not even one at a time.
>
> HUSBAND

The loss of intimacy in sexual interaction and the replacement of intimacy with thrusting and contractions was reported by 244 of the men. They felt that their sexual experience had become pelvic and that they were addicted to their need for pelvic release. Sex for them was not sex if there was no pelvic contraction.

> I can get it done well. I am very responsive . . . hyperresponsive . . . a nymphomaniac maybe. I love to do it. I ride him fast and hard. It's like I devour him. I'd like to get every stud I could. You know what they say. The more the better.
>
> WIFE

One hundred and two women reported the problem of pelvic-reflex addiction. Their vocabulary revealed a genital focus, an emphasis on contractive release that distracted them not only from intimacy but sometimes from daily life activities. Whether or not men and women can truly be "addicted" to sex is not clear and is now debated in the research literature. My couples indicated that there was a habitual focus on pelvic contraction at the expense of partner or relationship focus that resembled the dibilitating life distraction of alcoholism and other substance abuse.

Cold Sexual Problems

At those times in your life when you are behaving in a defeated, passive manner and feeling inadequate, helpless, and hopeless, you may experience some of the same problems in sexuality as the husbands and wives below.

> **DIMINISHED PRE-EJACULATORY FLUID:** I used to feel real full, like my penis was ready to explode. My underpants would be wet even before I came. Now I just don't notice that feeling. I just don't see much of the fluid.
>
> HUSBAND

While the aging process accounts for some diminishing of pre-ejaculatory fluid, emotional and interactional factors can also inhibit its emission. Sixty-three men reported experiencing this problem.

> **DIMINISHED LUBRICATION:** I used to be too wet sometimes; now I just feel dry. It hurts when he enters. I feel turned on, but I'm dry.
>
> WIFE

Aging, hormonal changes, some disease processes, other factors affect lubrication of the vagina, but emotional factors are also influential. While amount of lubrication does not indicate amount of arousal, a noted change in amount of lubrication can signal emotional states incompatible with this response. Five hundred sixty-five women reported problems with lubrication at least occasionally.

Prior work in the field of sexuality has equated male erection problems with female failure to lubricate. Female clitoral erective problems were essentially ignored. As you read above, male and female erective difficulty is related to hot-running times, to hyper-arousal. Inhibition of secretion of lubricatory fluids in men and women is related to the cold-running times, those times when there is a lack of life energy, eagerness to be close, to merge. We don't need to lubricate if there is little likelihood of the joyful friction of joining and staying together.

> ABBREVIATED ORGASMIC CONTRACTIONS: It's like it doesn't really completely fire; you know what I mean. It doesn't throb like it used to. They're there, but not the same.

> I can't get that feeling. I just don't feel it thump or pulse like it did. I mean, it does throb, but not fully.

Can you guess which is the man and which is the woman? The first report was from a wife, the second from a husband. Aging can diminish the intensity of the pelvic contractions that accompany orgasm (though does not diminish psychasm), but premature diminishing of this reflex is related to emotional state; an emotional looseness is translated to a genital response. When your emotional energy is drained, the pelvic contractions decrease, too. Four hundred forty-three men and 388 women reported this problem.

You can already see the numerical overlap in this problem report. The more I talked with the couples about this model of sexual response and understanding sexual problems, the more they shared a range of feelings about sexual experience. They were no longer limited by the genital focus.

> ABSENCE OF ORGASMIC CONTRACTIONS: I can enjoy the whole thing, but I do not come. I can go on and on, but I will not, I cannot come.

> It gets so bad that I am actually screaming inside at myself to come, come, come. My partner says it. Come, come, come. I can't, can't, can't.

Guess again which report belongs to which gender. The first is a wife, the second a husband. The similarity of sexual response and problems seems clear. Both genders reported problems with orgasmic contractions. One hundred fifty-five husbands and 344 wives reported such problems. When this problem occurred, it took with it in many cases the possibility of psychasm, for these people were taught that orgasm was the ultimate goal, the only goal of the sexual encounter. Without pelvic contractions, there could be no "fulfillment." This is not true, and, in fact, these spouses learned to enjoy psychasm independent of contractions. When this happened, and the defeated, angry orientation at the center of this problem was removed, orgasmic contractions returned.

> **DIMINISHED F- AND/OR R-AREA SENSITIVITY:** Somebody turned off the switch on me. I cannot feel much down there at all. I was kicked hard there once when I was a kid, and it was numb for hours. This is something like that. I have almost no feeling.
>
> HUSBAND

In the absence of medical problems, this male problem relates to the parasympathetic mediation associated with cold-running times. When we run cold, we tend to run nonreactively, and our response level to life, to sex, decreases. Seventy-five men reported this problem, and twenty of these men were shown to have a medical problem (see Chapter Eleven). The rest had unwillingly and unconsciously anesthetized their genital area. One of the men tried a vibrator, which he strapped to his hand, reporting, "I tried to force some sensation, and it made it worse." Sexual enjoyment cannot be force-fed; it must be received by an open and balanced life-style free of the learned helplessness of the cold reaction.

> **DIMINISHED G- AND/OR C-AREA SENSITIVITY:** He bought every sex toy in the catalogue. He even tried a Water Pik, and shot water at my clitoris. Nothing. I just don't feel down there. Then he went after the G spot. I don't have one of those either.
>
> WIFE

Seventy-five wives also reported diminished G- or C-area sensitivity. Once the women were educated as to the mythology about a magic G spot that swelled when touched and produced ejaculate, they learned that their bodies, all bodies, change from time to time, sexual encounter to sexual encounter. Some then continued to report a lack of pleasing sensations in the genital area. Eight of these women had medical problems that you will read about in Chapter

Eleven. The rest were at cold times in their lives and relationships, as psychologically anesthetized as their male counterparts.

> **PROLONGED CONTEMPLATION:** I think I start to think things over before it's over. That is, I start to feel empty even when he's in me. I think, Oh well, at least I'm getting held. That's more than I usually get. I even start to cry, but I cover it up by faking arousal.
>
> WIFE

> When we are lying there after, I just think to myself. I think about life, work, us, the kids. I don't know why, but after sex, I get very reflective, very philosophical, kind of funky.
>
> HUSBAND

Seventy-five women and 109 men reported this prolonged contemplation. Cold-running times are often accompanied by long periods of introspection, often negative introspection of missed opportunities and goals. Fewer women than men reported problems, with prolonged contemplation, perhaps because they were more comfortable with or more acclimated to such reflection and thoughtfulness about sexual intimacy. Of course, the men and women were all in therapy, so introspection was to be expected. As I pointed out in the introduction, I am including numbers here for illustration, not documentation. The numbers cannot tell us how often these problems occur in the general population, but they can help us understand about the gender overlap, generality, and life-systems orientation of sexual difficulties.

I noticed that the women reflected on the marriage, the relationship, the loving. Men tended to reflect on life in general, as if forgetting the sex and moving on to unresolved daily problems. This finding, as with all of the findings in this subjective report, is certainly not true of all men or women, not gender-caused. However, some of the difference may be related to expectations and views of sexual experiences and the effect of our love maps. The colder we are running in our life, the more we may freeze up a little after sex.

> **DECREASED AROUSAL:** I can tell you now that I have lost my sex drive. I just don't feel like it, want it, or really even want to talk about it.

> There isn't much time for that sort of thing anymore. My mind and feelings are on the kids right now.

The first report was a wife's, the second from a husband. Five hundred eighty-eight men and 678 women in the sample reported some problem with the arousal axis of the sexual-response system. Some of these same persons at times experience hyperarousal as well, so life phase was an important predictor of sexual response. Most clinicians report that diminished sexual arousal (what they call sex drive) is the most frequent sexual difficulty. I found that there was no one dominant problem and that no one problem stood alone. At cold times, sexual arousal cools down as much as it may heat up at hot times.

A word of warning here. The hot and cold dimensions overlap. You can, as I have said, be "hotly cold" or "coldly hot." You can be as vigorously depressed as you can be passively agitated. At such times, the apparently "cold" person may be showing the "hot sex problems," including hyperarousal, while the apparently "hot" person may be displaying the "cold sex problems," including diminished arousal. In operating your own sex clinic, and particularly at this step of understanding your marital relationship style and any areas you both wish to correct or enhance, you may want to read my book *Superimmunity*, in which I describe hot and cold life-styles and provide several tests related to these orientations.

> **ABSENCE OF PSYCHASMS:** I don't feel like I really have an intense emotional experience. I don't feel like I have really gotten into and out of something.
>
> It seems like my body comes but I don't.

The first report is from a wife, the second a husband. Absence of psychasms, that is, an absence of the alteration of conscious and emotional experience through intimate bodily contact with someone else, is related to both hot and cold times, for unless we are in balance in our lives, we are not free to enjoy a variety of consciousness experiences. To do so, we may turn to drugs to help us accomplish such uplifting and mind-altering experiences, but drugs never really work. Only through intimacy and spiritual development can we really transcend the material, physical limitations of day-to-day life. The 881 men and 492 women who had trouble with psychasm were equally distributed in their hot and cold orientations to life both in my sample and in their own daily lives, running both hot and cold at various times.

DIMINISHED SEXUAL INTEREST: I don't think about sex unless it jumps up and bites me. I guess I don't think of much unless it hits me over the head. I just go on leading my life.

HUSBAND

How can you really think about sex when you have a million problems in your life? You can only think so much, you can only have so much energy. I am drained just dealing with life.

WIFE

There has been a tendency in sex research to focus on behaviors, sometimes feelings, but seldom thoughts. How we think about sex influences our entire sexual system, and when we are running cold, we tend to lose sexual interest. One hundred fourteen men and 245 women reported problems with sexual interest, and the frequency of sexual-interest differences in marriages is probably much higher than these numbers indicate. Remember, these couples came to the clinic for help with the sexual dimension of their marriage. They had enough interest in sex to try to improve their sexual relationship.

LENGTHENING OF REFRACTORY PERIOD: I am wigged out, flaked out, spaced out, dead. After sex, I just am drained. I need the intensive-care unit. It's always a long time before I can have, even think about having, sex again.

HUSBAND

It almost seems like having sex decreases our sex life. When I have it, I just don't want to have it again. I feel like all the energy is gone then.

WIFE

One hundred and nine men and 59 women reported that their refractory periods seemed longer than other times in their life. When we run cold, there may be a tendency to overdo it when we finally find the time and energy for sex. When we become contemplative, we also lengthen the refractory period by avoiding behaviors that may lead to re-arousal. Since the cold reactor is in a perpetual emotional refractory period, it seems logical that such a life orientation would enter into the sexual system.

What about your own sexual system? In terms of this new diagnostic system, what types of problems is your sexual system experiencing at this time? Don't deliver a verdict. Think about your sexual functioning to determine who is the matter with the sexual system. You are not assigning blame or responsibility for the problem, for each partner is responsible for self. It means understanding that it is "who," not "what," that matters in achieving super marital sex, the who of the combination of you both. It is how we are and who we are as people who relate that really matters.

Step Five: Getting Fixed up Sexually: Thirteen Prescriptions for Sexual Health

Now that you have set up the place, hired the staff, completed the evaluation, and reviewed your sexual problem, you are ready for super marital sex. The steps are simple, but you must commit time and personal involvement to each one. These techniques are called "sexual sigs" from the medical shorthand for prescribing, "signifying." In case you have been wondering, these steps also include the posture of the future. I hope you and your spouse are helped by each "sexual sig," and that you will make time and take your time to enjoy and experience each one.

Sexual Sig Number One: The L.O.V.E. Technique

This is the *l*isten, *o*bserve, *v*erify, and *e*mphasize technique. As you begin your super marital sex program, a key rule is never, but never, to respond to a feeling statement from your spouse without first reiterating that statement. Below are examples of the experiences of various couples from the thousand in the clinic program to illustrate the sexual sigs.

"I really want badly to have a new couch," said the wife. Her husband's reiteration, done only at my insistence, was, "I understand that you don't like the furniture I bought." The wife responded, "That's right. You've got it." There was no listening on either side, no observing of body language and facial gestures, no real verification of message or empathy for the partner. The L.O.V.E. technique is a prerequisite for sexual problem-solving.

Practice together at least once a day in your sex clinic. Send and receive messages with an emphasis on learning and listening, an emphasis on watching your partner while he or she talks, on trying to feel what the other is feeling while he or she is talking. "Try again," I asked the couple. "This time, really watch each other and try to feel what is said, not just hear it." "Okay," said the wife. "I really, really want a new couch, just a new couch." The husband reiterated, "I hear you saying that you really want a new couch." He looked at me and shook his head. "Now what? She wants a couch. That's no big deal."

The husband was wrong. His wife said something, he heard it. That's as much a start for learning good sex as not hearing a simple message is a start toward bad sex. The trick is to employ the L.O.V.E. sig when it counts, when important issues are being discussed. Always remember to listen, but also to watch each other, verify before responding, and emphasize empathy, trying to get the feeling, not just the words. Listen for each other, not from each other's personal biases. Much more intimacy can result. It all starts with listening.

Sexual Sig Number Two: Secret Touching for the Secret Spot

Lie naked in bed and take turns trying to discover the tensest spot in your spouse's body. Use lotion to lubricate your searching touch while your spouse tries mentally to guide you to the single tensest area. No talking is allowed, and even though the genitals or other erotic zones might be the tensest areas at a given time, remember to touch everywhere so you don't miss a spot. Couples reported that they could learn to lead their spouses right to the spot.

One husband stated, "What I liked was not touching just for sex. It was fun, almost a game, but we sort of merged, my hands, her hands, our thoughts. She led me to my spot, too, or I directed her with my thoughts. We just both knew when we found the spots. Just like you told us, when we found the spot, we gave it a gentle kiss and then switched who did the touching and who had the spot."

Nongenitally focused touching, mutual cooperation, combining physical and mental processes, and learning to cooperate sensually can all result from this procedure.

Sexual Sig Number Three: The Spouse Spa

Set aside one morning for the spouse spa assignment. It must be a morning and not a late-night encounter. You must be alone and in your private intimacy place. Hire a babysitter if you have to, and take some time off work. You must make this program a priority, for as I pointed out in Chapter One, failure to do so will eventually rob you both of sexual fulfillment. On two different days, one day for each of you, give your spouse a complete spa treatment. Bathe him or her, wash, dry, and comb the hair, provide a massage that your spouse might like, and wrap her or him comfortably in bed. Bring food, turn on some music, and then read aloud a short story. Do some research for all of this. You will have to interview your partner to be sure it is a spa day he or she will like and not your version of the day. Find a short story that conveys an important message about your relationship.

"Now you're talking. I loved that day. I have never, ever enjoyed anything as much," reported one husband. He was talking about being the spa-er, not the spa-ee, about providing his wife with this opportunity.

"I loved it, too, both parts," reported his wife. "I don't know why we didn't think of it before. I don't remember getting so turned on."

There is no rule about not having sex at this time, but the focus is on the spa experience, not the sex. I have not found it helpful to delay sexual interaction in the treatment program, but I warn that anything that was wrong might still be wrong, so the sex just happens. The spa is not a test. If you are thinking of testing your sex, then don't have sex. Just do the spa experience. If sex is delayed as some type of ultimate end goal, the "real" thing, it is taken out of its natural, intimate context.

Sexual Sig Number Four: The Wisdom Walk

I mentioned the importance of walking together as a couple every day. For this "sexual sig wisdom walk," one person talks, the other listens on the entire walk. Next walk, change roles. The listener uses the L.O.V.E. technique while the talker discusses anything at all. There is a wisdom in all of us, and, as Buckminster Fuller once said, "All of us are geniuses. Some of us are just less damaged than most."

One wife reported, "I had a hard time at first getting used to being the talker and then just a listener, but it was something. I looked forward to both roles, but hearing him talk while we walked, talk about trees, work, kids, neighbors, whatever, without reacting to me was a real trip."

"I realized how much I interrupt and control the conversation. While we walked, it seemed easier to listen and not take over. We kind of got in a rhythm," said her husband.

Sexual Sig Number Five: The Love Library Technique

Go to a well-stocked bookstore and select two hardcover books. Pure fiction only. No "how to do its." Buy two different color markers and underline interesting parts of the first of the books you read. If you don't have time to read, you are too stressed and must make more time before you make more love. Make time to talk about the books and the sections that are underlined. Notice your partner's underlines when you exchange books. Wonder why he or she underlined a given section, how he or she might have felt when reading that particular part.

One husband said, "I noticed at every hotel we stayed at that the women would be reading books more than the men. Just taking time to read nonfiction was a major step, but to read my novel and hers and discuss the same books was a first for us. I got so I felt I was reading along with her when I read the book she underlined."

"I found it that way, too," responded his wife. "The worst part was finding time to read. We had to struggle with that, but as you said, that was part of the sig, to use the reading requirements as a test of whether we would make the time for each other."

Sexual Sig Number Six: A Theme from Your Own Love Story

"Shopping together for a theme song, a love theme song, was not easy. We had songs that we liked before, sort of 'our songs' of the past, but it was hard to find a new one," said one wife. I had instructed them to find a song that could signify their own recommitment to their relationship. It had to be mutually selected and one in which they could understand the words.

"I thought it would be a romantic song. I thought sure we'd get something like the theme from *Love Story*," said her husband. "We got 'Love Lifts Us Up Where We Belong' from the movie where that guy fights with his drill sergeant. What does that say about us anyway?" He laughed, but the words they copied from the song and learned by heart continue to be special for them. "Every time I hear that song on the radio, every time I even see Joe Cocker, I think of us. Is that strange or is that strange?"

Sexual Sig Number Seven: The Spirit of Sensuality

Belief systems are as important, perhaps more important, to sexuality as any other area of life. Developing a shared belief system is central to super marital sex. This is why marriage offers a unique opportunity for intimacy, for it provides the time and opportunity for spiritual growth through life changes.

I ask my couples to find a belief system that they can share actively, either by going to a church, synagogue, or other place of worship or doing volunteer work or other activities that make the belief system come to life. While therapists seldom discuss such issues with their patients, I find this one of the most if not the most productive area for improving intimacy.

This sig has been one of the most rewarding and one of the most difficult for the couples. "I have been a noninvolved Catholic all of my life. I don't know what I can do about it now," said one husband.

"I'm a cultural Jew," answered his wife. "I don't believe in institutional religion."

I asked this couple to talk things over together for a while, perhaps on their walk. To achieve super marital sex, you need a commonly acted open belief system, a transitional life philosophy that binds you together beyond problem-solving and day-to-day living and loving. Talk to a rabbi, a priest, or clergyperson you can both relate to. Do not neglect this part of your relationship. Retrace together the origins of your "life philosophies." These philosophies are related to the couples' love maps.

To help with this, I suggest a once-a-day mutual prayer during which both partners sit or kneel silently and listen together, receive together a sense of connection, a sense of oneness. It is nonpetitionary because it is not a way of asking for something, but a way of tuning in to the connection between the relationship and the universe. It allows for a quiet, steady time together that may help in the development of a strong mutual belief system, even if the religious backgrounds of the spouses are very different.

A recent study by Patricia Weenolsen of Seattle University suggests that we are constantly re-creating the relationship between our inner selves and our outer world. She discovered that people fell into four categories regarding this issue. One group focused on the idea of a supreme being and cosmic purpose. A second stressed a cosmic purpose of transcendence, a spiritual view of life not associated with a deity. A third group ascribed the meaning of life to an individual goal for living, such as making a certain amount of money. A fourth group focused on individual goals of a more general nature, such as being happy or loving. I have used this framework to help some of the reluctant couples begin their discussions about "the meaning of life." In the order of the examples of Weenolsen's categories, are you cosmic-specific, cosmic-general, individual-specific, or individual-general in your view of the purpose of life?

"It was so awkward at first, but after a while, it was almost magic, almost mystical. We could feel it together," reported one wife. "It wasn't like religion, or just a ritual. It was ours. I guess we were both cosmic-general and didn't know it."

The husband reported, "I thought it was really proselytizing at first. I thought you were selling the church, passing the plate. But it turned out to be something very special to us. We don't really have a common belief system like you said, but we are closer. That quiet time is special. There is no other word for it, just special."

This sig is a key to making your marriage, as stated by Shapiro and Shapiro, "valued by both partners as a kind of miracle." If marriage and sexuality are systems, they are systems within the larger system of everything else. Maintaining that connection is vital to living intimately. As you learned in Chapter Two, the laws of the universe are the laws of marriage.

Sexual Sig Number Eight: The Single Sig

Couples in the clinic program are asked to spend one weekend alone, away from the spouse, taking time to think about the relationship, their spouse, and their feelings about self in the context of the relationship. They are asked to be alone during the weekend or whatever two days are picked, and not to take friends along. If possible, they are asked to go to a place that the couple has visited together. This revisit seems to help in the contemplation and meditation about the meaning of the relationship.

A wife reported, "I hadn't done that for a long time, really been alone. Even in college, I was always with someone. I felt like something was missing. It wasn't like absence made the heart grow fonder, but that I seemed to see the relationship in a different way. It's really something to be alone, not to call home, not to be a couple after being a couple for years."

"I got kind of sad," reported her husband. "On business trips, I am always with someone or busy or tired. I always call home.

This time, I went to the same fast-food store that we went to together in Toronto and I seemed to sense her absence strongly."

Sometimes, marital therapists suggest formal or legal separation as a means of learning. I have never found this strategy effective and have seen partners learn only how to be even more distant from one another. The sexual sig I am suggesting here is not for separation, but for closeness, a chance to step back, just as one moves back to look into the partner's eyes before an intimate kiss. This separation is not a test, but an opportunity to learn the impact of the partner when the partner is not physically close.

You might like to try "marital telepathy" during this single sig. Even though you don't call, try sending messages. Set aside a mutually agreed-upon time of day and sit down for a few minutes. Try to send and receive, to sense and be sensed. Russell Targ and Keith Harary collected scientific research on such "sending," and concluded, "Scientific evidence does strongly suggest that the ability to function psychically is a genuine human capacity which, for many people, seems to improve with practice."

"I can tell you now," said one husband, "I am convinced we are getting better at this sending thing. I lay there in bed and could almost hear her talking to me. When I got home, I asked if she sent a message, the names of our three children. Tell him what you said."

"This is like the Twilight Zone, but, yes. I thought I would try it like you said. We picked the time and I sent the name of the three kids. He got them in the same order I sent them, which was not by age. It's probably just coincidence, isn't it? I mean, of course we would both think of the kids."

Why would coincidence make it any less important?

Someone once said that a kiss is nature's way of getting two people so close together they can't see each other's flaws. This sexual sig is an opportunity to be apart so that you may become even more aware of the bond that holds your marriage together.

Sexual Sig Number Nine: The Cycle Sig

Couples fall into patterns, obligatory daily cycles that can destroy intimacy by boring it away. This opportunity requires a time-schedule change. Couples are asked to "find an hour for intimacy." My interviews indicate that the day-to-day requirements of living in our society either erode opportunities for intimacy or numb us to them. I ask the couples to schedule intimacy as follows:

1. You must find one more hour, either by getting up earlier or going to bed later, or taking more time from work, or from wherever and however you can steal an extra hour.

2. Circle days on the calendar that will be scheduled sexual-intimacy days. These times don't mean intercourse necessarily. On these days, except for illness, nothing will prevent holding, touching, and intimacy. It may not be at night, but it will take place.

3. Let the kids know it. The calendar does not just have to be by the bed, it can be on the refrigerator. You come to behave as you feel, so behave intimately. If you don't schedule it, it will not happen over time.

4. Always, but always, rise together and go to bed together. Eat breakfast together if possible. There is no such thing as too much intimacy. Ignoring the development of a mutual cyclicity will eventually lead to marital lack of coordination, a relationship clumsiness that ends in separation either in fact or by circumstance. This rising and going to bed at the same time was one of the most difficult of tasks for the couples, but one of the most important. It is not necessary for a good marriage, but it is basic to a super marriage.

5. Spontaneity will take care of itself. Just because you schedule intimacy does not mean that extras can't happen. It is not unromantic to schedule intimacy. Loving and sexuality is as volitional as it is emotional. Getting on a sex cycle together will help you to find your own sexual Tao.

"What a thing this is," stated one husband. "I was used to sleeping in an extra hour. Now I get up two hours before I have to just to have breakfast with her. But you know, it has added one whole day a week to our marriage. We have gotten kind of arrogant about it and we like to tell our friends. They can't believe it."

His wife added, "He's right. We don't talk much. We mumble and stagger around. He reads the paper, I get ready for work, and we both yell at the kids. Actually, we take turns yelling at the kids. But now there is that early time for just us to say hello."

Sexual Sig Number Ten: Play for Your Marriage

"I want you to learn to juggle together, to jump rope together, to play jacks, do puzzles, play board games, and generally get back to being playmates," I said to one of the couples who seldom smiled.

"Do you mean go to Toys Я Us and get games? We don't have to. Our kids have enough to open their own store. Toys Я Them," said the wife.

"No. I want you to get your own toys. These toys are for you. Keep them in your private place. I know you play with the kids, but now I want you to play with each other." They looked at me, smiling.

At the next visit, they brought three beanbags and demonstrated their juggling skills. They laughed as they repeatedly missed the bags. "I love this," said the husband. "I can't remember playing, and certainly not with her. I play tennis and golf, but this is all different. We're playing like kids, really playing, not just having recreation."

The couple experienced this opportunity as different because it is based on the concept of "neoteny," Ashley Montagu's term for the return to some of the characteristics of childhood. It is a way to laugh, play, and salvage lost opportunities from the health of youthfulness. Perhaps we age because we don't play as we get older.

I ask couples to keep a large family puzzle going at all times. Have it on a table in plain view. Put it together slowly. Everyone should work on it. You will be surprised how stress-reducing this can be, unless someone gets trapped into trying to beat everyone else by finishing it alone. The rule is that no one can put in a piece without someone else from the family present.

Sexual Sig Number Eleven: The Edu-Sig

I ask couples to get books, videotapes, audiotapes, and other materials they find interesting regarding sexuality. Some couples find carefully selected and mutually acceptable X-rated videotapes arousing and educational. Some find them degrading and dumb. It is a matter of personal and marital choice, but now is the time to experiment and learn. Try some old romantic films or comedies, whatever seems interesting to both of you.

Most of the couples invested in a video-cassette player and often watched comedy tapes together. Laughing can be one of the most powerful of aphrodisiacs. There would be much less suffering in marriage if we made more time for laughter and fun. Have you ever noticed the happy looks and laughter from people who are helping others? Have you seen the laughter and joy in the entertainers who gather for a charity event? Giving and sharing seem to be very healthy emotions, and they almost always result in hugging and holding. Again, we do tend to feel as we behave, so learn to laugh. Whatever type of tape you watch, discuss it and learn together.

"We watch those tapes, and I think they stink. But we talk about them. I saw a few things to try, too," said one wife.

"I used to sneak to watch the X tapes. I love to share them with her. We have learned to be real selective. They mostly stink. When we get a good one, one with something we both like, then we get turned on." This husband was the initiator of the tape-viewing, but his wife added, "As long as you want to read those romantic novels with me and watch the old film classics, watch the romances, then I'll watch the junk with you. We can learn from anything, I guess."

Interest in sex is maintained only by thinking, reading, and talking about sex. If you speak only of work, school, problems, and bills, then sex will gradually leave the marital agenda.

Sexual Sig Number Twelve: Building the Sexual Vocabulary

Many of the couples lacked effective verbal communication skills regarding sex. "I want to tell her to suck me down there, but it sounds dirty," said the husband. "I hate the sound of that," answered his wife. "It just sounds crude." To help with this problem, couples are asked to play the sexual-synonym game. They write down all the words for the genitals, breasts, and intercourse that they can think of and talk about them. This exercise helps in the building of a marital sexual vocabulary, not to mention the fun of the marriage. "She said her synonym for penis was 'Richard' because the word 'dick' was too dirty," said the husband, laughing. "Right," said his wife. "But I really broke up when you called cunnilingus 'eating at the Y.' "

"Okay," responded the husband. "You want to reveal your creative name for the penis and the testicles? It is really quite artistic. She called them the light tower on the rocks."

This banter came from the same couple who weeks earlier could not discuss sex in other than the most cryptic of terms.

Sometimes spouses became trapped in projected roles, seeing themselves in ways they feel they must behave rather than allowing themselves to change and develop sexually. "She would never in a million years say the F word," said the husband. "I would, too," answered his wife. "The trouble is, you use it too much and always in anger." By talking about such differences and perhaps false expectations and assigned roles, years of barriers to sexual expression can begin to fall.

Sexual Sig Number Thirteen: The Posture of the Future

You have learned about a new sexual system. You know that there is no reason to limit yourself to the old views of sex that emphasized penetration, thrusting, orgasm, timing, energy release, and ejaculation. To learn more about this, you may want to try a posture that emphasizes the new sexual system, one that stresses closeness, time-free interaction, pays no attention to erection, penetration, ejaculation, or orgasm, but allows for intense and mutual psychasm.

Place all of the pillows you bought for your private place into two wedge-like piles about one body length from each other. When the pillows are all arranged, each of you sit with your back to one of the two wedges, face to face, nude. Test them for comfort and support. The wife's wedge can be a little lower and she can be a little more on her back than the husband as they face each other in this seated position. Both of your genitals should now be next to each other, the legs of one partner comfortably over the legs of the other.

In this position, the wife can reach forward or the husband can reach down and move the penis into contact with the vaginal area. Erect or not, the man can now contact the F area or the R area with the C area and use his finger in the G area if his wife desires. Face to face, partners can now communicate with each other, insert the penis if desired, or continue to contact the F and C areas, the two most sensitive genital areas. Each partner can caress the other. Adjust the posture so there is no stretching or muscle tension involved. Look in each other's eyes, talk together, rest, move closer and embrace, move back and feel. Use artificial lubrication if desired. Use lotion and caress the legs of your partner now at your sides. You are sitting face to face, legs spread, comfortably resting against your own pillows.

Look at each other completely. Think about each other, about the tests you have taken to this point, about your feelings for one another. Feel the physical and emotional sensations of intimacy. Feel the contact of the two most sensitive physical areas of the body without the pressure or tension of thrusting or working for orgasm. Talk, share, and feel for as long as you choose.

Sitting face to face, embracing at will, with genitals positioned next to one another, learn and experience the fourth perspective of human sexuality. This is the perspective of pressure-free sex, intense physical intimacy without imposed expectations of erection, lubrication, or orgasm. It is a perspective of freedom to feel one another, merge with one another without the "foreplay, do it, and stop" sequence. And most important, it is a perspective of love, a love of commitment and a marital sex of male and female equality in the opportunity for personal fulfillment.

The posture of the future allows for more practice of your "telepathic sex," a sending of messages beyond the see/touch world. Scientists are now turning their attention to the subjective, the possibility of communication beyond words and sound waves. All of us know that we communicate on many levels, that we sense each other. We know that this "sense of one another" can be particularly profound between lovers in long-lasting relationships. In this new posture, try to develop your sexual psychic powers. Be open to feelings coming from your partner and send them back. It will take time, but you will see that telepathic sexual arousal is as "sendable" and "receivable" as any other emotion. You will begin to feel a telepathic turn-on. Psychasm is the sensation not only of your own conscious and emotional experiences, but of those of your partner as well.

This is what super marital sex is all about. The posture of the future can help you both learn to develop your own form of sending and receiving free of the sexual prescriptions. The posture of the future is really your posture, so don't worry about "getting it right." If it feels right to both of you, it's right.

"The first time we rushed it," said the wife. "We stacked the pillows, got naked, and tried it. It was terrible. Then we took our time. We moved the wedges around, changed distance and angles several times until we found the right face-to-face sort of semi-sitting postures. The lighting helped, because we had never really seen each other like that, actually looking right at each other and our genitals. The telepathy worked. He got a drifty look on his face that drove me crazy. I was really turned on. His F spot—I mean, area—was right there on my area. We almost quivered together. It was like in the movie *Cocoon* when that man and woman are in the pool together and he says, 'If this is foreplay, I'm a dead man.' It was very much like that scene. We felt each other on every level."

Her husband added, "Never, never in a million years would I have thought this posture was anything special. I can tell you now that it just cannot be described. We insert the penis sometimes, I ejaculate sometimes, we have orgasms, psychasms, breastasms, I tell you, we just merge. With the music and the light, it is just another world for us. If you would have told me that erection or insertion was not necessary weeks ago, I would have thought you were crazy. I see now that it's not really the posture, it's the whole system.''

Try the posture of the future. You cannot do it wrong, because the two of you are doing it, sharing it, changing it, learning it together. The posture of the future, the marriage of the future, will evolve from a new emphasis on intimacy and the integration of sexuality into the whole of the marital system.

Step Six: The Marital R&R Trip (Recommitment and Re-Creation)

I often tell couples to select a weekend soon, a time when you can go away together and not receive any phone calls. You may not take your watches. This is a trip only for one another and based on the marriage, not the clock. You can ask for wake-up calls and check clocks anywhere, but on this trip, no watch-watching. You must make sure that all of your concerns about home are taken care of. Start planning now, because this trip is difficult. This will be your R&R trip, a trip to recommit to the marriage and celebrate its re-creation. Couples generally appeared eager but confused.

''Do you mean just a weekend away?'' asked the husband. ''We do that often.''

No, this is not just a weekend away. This is a re-honeymoon trip, a special marital trip of intimacy. A celebration. Each partner should buy a gift for the other that costs a total of less than five dollars and will last forever. You will exchange this special symbolic marital gift with a personal note during the trip. I would like each of you to write out special new vows to one another that you will exchange. The selection of the gift is important and difficult. The price limit will cause you to think about this.

This couple selected Toronto for their trip. They had been there several times, usually with friends. They selected a play to attend and a deluxe hotel. Your own trip could be down the street, just so long as you are alone together away from everyone and everything. When you check in, make love before doing anything else. Sexual intimacy should not be the last thing, but the first thing. Remember your daily walks, remember the posture of the future, and remember to set aside time for your own private ceremony of recommitment.

One wife described the ceremony she shared with her husband.

"We lit a candle, but the damn smoke alarm went off. We decided to turn off all the lights and open the drapes so the city lights would light our room. We got in the posture of the future, naked, but we didn't touch genitals. We looked at each other. I don't know how long, we didn't have a watch. Time just didn't matter. We shared our vows and we cried. Really cried. We sat closer and held each other. Later we exchanged gifts and little notes."

Her husband added, "She gave me a picture she had framed. Just a snapshot of us at the beach when we first met. Do you know what I gave her? You would never guess. I gave her two things. First, I gave her a cheap little painting of a light tower. She couldn't stop laughing. [Remember the sex word game? This was the creative wife who had a new name for the penis and testicles, the light tower on the rocks.] Then you know what? I gave her a little painting I did myself with a plastic frame. Five dollars doesn't go too far. I painted a picture of our house. Just our house with a big sun behind it. We laughed and cried. We knew we were making memories."

The wife added, "We just sort of nodded our heads when we shared our vows. The words didn't seem to matter." The communication of this couple was on a level beyond words, in a language unique to their marriage, to their love.

Step Seven: Follow-Up for Foul-Ups

No one program changes anything permanently. I told the couples that their treatment began when their visits to the clinic ended. I saw them all several times at intervals until the five-year follow-up, but more important I asked them to conduct their own follow-up. All marriages have severe conflict, disappointment, life-cycle changes, and daily pressures. To cope more effectively with such pressure, mark on a calendar a time for one brief trip every three or four months. This R&R trip does not have to be expensive, but getting away together not for vacation but for marital recommitment is important to continuing the gains you have made in owning and operating your own sex clinic for super marital sex.

Every New Year's Eve, your first and foremost task is to select those dates for follow-up trips to deal with and prevent foul-ups of your super marital progress. Give priority to these dates and schedule work and other obligations around them as much as realistically possible. As I stated in Chapter One, so long as we continue to put marriage last, to allow all other events priority in our life schedule, marriage will continue to reflect this place on our commitment list. Once you have the dates, they should be considered as fixed and as important as any other events that may come up. For super marital sex, these dates should be considered even more important than most other events, a form of marital rebirth-days.

"People seem to get almost angry that we have those dates," reported one husband. "They ask if this is our vacation, I tell them no, and they cannot understand just going away to recommit. Maybe it's a form of marital jealousy, because they tell me later that they wish they could do it. We stopped wishing and did it. One guy at work even said I was more dedicated to my marriage than to work. I agreed, and he almost had a seizure."

His wife added, "Of all things, a woman at work asked if I was trying to make a super marriage. A super marriage. Can you believe that? I am sure she meant it sarcastically, but she actually used the word."

Step Eight: Postal Sex

Another way of following up on your marital learning is to correspond together regularly by letter. Marital therapists and marriage-encounter groups use this technique, and I find it helpful to the couples. The rules are simple:

1. Write a one-page letter only. No typing, so write slowly and clearly.

2. Proofread your letter before sending it. Make sure it reads just the way you want it to.

3. Buy and use your own special stationery for this assignment. This gives the letters a special personal touch.

4. Mail the letter. Don't just give it to your spouse, but send it to him or her.

5. Never discuss the letters. Write to each other about them.

6. Write only from the "I," using "you" only as the object of the verb, not the subject. "I love you, I would like to take you to . . . I would love it if we could . . . etc."

7. If you send a letter about a problem, remember to avoid what I call SSAADD language. Do not use *sarcasm*, *surrendering* comments, *accu*-

sations, *a*ssumptions about motives, *d*emeaning statements, or *d*emands. Tell what you like and want, not what is not happening or what fails.

8. A basic rule is that you must answer the letter you receive within two weeks after the date on that letter (so remember to date each letter). Keep a file of your letters as they are received so that dates can be remembered. If you don't get an answer within four weeks of the date on the letter you sent, you may then send another, but do not discuss the issue or question your partner about the letter. This postal assignment is a supplementary assignment. Don't use it as evidence against or for each other or the marriage.

9. If you get very busy and feel you cannot write to your spouse for a while, tell her or him by letter. Keep this assignment going in the mail, never the bedroom.

10. Change the rules of the letter-writing only by mail.

"I never write longhand and I never write letters," said one husband. "When I tried, though, it really helped me think things out about us. I kept my attention on us. One page was nothing. I could have written much more."

His wife added, "At first I was sending complaint letters or trying to be cute. Now we write only every two months or so and the letters are two pages. We worked all that out by mail. Now we send love letters except for one period when we carried on a several-week fight by mail. When I proofread my fight letters, two things happened. First, I wasn't as angry once I wrote it out, so I had to write again. Second, I found out that I was always angry about feelings, not facts or issues."

Step Nine: "Managed-À-Trois"

There is no spelling error in the title of step nine. I suggest that couples "manage" a threesome. This is not a sex threesome, but dinner or some activity with another man or another woman with the spouse present. It is a chance to involve spouses in business relationships and other friendships that they would not otherwise be a part of.

We live in a time when the complexity and anonymity of life provides temptations for sex outside of marriage. We are exposed to attractive, available potential sexual partners almost every day. We typically relate to these people when we are well dressed, impressive, demonstrating our social or occupational competency, energetic, and without our spouse. In our marital life, we may feel spent, de-energized, dressed for comfort. The managed-à-trois is an opportunity to see our partner at his or her best, being reacted to and reacting to other attractive, interested, and interesting persons. With both husband and wife present, the temptation or competition of outside relationships is reduced, while the positive effects of newness and energizing input from others is available.

If there is someone important to you whom your spouse does not know, super marriage depends upon using this managed-à-trois opportunity to acquaint your spouse with that person. A good marriage does not require this all-inclusiveness of the partner, but super marriage does.

"We went to a play with my friend. He loved it. He walked in with a woman on each arm. We had dinner and talked. It was really fun," reported the wife. "People weren't used to seeing that, and he was proud and smug as hell."

"We went a step further. I went out with a married couple we both know and she did the same last month. It really breaks the pattern and gives us a bunch of new stuff to talk about," said one husband. "It's probably not surprising that the stronger our marriage gets, the more independent we feel. This 'managed-à-trois' assignment is just good fun."

Marriages tend to stick with marriages, to go to the theater, to parties, to dinner as couples. This opportunity provides the chance for a different pattern, for relating outside of the "two with two" pattern. Couples report a different view of their spouse when they see her or him in this context. Couples develop friendships with one person instead of just couples, developing a wider friendship circle outside the confinement of "couples only."

Step Ten: Hiring a Marriage Sitter

"We used to always get a sitter and go out," said the wife. "Now we get a marriage sitter. The sitter makes us dinner and puts the kids to bed for us. We just live in our house. The sitter does dishes and everything. Why waste a sitter on the kids? We should get taken care of, too."

Marriages can learn to enjoy themselves at home as well as outside the home. I assigned a marriage sitter to all of the couples, and they reported it helped in organizing the house and provided a respite from the constant and hectic daily schedule. It's a good idea to get the marriage sitter during the week. He or she might be able to help the kids with homework, too, while you two sit and do nothing or take your walk together. If you are very courageous, you might go up to your privacy place and put in a little practice time on the posture of the future while the marriage sitter protects your privacy for you.

"I think at first it blew her mind," said one husband. "We had her come over one Thursday a month. She made dinner for all of us, put the kids to bed, and answered the phone. We had her do one household chore that we both hated, like fold clothes or something. She stood lookout for us while we were in the bedroom. She never said a thing, but I'll bet her parents heard about those perverts who stayed home when the babysitter was there and even went into their bedroom alone. We got some strange looks from her mother at the grocery store the other day."

It takes courage to make a super sexual marriage. You have to be willing to stand out as a marriage, to break away from the established pattern. After a time, however, my couples found that other marriages were coming to them for guidance. In effect, they were being asked to expand their sex clinic. I told them to avoid telling anyone what to do, but to enjoy their new advisory status by talking about what they did in their own marriage. Tell them anything you like, but keep the posture of the future a secret. Although it does serve as a marital attention-getter, it's a symbol for more basic and substantial marital and sexual changes. It might help others become curious enough to make their own changes and open their own sex clinic.

Step Eleven: Making M-Rated Tapes

If your clinic budget allows, buy a simple black and white video camera and tripod. Make some tapes of your marriage. Make tapes of the family, the kids, the house, the cats and dogs, but most important, make some private tapes of your marriage.

"Are you serious?" asked one wife. "You want us to make our own X-rated tapes?"

That's up to both of you. I am suggesting short tapes of the two of you talking, dancing, doing things together. If you check your family pictures and movies, most of them do not contain pictures of the two of you together. Videotapes of your communication, of dinners and other interactions could teach you much about your pattern of interaction. The videotapes of couples communicating in the clinic are among the most helpful of clinical tools, especially when the couples review them carefully. By discussing the tapes, each partner becomes aware of the other's style of relating, emphasizing self-analysis and the responsibility of each partner to the interaction. The communication styles reflected the reports of sexual styles. Videotapes can be to marriage improvement what X rays have been to medicine. They can be abused and dangerous if overdone, but if carefully used in moderation, they can help us see through a lot of marital problems.

It may be helpful to set up a role-rehearsal tape where there are preassigned situations, such as a vignette in which one or the other partner must announce something to the spouse that the spouse typically gets angry about. Study your marriage and see if there are not some good role-rehearsal patterns you could use.

More couples make their own sex tapes than are willing to admit it. Fifty-six couples of the thousand stated that they did so. Watching yourselves make love can teach much if the couple approaches this opportunity with humor, sensitivity, and mutual concern for intimacy and respect. If one partner is "just going along" with this idea it is probably not productive to do it. M-rated ("M" for marriage) tapes are certainly of much more value than the X-rated tapes of complete strangers, because they are modeling the sex of the first three perspectives while you are trying to learn a fourth. The tragedy of the couple in the introduction to this book was that they were looking to the couple in the tape to find the intimacy that was right there between them, they failed to realize they are the stars of their own intimate drama.

Step Twelve: Building Foundations for Further Growth

We haven't been to church together in so long that I don't think we know where it is.

WIFE

Many of the couples in the super marital sex program found it meaningful for them to attend a religious service together. Where differences in religions existed, couples were asked to visit the church or temple of each spouse at least once. Whether or not formal religion was a part of a couple's life, most husbands and wives had attended church as a child. Revisiting their place of worship as a shared gesture of commitment was of value to the spiritual communication system within the marriage.

I asked the couples to discuss their belief systems, the answer to questions about the meaning of life and death, about their prayers, hopes, and fears. Some couples requested help from a clergyperson at this part of their program, and in some cases the couples returned to more regular involvement in religious services. Whether or not such reinvolvement took place, the rediscovery of the value of discussing philosophies of life and living was a unifying force in the relationships.

If you have followed along with this program, if you have established your own private sex clinic, you have taken the major strides toward finding super marital sex in your relationship. Even if you have tried and found problems, you have moved closer to changing things for the better. As you prepare to read the final section of this book, dealing with the problems of everyday living as they affect sexuality in marriage, remember what the couples came to call the four "P's" of super marital sex clinic operation:

*P*erspective in your approach to sexuality. Remember that your living style, your tendency to run hot or cold at various times, is a key part of your sexual life. A wide perspective on the sexual system is necessary for understanding the fourth perspective of sexuality.

*P*atience with your self and your relationship. All human growth and development takes place over a long period of time and in waves of progress and regression. Be at least as patient with your marital sex as you are with your children and others you love.

*P*ersistence in your attention to the intimacy within your marriage. Starting to improve, then surrendering, getting distracted by other "more important things," or getting involved in "fads" of self-improvement only detracts from the task of building intimacy. Take the tests in this book, follow up on their indications, and stick with the changes you select.

*P*ride in yourself and your marriage is important for continued growth. Our society has valued self-esteem, but marital esteem is every bit as important. If you have tried the many suggestions in this book, you deserve a standing ovation. Maybe a good, strong, long hug would be even better.

Super Marital Sex Opportunity Number Eight

Now is the time to come out of the closet. Let people know about your recommitment to your marriage, to your intimacy. Throw a party and send out announcements. This is not an anniversary party, it is a celebration party. It salutes your marriage and your day-to-day life together. You are acknowledging the fact that your marriage provides the one system that can help you cope with daily problems. It celebrates the art of loving and sexuality in a society that emphasizes independence rather than interdependence. You have opened your own super marital sex clinic, so let it be an open house to celebrate this new beginning.

Ask each guest to bring one handwritten statement about the meaning of marriage. Pin their statements up on the wall as they arrive. Let them all know they have come to a house that values the relationship that built it, that made it a home for the growth of intimacy.

PART THREE

Living, Learning, Teaching and Protecting Super Marital Sex

A terrible thing happened last night . . . nothing!

PHYLLIS DILLER

All sexual activity except for our purely private dreams and fantasies can unintentionally or intentionally offend, disturb, and harm others.

RENÉ MAGRITTE

When we are sexual together now, it is like we don't come "together," we merge with each other. It's like is a part of our living and we merge with every part of each other.

NOTE CO-SIGNED BY HUSBAND AND WIFE

This final section explores the relationship between super marital sex and holistic living. You will learn about the relationship between problems of daily living and ways in which sexuality can help us through our transitional life crises. You will read about twenty of the most often asked questions from people coming to a sexual-treatment program and the most frequent causes of their sexual problems. You will read about several health problems and their relationship with sex. Finally, you will learn how to learn and teach about super marital sex, how to communicate specifically and clearly about a new sex for a new time. You will learn that the ''super'' part of super marital sex refers not just to a new form of sexual pleasuring and mutual sexual enjoyment, but to the relationship of sexual intimacy to the world and to the spirit. You will learn that the treasure at the end of your love map is the sharing far beyond the erogenous zones, into the infinite loving zone.

Chapter Nine

◉◉◉

Sex and Problems of Daily Living: Why Nobody Has a Sex Life

Meet twelve people who almost lost their sexual intimacy for the rest of their lives.

WIFE: "We were having sex. We fell asleep in each other's arms. I just had a feeling, an eerie feeling that I should check on the baby. She was dead. Sudden Infant Death, they called it. We had her and then we lost her. We never made love again."

WIFE: "There is no time left. Kenny's allergies are so severe that he is awake almost every night. Deana sleeps so light that I know she would hear us if we made love. Steven is so emotionally upset, so absolutely hyper, that we can barely keep up with him. We don't have a sex problem. We just don't have sex."

HUSBAND: "My father expects me to take care of him. My mother would have expected it. He lives three doors down, and I take food to him. He is getting senile, and there are times that I have to dress him or he would go out naked. I take care of him, and it's worse than another child. You add that to my family and my job and sex is about nonexistent."

WIFE: "Now that I finally have my own career, every second counts. I take a lot of work home, and when I'm not working, I talk with the kids. I know I neglect my husband. I have to run twice as fast just to stay even. When you are a woman and a CEO [chief executive officer], you have to prove yourself every day. I'm just too exhausted to have sex most nights. Even when we have it, I am usually thinking about a damned work problem."

HUSBAND: "I really think sometimes that we could end up broke. My wife makes much more, I mean much more, than I do, and if she didn't, my teacher's salary would never keep us living like we do. Ever since she started making that money, our sex life changed. The roles are just different. I know it sounds small of me, but I just don't have the pride, the assertiveness I should have with her in our lovemaking. She's like my superior. I even hate it when she is on top."

WIFE: "I need friends. He complains that I am always on the phone, but I really give them support and they help me. He thinks I am more into them than into our marriage. He said he waited up one night until midnight while I talked to Cindy. He just stopped wanting sex and he says it's because I am distracted and ignore him. He resents my involvement with anyone but him. It takes away my respect for him."

HUSBAND: "I golf. I would golf at night with a coal miner's hat on if I could. She doesn't golf. She isn't even athletic at all. She is angry because she wanted to make love Saturday morning and I was late for a golf game. It's my only recreation, my only escape, and I think she is just jealous. She should find her own interests."

WIFE: "This is our third move in five years. New friends, no old friends, no family, new schools, new stores, same old house problems of moving in again. You can't spend much time making love if you are never really unpacked. Would you believe that one night I just could not find my diaphragm. I had packed it up somewhere and started tearing through every box in the house. When I came back empty-handed, he was mad and told me to forget the whole thing."

HUSBAND: "Everybody jokes about retirement; the old gold watch routine. Well, I just don't know. I lost my energy with this early-retirement thing. I worked twenty years for this, and now it all seems kind of empty. We don't have sex and we haven't had sex. As soon as retirement neared, I lost my reactions and my sex drive. If it's in my head, I still can't do a thing about it. I'm in sexual retirement, too, I guess.''

WIFE: ''You said to schedule sex. You said to get up an hour earlier. We did and we do, but now the hour is all used up. Any time we have gets sucked right in. We really don't have time for sex. We really don't have much time for doing much of anything. I swear, someone once said that life is eighty percent maintenance, and for us, it's more like ninety-eight percent.''

HUSBAND: ''Now I have to file my taxes four times a year. I have to go to school conferences, doctors' offices, kids' activities, business meetings, call repairmen, pay bills, and it is all so frustrating. The school, the IRS, the dentist, and the plumbing and heating guy all screwed up on the billing. I have written four letters to the phone company about a bill on a phone I don't have, and now I'm getting a penalty charge on this stupid bill I don't even owe. What's worse is I can't talk to anybody. When I do, they don't seem to give a damn. They even criticize their own company. I am so distracted and trapped that it's no wonder I can't come during sex. I just feel all uptight.''

WIFE: ''After twenty-seven years of marriage, I still go to church alone. We don't even talk about it anymore. He hated the church and I love it. It has always been a part of me. He wants sex but I can't do the things he wants to do. If he can't even go to church with me, how can he expect me to make love with him? It's cheap, just cheap thrills. If he loved me, he would be part of my life and my religion. I can't respect a man who doesn't honor his faith, any faith.''

These twelve quotes illustrate the ''dirty dozen of daily living,'' twelve general problem areas that get in the way of sex. Any hope for super marital sex depends more upon our living than our genitals. No one really has a sex life. We have *one* life, a life we lead as a part of a system, and the twelve problem areas below can be transitional or even permanent blocks to our intimacy.

Try to match the problems below with the statements of the spouses above.

Sexuality's Dirty Dozen

1. Loss

2. Parenting

3. Parenting parents

4. Work or career problems

5. Financial problems

6. Balancing outside relationships with marriage

7. Problems fitting recreation into relationship

8. Relocating, moving to a new home

9. Problems with transitional life phases

10. Insufficient time or poor time management

11. Counterproductiveness and ineffectiveness of institutions

12. Difficulties in living and loving according to morals, values, attitudes, and beliefs

The husbands' and wives' quotes were reported in the same order as the problems list above. This list represents some of the major obstacles to super marital sex. Go through the list one more time and assign points for your marriage on each item on a 0-to-10 scale, with 0 representing no such problems now and 10 representing severe problems in that category. Talk it over with your spouses and decide on a number value for each item.

The average score for the thousand couples on this test was 68 points of a maximum 120 "sexual stress points." The average for four thousand other couples who took this brief test during some of my lectures was 53. The couples found it helpful to convert this score to a percentage by dividing their score by the total possible 120 points, resulting in about 44 percent of possible sexual stress points for the lecture groups who were not coming for specific sexual help and 57 percent for the clinic group. At five-year follow-up, the clinic couples averaged a score of 24, or 20 percent. Their stress points were significantly reduced because of time, treatment, improved sexual life, or change in life circumstances. I have never seen a couple accomplish super marital sex without significantly reducing their percentage on this test. This chapter is about ways in which you may reduce this percentage together as another step to super marital sexuality.

I tell my patients to remember three "grabbing" techniques when facing life's transitional problems. These techniques include *supporting* each other, *holding* on to your sense of humor, even at the worst of times, and *clinging* to your belief system and the faith that your super marriage will be able to cope. Remember these factors as you review the twelve problems below.

Losing, Loss, Lust, and Love: Death, Endings, and Sexuality

> I felt anger. When my uncle died, when he died so quickly, so suddenly, and he was so close to me, I just got angry. I couldn't cry. It's sick, but I wanted to screw, screw all night long. I feel so guilty that the night he died I just wanted sex.
>
> WIFE

Grief is a natural response to the end of a bond that lasted long enough to leave one of its members intensely alone. It is a natural physical and emotional reaction to bereavement. It always involves protest of the loss followed by some form of surrender and, we hope, adjustment and resumption of personal and social growth and development. All of us have felt it, but little is written of the impact of grief on sexuality.

Any strong emotion results in alteration of body chemistry. The master organ, the brain, alters the entire neurohormonal system whenever we experience strong emotion, and grief is one of the strongest emotions possible. The couples reported that grief had a distinct and traceable impact on their intimacy patterns. Here were the most frequent patterns of the sexual impact of grief:

LUST REACTION: Although it may seem incompatible with grief, lust can result from loss. As if symbolically attempting to re-create, to produce, to generate at a time of absence, emptiness, and loneliness, some of the spouses reported a strong need for sexual release at the time of a death or other loss. The buildup of stress chemicals may play a role in this reaction, as does the excitation of sudden change and challenge to the life system. Sex may be one of the ways some persons attempt to discharge their grief and the toxicity of built-up tension and stress.

If there is a supporting partner available who understands this temporary state, this form of heightened sexual activity can be therapeutic. If the partner feels used or is critical of the bereaved partner, breakdowns in communication and sexual distance can occur.

One of the seldom discussed dimensions of losing a spouse is the "lust response" that comes with psychophysiological shock in the absence of any acceptable outlet for its expression. Bereaved spouses are as much as twice as likely to become ill themselves in the aftermath of their loss, and a part of such illness may come not only from life-style changes and other emotional consequences, but from sexual frustration and related guilt.

LOVE REACTION: Loss can emphasize the value of the presence of others, and the bereaved spouse may turn to the partner for a renewal of intimacy and love. If the partner is puzzled by such a need, by a request for romance at this time of sadness, or if the partner overtly or covertly rejects such a longing for love and its manifestation through sex, hostility and anger can result, worsening the grief reaction and even jeopardizing general health.

Sometimes the grieving partner "tests" his or her own relationship for love at the time of loss, making sure his or her most important source of social and intimate support is still intact. An unsuspecting partner may "flunk" this love test, never knowing that he or she has been tested, and the grieving partner sinks further into depression at what he or she sees as yet another loss.

SEXUAL WITHDRAWAL: Bereavement brings with it a range of physical and emotional reactions. Nausea, disequilibrium, muscle and joint pain, chronic headache, sweating and chills, bowel and urinary disruption, and other symptoms of bereavement are not uncommon and may delay return to sexual intimacy.

Emotionally, guilt or self-blame regarding the loss may result in a self-imposed compensatory celibacy, a paying of penance for imaginary or real responsibility for the loss. The partner's attempts to break through such withdrawal may be perceived as insensitivity, and the partner may become a target for projection of the blame and self-recrimination felt by the bereaved.

Sometimes a compulsive searching is part of the grieving process; searching for the lost person and the feelings lost because of the bereavement. This cognitive and emotional wandering results in a distractability that represents yet another form of sexual withdrawal. It may show in listlessness, lack of attention, fading in and out of attention, failure to listen, and long periods of passivity and contemplation. This natural phase may be mistaken for sexual rejection for the marital partner.

SPECIFIC SEXUAL PROBLEMS: With the complexities of metabolic and neurochemical reactions that accompany grief, it is not surprising that specific transitory sexual problems can result. Fatigue, failure to eat and exercise, and disruption of sleep and other life schedules can impair sexual reflexes. If both partners are aware that time will usually take care of the problem, sexual function will return to normal as the grieving response diminishes. If, on the other hand, the sexual problem is viewed as "just another crisis related to the loss," it may become more established in the sexual interaction pattern, a permanent side effect of the misunderstood grief response.

LOSS OF SEXUAL SELF-ESTEEM: Grieving is a de-energizing process that must take place whenever a relationship ends. When life energy decreases and the bereaved partner feels weak, drawn, and listless, she or he may also feel that personal sexual attractiveness has been lost. During grieving, there may be a period during which self-care and attention to hygiene, dressing, posture, and general self-presentation are ignored or neglected. The bereaved partner may present this "grieving mask" to avoid intimacy, to hide from what he or she perceives as premature, even insensitive sexual overtures. When others seem unattractive to the grieving person at this time of loss, it is easy to neglect one's own physical appearance.

FEAR RESPONSE: Some of the spouses report a fear of returning to sexual intimacy following a loss. Whenever we experience a death close to us, we question our own mortality, and we may become so focused on the fear and ruminations about living and dying that there is little room for the renewal of sexuality. The intensity of loss can result in a fear of all intensity, including the intensity of sexual intimacy, and fear can replace positive anticipation.

SEXUAL TITHING: Some partners deal with their grief by consciously or unconsciously giving up some of the joy of their own living. Sometimes the sexual area is the area of joy that is sacrificed. One husband had promised in his prayers that if his father was spared from death, he would not continue to have sex with his then fiancée. His belief system, one he was willing to modify prior to the stress of his father's illness, dictated against premarital sex. Following marriage and for the six years of that marriage prior to the couple's treatment in the super marital sex program, no sexual interaction took place.

Other couples report that a percentage of their sex life seemed to end with the loss experienced by one or both of the partners. This "tithing" may not be as overt as in the example of the husband just mentioned, but it is a factor in couples who felt that they were compromising their values sexually and then experienced a loss they perceived as punishment or a "sign" to pay for their indiscretion.

There are many forms of loss other than death and illness. Separation, divorce, a child moving away, placing a parent in a nursing home, or change of job may be perceived as loss, even when there is apparent gain, and may disrupt sexual functioning. Here are some ways to maintain sexual intimacy at times of significant loss.

1. Remember that all of the above reactions are natural parts of the grieving pattern. We all go through them. We must go through them.

2. Just as sex is not separate from life, it is also a natural part of endings. Touch, intimacy, and fulfillment can help soothe the grieving process while allowing it to take its natural course.

3. Medicating away the symptoms of grief can have negative physical and emotional effects. The natural body response to intimate sexuality allows grieving without the numbing effect of artificial substances.

4. As discussed earlier, all love carries within it its own end. The more the loving, the deeper the grief. Seeing life and loving as cyclical does not prevent the pain of loss, but it does allow the hope of new beginnings.

5. Examine your feelings and those of your partner regarding mortality. Discuss your relationship and its future. No one is ever prepared for loss, but the process of losing can be less destructive if it is discussed directly and openly before it occurs. It is just as important to discuss love insurance to prepare for emotional endings, as it is to carry life insurance to prepare for the financial aspects of loss. If you are the bereaved partner, remember that no one else will ever feel the loss as you feel it. Don't expect your partner to grieve to the depth that you do. Invite him or her to be with you during loss.

6. Your partner's sexual needs remain even when you are hurting. Be aware of those needs and be available for sexual expression for your partner. One of the best antidotes for grief is giving, and that extends to the sexual relationship as well. As difficult as this may sound, it is one of the most important things you can do for a super marriage.

7. The emotional and physical symptoms of grieving will diminish. Contrary to popular mythology, there is no set sequence or set of stages for adjusting to loss. Time and touch, the touch of and by a loving partner, are the best that life has to offer at times of death, dying, and loss. We must lose lovers, but we do not have to lose loving.

Parenting, Pressure, and the Posture of the Future

I'd like to know how anybody with kids ever has sex.

HUSBAND

If having sex was as hard to do before we had kids as it is now, we would have never had kids, because we would never have had sex.

WIFE

In a sense, all sex in a crowded home becomes group sex. Privacy, quiet, and confidentiality are luxuries that few families have, and the more loving, open, and involved the family, the less likely it is that the parent can find much time to have open, free, expressive sex.

Here are some of the types of sexual adjustment to kids and parenting that I noted in the thousand couples. As you read these types, remember the words of David Lodge: "Literature is mostly about having sex, and not much about having children. Life is the other way around."

The Sneaks: This is the couple who is ever vigilant for an opportunity to "do it" when the kids aren't around. Their sex life ends up determined by the kids' schedules, with husband and wife sending immediate "urgent" signals when the kids might be gone for a few hours. Unfortunately, the home schedule may be so hectic that even the "sneaks" run out of time before they run out of chores, and this involuntary "sneaking" for urgent sex can disrupt a more natural flow of sexual interaction between husband and wife.

The Parental Celibates: This couple has given up on sexuality, holding out for the time when all children are gone from the home to college or career. By mutual and usually covert agreement, they have decided that the effort to fit sex in secretly is just too tiring, or detracts too much from enjoyment of the experience. There may be a few "celibacy slips" when sexual expression is enjoyed, but these events are few and far between.

The Hostages: This couple has children who covertly control their parents' sexuality. The kids know that the parents have sex, and if the parents are very, very good, and pay the ransom of cab service, snack preparation, junk-food donations, and tolerance of deterioration of chores, the kids will "turn the other way." They may go to bed early and actually fall asleep. Better yet, if teenagers are involved, they may decide to play their music, which guarantees their temporary deafness.

The Defiants: This couple decides to crash head on into sexual liberalism by making love loudly and deliberately while the kids are awake. Unfortunately, one partner usually feels embarrassed and tries to monitor the sexual activity. Pillows over the face to muffle sounds, contortionistic over-the-head arm pushes of the backboard of the bed away from the wall it has been slamming, and frequent coughing, clearing of the throat, turning on of water, flushing of toilets, and increased television volume are some of the maneuvers used. Morning-after cover stories are offered to smirking young sex experts who will probably repeat them to school chums.

As explained earlier, establish a private place to make love and tell children that you love each other and make love and do not intend to keep those facts a secret. This "marital coming out" takes courage, not defiance. Good and effective love education requires openness. If you sneak, lie, and distort your lovemaking, your children will probably do the same with their love life. The rule of thumb is that privacy is not secrecy. What you do sexually in your marriage is nobody's business, but you will never hide the fact that you have a sexual marriage. Such openness may be our last hope for sincerity in the sexual development of our children, for they care much more about what you do than what the birds and bees do.

Don't forget that the posture of the future can be done quietly, comfortably, and with an emphasis on a "sexual telepathy" that few children will be able to tune in to.

Parenting Parents and Pleasing Partners

> He had better make up his mind. He is either my husband or her son. He can't be both anymore.
>
> WIFE

> She is making a love triangle out of this whole thing. She is making me choose between her and my mother. Screw them both!
>
> HUSBAND OF ABOVE WIFE

Even though the elderly are living longer, we have done little to improve their health. They tend to be malnourished, overmedicated, and neglected. We view them as a new national obligation rather than a treasure and a part of our life.

Sexuality remains throughout the life process. There are some physiological changes in the form of slower, sometimes less firm erections and decreased lubrication and some changes in stamina and orgasmic contractions, but sexuality in aging remains intact. The fact that our parents remain sexual and have needs to be touched, loved, visited, talked to, and taken care of spiritually as well as physically has caused problems for some of the couples. Here are some of the responses to attempts to parent parents.

The Caretaker: This spouse assumes the role of medical specialist, advising the parent on all health issues and focusing on the survival rather than the thriving of the parent. Caretakers want to avoid guilt later for not having done enough now, vigilantly monitoring the parents' health at the expense of the intimacy of their own relationship and the intimacy needs of the parent. The Caretaker seems to be attempting to preserve parents more than love them.

The Surrogate: This adult, whose parent is widowed, serves in the role of the lost partner, attempting to meet the parent's emotional and survival needs at the expense of the adult's spouse. The spouse tends to become angry and jealous. Intimacy can be directly affected, with verbal, even physical, battles resulting.

The Nest Filler: This is the spouse who symbolically returns home, fills the empty nest while trying to maintain his or her marital and family life. The Nest Filler returns to "dating" his or her spouse, fitting him or her into a new "home life." The Nest Filler feels guilty when with the parent and guilty when with the spouse. This guilt gets in the way of sex with the partner as the Nest Filler tries to please everyone but him- or herself. The guilt also prevents enjoyment of time with the parent.

The Nest Filler tends to regress, becoming more childlike, dependent on the parent being cared for, and defaulting in their parenting and spousing duties at home. He or she may feel trapped, unappreciated, taken for granted, and overtly or covertly angry at his or her own lack of personal growth.

The Converter: This spouse feels so trapped between the parent and the spouse that he or she decides to have two spouses (parent and the actual spouse, regardless of gender of the parent) or two parents. This distortion of roles results in the parent, the spouse, and the children resenting this alteration of perception. Serious communication and sexual problems can result. The spouse's own children may rebel through school problems, delayed development, or depression. The child may begin to resent the parent's parent, causing a counterreaction by the father or mother, especially since the child may be expressing the feelings that the Converter has repressed. Serious family problems start to brew. Sexual intimacy never flourishes when there are unresolved family conflicts, or when anyone is "converted" to artificial roles.

The couples used the following ideas to confront the problem of parenting parents:

1. The only approach to resolving the multigenerational family is a systems approach. One sibling cannot do the job. Even in the case of an only child, some type of support system is needed. Nobody can do double-duty daddying or multiple mothering for long.

2. The marriage must deal with the parenting-parents issue. If one spouse takes on the responsibility, then the other will end up in resentment or isolation. Talk the issue over and approach it together. The argument that "Well, it's your mother or it's your father" never works. Marriage changes the whole deal. Both spouses owe caring to both sets of parents to a degree of balance that both spouses can agree upon. A key point I have stressed throughout this book is that sexual health, all health, depends on our understanding our lives as inseparable, holistic systems, and the system includes everyone everywhere.

3. Remember that your children can help by "childing" your parents. Get them involved through chores such as driving, calling, visiting, and supporting as their own development needs will allow. Teaching your children

to love your parents and to act on that love is an important sex- and love-education lesson.

4. You cannot provide total health and financial care for your parents and still raise and develop your own family. Unless you are very well off financially, you will have to spend time planning with someone who knows the laws, insurance, Social Security, legal rights of the aged, and related issues. Time spent in such planning is as much a part of showing love for your parent as actually providing direct help yourself. It has been said that anyone who has enough money is not taking good care of his or her family, and parenting parents illustrates the validity of that statement.

5. Finally, there is no amount of caring or helping or loving that will ever prevent you from feeling you could have done more. All children feel some guilt when they lose a parent. It is a natural part of grieving. Don't work yourself and your marriage to the bone trying to do everything humanly possible so that you will have "a clean conscience." If you love your parent or parents, do what you can do for them and with them, and then invest your love and energy in your own marriage and family. You have given your parents the greatest gift of all, the gift of passing on the love they gave you.

Clarence Darrow wrote, "The first half of our lives is ruined by our parents and the second half by our children." In our present society, life is no longer so divided, and parenting parents is a major challenge of living today. Bette Davis reminded us, "If you have never been hated by your child, you have never been a parent." Remember that the reverse of her statement is equally true.

Working in Sexuality

> I think the only people who can have a career and have a lot of sex must be prostitutes. They do it for their living. I have to make a living and then try to make time for sex, and there isn't much of that at all.
>
> WIFE

Working and the workplace are two of the major sources of stress in our society. They take a physical and emotional toll everyday of our lives, sometimes leaving us with little time or interest in other areas of daily living. My interviews indicated that, unless we are able to enjoy our work, little else will bring us happiness.

Although there were exceptions, men interviewed tended to view their work as closely related to their self-esteem. They often felt sexually invigorated by some "conquest" or "victory" at work. "I can tell when he's made a big sale," said one wife. "He comes home horny. He wants victory sex.'' "That's true," responded her husband. "When I'm on my game, I want to get on her." Even though both partners laughed during this exchange, the male success-object orientation is often seen in the work/sex connection.

Women are equally involved in their careers, but they continue to be expected to "add" career or working outside the home "to" their lives. The men interviewed tended to be more supported in their work, and more adjustments were made for their working than was true for women. Women were expected to find more hours in their day, to add to an already heavy home workload. Sometimes token, sporadic chore-sharing on the part of husbands was the only accommodation made for the working wife. The increased frequency of wives working outside the home is more an addition to rather than change in the role of the married woman.

I recently asked an all-male audience how many of their wives worked. Several hands were raised. I then asked how many of their wives worked outside the home. Many of the men were perplexed, even embarrassed at their own sexism, which resulted in their failure to see work done at home as "real work." This same sexism causes many wives to attempt to carry an unhealthy burden of career development, income production, and almost solo home maintenance.

Recent data indicate that over one third of women with master's degrees in business administration "opt out" of the business world. More likely they are "pushed out" when they hit the ceiling of resistance to women in high positions, and confront the inevitable sexist assumption that they, more than men, have "other things" that are more important. An increasing health risk exists for women unless the "Wonder Woman" syndrome of doing it all is addressed. Doing it all can seldom allow for fulfilling sexuality.

"I feel like I'm drained," said the wife. "At work, I get calls about the kids' school and even think about dinners, entertaining, house issues. At home, I hardly have time to think. I certainly don't have much energy left. Sex takes energy, so it gets on the agenda, reported in the minutes only when we can both find some time."

Dr. Susann Kobasa researched what she calls "psychological hardiness." She found that men and women who showed commitment to their own development, felt control over their life, and continued to be challenged by changes in their day-to-day life enjoyed a degree of psychological, even physical, immunity to stress. My interviews supported this, and I extended her "three C's" to "Ten C's of Working and Still Being Sexual." Here is the list as it evolved from the couples' interviews. You might want to score yourself on a 0-to-10 point system for each item, with 10 indicating that you are near perfect on a given item and 0 meaning you do not enjoy or manage that aspect of working at all.

Ten C's of Working and Still Being Sexual

1. Are you challenged by your work? When problems occur at work, do you feel excited and activated rather than overwhelmed and helpless? _____

2. Have you maintained a balance between commitment to work and commitment to self, including family, life, loving, and sexuality?_____

3. Do you have a sense of control over your work and family life? Does that sense of control allow you to feel that you are running you instead of being run by things and events?_____

4. Do you feel competent at work and still maintain a feeling of competency at home? There was a direct correlation between feelings of competence in bed and at the desk or counter at work._____

5. Have you maintained a sense of concern for your job and those persons you service? Are you still concerned for the job you do? Some people deal with work stress by adopting an ''I could care less, I put in my time'' approach that only worsens their stress and may affect their sexual life as well._____

6. Have you maintained your ability to communicate at work and home both professionally and intimately? Some people spend all their communication energy at work, leaving little for intimate exchange with the spouse. _____

7. Do you feel a sense of connection between work and home? To be healthy, life must be an intergrated system. Are you able to integrate working and loving, sharing feelings about both in both places? Being a ''completely different person'' at work than at home is one clear symptom of increasing stress and an ineffective strategy of adjustment to one place or another. _____

8. Are you careful both at home and at work? If you find that you are having several little accidents, forgetting your turn-off on the expressway after driving the same way for years or slamming your finger in the same kitchen drawer, you are showing signs of poor balance between work and loving. Are you aware of being careful?_____

9. Do you have a feeling of being complete at the end of the day? Things are never done, but you should have a feeling of closure when the day ends instead of thinking about tasks left undone or new tasks coming up. _____

10. Would your colleagues and your family, particularly your spouse, describe you as cheerful? Is your report of "Good Morning!" when starting the day at work or home a greeting or a ritual? "When I walked into work," reported one of the wives, "Sam came up and said, 'Hey, a smile is the one curve that straightens everything out.' He's lucky I didn't straighten his mouth out with a punch." Are you more cheerful than this wife? Happiness and the desire to be intimate are interconnected. _____.

Any less than 80 total points, and work or career is probably getting in the way of a super marital sexual relationship.

All ten C's are needed for super marital sex, so practicing them at work and in daily living is necessary if they are going to be present in marital intimacy. Here is the same list presented as the C's apply to super marital sex. Use the same 0-to-10-point scale and see how your scores compare.

Ten C's of "Coming" Together

1. Are you still challenged by your sexuality, putting effort into invigorating and energizing sex at least as much as working at your work?_____

2. Are you committed to your sexual life, to keeping it alive by scheduling it if you have to, finding and making time for intimacy?_____

3. Do you have enough control over your sex life to make sure both you and your partner are having your needs met? (Have you prevented work from controlling your sex and marital life?)_____

4. Do you still have your sense of sexual competence, not allowing set-backs at work to become sexual setbacks as well?_____

5. Have you maintained a sexual concern for the intimacy of your marriage? Healthy living depends upon multiple concerns, a concern for work as well as a concern for loving._____

6. Do you still communicate about loving as much as or more than you communicate about working? Are there fewer work war stories than there are marriage love stories?_____

7. Do you feel emotionally connected to your spouse even though both of you might be struggling to develop or maintain careers or jobs? (One wife reported that her husband was "electronically connected to his computer. He gets into that much more than he gets into me.")_____

8. Are you careful of your spouse's feelings, treating him or her with more respect than strangers or work colleagues?_____

9. Is your sexual interaction complete? Do both you and your spouse feel that your needs for intimacy are met?_____

10. Is there still joy, cheerfulness in your intimacy? Have you allowed your sexual relationship to become devoid of emotion or passion?_____

Freud is quoted as saying that the secret of psychological health is "to love and to work." Without either one·of these, we suffer. When one robs the other, we lose both.

For Love and Money

> You would think we would be able to deal with money. There isn't much of it anyway. We spend more minutes on money than we have money. I wish we got paid to worry about money. We'd be rich.
>
> HUSBAND

There are several books that trace the relationship between love and managing money. Carol Colman's book *Love and Money* explores some of the patterns that evolve in marriage related to financial issues. Money seems to be the great quantifier of worth in our society and even in our marriages. Earlier in this chapter you read about the man who had sexual problems because of his wife's higher salary. Several of the couples reported problems in this area.

Here are some of the adjustments couples made to issues of money and sex. Discuss these and the other problem issues in this chapter, remembering that super marital sex is a process, not a goal.

The Banker: This spouse feels that his or her entire self-esteem is measured by his or her control of the family finances. He or she controls the checkbook, saving books, all shopping, buying, allowances, and investments and seems to get more enjoyment out of a balanced checkbook than a balanced love life. Super marital sex cannot survive if partners exclusively assume any one marital task.

The Client: This is the spouse who is married to the Banker. He or she may criticize the lack of money, poor investments, missing checks, the size of the grocery bill, but make little effort to share the financial responsibility. The Client defaults financially, and so ends up defaulting sexually, feeling unfulfilled but helpless to correct the problem because the spouse "is responsible."

The Absentee Landlord: This spouse earns and provides most of the family money, turns it over to the partner or "broker" who is assigned more than assumes the task of money management. The Absentee Landlord feels his or her job is to provide and the spouse should manage. His or her contribution is in the form of a "buy-off'' that purchases personal freedom from other marital obligations. In the process, this spouse loses contact with the real financial world, even the real everyday marriage and family world. One husband stated, ''Where in the hell did all that money I gave you go? You took almost fifty dollars to the grocery store and came back with one bag.'' Obviously, this Absentee Landlord spouse has not been to the store in the last decade or he would realize that the paper bag itself is a luxury. This same lack of involvement or awareness seems present in the sexual life of such a couple.

''I give her sex. We have it as much as or more than anyone else, I'm sure. What more does she want?'' This husband felt that sex was a form of donation, an investment made and left to take care of itself. He was absent not only financially, but intimately.

The Impoverished: This is the spouse who, no matter how much money there really is, complains about impending financial disaster. Maybe he or she grew up poor and now feels that everything can ''crash'' in a matter of seconds. The Impoverished feels any purchase that is not life-maintaining is extravagant. This same insecurity is noted in the sexual life of the couple, with fear blocking much of the spontaneous affection.

The Gambler: This spouse shows little concern for money. He or she may spend far beyond the couple's income. The more responsible spouse becomes angry and frightened, and these emotions extend to sexual interactions in the marriage. The irresponsibility and oblivious risk-taking of the gambler erodes the trust necessary for mutual sexual fulfillment. The gambler may even overspend as a not so subtle form of punishing or getting the attention of the spouse.

The Accountant: This spouse feels that money is the measure of meaning in the marriage. The more spent on himself or herself, the more love there must be. When such an emphasis on the tangible characterizes a relationship, the less measurable and subjective aspects of sexual intimacy can suffer. Here were some of the recommendations given to the couples regarding the money issues. Remember the warning of Jackie Mason, who said, ''I have enough money to last me the rest of my life, unless I buy something.''

1. Money is a token, a token for trading a measure of some of your work or earnings for things you want or need. It has no meaning other than that. Do not allow its amount or use to symbolize anything more than that.

2. If you're fighting over money, you're not! When you fight over money, you are doing so because money provides a target for interpretation, misinterpretation, and "proving something." Look deeper, because the money is not the issue.

3. Money relates directly to roles in the marriage. If there are problems with money, consider altering the roles. All role changes should be for a prearranged period of time followed by scheduled reassessment of how the new roles worked out.

4. When money problems are severe and arguments are getting bitter, sex will no doubt suffer. This is the time to reconsider goals, hopes, and aspirations for your marriage. When such dreams are vague, unshared, or forgotten, money and money issues seem to take on a life of their own. Couples may have a financial plan, but they need a shared life dream, too.

5. The key first question in money management in marriage is not "Can we afford it?" or "Who will pay for it?" or "Who's money is it?" but "What do *we* want to do and what do *we* need to do it or get it?" After this question is discussed, then money can be the focus as a shared problem, a means to an end. Most couples want money to be able to "do" things, to "buy" time, rather than "get" things.

6. In a super sex marriage, all money is "us" money. It comes from and belongs to the marriage. Any other arrangement will prevent the type of intimate trust necessary for the type of sexuality that I am discussing. For a super marriage, all major purchases must be mutual, with intense shared review and discussion. Deferring to a partner on major investments will always come back to haunt you. It doesn't matter who knows more about money. What matters is that both of you have feelings, and money issues are never separate from feeling issues.

Love Polygons

> There is no love triangle in our marriage. There are more people involved than that. My wife knows almost everybody in the world. The police should call her if anyone is missing. She either knows them or would know someone who did.
>
> HUSBAND

One of the most difficult tasks for the thousand couples was balancing commitment to their spouse while maintaining outside friendships. Our society seems to divide itself into "married couples" and "single people." When a married person tries to have other married and single friends separate form the marital relationship, problems can result.

Each couple has to find its own solution to how many "other" people can be included into the marital life. There were two major dangers that seem related to this problem in the interviews.

First, when one of the partners is searching for more and more friends or is turning almost exclusively to a "friends advisory group," this outside focus signals marital problems. What needs are being met outside the marriage that cannot be met from within it? Friends are necessary for healthy living, but marriage is the one place for total vulnerability and intimacy. If you are telling your friends things you will not or feel you could not tell your spouse, you will never achieve super marriage or super marital sex, for both of these require exclusive intimacy rights.

Second, if the couple factor is decreasing, with any social event creating more distance than mutual enjoyment, problems may be brewing. When you go to a party, do you see as much of your spouse as you do other people? Or do you and your spouse split up only to "meet up" at a prearranged time to leave? Do you have to search out your spouse and almost drag him or her away from others? Does your spouse seem more "on" and "up" when she or he is with others than with you? These are signs of problems that may require a system re-evaluation.

"I only ask that he gives me what he gives to others. Everyone loves him. I love him, too. He seems to value their love and respect more than mine. He just takes mine for granted. Maybe he just doesn't care anymore." This report from one of the wives illustrates the "polygon" issue. This is not the "love triangle" affair discussed when I reviewed the two types of extramarital sex. A polygon is a many-sided figure with no real base, and the issue here is multiplicity, extent, and priority of involvement with others outside of the marriage, resulting in dilution of intimacy.

Here were some of the recommendations in this area.

1. Your spouse should be introduced to all of your friends at least once. Each of us needs distance and our own chance to be free and be a "non-spouse" once in a while, but super marital sex depends on total disclosure. Make sure your spouse knows everybody you know.

2. Never, but never, criticize your spouse to someone else or in front of someone else. Marriage is for intimacy, and that includes the dignity of both sexual and problem-solving privacy. One angry wife stated, "Unless you want to have sex with me in public, don't try to screw me in front of our friends." Take your spouse with you when out with your friends sometimes. There is no rule that all groups must match up gender for gender, couple for couple. Maybe your spouse could become a different type of friend to

you by seeing your friends and relating to them in different settings. This was the idea behind the "managed-à-trois" assignment discussed earlier.

3. If you are putting more effort into your friendships and into your interactions outside of marriage, stop and ask why. Your primary energy, including your emotional and physical presentation of yourself, should be for the marriage.

4. When your spouse is available, take advantage of it. Time is always a problem, so talking on the phone or spending time with friends while your spouse "waits" can cause subtle and sometimes not so subtle messages of lack of concern or feelings for your partner. Try to schedule most of your calling and visiting when your spouse is not available or when you have mutually planned some time for other friends.

5. You do not have to be inseparable. Go to some couples' parties without your spouse when this seems convenient. One reason for friends is that they provide variety, different points of view and feelings. If one or the other of you feels that you are going to a dinner or party reluctantly or as a favor, discuss the possibility of going alone. Your host or hostess will probably be shocked at first, and rumors of your impending divorce will start immediately. You know better, and that is what really matters. Show off. Show them that your super marriage is strong enough to allow for independence.

I have described six of the "dirty dozen" problems that can affect super marital sex. You and your partner have reviewed each issue together and come up with some of your own plans for dealing with these problem areas. Dealing with loss, parenting, parenting your parents, working and loving, finances, and working others in and out of your marriage are strong challenges in themselves, so take a break here before going over the last six problems. Stand up and hug. If you have some time, have some super sex. You've earned it.

Personal Play and Marital Pleasure: Spousehood and "Spersonhood"

It is always tennis. Morning, noon, and night, it's tennis. He has tennis cuff links and he doesn't even have French cuffs on his shirts. I hate tennis and I couldn't play it anyway because of my knee. I mean it. To him, love is just a tennis score.

WIFE

Balancing our needs for recreation and the needs of our marital relationship is a relatively new concern in our society. The day-to-day pressures of surviving used to take up all the time there was. Now we are told to exercise, to play, to have fun because it is healthy. We do want to play, but how do two people play together if interests and capabilities are different?

It was the rare couple in which both partners were equally involved in a recreational or avocational interest. "He golfs, I drive the cart. I enjoy the scenery, but he never sees it," reported one wife. "To him the landscape is just a place to lose his golf ball." As this example illustrates, sometimes a spouse will try to "go along" and enjoy the spouse's enjoyment, but rarely does this completely fulfill one's own needs for recreation and fun.

Our public schools seldom emphasize couples play. The boys and girls are separated into different gym classes. The activities are typically individual or team sports, seldom a boy and girl playing together. Even in team sports, the individual seems to be the focus in a society that values stars more than constellations, independence and the ability to stand out rather than the important skill of fitting in to enjoy a common purpose.

So how does super marital sex survive the distance that may result by different recreational involvement? One husband reported, "About the only thing we do together is sex. And then, we really have been doing it to each other." Sex therapists typically ask about individual reports of fulfillment, the most popular question being "Are you orgasmic?" Couples are less often asked about their mutual interaction, the results of togetherness. The only hope is to change, or at least broaden, our view of play to include dyads, two persons playing together.

Here are some suggestions for improving recreational time together.

1. Select an entirely new activity that neither one of you has ever done before, even in childhood. There are hundreds of possibilities.

2. Decide what type of recreation suits your "unit." If one of you is very athletic and the other more artistic, the activity will have to stress other skills, leaving these for individual enjoyment.

3. Start the activity together and develop it together. If one or the other partner tends to "get ahead" in most things, make sure you learn together. This one activity is only for the two of you. You can still have your golf, tennis, running, or whatever other activity you may enjoy as an individual.
One wife reported, "We came up with something. It's sailing. We both can't swim, have never been on a boat, and don't like the water. We couldn't

come up with anything, so we picked the one thing most unlike both of us. It's working out slowly. He tried to be the captain and make me crew, but I think we worked that out after he fell off the boat while trying to tell me to be careful. There he was, mouth full of water, his captain's hat floating beside him, and trying to tell me how to save him.''

4. Remember that individual activities are still important. One husband stated, "We have spouse activities that include tennis and walking. Then we have what we call 'sperson' activities, individual things we do with other people. She golfs, I golf, but we're at drastically different levels of ability there. I will never be the golfer she is, so we each enjoy it to our own level with other people more at our level.''

The marriage that plays together and plays separately is most likely to find super marital sex, for the joy and energizing aspects of fulfilling play can enter into the sexual relationship. As you consider this possibility, remember that a mutual involvement in a "mini-career" could also be a form of play. Noël Coward said, "Work is much more fun than fun.''

Relocation and the Misplacement of Sex

> If you have never moved, then you cannot imagine what happens. You literally are spun around. You might want to go to bed, all right, but not for sex. It just becomes a place to hide. At least most times you can find the bed even if everything else is lost or in a box.
>
> WIFE

Almost half of our population changes residence every five years or so. We are a mobile, relocating society. Every psychotherapist knows that moving, changing where you live, is one of the most disruptive of life experiences. I noticed that the inpatient unit at my hospital typically contained patients who had moved relatively recently. The move itself does not cause their emotional problems, but the stress accompanying moving probably exacerbates any propensity to fail to cope.

Early in the super marital sex program, some couples who seemed to be making excellent progress regressed during the five-year follow-up. One factor often mentioned was relocation. They reported an almost complete upheaval across their life experience, and their sexual relationship suffered from either neglect or situational disruption.

At a recent professional meeting on marital and sexual therapy, one of my colleagues questioned the possibility that moving could really cause sexual problems. He felt that such problems were caused by what he called ''deeper-seated problems within the marriage.''

This question misses the point that most problems causing marital and sexual difficulties are ''transitional problems'' common to all of us. To assume that moving is not stressful enough to disrupt sexuality is to fail to realize that any system, particularly a marital system, is affected by change. How the couple copes with the change, and the couple's ability to preserve emotional intimacy even at times of more mechanical, mundane requirements, is a key predictor of the adaptive strength of the marriage.

Moving alters social support systems and parenting responsibilities; it heightens feelings of vulnerability and causes feelings of ''temporariness.'' It is not just the stress of moving that makes relaxed, intimate sexuality difficult, but memories or unresolved issues associated with places and people left behind. The couple may move closer to or farther from one set of parents and may feel resentment. ''I don't really think it was a factor,'' said one husband, ''but when we moved from Boston to Chicago, we were that much closer to her parents, who live in Hawaii. It sounds ludicrous when I say it, but I'll bet it played some part in why she took this new job.'' The lack of communication and trust in this statement was playing itself out in the sexuality of this couple. The wife reported, ''Since we moved, he has been kind of cold, distant. We have sex, but not quite like before.'' If this is what the colleague who questioned the impact of moving meant by ''deeper'' issues being at work when marital problems result, then certainly these are important to intimacy, but this was and still is a strong and loving couple who was disrupted by the move and for whom the issue of moving brought up issues that would otherwise not have been so intrusive.

These are some things to consider if you are contemplating a move.

1. Review all of the positives of where you live now. What characteristics of ''how'' you live where you are would you like to take along with you?

2. Discuss the positives of the move emotionally as well as pragmatically for both partners and the entire family.

3. Discuss the negatives, the fears. Even if your fears seem unreasonable or immature, they are still your fears. By raising them now, you will be better prepared for conflicts that arise later.

4. You will forget something when you move. No matter how careful you are, all moves get messed up somehow. Don't blame yourself or your partner.

5. Don't mix the move with an attempt to purge all of your "stuff." Moving is difficult enough, so don't make the move a complete reappraisal of your marital collection of "things." If you do that now, when you are rushed, you may throw out something you wished you hadn't, and that will make the adjustment to moving just that much more difficult.

6. Try to see the move as a change and not a dumping of a prior life. Homes are emotional feelings, not wood and brick buildings. Talk about the feelings.

7. Don't try to have sex as soon as you move in. "We tried to christen the new bedroom after a day of stacking, moving, and cleaning. It didn't work. We should have just held each other and slept." This report from one of the husbands is good advice and in keeping with the warning never to force or test marital sex. If you are thinking of having sex as a test or for any reason other than joy and intimacy and closeness, don't do it.

8. Assess together what the move does to your support systems. Moves can come to mean new beginnings or cause rehashing of unresolved issues. Attend beforehand to the emotional dimensions of moving and there will be fewer, but still many, problems. As bad as it may seem, this move most likely is only practice. You will probably move again in a few years.

Moving Through Life and Keeping Sexuality Moving

When I left my department-manager job and took over the whole store, everything changed. I felt different. Happy and sad at the same time. I was proud and excited, but sad that there was no going back. I would never be quite like I was before. I know that adjustment affected our sex. I was sort of afraid to have sex for some reason after the promotion. I don't know if it was superstition or not, but it was like I was insecure, didn't want to rock the boat, jinx myself. I got so busy trying to prove to everybody that I deserved the promotion that I never thought about deserving my wife or what she deserved.

HUSBAND

As I indicated earlier, mid-life crises are life crises that are finally getting our attention. There are as many books on transitions in life as there are transitions. Attention to sexual intimacy at times of change, no matter what "stage" we feel we are leaving or entering, preserves and enhances our intimate relationship and helps us through any transition.

I have listed some of the most recent sources of research on transitional life changes and adult development in the notes for this chapter. One of the most carefully researched approaches to adult development is by Dr. Gerald Levinson. He mixes sound research with interesting insights about the fact that development is not just something children do.

I noticed that at every major professional meeting on sexuality, professionals talk about overall life development more than about genitals. They do so because sex and development are one and the same. I have designed my own informal "adult sexual development cycle" that was used by the couples to discuss their own feelings about their sexual "place" at various times in their own lives. These are not steps or stages. Each phase is more like an overlapping spiral within which we move back and forth. Adults, like children, never "enter" a stage. They encounter life challenges and cope using their available resources at that time. So, as you look at each adult sexual cycle derived from my interviews, view them as reciprocal and interwoven, as stimuli for more learning, not places or stages.

SEXUAL PASSAGES: CYCLES OF THE DEVELOPMENT OF INTIMACY	
Early Childhood	Integration of physical and emotional sexual sensations, combining touch with feelings
School Age	Overcoming sanctions against sexual self-worth and enhancing sexual self-esteem
Preadolescence	Developing sensitivity to and for other gender and accepting sensitivity to same gender
Adolescence	Integrating love needs with sex needs
Young Adulthood	Expressing vulnerability and transcending needs to withhold
Adulthood	Learning value of stability and coping with pressures for variety
Mature Adulthood	Enjoying inclusivity, sharing in balance with autonomy and individuality
Aging Adulthood	Remaining creative in balance with accepting and tolerace

The sexual histories and the multiple therapy visits of the couples, as well as the thousands of other interviews of persons coming for sexual help, revealed a pattern of recurring sexual cycles that related to the development of each spouse's love map. Here are the eight cycles briefly outlined. The future of therapy for sexual problems rests in this family and developmental approach more than the discovery of new techniques, postures, and genital reflex controls.

Early Childhood: Pelvis vs. Personal Stage

All of us become aware of pelvic sensations earlier than we are able to recall without extensive and very open self-examination. Think back to your sexual development and you will remember pelvic throbbing, sensations of warmth or tingling in the genital area. Depending on what, how, and by whom you were then being taught and role-modeled, you learned that such sensations were wonderful forerunners of a future of intimacy and fulfillment as an adult, or that these were the devil's own work that had to be controlled as somehow separate from you. Do you recall how you resolved these issues? Were you able to personalize these sexual sensations as a healthy new dimension of the emerging you, or did you or others try to cast them out, group them with the other, somehow nasty adult secrets?

School Age: A Sexual Self or Shameful Sex

Once we entered school, we discovered by the universal peer-group sex-education system that everybody else had sexual feelings, too, even those members of the "other gender." We learned to see our sexual feelings as private signs of our membership in our own peer culture, or we learned that we were different, did not fit, that our sexual feelings were not normal or like everyone else's. Shame was the lesson, shame for what we felt and even who we were, because at this phase of the cycle the sexual feelings are becoming one with the self-image. Those early boy-group, girl-group, and cross-gender-group discussions and explorations and adult reactions to them did much to forge our sexual and personal self-worth.

Pre-adolescence: Bi-Gender Comfort or Gender Fear

If you listen carefully to pre-adolescents today, kids about nine or ten years old, you will hear the word "gay" used quite frequently. We all have sexual feelings about both genders, and all the men and women I interviewed had clear memories of their first sexual encounters and feelings about the opposite- and same-gender friends. We learn to accept our sexual feelings for both genders and the strong ones most of us feel for the opposite gender, or we learn to fear them. In all of my interviews, the stronger the fear of homosexual concerns, the stronger the underlying fear of sexual interaction with the opposite gender. These feelings develop in tandem, and when we or our culture imposes sanctions against same-gender and/or opposite-gender sexual feelings, our natural flow of sexual development becomes disrupted.

Most research indicated that by this age gender orientation is pretty well developed anyway, so fears that same-gender interest will cause "homosexual tendencies" or "perversion" or promiscuity are unfounded. If we cannot accept a range of feeling about everybody, we will always have trouble accepting any feelings about a special somebody.

Adolescence: Feeling It vs. Doing It

Adolescence is so sexually problematic not only because of resistance to allowing our young people to enter our adult world, but because the first three stages of sexual development are difficult for most children. When adolescence is taking place, the focus can be on "doing it" if the sexual self-concept and emotional response to sexual feelings have been disrupted or delayed. In a society that values action over feeling, doing over thinking, acting over reflecting, it is difficult to come through adolescence with an integration of love and sex. We teach our teens to be a man or woman rather than experience their own personhood and the personhood of others. We teach them to fear anything but the strictest of gender division lines.

You have already learned to read your love map and I have discussed these adolescent concerns, but reconsider now your own ability to unite sex with love. Would you say, would your children say, that love and sex are the same? They are, but our society teaches that they are different because our society seems stuck at this developmental phase itself, continuing to separate doing from feeling.

Young Adulthood: Telling It Like It Feels vs. Telling What You Feel Like Telling

You have traced the courtship ritual in our culture, and have learned that vulnerability has received a bad name. Instead of learning to value people because they are vulnerable, fragile, open, and disclosing, we learn to think of them as foolish and immature. We see them trying too hard and showing too much of themselves. A key lesson for super marital sex is to be able to open it all up, to share every feeling as you feel it. The real outside world doesn't allow this openness, but it is available to you in the privacy and safety of your own marriage place. The young adult must resolve this conflict, take the risk, get hurt, bounce back, and eventually learn that only through vulnerability will lasting love and fulfilling sex be possible.

Adulthood: The Saneness of Sameness vs. the Quest for Newness

From early childhood, we learn that new is always better than old or used. Same is not as good as different, unique, or unknown. We learn that variety is the spice of life. At this adult phase of development, we must learn to countermand these cultural orders, to learn to value sameness, reliability, predictability, history, and a long-lasting, predictable sexual relationship.

Somehow a cultural myth evolved that people must "sow their wild oats" before they can "settle down." Sexism has translated this myth to males doing the sowing and females avoiding the reaping. Finding someone to love, to have sex with over a long time does not have to follow anything else. Those people who negotiate through this stage learn the lesson that movement toward love does not have to include a sally into promiscuity.

Mature Adulthood: Us vs. Me

The term "inclusivity" refers to sharing activities and life endeavors. This phase of sexual development requires striking a balance between autonomy and individual identity and finding such identity with someone while he or she is finding his or her own. Watching a lovely sunset can be a strong individual, almost spiritual experience. It can also provide for a sharing, a mental, emotional sharing or telepathy. The balance of independence and interdependence is the challenge of mature adult sexuality.

Aging Adulthood: Making vs. Monitoring

Of course, we are all aging all of the time. This phase of development, the sexuality of our later years, involves making an emotional and cognitive choice between sitting back and allowing sexuality to diminish or continuing to make the effort, the time, the risk to reach out for sexual fulfillment in our last decades. There is nothing in the physical development of the human that precludes sexual activity until death. Who knows what goes on after that?

As we mature, we are able to accept what life is giving and balance that with what we do not want to take. You may have more time in your later years to monitor those who are still trying to save or destroy our world. Watching, reporting, writing, and serving as a watchperson for social values can be a healthy phase of life no less important than the more physically active tasks of younger years. We don't have to sit back, but sit up and take notice. If you don't do it, who will? Younger people are too busy doing things to pay much attention to what they are doing and its long-term impact. They don't have the perspective of the older adult. The same holds true sexually. A slower, less physically vigorous sexuality is not the only sex available during our later years. It is an option all of us should consider at any time in our life.

After you have discussed these phases with your partner, sit back—better yet, lie back—and review each phase silently. Where are you now anyway?

Timeless Loving

> I just don't know where time goes, but it goes somewhere. It moves faster and faster. If you talk to anybody, they will tell you that time seems to be going faster and faster, seasons merging into seasons. No matter what else we do, there just isn't much time for sex if there isn't much time for anything.
>
> WIFE

Our concept of time is tied directly to our concept of life and living, how we view our world, those we love, and what we hope for and expect out of life. I have discussed the time issue in earlier chapters, but there is one central point the couples raised that can help all of us view time in a somewhat different way.

"When we are actually having sex," reported one wife, "while we are doing it, there is no time at all. I mean, time doesn't stop or go, it just isn't. Now, after we have sex, we sometimes lean over and check to see what time it is, but during our sex, that is the only time there is no time."

This wife and other spouses interviewed indicated that sexual intimacy, the total involvement and merging with another person, is not tied to the time dimension. As pointed out earlier, modern physicists, including Einstein and other so-called new physicists, have documented that time is not a concrete, easily measured "thing." It is, rather, a highly abstract concept that depends on where we are, whom we are with, and what we are doing. During super sex, we are with the person we love, doing what we want to where and when we want to do it. Our consciousness is altered. We are more into someone, responding to that someone rather than carried along by the ticks of a clock.

Perhaps time seems to be going so fast because we watch it so much. The abstract, subjective nature of time is reported by the following spouse with cell disease: "I have learned to sit and do nothing or to make love with my husband. Then time stands still or seems to go slowly. When I first learned I had cancer, I started to do everything I could to stay active every moment. I think I was speeding up time, because the more I did, the less time there was. Now just sitting, even being bored, seems to make more time." We do not have to be victims of time if we set the rhythm of our own living.

Whenever you want time to slow down, try some super sex. Make sure you "make time" for this opportunity, then ignore time altogether. As I pointed out earlier, all sexual problems as described by the early sex perspectives were related to a timed orientation to sex. When we free ourselves of this limitation, we have all the time in the world for loving and living.

All disease relates to disorders of time. We are too rushed or too bored. We hurry or we feel trapped. When our blood rushes to keep up with the demands we place on it, our blood pressure goes up. When we eat too fast, our stomach gets sore. When we control time, we control illness.

Another point the couples raised regarding "time for sex" was the issue of priorities. When we divide our life into segments, few of which are related to what we really want to do, we find ourselves watching the clock for "permission" to finally "do our own thing." If we are clear on our priorities, and most of what we do relates to what we want to be doing, time ceases to be the single controlling factor.

I have presented papers at conferences on substance abuse and the relationship between my work with sexuality and drug use. I report that my interviews indicate that much, if not most, of the substanace abuse I have heard about from my respondents relates to their attempts to "buy time," to stretch out and intensify life experience. Even if they seek a "rush," it seems to be in the attempt to get more out of every moment. Perhaps if we all learned to listen for the ticks of our internal clocks, we could take time into our own hands. We could be the hands of time.

Institutional Insanity: The Industrialization of Sex

> Well, as far as I'm concerned, we will never have sex again. You know why? Because we aren't. I mean, we don't exist. There's no us. The insurance company says so. I wrote to them and they said we never were insured with them. I guess I have been sending bills to outer space for these last eight years, then. They are slowly driving me insane, but I could never get into a mental hospital. I either don't exist or I don't have insurance to cover it. One or the other.
>
> INVISIBLE HUSBAND

Most institutions seem to be able to accomplish only with gross inefficency some of what they are designed to accomplish and with remarkable efficiency the exact opposite of what they are supposed to accomplish. Schools cause what some researches refer to as "pedogenic illness," actual mental or physical health problems related to just being in school. Hospitals cause what are referred to as "iatrogenic" health problems, negative effects on health due to being in the hospital. Telephone companies struggle with "disconnections" even though they are supposed to help us connect, reach out and touch somebody. Car companies produce "lemons," banks issue "false statements," and most recently our national government reportedly has been dealing in what some politicians call "disinformation," even though our entire democratic system is based on information.

The only strategy currently available to couples to cope with institutions is to reduce the number of them we deal with and to learn to play by the rules of the ones we must deal with. It may not sound at first as if keeping careful, accurate records has much to do with sex, but only by organizing your own files regarding the complexities of daily living will you be able to free yourself from distractions that can lessen sexual activity and enjoyment.

In the counseling program, couples were taught to do a monthly joint review. The stress of year-end or tax-time record organizations can overpower any sexual interest. The small-step approach helped the couples feel a sense of control over the endless record-keeping and required institutional-response requirements, and such control removed some of the pressure and distractability from their intimate relationship. One afternoon each month, both spouses readied themselves for the frustration of re-creating the past four weeks of activity. Sharing the responsibility reduced blame and guilt, and the monthly adjustments eliminated year-end panic that resulted in family arguments, accusations, and feelings of carrying too much of the burden.

The couples also were taught to share all record-keeping responsibilities. At first, this task was awkward and led to arguments about whose style of organization was best. With practice and patience, the mutual approach took pressure off the marriage. It also lessened the fear of having to deal with such issues alone for the first time should something happen to the partner.

Unless you attend to and plan together for the never-ending institutional requirements of daily life, they will rob your marriage of the opportunity to relax and enjoy itself. A small-step, shared approach worked well for the thousand couples.

Believe It or Not

Chapter Eight discussed the importance of a mutually acceptable belief system that is acted upon daily by both partners. Our daily living style makes little room for beliefs, and clinging to morals that many view as old-fashioned has become difficult. The fear of AIDS has resulted in some people attempting to modify their sexual behavior to prevent illness or death. While behavioral change is necessary during the crisis of AIDS, we should also be busy asking ourselves about the meaning of sexual intimacy. We should be busy not only trying to prevent the spread of a deadly disease, but busy spreading a value system that teaches the emotional and physical immunity provided by mutually pleasing, exclusive sexual intimacy. If we fail to learn from AIDS and other sexually transmitted diseases, another disease will simply replace AIDS after it is conquered medically.

The couples were asked early in the program to make at least one time a week "worship time." It didn't matter what they did during that time, but they were asked to go somewhere and worship living, love, and life together. One wife reported, "You know what we did? We did every church and temple we could find. We took the kids every Saturday or Sunday morning and went to any place of worship. Just sitting there together was relaxing. It was really the only time other than watching television, or going to funerals, or weddings that we have ever sat together quietly, respectfully, spiritually and just were together."

Super marital sex is the most highly advanced, exclusive, high-level form of human relationship possible. It requires attention to all of the dirty dozen. It requires an effort, commitment, and willingness to change first and think about it later. Unlike the first three perspectives of sexuality, the fourth perspective upon which super marital sex is based emphasized a totality of life involvement, a cleaning up of the dirty dozen.

Super Marital Sex Opportunity Number Nine

Start a special one-year "Twelve Problems" program now. Sit down together and put the twelve problems in order from the one problem that least pertains to your marriage to the twelfth problem, which for your marriage is the most difficult and imposing. Write the problems in this order on a calendar. The next month is the first month of your twelve-month problem-reduction program. Work on one problem a month, starting with the "easiest." You are not really trying to solve each problem. You and your spouse are trying to focus on that one problem area during that one month.

Now that you have studied super marital sex and its relationship to daily living, it may be helpful to read about the most often asked questions heard in my sexual-treatment program. By looking at these questions, you may gain more insight into how to apply the assumptions and perspectives of super marital sex to your own marriage. Before turning to Chapter Ten, what would be your first question about sexuality? After reading to this point, how would you answer it? I hope you thought of answering the question as a couple, as a system, because that is the central idea behind the answers to the twenty questions in Chapter Ten.

CHAPTER TEN

☙❧☙

The Twenty Most Often Asked Questions in a Sex Clinic: Super Marital Sex Answers

In an attempt to relieve some of the anxiety and misunderstandings about solving sexual problems, and to illustrate the fourth perspective that underlies super marital sex, I present the twenty most frequent questions asked by spouses in my study. The questions express the innate wisdom and courage of all of the patients, their vulnerability, and their infinite struggle to continue the development of their love maps and grapple with the complexities of marriage.

After reading and discussing the information and tests in the first nine chapters, practice being a sex-therapy team. Answer these together as if the person asking each question had consulted you in the sex clinic you built for yourselves in Chapter Eight.

Just before you get to the list, guess what is the number-one asked question, the single most often raised concern. It's number one on this list of twenty. The other questions are not presented in any particular order, because they were raised at about equal frequency.

1. Why does he/she want more sex than I do?

The "frequency and interest" issue tops the list. The question may be asked in a variety of ways, such as "Why does he avoid

272

me sexually?'' or ''Why am I so much more interested in sex than she is?'' or ''Why am I always the one who has to start it off or think of it?''

2. Why won't he/she do oral love (fellatio/cunnilingus)?

3. Why does he/she have a ''fetish'' (for an object or activity)?

4. Why does or doesn't he/she get turned on to pornography?

5. Why can't I (he) slow down my (his) ejaculation?

6. Why can't I (she) come quicker? (And why can't I get and stay erect or wet?)

The ''sexual reflex failure'' questions were asked in many forms, but all contained the same concern for the breakdown or change in a natural sexual reflex, including pain in intercourse.

7. Why can't she (I) come in intercourse?

8. Why can't we come together?

9. Why does he/she talk (or not talk) during sex?

10. Why won't she let me (why does he want to) have anal sex?

11. Are you sure he/she isn't homosexual?

12. Why is sex so much better on vacation or when we are away from home?

13. How can I have sexual enjoyment when it goes against my religious principles or upbringing?

14. Is he/she having an affair (and that is why there is a sex problem)?

15. Can I ever get over the sexual abuse I experienced?

16. Does PMS (or other menstrual issues) affect sex?

17. Isn't that sex fantasy sick?

18. Isn't masturbation very bad (or very good) for you?

19. Why am I not sexually attractive to my spouse (or how could I ever be as sexually attractive as she/he would like)?

20. Is this normal? (Whatever ''this'' is.)

Even though it will take some time, sit down and try to answer each question out loud as a couple. Discuss it first before you give your answer. Keep your answer brief, related to the fourth perspective of super marital sex if you can, and be as direct as possible. If the question is too vague (and they all really are), restate it to a form you can answer.

Here are my answers to each question. I have included the specific question as asked by one of the spouses and tried to select a typical question in each of the twenty areas. I have highlighted the super marital sex rules that apply to each situation.

1. "Why am I always the one to start sex, to make the gesture or the first step? I always do it. He responds most times, but I seem to be the one who really wants it most. Why can't he start it sometimes? Why doesn't he want me like I want him? Why is his sex drive so much lower than mine?"

ANSWER: It's not, because the issue is not sex drive at all. We have to refine this question before I can answer it. We have to find out what "always" means, we have to find out how you both feel beyond the actual sexual gestures, and we have to get more information on the differences between wanting, needing, interest, arousal, excitement, and other aspects of sexuality. Once we get all of that information, you may find that it doesn't matter who starts it just as long as both of you enjoy it. You also will probably find that the entire sexual-response system changes over time, and your roles will change along with it. Overinterpreting what is happening now neglects the years of changes in sexual interaction that take place in marriage. That's one of the advantages of marriage over other short-term sexual relationships. There is always time for change. Interpreting sexual motives and feelings is always dangerous. *Remember the super sex rule that you will feel as you behave, so patterns of behavior can dictate feelings, and feelings can be changed by behavioral pattern change.* Finally, remember that you are starting fresh, are going to be reintroduced to one another sensuously, so who knows what new patterns of invitation and receptiveness might develop. There is nothing wrong with either of you, but your system of interacting sexually can change in directions that both of you prefer. Look first at what is happening between you, not what might be going on within each of you. That's where you can make the real progress that can actually change how you feel.

2. "I love it when he kisses my vagina and my clitoris. I have my best orgasms that way. He won't do it anymore. He says it smells and tastes bad. Does that mean I will never be able to have it with him?"

ANSWER: If by "it" you mean cunnilingus, then, yes, you will be able to enjoy it with your husband. Based on what you just shared, make sure you do not have any related health problems that could account for any unusual odor or taste. Check out your husband's health, too, because taste and smell are interactional and depend on two people. Changes in either of you, some type of reaction between you might, although not likely, be getting in the way. *A super marital sex rule is that both partners in the marriage must get everything they want sexually. That's what makes it super sex, not compromised sex. Another rule, though, is that all change takes place by small steps, steps that are approximations,* in this case something like cunnilingus, such as kissing the thighs, stomach, and pelvic area and gradually learning or relearning to enjoy this activity mutually. Talk further with your husband about his feelings about fellatio and the issue of reciprocity of oral love. I know it doesn't seem possible that both partners can really get everything they want, but the small-step process usually leads to a new system of relating that pleases both partners in ways they might not have thought of before.

3. "Why does he have this fetish for doing it doggy-style? He wants to get on me from behind. It's all he ever wants to do. Why is it such a thing with him?"

ANSWER: *A rule of super marital sex is no problem is just with him or with her.* It will help if we phrase the question a different way. Why do you find yourselves in conflict over the frequency of one posture? This question raises several mini-questions, such as how you both feel physically and emotionally about the posture and about postures that are not used and how and why this one posture became so frequent. One more thing. A posture is never a fetish, and people don't "have" fetishes. They behave in various sexual ways that involve a range of stimuli. When one stimulus preference gets in the way of mutual enjoyment, there can be a breakdown in intimate communication. Remember that sexual preferences, even very strong preferences, are not fetishes as long as they do not physically or emotionally harm the partner. When a preference for something becomes a substitute for intimacy, professional help may be necessary on an individual basis first before working on the marital relationship. What you describe is not a perversion. It is a temporary mispositioning within your sexual interaction, not within him or you, that is correctable through open communication.

4. "I think porno is the most humiliating, sick, pathetic junk in the world. She would watch it all night. She gets turned on to it and even wants to try some of the stuff. She reads those sex magazines and gets all turned on. Why does that stuff get her?"

ANSWER: That stuff doesn't "get" her. She is not responding just to the erotic material. Her arousal, as yours, comes from within, and something about some of this material touches a part of the love maps we discussed. Sometimes just the fact that this material is forbidden is part of the arousal factor. If she feels isolated from you because of it, this isolation will not diminish her interest in it. There are two options here. One is to explore the possibility of setting up your own mutually accepted "erotography" collection, one that you can both accept without labeling each other or criticizing each other's preferences. Second, *a super marital sex rule is that not all sex has to be shared sex.* If you cannot, and you certainly do not have to, develop a tolerance or even enjoyment for some of the material she finds arousing, then you should encourage her to enjoy the material in privacy, without overt or covert censure. Her arousal is a part of her and your marriage. It is not determined by or corrupted by this material. The sex you have together is just yours, no matter what factors might have resulted in arousal.

5. "I can't hold back. No matter what, I come. Isn't there something I can do to hold back until she finishes at least?"

ANSWER: Concepts such as "hold back," "finish," and "coming" are leftovers from old ideas about sex that emphasized the mechanical, reflex parts of sexual response. If you mean by "coming" ejaculating, then there is much you can do to ejaculate when you want to. Making sure your bladder is empty before sexual activity will help, and learning to thrust with your whole pelvis instead of squeezing the muscles of the buttocks together and tensing the area between your legs is another idea. Most important, however, are *two rules of super marital sex. First, since ejaculation is the body's reflex to arousal, your whole life-style affects that body response.* If you live fast and pressured, you are setting the stage for all body processes to accelerate. Slowing down in living is as important as slowing down in loving. Second, a posture in which your most sensitive area of the penis, the F area, is contacting your partner's most sensitive area, the C area, is less likely to throw off the timing of this reflex. The posture of the future will help in this regard. And don't forget, orgasm and psychasm are different. *Fo-*

cusing on coming or not coming only leads to more focus and less *fun*. Since psychasm is emotional and mental, it is impossible to think or feel too soon.

6. "It takes me forever to climax. I get close, then fade away. Get close again, then fade away. After a few times of that, then I don't get close. I just fade away. How could I climax sooner so my poor husband doesn't have to work so hard and hold back so long?

ANSWER: Probably the worst word in the sexual vocabulary is "climax." It has become at the same time a goal, a purpose, and an end of sexual activity. *A super marital sex rule is that the journey should be as important as or more important than the destination.* Learning to focus on what is happening instead of where it is leading you will help. The physiological reflex or orgasm, like any human response, always involves an ebbing and flowing of sensation, of getting close, then not so close, then close again. What you report is perfectly natural. That's the way all body processes operate, and sex is no different. Learning to enjoy the fading will also help, because there is no need to follow a "one way only" sexual system. If you want to experience an earlier orgasmic reflex as part of, but not the goal of, the sexual interaction, there are a few things to remember. First, learn about your sensitive areas, the C and G areas. Learn what type, speed, intensity of stimulation you like and teach it to your partner. Some people report a "withdrawal from the edge" response when they get close to pelvic contraction. Practicing alone to go over that edge can help, but most important, psychasms can help take you over. Remember your capacity for both types of response and pressure will reduce. Pushing yourself when at the edge only causes more withdrawal. Letting the edge draw you over, letting the psychasm carry you over, can also be learned.

7. "I never come in intercourse. Why not? My husband sure does."

ANSWER: Many women do not have orgasm in intercourse. Most men seem to. Not having orgasm in intercourse is not a malfunction. Having pelvic contractions in response to the penis in the vagina is not always easy, because your most sensitive areas, the C and G areas, may not receive enough stimulation for the reflex to occur. Your husband may be having easier pelvic contractive reflexes in response to coitus because his F area and even R area are receiving intense stimulation. Of course, you could have psychasms, because that depends on consciousness-altering with your partner, not just pelvic reflex. It may be that women have more trouble having orgasms in coitus, but more often have psychasms, and that for men the reverse may be true. Talk it over with your spouse. The posture of the future helps both of you receive an equal amount of genital stimulation, and that should help with your concern, too.

8. "Why can't we come together? We have tried every trick in the book. We never climax together."

ANSWER: Nobody ever comes together if by that you mean simultaneous pelvic muscle contraction. If it does happen, it is rare and an accident, mere chance and luck. The effort to accomplish this mutual reflex would be like trying to sneeze together. You might be able to do it, but you would wait a long time, and even if you did it, you would wonder why. Trying to have pelvic contractions together only gets in the way of enjoying psychasms together, which is much more satisfying because they are much longer and easier to share. Remember that orgasmic contractions last less than fifteen seconds. It makes little sense to spend most of the sexual encounter to synchronize your fifteen seconds. *A super marital sex rule is that where you are going together is much more important than trying to end together.* It's too bad the word "climax" was ever used. A better word might be to "preamble" together, to start instead of end. You might try using a less motion-oriented vocabulary of "come," "get," and "do" in favor of the more experiential terms of "share," "feel," and "be."

9. "Why does she talk like that in sex? She says things that just send chills through me. It's not her talking. She seems possessed or something. It's dirty talk. It's a turn-off."

ANSWER: One of my other patients once asked why her husband yawned so loudly. The answer to that question is the same as the answer to this one. We all express ourselves differently. The words that bother you so much are just expressive sounds. They mean nothing about you or her; they are reflexes just like any other. Such expression is arousing or exciting to some people, but if these words bother you, suggest the words you might like to hear. It will take some time, but such words might work their way into her "reflexive vocabulary.'' Remember that the words are reflexes, not messages, and maybe you won't be so bothered. It's a compliment to you, really, that she feels comfortable and safe enough to let loose, to be free in her sexual reflex vocabulary.

10. ''He wants to put it up my butt. I hate it. It hurts. Why would anybody want to do that?''

ANSWER: Even though the rectum has connotations in our culture that make it seem dirty and corrupt, it is actually a very sensitive area. You know that, because you know how much it hurts you when he tries to enter you there. There is nothing unnatural about anal penetration. It is purely a matter of two things, preference and knowledge. The issue of preference can be addressed only by open communication. The issue of knowledge may help in this situation, because the facts may help you both to come up with a solution to your differences. The tissue in that area of the body is not only sensitive but can be damaged easily. Lubrication is important, so if you ever decide to do it, use a well-lubricated condom. Infection can be a problem, too, so make sure there is no cross-stimulation from the rectum to other areas of the body. Finally, it takes practice and cooperation to accomplish penetration of the anus. Practicing with slight insertion of the little finger and moving on to more and more penetration can help, and learning to relax the muscles in that area facilitates entry. Super marital sex rules indicate that the small-step approach can help here, with approximations of penetration aided by verbal fantasy of penetration. Surrendering or forcing only causes you both to relate such activity to the cultural orientation of ''a pain in the ass.'' *An important super marital sex rule is that there should never be intentional mental or physical pain or coercion during any sexual interaction.*

11. ''Do you think he could be a homosexual? He doesn't want to do it as much with me anymore.''

ANSWER: No. Absolutely not. If your feelings about this are based on sexual interest or desire, then the issue of gender is irrelevant. Male or female homosexuals have the same range of feelings and desires as anyone, may or may not want a lot or a little sexual relationship with the same or the opposite sex, and have as much healthy and unhealthy sex, as many problems and sexual joys, as anyone else. *We must learn to stop labeling people or ourselves by what we do sexually.* This is a basic super marital sex rule. The homosexual couples I have treated sometimes report the reverse concern, that diminishing interest on the part of one partner may mean that he or she is a "latent heterosexual." It is one's feelings, general hot or cold lifestyle, overall health, values, morals, fears, hopes, and relationship status that affects interest, desire, and arousal, not gender identity.

12. "Why do you think we have such good sex up north [at their cottage] than at home? We're the same people."

ANSWER: That's exactly the point. You are the same couple, so the trick is to look at how you relate and what you do up north compared to what you do at home. Most likely you have more time, less pressure, and you make sex a priority away from home. You should know, however, that this is very good news, because vacations are also times when couples fight, draw further apart, and exaggerate their problems. The fact that time away becomes time together reflects a strong relationship just waiting to get some of the same attention and priority at home. One more thing. Different places for sex seem to be invigorating, and you don't have to go all the way up north for that. Try going downstairs at home, even out to the garage.

13. "I can't help feeling that I am doing something wrong when I have sex. Years of upbringing can't be overcome. I'm still a Catholic boy at heart."

ANSWER: There is no need to overcome those important years. The idea is to incorporate your feelings and memories and values from those years into your sexual life. If this seems almost impossible, I suggest you consult a clergyperson. *Examination of belief and value systems is a key part of developing super marital sex for all couples,* so your orientation gives you a head start here. The challenge will be in learning a new sexuality that is comfortable and nonoffensive to you both. I can assure you that in the years I have been doing therapy, I have never encountered a religious system that prohibits sensitive, caring intimacy between married people. The problem is usually not the religion, but the religiosity, the *way* it was taught and not *what* was taught. We must learn to look for the deeper messages in our value system, the messages *about* and not *against* sexual intimacy.

14. "I am deathly afraid that he is having an affair. He just doesn't want that much sex anymore. Is he?"

ANSWER: Frequency of and interest in sex is not a symptom. It does not "mean" anything if medical problems are ruled out. It is a means of sharing and expression that stands in and of itself. Looking for outside affairs only avoids the real issue of strengthening the marriage. Even if an affair were taking place, the issue would still be to strengthen the intimacy of the marital relationship. To enhance the intimacy of your relationship, particularly at times of outside stress on the relationship, devote for a period of time almost all of your mental and emotional energy to this relationship and suspend other relationships, even friendships and family ties. This doesn't mean give them up; it means announcing that for a few weeks you are giving your full attention to your marriage. After that, you will be back in all relationships you value, even more ready to be close to others because of your new trust in the closeness of your marriage. I have found that there is little interest in returning to relationships that are only approximations of what super marital sex can be. If after these few weeks there is still a trust problem or other difficulties, look inside, at the marriage, for the cause, not outside at other factors.

15. "When I read about sexual abuse, I knew it was the same for me. Will I, does anyone, get over the terrible scars of the abuse?"

ANSWER: No, nobody "gets over" them, but one learns to put them to work in favor of a new intimacy. Those who have suffered abuse learn the contrast between sharing and abusing, and they seem all the stronger for the pain, for they have seen both sides of the issue. They have felt the guilt, self-blame, and anger of sexual abuse and learned the contrast between that and the love, trust, and safety of sex in marriage. Just as someone who never has been really sick may never fully know what it is to be very healthy or at least fully appreciate and value health every day, so it is with sexual abuse. You have seen and felt the pain, so the joy and freedom is all the more valued.

16. "I have terrible cycles. There is a brief period of time when I am turned on sexually, but other times I just hate it. It could be PMS, couldn't it?"

ANSWER: Premenstrual syndrome continues to be researched, and there is much left to learn. There is no doubt that some women, indeed some men, have strong and marked periods of emotional, physical, and intellectual changes related to neurohormonal patterns. There is also no doubt that sexual response is related to all life cycles. The best thing to do is to graph not just menstrual cycles, but any cycles you feel are taking place. At the same time, make a graph of your couple cycle, how the two of you are relating. See if there is any pattern or relationship. If there is, consider a medical checkup. There are dietary, exercise, and other tactics that can be tried that may help. Most often, though, there is a strong interaction between life stress and life cycles. There are usually good reasons why we feel sexual or do not feel sexual, and usually these relate more to how we are living than any innate predetermined pattern. Graphing the couple and spouse patterns, talking this over, and reducing general life stress are important steps. When sex problems are attributed to PMS, or to any one factor or partner, we fail to understand the systems nature of sexual intimacy, the MMS, *m*eaningful *m*arital *s*ystem.

17. "Fantasizing me having sex with another man is really sick, isn't it? I mean, I'm his wife, for God's sake."

ANSWER: Fantasies are the most intimate and personal of sexual issues in couples, even more so than actual behaviors. What we think we might like to do or dream about doing seems to threaten spouses more than what actually takes place. No fantasy is sick; only hurtful behaviors are sick. The fantasy you describe is very common. Even though some couples find this hard to do, you may want to buy a few issues of one of the more explicit sex magazines and read the letters to the editor or other sex letters. As strange and artificial as these letters may seem, you will see that some of them are similar to some of your most forbidden thoughts. Rest assured that someone has already had your fantasy. Blocking fantasy by a spouse only raises anxiety and causes withholding of feelings and private thoughts, both of which block super marital sex. Fantasies are related more to how we learned about sex than they are to our feelings about our partner.

18. "Isn't masturbation a bad thing to do? Doesn't it mean that you are not having a very good marital sex life?"

ANSWER: No, masturbation does not mean anything good or bad about your marital sex. Whether masturbation is bad or good is a moral decision. Some evidence does indicate that persons who do masturbate without guilt are able to be freer in their heterosexual life, more aware of the nature of their own individual sexual response.

19. "He thinks I'm too fat. Can I ever be sexually attractive to him like this? I just don't think I can ever keep much of this weight off."

ANSWER: The range of healthy weight seems to be much wider than once thought, and general health, not sexual attractiveness, should be the determinant of weight. *One important super marital sex rule is that arousal comes from within, not without.* We are all responsible for our own arousal and appearance. To blame our partner for our own sexual feelings only blocks progress toward total personal and sexual health. A rose is a prickly, thorny, smelly, red thing that blooms only sometimes and is overpriced in flower stores. It can also be a symbol of love, a beautiful, soft, perfumed living symbol to be purchased for what it means, not just for what it costs. As has been said, all perception is mere hypothesis. Super marriage provides the opportunity for developing a hypothesis beyond the physical appearance. The more we look at bodies, the less we see the interaction and the system itself. It is important in super marital sex to *be the partner you would like to be married to*, and to be that partner in every way, including but not limited to the physical appearance.

21. "Is it normal to want to rub his penis on my breasts, between them until he comes?"

ANSWER: Someone once said that "Norm" is the name of a guy who lives in Brooklyn. If you can do it, it is a natural part of life. The right or wrong of things is a matter of personal and marital negotiation, but negotiate on the basis of wants and needs, not rights or wrongs.

The above answers review many of the issues raised as I discussed the development of individual love maps. Each answer to each question tried to do four things.

1. State the facts in positive terms to compliment the marital relationship.

2. Correct any misunderstanding or "myth-information" about sexuality. The myths revealed above related to the Ms. and Mr. Myths described in Chapters Six and Seven. Did you remember the facts?

3. Suggest steps to take to deal with the problem by reminding the spouse or couple about a related super marital rule. Did you recognize these?

4. Avoid self- or partner blame and, where possible, reduce guilt and increase hope and confidence in the possibility of positive change.

The answers to these questions were followed by more specific discussions related directly to each couple. They are incomplete in the context of this chapter, but the answers illustrate an orientation to super marital sex that all couples can learn.

Before moving on to Chapter Eleven and a discussion of more specific medical concerns as related to sexuality in marriage, I outline here the twelve most frequent causes of sexual problems for the couples group. You can see these problems within each of the above twenty questions. While the problems varied, they could be grouped in the following twelve categories. I have matched each category with an "opposite," a potential key to super marital sex. Review this list with your spouse as one final review of your own sexual status.

Twelve Causes of Sexual Distress

IGNORANCE: I found a profound lack of sexual knowledge in the couples and, even worse, the possession of "myth-information" based on the first three perspectives of sexuality. Super marital sex requires first and foremost knowledge, a knowledge that integrates all four perspectives of sexuality. Knowledge is the first key to super marital sex.

FEAR: Spouses were afraid, afraid of failure, embarrassment, of not living up to their partner's or even society's "sexpectations." Confidence in self and in the marriage is necessary for our natural sexual-response system to flourish. Confidence is the second key to super marital sex.

OBLIGATION: Spouses reported feelings of "ought to's" in their sexual system that took away from the opportunity to experience what they would like to experience. Natural sexual response is blocked by conscious attempts to "do something" that "should" be done. Freedom is the third key to super marital sex.

VOYEURISM: This is a form of "group" sex in which each partner is busy watching self, other, and "us" rather than experiencing and sharing in the sexual interaction. Involvement is the fourth key to super marital sex.

WITHHOLDING: This was the "economic problem" for the couples, feeling that one or both spouses had to "earn" sexual fulfillment through sexual expertise and good timing or activities outside the sexual area traded for sexual favors. Trust that you are accepted and desired sexually for who you are and not what you have done is necessary for spontaneous sexual response. Trust is the fifth key to super marital sex.

PERFORMANCE: Masters and Johnson felt that an orientation toward performance interfered with sexual response, and my interviews verified this. Making sex an event instead of an experience can destroy any real joy in the interaction. Sharing is the sixth key to super marital sex.

DYSCOMMUNICATION: Breakdown in verbal and emotional communication can also block super marital sex. Dyscommunication is inaccurate communication. Malcommunication is hurtful communication. Discommunication is communication without mutually shared purpose. Acommunication is no communication at all. Hypercommunication is overemphasis on intellectual and verbal communication in the absence of emotional sharing. Vulnerable sharing of feelings is effective Communication, the seventh key to super marital sex.

OUT OF CONTEXT: Sexual interaction out of the context of loving, sharing, and mutual concern for partner, as a negotiation, trade-off, even payback destroys any chance for super marital sex. Loving Context is the eighth key to super marital sex.

IATROGENIC PROBLEMS: Physician-caused problems, through misinformation, fear, or refusal or inability to raise and answer sex questions can remain a lifelong handicap to sexual fulfillment for the patient encountering such a physician. Responsive, comfortable, knowledgeable professionals are the ninth key to super marital sex.

POOR GENERAL HEALTH: Running too hot (hostile-competitive-impatient) or too cold (depressed-inadequate-passive) or having untreated health problems can prevent sexual fulfillment. Good overall holistic health is the tenth key to super marital sex.

SEXISM: Relating any element of the sexual-response system to preassigned sex roles for either gender imposes artificial and destructive limits on sexual intimacy. Androgynous, nonsexist life orientation is the eleventh key to super marital sex.

SEXUAL ANESTHESIA: Closing ourselves to incoming stimulation from multiple sources, including sensory, extrasensory, physical, emotional, and cognitive stimuli, limits sexual sensitivity. Sensuality is openness to the sending and receiving of a wide range of stimulation. Broad, holistic sensuality is the twelfth key to super marital sex.

All marriages experience some of these problems sometimes. Being aware of the potential for such problems and of the difficulty in achieving and maintaining super marital sex is one major step to mobilizing marital strength to solve these problems. I will present a very special "thirteenth key" to super marital sex in Chapter Twelve, but for now, use the twelve keys above to open the door to your own super sex.

Super Marital Sex Opportunity Number Ten

Take a sexual look back at the development of intimacy in your marriage. Using the twelve keys to super marital sex and the twelve problems above, talk together about times in your relationship when some of these problems and keys seemed to evolve. Look back on what helped and hurt the intimacy of your relationship.

Chapter Eleven examines some of the health problems that the thousand couples experienced and some suggestions for healthy sex, even healing sex, even at times of dis-ease within the person or the system. The twelve keys are even more important when there is a challenge to the marital system, so take the time to review them through super marital sex opportunity number ten.

CHAPTER ELEVEN

❦❦❦

Sexuality, Illness, and Health

You have to actually feel good to really feel anything.

HUSBAND

Not a problem in the world. Both spouses young and in perfect mental and physical health. Never a physical symptom of illness, always feeling energetic, well nourished, and well exercised. Two people glowing with health; hale, hardy, and feeling good every moment of every day. If this describes the two of you within your marriage, you are unique, for most of us have transitional minor health problems throughout our lives. Many of us have major health problems with which we must cope. This chapter is a home health guide for maintaining intimacy at times of illness, for people who fall into any one of the following four categories.

Feeling good and having no health problems now. All people get sick sometimes. There would be no wellness without illness, for illness is as natural a part of living as health. Sickness comes with being human and can directly affect your sexuality. Sexual intimacy can also help in your recovery from illness. Understanding the impact of illness on sex and sex on illness before we are ill can be effective preventive medicine, so even if you have no noticeable health problems now, the material to follow can be of help to you and perhaps to someone you know if you share this knowledge.

Not feeling too good but having no detectable health problems. Medical measurement techniques are all vague estimates of body processes that can never be directly assessed. We can only compare some body response, count of cells, or appearance of body products with some arbitrary numerical standard. When your "count" falls within pre-established limits, then cosmopolitan medicine says there are "no remarkable findings." (Actually, the human system is far beyond remarkable, a true, infinitely complex miracle.) Even when medicine says you are fine, you may not "feel good." Too many times, physicians either ignore the sexual dimensions of our health problems or are too uncomfortable to deal with them. Physician Harold Lief reports that the instance of patient report of sexual difficulties is predicted by the willingness on the part of the physician to talk about this important area of life. Another doctor, Richard Green, writes that to ignore sexual health in attempting to treat any health problem is incomplete, even unethical health care. "Not feeling too good" affects and can be affected by our sexuality.

Having a health problem and not feeling good. Just as times of being and feeling healthy are transitional phases of life process, so it is with times of sickness. All life systems go through periods of change, adaptation, "breakage," wearing out, and responding to internal and external challenges to our immune system. At such times, we may feel terrible, because this is nature's way of telling us that some response or alteration within our system is taking place. Sex is affected at these times, too, and can even help us through such crises by helping mobilize our internal natural healing processes.

Feeling good and having a health problem. We can thrive even when we are sick, particularly if we remember that sickness is part of health, part of the natural rhythm of life. Our health-conscious society has mistaken wellness for absence of medical problems, resulting in a defensive approach to daily living, a "preventive" life-style of running from the fear of illness. We must learn not only to live "well" even when we are sick, but to rally in the face of challenges to our system. Sex can be one of the most constructive ways of dealing with illness, yet few doctors provide prescriptions for love. In fact, most hospitals seem to go out of their way to prevent intimacy, the healing touching we all need when we are sick.

If we consider sex the sole prerogative of the "totally well," most of us are going to miss out on the most fulfilling of life's opportunities. Sickness is affected by sex as much as it affects sex, and I hope this chapter will help in clarifying this vital life relationship. As a starting point, I provide a Sexual Health Status Examination, the equivalent of the annual physical exam. The problem with the physical exam is contained in the name of this procedure. It is "physical" and tends to ignore the mind/spirit/body/feeling interrelationship. It is an "exam" instead of a learning experience, a test without a lesson. Even though the word "doctor" itself derives from a root word meaning to teach, too few physicians actually teach anything at the physical examination. If a problem is found, sex is seen as, according to one physician, "the last thing patients should be thinking about when they are sick." Actually, we may be sick partly *because* sex is one of the last things we are thinking about.

A Sexual Health Exam

I've worried about this for almost ten years, and now you tell me it is absolutely normal that my left testicle is a little larger and hangs lower than the right? I always thought it meant that I was a little less fertile or that maybe I hurt it that one time I fell off the seat on my bike and cracked my nuts on the crossbar. I always sort of hide it whenever I shower at the club. I really don't think my wife even knows.

HUSBAND

He has always acted funny about his genitals. He never lets me really see them or touch them. I touched his testicles one time and he pulled away like I had killed him. Why didn't he ask the doctor?

WIFE

I did. He just laughed and said maybe I had pulled on one for too long. I never mentioned it again.

HUSBAND

Several of the husbands and wives reported similar instances of worries and misunderstandings that were never clarified, even made worse, by the lack of comfort and sexual knowledge of the medical field. As with all of the tests in this book, taking the sexual health exam together is the best way to learn about each other and yourself.

Dr. June Reinisch, director of the Institute for Research in Sex, Gender, and Reproduction, reports that questions to her nationally syndicated column often contain misinformation and a refusal by physicians and other health professionals to respond openly, comfortably, and directly to sexual questions from their patients. Any doctors who don't hear such questions in their practice can be sure that they have stopped them through their own discomfort with the topic.

1. DO YOU HAVE THE ABILITY TO BE SEXUAL WHENEVER AND HOWEVER YOU WANT?

This is the mechanistic aspect of the sexual health examination. Whether or not you are experiencing illness at this time in your life, assess your ability to move, to actually "do" the things you would like to do sexually.

"I know this sounds like an excuse, but I get terrible cramps in my legs whenever I'm on top," reported one wife. "I start out okay. Then, after a while, they start to ache at the thigh and then my feet get these terrible cramps."

"I can't control my movements when I thrust," said another husband. "My back tends to go out on me sometimes, and I sort of hold back so that won't happen."

In these two examples, prescription of special exercises and sexual-posture adjustment corrected the problems. Following medical examination to rule out any factors that might have contributed to her cramping (always a necessary first step), this wife was told that there was no reason that she should stop using the posture she preferred. She had not tried this position in five years, but when she was taught to push her open hands against her husband's hands as he pushed up against hers, the cramps disappeared. The problem was approached with both partners as a team, a system, and the obstacle was removed.

The medical examination of the husband revealed a kidney stone that had not been diagnosed. The doctor decided that the stone could not be removed at this time, and the patient was instructed with his wife present that any coital movements would have no effect on the stone and certainly not cause problems for a back injury he never really had.

So take a look at the ability factor, your range of sexual motion, stamina, and incoming/outgoing stimulation capacity. My work with paraplegic patients resulted in what those patients came to call the "top to bottom and back" test. Try it yourself:

Lie down in bed alone and start at the very top of your head. From that spot, mentally and, where possible, physically with your own hands scan down every part of your body and back up again. These are the questions the paraplegic patients used, and I found that they help patients with any disease process and persons without current disease to understand the "doing" aspect of sex.

1. Can I move the way I want here?

2. Can I feel here?

3. How could I please a partner with this area of my body?

4. How might a partner please himself or herself with this area of my body?

5. How do I feel about this area of my body?
    Healthy?
    Strong?
    Safe?
    Soft?
    Attractive (to myself and my partner)?

6. How does this part compare to other parts of my body?

7. How has my disease or health problem affected this area of my body, if at all?

8. How has this part of my body changed over the years?

9. What is the range of capacity for this part of my body (range of motion, posturing, etc.)?

10. How could I use another part of my body to compensate for a problem somewhere else?

11. What might I do to help out this part of my body? Is there a postural, positioning, even lighting or furniture change that could help?

12. Lie quietly and feel your body as a whole. How do you feel, how does it feel to you at this time of your life?

Other mini-questions may occur to you as you explore your sexual ability. This is the "what am I able to enjoy sex with?" part of the sexual health exam, and any questions or concerns about health should be brought to the attention of your doctor. This is not a question of cosmetics or assessment of your place on the sexual attractiveness scale. It is an opportunity to check out the "hardware" of the system before you look at the more important "software" issues.

2. WOULD YOU LIKE TO MAKE LOVE WITH YOU?

The reason for starting with the mechanical question is to get it out of the way so that you can look at the more important relationship issues, for these are the areas where disease and handicap have their most profound influence. If we keep taking our banged-up cars into body shops for repair without looking at how we drive in traffic, we will end up with more and more banged-up cars. So it is with disease that, as one paraplegic man stated, "The system is more important than the thing."

"I just sort of became the chicken-soup type. I mean, I turned over my life to everyone else. My wife became a caretaker, and caretakers are not supposed to screw their patients." This statement from a husband with multiple sclerosis illustrates the importance of sexual self-concept. Try to answer question two not in terms of skill or attractiveness but on the basis of "how" you are as a person when you are trying to be intimate. If you are experiencing disease, what has the disease process done to your relationship skills. Have you become more dependent, more aggressive, less assertive, more or less withdrawn? What has been the major impact of your illness on you as a person? How people experience disease and illness tells more about how they really are as persons than how they experience health.

I have my patients who are experiencing disease calculate their "N/S Quotient." This is the balance between nurturance—taking care of someone else—and succorance—being taken care of by another person—that I discussed in Chapter Four. One of the most healing of human experiences, one of the healthiest things you can do, is to help somebody else. When you are sick, you must continue at some level to help others. How would you say your balance is? Do you still profit, even if you are sick, from all the good healing internal chemicals that come from the joy of supporting and helping someone else?

There have been research articles (not many) describing the impact of disease on sexuality. There have been very few articles about the impact of sexuality on disease, on sex as healer, on sexual shamanism. Maintaining and enhancing intimacy throughout the challenge of disease is not only possible but necessary for getting better. Remaining sexually active can actually slow some aging processes, protect the genitals to some degree from aging changes, and possibly offer a boost to your immune system. Research has clearly shown that immunoefficiency increases when you love and are loved.

3. ARE YOU ABLE TO RETAIN SELF-RESPONSIBILITY AND RESPONSIBILITY FOR OTHERS?

> "I hate that she has to undress me. I can't undress myself anymore," reported the husband experiencing multiple sclerosis. "I think that's the worst part of this whole thing. I know that doesn't make much sense, but I feel like a child being undressed and dressed."
>
> PARAPLEGIC HUSBAND

All disease requires some sacrifice of autonomy as much as it requires self-responsibility for healing. We all have to turn to someone for help, support, covering for us at work, bringing the chicken soup, pushing the wheelchair in some hard-to-go places, holding the door while we struggle with a cane or crutch. Disease reminds us firmly that we all belong together, and healing depends on acting as if we really believe that.

"Is it that you are being undressed or that you can't undress your wife, too, that really seems to bother you the most?" was my question to this husband.

"Well, she undresses herself, and I watch her, but when she turns to me and has to do me, too, that's what gets me," he answered.

"I have two suggestions, and they both may seem crazy," I answered. "First, why take your clothes off every time anyway? Dress in clothing sometimes that is comfortable and allows for stimulation you enjoy. Maybe some clothing might even feel good to you. Ask your wife to do the same. Some couples wear jogging suits of a material they like and they don't wear any underwear. Then, when you feel like sex, no dressing or undressing may be necessary. Second, maybe you have failed to change your sexual pattern to adjust to this disease experience. Making love at the end of the day with your wife getting you undressed was an old pattern. Disease requires change. In fact, some philosophers suggest that this is the purpose of disease, to cause change and growth in the long term. I know it doesn't matter much in the short term that all disease leads to overall change, but your sex life must reflect this fact. If you are undressed at night, then sleep naked and have sex in the morning when no dressing or undressing is necessary. And remember, you spent much of courtship undressing her. Maybe this disease can cause some role reversal you might enjoy once you get used to it.''

"All of those ideas are crazy but one," he answered. "I never thought of staying dressed for sex. I guess that could work out. I think we'll try it. Maybe I'll market these things. Instead of jogging suits, we'll start a new yuppie fad. Sex suits. It might feel neat."

The process of reconsideration of the relationship between sexuality and illness starts in just this simple fashion. Talking, sharing, modifying, being creative, and designing and redesigning your sexual patterns is part of the healing process.

Since all disease happens within a system, it is important to look at the responsibility issue from the perspective of both partners. "I don't know what he's talking about," said the wife of the man in the example above. "I love undressing him. I just wish he would make more of an effort to solve our problems instead of surrendering or deferring to me. It's not the undressing part that makes him seem childish, it's his attitude. I married him for his brains, not his wardrobe-changing skills."

4. CAN YOU BE INVOLVED IN A MUTUALLY PLEASING AND FULFILLING SEXUAL EXPERIENCE?

"Ever since the heart attack, he seems to be trying too hard. I mean, he wants to please me, prove something, I think." The wife described her feelings about the impact of a life-threatening disease on her husband and her marital sex. "He used to really enjoy me, but now he seems to be worried that I will see or think that he is fragile or something." With catastrophic illnesses, some patients adopt styles that prevent a mutually pleasing sexual interaction. Here are some of the styles, based on my interviews.

The Accepter: This person acts as if the disease is deserved, another negative in a disappointing life. There is little effort to fight back, to change, to adapt, to protect sexuality. Rather, there is surrender and sacrifice of sexuality to the disease process. "The doctor told me that diabetes could cause impotence. He said it, and he was right. So I don't know why you are asking me about our sex life. I can't have one," said the husband. When I asked how his wife felt about that, he responded, "She has no more choice than I do. It's just in the cards. A bad deal, a rotten deal." When I suggested that there was indeed much that could be done even if there was no erection at all, the man responded, "Look, you learn to live with what you are given." To paraphrase T. S. Eliot, if you fail to look inside for the strength to grow at times of crisis, then you must accept whatever life gives you. As this chapter continues, remember one basic principle: No disease prevents sexuality. The Accepter has forgotten this fact.

The Denier: This patients minimizes all illness, indeed all negative events, and in the process sexuality leaves the marriage. This minimizing interferes with sex because the maintenance of intimacy depends first on acknowledging any blocks to that intimacy. "No stroke is going to bother me. It didn't even faze me, really. We just keep going," reported the husband. "No way that's true, Dave," said his wife. "Can't you see that we haven't had sex in months?" The husband could not believe his ears. "It could not have been that long. I'm just as sexy as ever." He laughed and pinched his wife's thigh. She slapped his hand and he continued to laugh. "It's not funny." She began to cry. "You're either a liar or a fool. I cannot live this way."

The Catastrophizer: This person pulls away from sexuality and most of life. The health problem becomes overwhelming, distracting him or her from any personal or marital strength that could save intimacy and contribute to healing. "When I lost my breast, I lost everything," reported the wife. "The cancer took more than my breast, it took my marriage." The husband offered help. "But, honey, your cancer was cured. There are no signs of it at all. You licked it. It's gone." She stared angrily at him. "You'll never know what it's like to sit on a time bomb like this. It could come back. If you want sex, go somewhere else. If that is all I am to you, even at a time like this, then leave me." The husband offered her his handkerchief for her tears and she threw it to the floor.

Unlike the Accepter, this person is defeated and asks repeatedly, "Why me?" While such concerns are a natural phase of illness, the Catastrophizer remains stuck at this phase, mistaking diagnosis for verdict. He or she may withdraw from sex as a form of self- or partner punishment in a misguided attempt to strike back at the terrible injustice he or she has suffered. The Catastrophizer is the innocent prisoner of their health problem, while the Accepter is more the overwilling victim.

The Hero: Heroes use their disease as a flag of battle. They become so involved in their war against illness that they forget or neglect the tenderness of intimacy. "No way I'll give into this," reported the wife with lupus. "I'll read every minute about it, I'll exercise, I'll see every expert in this world or any other." Her husband could not understand this total involvement in the battle against the disease. "I know we have to fight this thing, but what about the rest of life? Can't we love and laugh too, love and laugh as much as we fight and struggle?"

"Maybe you can, but I'm the one who will prove them wrong. I can handle this alone if I have to," was the wife's response. "I haven't got time to play around. Every minute I waste is a minute I give to the disease. I'll feel like making love after I feel like I take care of this first." She failed to understand that "taking care" of this disease depended in part on taking care of her marriage and sexuality at the same time. Heroes find themselves eventually alone, even in victory over the disease. They become victorious warriors with no one to share the victory.

The Sweetheart: Sweethearts seem to be trying to "sweeten" the disease away by overcompliance to any and all medical suggestions and requests. This same pattern continues in the marital sex, as they attempt to please their partner. "I have never turned him down. Even when I am sick as hell from the chemotherapy, I'll still do something." This wife reported a continued effort to be "nice" sexually and in every other way. "The doctor forgot what he told me about the medicine, but he is a very busy man. I am not his only patient. I understand."

Research in healing indicates that such compliance is as potentially detrimental to coping with disease as is the unrelenting battle of the Hero. Providing sex as a favor, as an obligation to a partner, only serves to alienate the spouse, who in turn may pull away sexually. A balance between compliance and educated, modulated resistance to the disease process seems to be healthiest for any patient, and such a balance is promoted by a continued sexual interaction where there is alternating give-and-take. "I wish she would be a little nasty sometimes, you know. She is so damned sweet I almost feel guilty having sex with her." This husband's report points out the need for balance and what can happen to the spouse of the Sweetheart patient.

The Sweetheart patient puts herself or himself at risk. The medical industry can kill you if you fail to represent yourself, fail to ask questions and hold professionals accountable. Being obnoxious in the hospital or when you are being treated will not make you popular, but being too nice might get you ignored. Again, the issue is balance.

There are certainly many other forms of adjustment to illness. Try to understand how you are being ill, your sickness strategy, and you will learn much about how you might get well.

5. IF YOU DID NOT HAVE OR DO NOT HAVE A HEALTH PROBLEM, WOULD YOUR SEX LIFE BE WHAT YOU WANT IT TO BE?

Some people "use" illness as a sexual excuse, an explanation for not having sex. As you will see shortly, you can have a fulfilling sex life no matter what illness you may experience if you define the sexual-response cycle from the fourth perspective, one free of the energy/erection/orgasm emphasis. Here is my definition of sexual health. Answer yes or no to each question:

1. Do you know how to have sex, really know, not just think you know? Do you understand the fourth perspective of sexuality?

2. Are you relating now with someone?

3. Are you with a partner of choice, not a partner of obligation?

4. Do you feel that you relate intimately (give the gift of self)?

5. Are you sexually responsible contraceptively and in terms of disease and integrity in your relationships?

6. Do you concern yourself with the interaction more than with self or partner? Are you behaving as a part of the sexual system instead of being in charge of or merely responsive to someone else?

7. Does your sexual life match your belief and value system (not in direct or hypocritical conflict with it)?

8. Are you proud of your sex life instead of embarrassed, guilty, disappointed in self, partner, or relationship?

No disease or illness totally prevents us from making contact with someone we love. Ignorance about the sexual impact of disease can block such contact. To help you understand the sexual impact of some of the major diseases, I will review some of the common illnesses of our time and what we know so far about their relationship to sex.

Sex and the Heart

> Would you risk it? I'm not going to die having sex. I'd sooner live
> without sex than die trying to have it.
>
> HUSBAND

Fewer than one person in four returns to "pre-heart attack" sexuality. Almost none of these persons have any physical or medical reason not to return to sexual activity, but fear, lack of knowledge, diminished self-concept, general depression, or physician neglect of this important area of their rehabilitation got in the way. There were seldom significant organic reasons to avoid sexual interaction, but poor education from their doctor and reluctance to communicate about sex with their doctor or spouse robbed them of the opportunity to return to intimacy.

My interviews suggest that depression, whether from lack of information, lack of self-esteem, or fear, is at the core of the problem. "Will I ever be able to work again, work like I used to?" asked one man. "I just can't imagine being like I was before." I have never talked with a patient who reported such concerns who did not also have sexual concerns, for sex cannot be separated from our concept of self, our work, and our sexual "workability."

The lack of specific discussion of heart disease and its relationship to sex implies a negative message to the patient. "I thought because he didn't say a word about it that he thought I'd be crazy to even think it, so I stopped thinking it. At least, I tried. Every time I had sex it was like I decided I would die for it if I had to." This patient expresses the concern of most of the heart patients with whom I have counseled: forget the whole thing or risk your life.

When some information was given about sex and heart disease, it was usually wrong. Wait about six months for the heart muscle to heal, was a rule of thumb, followed by the now infamous "two flights of stairs" advice. If patients could walk up two flights of stairs without heart symptoms, they could have sex. Medicine apparently assumed that climbing stairs is the closest analogy to having sex. It makes one wonder how doctors have sex. The effect of such advice was to raise anxiety, as the patient waited for the weeks to pass to attempt the stair-climbing. Few health-care workers thought to study the effects of the anxiety caused by such delay and anticipation, the effects that such an emotional state could have on the healing heart.

Research data indicate that maximal heart rate during a typical workday is actually higher than that achieved during orgasmic contractions. Blood-pressure changes with sexual activity also are not at a risk level in the absence of other illness factors. Of course, each case is different, but unless the doctor can tell you why you should not have sex, then you would probably benefit from sex, not just survive it. I have never found that waiting for healing was helpful in any illness. Getting better is an active, not passive state, and diseases of the heart may be healed more easily by loving than waiting.

Here are some rules of thumb to apply to the issue of heart disease and sexuality. Remember, talk to your doctor first!

1. Talk with your doctor as a couple, not individually. Your healing takes place within a system, a relationship, so give your doctor the opportunity to talk to both of you. Talking together prevents some of the problems of "interpretation" from spouse to spouse.

2. Talk as a couple and with your doctor about sex and about concerns about the heart disease. There are many types of heart disease and very little research on sex and heart disease, so communication and mutual openness is important. Everybody who has ever had heart disease wonders about sexual issues. You are not alone in your concerns. Anxiety is worse for the heart than embarrassment, so take the risk and share your concerns.

3. Don't try to prove you are "all better" by trying a sexual marathon. Return gradually to the sexuality the marriage desires. Sexual tests always flunk anyone who tries them.

4. With or without heart disease, it is better to be sexually active when you are in good general health. Look at this issue as a general issue, not just one related to the heart muscle. Sexual health is a cornerstone of general health.

5. Avoid alcohol and heavy, rich meals. We all should do this anyway, and the risk factor for stroke or heart attack is increased for anyone when he or she drinks, eats a lot, and has sex.

6. Don't watch or feel for symptoms. They will get your attention if they occur. If they do (tightness in the chest, chest pain, shortness of breath), don't panic. Just slow down, hug, rest, and talk. Report these symptoms to your doctor, but remember, many such symptoms are insignificant or not as pronounced as you may think. Always call the doctor, but do not jump to conclusions. Don't lie there alone and worry. Share with your

partner. Your doctor will probably reassure you anyway. If you continue to worry, both of you should watch as the partner with the heart problem exercises vigorously under carefully monitored medical conditions. Have the doctor explain to you what all the tracings mean. Healing can be taking place in the heart even when there are some abnormal findings, even when symptoms persist. Symptoms do not necessarily mean a setback in healing. If you still worry, suggest that the doctor send the spouse with the heart problem home with an ambulatory heart monitor attached. Have sex, record when you had sex and any symptoms you might have had, and go together to discuss the results. You will probably be very relieved.

7. Your doctor will prescribe an exercise program. The days of staying in bed after a heart attack are over. Activity heals, but only at a medically monitored and prescribed rate, and that includes sexual activity.

8. If you have pain, ask about using nitroglycerin, long-acting nitrate preparations, or other medications. Be sure to ask when and how these medications should be used. Some should be taken at regular intervals, while others should be taken several minutes before sexual activity.

9. Remember, there is much more to sex than intercourse. Talk with your doctor about all of sex or he or she might assume that sex equals coitus. No single sexual activity is more dangerous than any other.

10. The spouse with the heart problem does not need a spousal nurse. He or she needs a loving sexual partner who expresses his or her own sexual needs vigorously and honestly. If the patient sees your comfort and freedom, he or she will learn the same approach. The patient must learn to protect himself or herself, and attempts by a spouse to protect the heart patient typically backfire into more fear, loss of self-esteem, and even resentment. Don't let any disease take the heart out of your sex life.

Sex and Cell Disease (Cancer)

I don't think he will ever want to touch me again. I feel like ruined property, damaged merchandise. I don't think I would want to touch me, to touch that thick, ugly scar where my soft breast used to be.

WIFE BEFORE COUNSELING

I love her. In some ways, I love her more now than ever. But I just can't bring myself to look at that part where her breast was.

HUSBAND BEFORE COUNSELING

It has come to be a symbol of sorts, I guess. He kisses me there and touches me there. It just doesn't seem as much a thing as it would seem. In fact, it means something special. We hate it in some ways, but it symbolizes us and our survival. It stands for our victory.

WIFE AFTER COUNSELING

When we make love, I don't try not to look at it or touch it and I don't try to touch it or look at. I don't try anything about it. But it's not hers, it's not like an "it," really, but the whole thing is us, a part of us. That was the biggest change, I think, when I stopped trying to adjust to "it" and she stopped waiting for me to or help me to adjust. It's that "holistic" thing, I guess.

HUSBAND AFTER COUNSELING

If we can have lung disease, heart disease, and other organ diseases, then we should refer to "cell" disease instead of the general and frightening term "cancer." I have never heard anyone refer to the "heart disease of crime," yet one recent commentator reported that "crime is the cancer of our country." Cells overgrow every day. They overgrow because so many cells multiply and divide in our body that some are bound to "go bad." They overgrow because of the toxicity of our world, our food, our style of living. Since cells are the building blocks of our body, cell disease can occur anywhere, and therefore there are many "types" of cell disease (actually locations). I discuss here some of the problems that came up in the couples group.

Mastectomy: Our society's limited view of erotic zones has resulted in the oversymbolization of the female breast. Research indicates that the woman's reaction to mastectomy, removal of the breast, relates not only to her own personal associations to her body, but to her perceptions of her partner's views as well. While over half of women who have mastectomy report wanting information on the sexual impact of this operation, only four of sixty women mastectomy patients in a recent study received such information. One third of another group of mastectomy patients failed to resume sexual activity more than six months after being released from the hospital. This is the case in spite of the fact that yet another research project has indicated that more than half of the men and women in marriages in which the wife received a mastectomy reported an increased need for intimacy. Here are some guidelines to help with this problem.

1. The wife should *not* see the scar from surgery. She should be helped to see her whole body, including the surgical site, while still in the hospital and with the husband present. I have the husband and wife look directly at each other's armpits. It tell them to stare at them and talk about what they feel. "It's weird. I mean, it seems weird to look at just one part,"

said one wife. That is just the point. If you look "at" the scar, that is all you will see. So look at each other, the entire body. Do it in private, but ask for more information from a nurse/oncology specialist after doing this or if you are unable to continue. I find the nurse/oncology specialists to be very helpful in these cases, good teachers and listeners and strong on empathy.

2. Change sides of the bed if necessary, so that the intact breast is first encountered when sexual contact is made. This change seems to help at first. After a time, it really won't matter.

3. Either you will grow from this problem or the relationship will suffer. It's up to you. Changing how you have sex does not mean diminishing it. Learning to include other areas of the body for sexual stimulation may enhance, not just "adjust," the sexual relationship.

4. Depression is a natural part of living, too. Talking it out together or with someone else can help. And remember, depression is like everything else in life. It does not last forever. One wife reported, "The depression is not so bad if I don't get too depressed about the depression."

5. There is no need to "test" things by trying to get "right back to sex." Being sick and in the hospital takes a lot out of a person besides money. Give yourselves time.

6. All sex does not have to be mutual sex. If one or the other partner wants sex, it is helpful to have some "special" experiences for one partner only. Try the "spa" experience I mentioned in Chapter Eight. Many of the mastectomy patients in my couples group found this helpful in learning to "re-accept" their body. Doctors don't usually talk about such things because they were trained in the third perspective that all sex is mutual and culminates in intercourse. You know better now. Reopen your own sex clinic.

7. There are some new operations for reconstructive surgery that are "one step" and do not require lengthy or multiple hospitalizations. Take some time first, and then consider that possibility if you think it might be helpful. As with the tubes they put in men's penises for erection, there is no "need" to do so. Such surgery is a matter of personal and marital preference.

8. Almost eight out of a hundred women may have breast cancer. Men can have breast cancer, too (at a lower rate). Do a breast self-exam every month. It is a necessary part of any wellness program. If you have breast cancer, you are not alone. Having breast cancer is like having high blood pressure; you are lucky if you found it out. Those who don't will suffer much more.

9. You don't have to be like the women on television. Recently there have been many movies and specials about breast and other forms of cancer and the extraordinary courage of some persons as they face this disease.

You are creating your own special. Adjust in your own way. Heroes are for Hollywood. Cry, complain, sulk, and yell if you want to.

10. Brief psychotherapy can be of some help if you hire the right therapist. If you feel things are moving too slowly, check Appendix II to determine when you need a therapist for sexual problems. Be careful and help the therapist focus on your problem. As one of my patients stated, "Just because I'm crazy doesn't mean I need a lot of therapy. I would just like to fine-tune my craziness a little. This breast cancer threw me out of whack. I just need a little adjusting."

Testicular tumors: Cancer, cell disease in testicles, is the leading form of cancer in men between twenty-nine and thirty-five. Men should do self-exams for this form of cell disease each month by taking a warm shower or bath and gently rolling each testicle between the thumbs and fingers of both hands. Feel for nodules, changes in consistency, swelling, or lumps. All men are different, so once you are used to doing this exam, you will know how you "should be." If you find something suspicious, go right to the doctor. It probably will not be cancer anyway, but it's a good idea to check. Eighty-eight percent of cases of cell disease in this area of the male body have spread before they are detected, so don't wait to go for a checkup.

Surgical removal of the testicle with overgrowing cells is usually the treatment of choice, and there are obvious sexual implications with such a procedure. Here are some ideas regarding testicular cancer and sexuality. Most apply to cancer of the prostate as well.

1. Some, but not all, surgery may directly affect ejaculatory capacity. Remember, this surgery does not mean loss of psychasm or even loss of orgasmic contractions. There may be a loss of the ejaculatory fluid, but this loss has no impact on sexual capacity.

2. The type of tumor will determine actual physiological outcome. If their particular type of surgery affects fertility, some patients decide to freeze some of their sperm prior to surgery so they may decide to have children after. Many types of surgery do not affect fertility.

3. There is no loss of erection that accompanies testicular cancer treatment. Sometimes, prostatic cancer surgery affects erective reflex to varying degrees. Of course, anxiety, depression, and other emotions will affect your body, and that can affect blood flow to the penis. Time and open communication, even the posture of the future from Chapter Five, could help with this.

4. Some patients report a diminished interest, arousal, or desire and other impact on their sexual-response system. If such states persist, ask your

doctor about a serum-testosterone test to be sure your hormone levels are within the appropriate range.

5. Short-term therapy, education, and reassurance can go a long way in preventing or correcting the emotional setback that may come with this type of cell disease. Again, hire somebody who will work with you on this specific problem.

6. Even though we talk about cancer as a curse and call persons with overgrowing cells "cancer victims," sexual activity does not cause cancer. It does not directly *cause* any form of disease, even though intimacy can transmit some diseases. Guilt will only slow the healing process. Self-blame will only get in the way of a return to intimacy.

7. Loss of ejaculate or reduction of fertility due to the drugs or radiation used in treatment does not decrease virility or manhood. Remember our fourth perspective in all of this. Sex is not a measure of anything, it is a response growing from within a system of interaction between two people. Cutting anything on the body does not have to cut off sex.

Chemotherapy and sexuality: Most forms of chemotherapy are designed to boost the body's own natural defense against fast-growing cells that are out of control. In the process, chemotherapy may result in side effects related to some destruction of your own healthy fast-growing cells (like the lining of your stomach or your hair cells). You can do much to reduce the sexual side effects of chemotherapy by conditioning yourself. Listen to pleasing music or smell a pleasing odor during chemotherapy treatment. The music or odor might become "paired" with the chemotherapy, and the sound or odor itself might actually help the chemotherapy by making it more effective with less of a dose. The principle at work here is the classical conditioning done by Pavlov, who taught his dogs to salivate to a bell. In this case, you are teaching your own defense cells to respond to music or an odor. This technique is still in the experimental stage, but there is no harm in trying it. Anything that doesn't hurt the treatment program could help it. Here are some issues related to cancer and chemotherapy.

1. Some chemotherapy may alter menstruation, fertility in men and women, and hormonal patterns related to human development, particularly during adolescence. Ask your doctor about the side effects in this regard. Just ask out loud, "What might this chemical do to my sex life?"

2. The whole process of chemotherapy and its administration is not conducive to comfort. You may become depressed as well as have other physical symptoms. Get a strong support system and make sure the setting in which you receive your chemotherapy is one that you can at least tolerate. Listen to

music, fantasize, play relaxation and imagery tapes. Help out the process! Go to your own internal pharmacy of natural healing chemicals.

3. It is not true that all chemotherapy causes infertility. Some types can, but not always. Teenagers I have interviewed sometimes assume that their chemotherapy makes them safe contraceptively. This is not true. Talk it over with your doctor.

4. The cell-disease patients I interviewed felt a stronger need than ever to be touched, held, stroked, and loved, and the more invasive the treatment, the stronger was the need. Never forget the power of the healing touch. "I can't say why or how, but his touch just soothed me after the chemotherapy." The wife reported that her husband could actually cancel out some of the side effects of her treatment. She continued, "He was on a sales trip once, and I had my treatment. I got sick as a dog. The next time, he was home. If we make love, like that time, I just don't get the nausea. Can that happen?"

There are forms of cell disease for every part of the body, but the principles above apply to each. If we take the fourth perspective of sexuality, we avoid the trap of a genital/breast focus on sex. When we avoid that trap, we have ample options to protect our sexuality. No disease destroys sharing, and sharing in the absence of the energy buildup and discharge model cannot be destroyed by cell disease. If we give up our sexuality at times of illness, we give the disease a power it does not have on its own.

Sex and Chronic Disease

My first involvement with patients experiencing chronic illness took place in a small room in the basement of a hospital. I had asked the head nurse on several of the units to offer group counseling regarding sexual health to any patients who were willing to come one evening and share some of their views and feelings about their situation. It was an open-ended offer, with no promises other than my willingness to listen to patients talk about sex and chronic disease.

As I entered the room, I noticed that nurses had accompanied the patients to the meeting. Wheelchairs, crutches, IV bottles, and various other medical paraphernalia were everywhere. "We could only fit in ten patients, but dozens more wanted to come down," said one nurse. "In fact, almost every patient we asked wanted to come down to talk about sex."

I wondered how I could start the discussion of this sensitive topic, but I didn't have to wonder long. A man was having trouble with the brake on his wheelchair, and said, "This is the kind of thing that drives me crazy. Your brake gives out and you're rolling helplessly down an incline while the woman you are trying to impress watches in horror."

"I know," said another male patient. "You are not impressive to women when you have to look up at them all of the time. I hate it on elevators. Your face is right at their butt almost. I can really cop a feel, goose their ass. When they turn around and see that I am in a chair, they just look up and watch the numbers. Any other guy and they would probably smack him in the face. But me, poor thing, they don't even think I am capable of sex. I must not have control of my hands and arms. It must have been an accident. What a joke. The day I get slapped in the face for goosing some broad on an elevator is the day I know that I am finally seen as a sexual person."

"They call us mermaids," responded another young woman patient in a wheelchair. "You know, nothing down there that works. All top and no bottom. If you think women don't see you as sexy, what about men looking at a woman in a wheelchair? They never say anything, but I know what the magic nagging question really is. It's always the same question."

A man next to me had braces on both arms. As he moved, he knocked over his glass of water from the tray attached to his chair. No one seemed to notice as the water poured onto his lap.

"Just what in the hell can she do? That's the question, isn't it? What can a par [paraplegic] really do sexually anyway? That's what they wonder if they take the time to wonder."

A nurse dried the water from his lap and he looked down. "Look at this. A sexy nurse patting my lap." He looked down at her hand as everyone laughed again. He did not laugh and continued, "You see. First, I didn't even know she had her hand in my lap. I had to see it first. I can't feel it. I'll bet Marsha [the nurse] would never pat someone else's lap like that without asking first at least."

The nurse pulled her hand away quickly as laughter continued. I hadn't said a word about sex and chronic illness, but the group was more than ready to talk and share, as if these issues had been waiting for the light of day.

"I guess you could say we are really off and sitting," said an older man from his wheelchair. "We're really a perverted bunch to be talking like this, but I love it."

"I would bet it's almost easier to have a noticeable handicap like you people in the chairs,'' said an attractive young woman with multiple sclerosis. ''It's not that noticeable for me, so I have the added burden of what I call 'the announcement,' sort of like coming out of the closet and telling people that you have a serious illness that can affect what might happen if you get sexual. At least with you, the announcement is visual. I feel like I am carrying this bomb ready to drop when I say, 'Hey, I have MS and sometimes I pee my pants. Now, let's make love.' ''

No laughter this time. Each member of the group seemed lost in a private replay of his or her own experiences. After what seemed like several minutes, the silence was broken by a blind woman. ''I don't know. I can't tell how people are reacting or what they are reacting to. You probably watch for signals, but I have to listen for them, sense them. You can't imagine how important visual cues are for relating to someone until you can't use them. What am I supposed to say? 'Hi there, I'm Jean, I'm blind in case you haven't noticed. Your voice sounds nice, but I hope you're not ugly. Just because I'm blind doesn't mean I want to make love to an ugly person. Now, let me run my hands over your face and body so I can tell if I want to go any further with this whole thing.' ''

Again, no laughter this time. Another blind male patient responded. ''You won't believe this, but I sat down on a bus bench and smelled this great perfume. It was magic. I sat for a few minutes, and then I thought, What the hell, I'll take a risk. I used the universal opening line. 'Hi.' I heard 'Hi' back, but it was a man's voice. I wasn't sure what the hell was happening. I didn't know where that great perfume was coming from. The bus came, and as I stood to get on, I bumped into a woman. 'Excuse me,' she said. 'I'm new at this.' She was blind, too, and it was her perfume I smelled. I still don't know where that man's voice came from. I started to board the bus and I heard someone say, 'Look, two of them.' That's all. We never talked again. I can still smell that perfume, though. God, I can smell it now.''

''Could you ask people to talk slower, please?'' came a question from a deaf man in the corner. He searched each person's face rapidly as they spoke, but I could see that he was losing track of who was talking and what was being said. His speech pattern was labored and unclear, but the group seemed to adjust immediately by raising an arm or hand or moving a chair forward when someone prepared to talk. Their ease and immediacy of empathy and compensation was remarkable.

''You know,'' the deaf man continued slowly, ''I have always wondered what a woman sounds like when she has sex. I wonder if it is like in those books, you know. Does it sound like a shriek, long repeated vowels, groans? How does it really sound? Can you tell me?''

"There isn't any one way," came the saving answer from the woman with MS. "That's all a myth anyway. Sometimes I don't make any sound at all, so you wouldn't be missing a thing. I talk so much after sex that you might be just the guy for me." Now the group laughed loudly, the deaf man laughing too loudly and in an odd rhythm that only I seemed to notice. It was clear that these people were responding to the essence of each message, not tone, style, rhythm, and other more mechanical things.

"You know what?" stated another blind man. "I have Cliff here [his Seeing Eye dog]. When a sharp lady goes by, he always growls and I feel it in his harness. I whistle out loud at her or yell something stupid like 'Baby!' My sighted friends tell me it works every time. The lady looks around, sees that I am blind, and walks away. My friend says it embarrasses him because the chicks think he puts me up to it. Cliff and I love it, don't we, Cliff?"

"Speaking of nurses, did any of you guys ever get a hard-on—I mean, erection—when the nurse is bathing you?" Another man in a wheelchair was talking now, and the nurses looked at each other knowingly and blushingly. "Well, I have that happen. The first nurse dropped the cloth and took off. They tried another nurse, an ugly one this time, but the same thing happened. It's just a reflex, because I can't feel a thing there. That's not always the case with pars, but I don't. They even tried a male nurse. They kept on sending them in, and I kept on going up. Now I notice that Joanne over there (one of the nurses who was trying to disappear behind one of the wheelchairs) is the designated erection washer. I don't mean to embarrass her. I want to thank her, to thank her for talking to me about it, not just pretending it didn't happen. I want to thank her for putting me in contact with Dr. Pearsall so my wife and I can talk about sex. No one, I mean no one, ever talked about it before. I almost lost my marriage before I learned, before I rehabilitated sexually. They teach about bowels, urine, spasms, and eating, but not sex. Come on now. Why are all of you here in this room tonight? Admit it. Aren't you hoping to have sex, some sex, sometime? How many admit it? Raise your hands?"

Another quadriplegic man (one who cannot move his arms and legs) asked out loud, "Hey, Joanne, come over here and help me raise my hand. You're an expert on things that go up." The loudest laughter of the night followed.

The group continued to talk for more than four hours. Persons with chronic illness struggle every day against bigotry, ignorance, insensitivity, and the discomfort of the helping professions with the topic of sexuality and disease. Here are some ideas related to sex and some forms of chronic illness. My teachers for these ideas have been the group you just heard from and all courageous hurt persons whose love has transcended disability.

Diabetes Mellitus

It's really a strange type of thing. I want to do it, I enjoy it, but my penis doesn't seem to be enjoying it as much as I do or it used to.

HUSBAND WITH DIABETES

More than two million men in the United States have diabetes. Approximately half of these men have problems with erection. Such problems in the case of male diabetes are not related to hormonal deficiency, but to microscopic nerve damage probably caused throughout the body by the accumulation of chemicals that damage these nerves. Some diabetic men have damage to the small vessels in the penis, because diabetes can cause the tiny vessels in the retina and kidneys and other organs, including the genitals, to function poorly (microangiopathy).

Just because a man has diabetes and has erection problems does not mean the two are causally linked. Some of the drugs used for diabetes can also cause erection problems, so a change in prescription might help.

First and foremost, tell your doctor about your problem! Second, remember that the problem is treatable. Third, remember that an erect penis is not a prerequisite to super sex. If erection problems are an early sign of diabetes, medicine and dietary management may help. If they don't, then do not assume that diabetes is the cause of the problem. The same hot and cold emotions that cause sexual problems for everyone can also occur in the diabetic. Some researchers feel that disregulation of the immune system in response to ineffective coping mechanisms relates to some forms of diabetes, so do not rule out emotional problems and professional help for these issues.

Diabetes does not have to affect interest, arousal, and the other aspects of the sexual-response system unless the diabetic allows it to by surrendering to the constant hassles of special diet, schedules of drug use, urine checks, and symptom vigilance. Even the symptom of erection problems may vary from time to time and may not be a static condition. Ejaculation, orgasm, and certainly psychasm will not be affected. Some of the couples I interviewed had stopped having sex completely because of unreliable erection. "We haven't done it for years. He just gradually lost it, the erection. We just don't do it," reported one wife in the group. Her husband continued, "It started to get a little flaccid and then there wasn't much at all."

I responded, "Yes, but sometimes these things change, and if you stop all sex, you'll never know what could be happening that you are missing. Let's look at other options to maintain sexual intimacy that are not dependent on erection so that you protect your sexual options." The couple learned much of what you read in Chapter Eight and noticed that sometimes there was an erection.

A very small percentage of diabetic men may experience retrograde ejaculation, a condition in which the ejaculate goes into the bladder instead of out the end of the penis. This is related to nerve damage that causes the internal muscles in the genital area to malfunction. This condition does not stop the sensation of orgasmic contractions, and all other aspects of the sexual-response system can remain intact.

There have been many advances in medical approaches for the more than ten million men who experience chronic erective failure, including new research on injection with papaverine hydrochloride and surgical insertion of prosthetic devices into the penis. Prosthetic devices include the fixed rod or inflatable implant, but any such surgery should be considered within the marital context. Remember that the erection is unnecessary for sexual fulfillment in the fourth perspective. As with any surgery, and particularly for the diabetic, there are always risks to be weighed against gains, and the whole process should be a team decision between marital partners and physician.

There has been much less research on diabetes in women regarding sexual functioning, although the effect of diabetes on female fertility has been studied for years. Once again, the biases of the first three sexuality perspectives dominates our medical orientation, including the assumption that women can always "receive" the male, so disease does not affect "them" as much.

Since diabetes can result in more frequent infections of all types, vaginitis is a particular problem for sexual functioning. Both partners may experience pain in intercourse related to this and other tissue infection. About one third of women with diabetes have problems with orgasmic contractions, probably related to the same neurological and vascular damage as in the male. Erection of the clitoris would also be expected to be affected. Diabetic women should check for recurrent mild urethral infections, cystitis, and vaginal abscesses. these are all treatable, so there is no reason to continue to have pain in intercourse. If you notice a decrease in natural lubrication (maybe due to microcirculation problems), check with your doctor. Again, do not assume that sexual problems are always related to your disease. If there is a lubrication problem, lubricants can be prescribed or recommended.

As with men, all areas of the sexual-response system remain intact for diabetic women. Interest, arousal, psychasms, and other dimensions do not have to be impaired if open communication and degenitalized approaches are considered and practiced.

Diabetes is like any other disease in that it is helped by positive emotions and intimacy, and hindered by fear and helplessness. Even if your diabetes gets worse, remember, you do not cause it to get worse. Even with your best efforts, diseases run different courses. None of these courses preclude intimacy. Every couple I treated in which one or both partners were diagnosed as diabetic were able at five-year follow-up to experience a mutually pleasing sexual life, even when the diabetes itself might have worsened. There were eighty-seven diabetic men in the sample and forty-seven diabetic women. While initially thirty of the men were considering implants, none of them went ahead with that procedure following counseling.

If severe genital problems have resulted from diabetes, there are still several things that can be done to enjoy sex. You read about some of these in Chapter Eight. One of the oldest medical jokes relates to a man whose arm hurts every time he tries to raise it. He tells the doctors about his problem and the medical advise is, "If it hurts when you do that, then don't do that." I would add, "If it hurts, check out why, if it can't be helped, try something else."

Ostomy and Sexuality

I just hate the thought that there is a hole right in me. I leave my T-shirt on during sex now. I could never stand the thought of my wife actually seeing the stoma [surgically created opening into abdomen]."
HUSBAND WITH COLOSTOMY

An ostomy is a surgical procedure by which an artificial opening is created in the abdomen so that the urine or intestinal contents flow into a collection sac attached at the sight of the opening (the stoma). There are three basic types of this surgery. A *colostomy* is most often performed because of cell disease (cancer) of the rectum or colon and in some cases of inflammatory bowel disease and diverticular disease. An *ileostomy* is most typically done in the case of inflammatory bowel disease. An *ileal conduit* is constructed to divert urine to a sac because of impaired bladder function, removal of the bladder, or neurological damage in this area.

The effect of the above surgeries is varied, but in general the sexual-response system as viewed from the fourth perspective is left intact. Depending on degree of damage to nerves in the area of surgery, some men may experience erectile problems, ejaculatory problems, or retrograde ejaculation. The ileal conduit procedure seems to have the most effect on erection, but even then more than one fifth of the men I interviewed (of a total of 122, including men not in the couples sample) reported no effect on erection. More than half of the men interviewed who had a colostomy (total 38) reported no erective or ejaculatory problems.

Women with ostomies may experience painful intercourse or some change in vaginal sensations. I found that postural adjustments helped greatly in many of the cases of coital pain, as some of the women were unintentionally compensating for the stoma and surgery by moving their bodies in ways that stressed different muscle groups. Of the forty women ostomy patients I interviewed, eight reported painful coitus that they attributed to the surgery. Thirteen, including these eight women, reported a change in vaginal sensations. As with the men, primary concerns were with appearance, partner acceptance, and odor that may come from the stoma.

I have found that the most effective counseling in these cases comes from partners of the patient talking to partners of other patients who have had an ostomy and resumed sexual functioning. This type of surgery requires some time before full physical stamina returns, so again the bywords are to take time, communicate, and move beyond the intercourse and mutual-orgasm orientation. I tell my patients that it is stamina more than stoma that will slow sex down at first.

Multiple Sclerosis and Sexuality

> I will never, I swear I will never in my life be used to walking with a cane. I'm twenty-eight years old, for God's sake. I'm walking with a cane, I have these tremors, and I am talking like a record stuck in slow speed. A real turn-on to my husband, isn't it. I'm more his patient than his lover.
>
> YOUNG WIFE WITH MS

This disease of the lining of the nerves continues to be a mystery as to cause and cure (although some patients have responded to treatment with adrenocorticotropin). Of the 167 men with MS (again these were men that included patients not in the couples group) that I interviewed, 43 reported erective problems. Of the 133 women with MS that were interviewed, the most common sexual complaint (44) was alteration or decrease in clitoral sensitivity. Both men and women reported decreased interest in sex, but interest level varied greatly over time. This variance is probably due to the ever-changing course of this illness, with symptoms coming and going with little or no warning. It is important for the MS patient to maintain intimacy, for the possibility of return of functions assumed lost always exists. One of my patients with MS stated, "I think MS stands for *m*uddled *s*ymptoms. You never know what will happen. I'm MS because I'm *m*uch *s*urprised most of the time."

Some of the patients reported spasticity as a symptom and had stopped having sex because of this problem. Counseling focused not on drug treatment of this condition (which may exacerbate sexual problems), but on integrating the spasticity into the sexual relationship. "I learned that slow, gradual, easy, and tender is only one side of the sexual coin. Movement, rigidity, shaking, and other movements feel good, too. Once I learned that, my sexual anxiety went down. When that happened, my symptoms seemed to decrease." This report from one of the husbands with MS illustrates the important interaction between feelings and symptoms in all disease, and emphasizes the importance of remembering that sexuality can help heal as much as be affected by disease. Sometimes couples can "use" symptoms and not merely try to overcome them.

"I am so tired most of the time," reported one wife. "So we have learned to be still, to have slow-motion sex. It's actually a turn-on. You should try it. We do everything at half speed, like a slow-motion film. When we stopped trying to do it like everyone else and do it like us, everything seemed to improve."

Arthritis and Sexuality

> I have learned to hate sex. It hurts, my whole pelvis hurts with every
> thrust. I just can't do it anymore.
>
>   WIFE WITH ARTHRITIS

Some of the symptoms that come with the various forms and degrees of arthritis include numbness, joint pain, weakness, fatigue,
and some muscular atrophy. The primary effect on sexuality seems
to be in sexual movements that accompany intercourse.

Of the 118 patients with some form of connective-tissue disorder
or arthritis, 26 had stopped having sex. Fatigue and pain were the
most frequent reasons given. I learned in the interviews, however,
that most of these patients were trying to have sex at night or in the
morning. These two times are typically the most painful in the cycle
of symptoms for most arthritis patients, particularly patients with
rheumatoid arthritis.

I suggested the following steps for the husbands and wives with
arthritis in the couples group.

1. Try a warm bath or shower before sex. The temperature of the water may
   lessen some of the pain in the joints and make movements easier.

2. Change the time of day you try to have sex. Late morning and early afternoon seem to be good times for less severe symptoms for my patients, but
   find your own sex time. Don't be bound by the nighttime trap.

3. Use warm compresses even during sex. Apply them just prior to posture
   changes, and incorporate them into the sex play.

4. Try the posture of the future. Mounting and thrusting are not sexual prerequisites.

5. If what you are doing hurts, don't only stop and change the activity, but
   discuss it later. There may be ways to make adjustments. Symptoms are
   always changing. What does not feel good today might feel great later.

6. Emotional state can affect some forms of arthritis directly. The stress of
   anxiety, fatigue, and work or family pressure is as damaging as postural
   pressures. Look to your emotional posture as much as you look to your
   sexual position.

Alcoholism and Sex

> I just drank it away. My sex drive, my erections, my job, my marriage.
> I just drank it away.
>
> ALCOHOLIC HUSBAND

A total of eighty-one men and forty-three women described themselves as alcoholics in the couples groups. Forty-seven of the men reported problems with erections and thirty of the women reported decrease in sexual interest. Even in cases where the physical examination did not reveal liver damage (a frequent consequence of alcoholism and one directly related to sexual problems because of impact on hormonal patterns), erective and sexual-interest problems were present. One woman reported, "I can't tell you if I am interested in sex or not. I do it a lot. But that doesn't mean anything. I go to work, too, but that doesn't mean I want to. When you're a drunk, you just do things. You're lucky if you remember what."

In addition to liver damage, neurological and circulatory problems occur with excessive drinking. Alcohol in the blood directly suppresses the sexual-reflex system. The body's immune system is seriously jeopardized by alcoholism, and the generally poor and deteriorating health of the alcoholic seriously affects sexuality.

Alcoholism, like all health problems, affects the entire family system. I have found that sexual counseling is not effective until the drinking problem and related family and marriage problems are confronted and remediated wherever possible.

We must recognize that our society's emphasis on the drinking/sexuality connection is strong. "A few drinks and I can really get it on," was one wife's report. She means that she experiences sufficient anxiety and insecurity that a chemical is needed to facilitate sexual interaction. The natural chemicals from our own brains are available to us if we will learn to relax, to share, to give a priority to intimacy so that we do not need "quick drugs" to depress us just enough that we can have sex. There is no human activity that is helped by drinking, and if you doubt that, you may be taking very early steps toward a drinking problem yourself. Drinking is ingesting small doses of a toxic substance that affects our nutrition, judgment, speech, perception, coordination, and ability to be truly intimate. It is one of our society's most serious problems, and the emphasis on the war against drugs should include alcohol as one of the major enemies.

During the treatment program for the couples, all alcohol was prohibited. Every one of the couples found that sex improved once they were free of their "habit." Our brains are preprogrammed to "get high," but our own bodies and brains provide the natural internal chemicals for that high. We seem to have a natural reflex, a joy response, and this joy response is blocked by alcohol, not enhanced by it. The couples found an immediate improvement in communication without alcohol, although at first some couples were awkward, actually in a type of mutual withdrawal state.

"It was like a first date. We just always used to have a drink or two before sex. It was kind of frightening at first, but we really rediscovered each other." This wife spoke for other spouses who at first resisted the sanction against drinking and then learned what it was like to respond drug-free in a sexual relationship.

If you have a drinking problem, even if you suspect one, get help now. You will not be able to stop alone later, and the earlier you get the help, the less suffering for all concerned. If you are drinking to change how you feel, you have a drinking problem. If you are fighting this issue as you read this material, you probably have a problem with alcohol.

Paraplegia and Quadriplegia

> If you are in a chair, people rule you out as a sexual possibility. I think the doctors did, too. My wife and I actually thought that our sex life was over. It's better than ever. Really. It sounds impossible, but it is better because it is not genital, can't be just genital.
>
> HUSBAND

The issue of spinal damage and sexuality has finally received more research attention. Anderson and Cole, in their book *Sexual Options for Paraplegics and Quadriplegics*, provide a list of guidelines for the physically handicapped that apply to all diseases. The list provides an excellent summary of the points that I have been making in this chapter.

1. A stiff penis does not make a solid relationship, nor does a wet vagina.

2. Urinary incontinence does not mean genital incompetence.

3. Absence of sensation does not mean absence of feelings.

4. Inability to move does not mean inability to please.

5. The presence of deformities does not mean the absence of desire (interest or arousal in my response system).

6. Inability to perform does not mean inability to enjoy.

7. Loss of genitals does not mean loss of sexuality.

There are so many different forms of spinal-injury impacts that I cannot discuss each specific type, but the rules above apply to each.

There are, of course, other diseases that I cannot discuss in this book. I have included the information I collected from the marital couples group and other patients with whom I have worked. One husband's statement has stayed with me as the best summary of the relationship between disease and sexuality. He is a mentally impaired man who has been married two years. He was engaged for sixteen years because, by his report, "Nobody thought we should or could get married. They thought it was a joke." He describes his love with his wife as follows:

"I know that people get divorced. I know I'm not as smart as most people. I'm not as smart as people who get divorced. But I can say I am smart enough to know something they don't know. I can say it. I can say that since I'm not so smart as they, maybe I am not as busy with all those other thoughts. Maybe I can love more because I don't think more, I'm not distracted from love. I'm not always thinking, but I'm always loving. Loving is easier than thinking because you have someone else to help you. Maybe people think too much and love too little."

A New Disease of a New Time: Aids and Faids

As I said earlier, the HTLV-III virus is related to, but does not cause, AIDS, Acquired Immune Deficiency Syndrome and the related disease ARC, AIDS-Related Complex. Both involve the weakening of our immune system. There is still no cure. It is the moral responsibility of anyone who has sexual contact with persons at risk of carrying the AIDS virus to be tested for the AIDS antibody. Persons who are immunopositive, who are tested carefully and with verification, should not exchange bodily fluids during sex until such time as they are proven to be no longer infectious. There is no safe way to have sex and exchange bodily fluids with an infected person. There are, as you have read, many ways to be intimate, to be sexual, including touching, holding, caressing, rubbing, self- and partner masturbation, and sharing of fantasy and sexual imagery. AIDS can be deadly, but it is still relatively hard to catch.

AIDS cases have increased 59 percent in 1986. There are now almost thirty-three thousand verified cases in seventy-four countries, according to the World Health Organization, representing an increase of twelve thousand cases since the beginning of 1986. Cases could increase tenfold in the next five years. I believe that enhancement of our natural immunity, emphasis on sexual intimacy and commitment over time, the use of condoms when sexually active with a new partner or partner who may have been exposed to the AIDS virus, and support, help, and understanding for AIDS patients are all important elements in the battle to survive this health crisis.

Marriage and sexual activity restricted to one exclusive partner is one of the best steps toward holding this deadly disease in check until a vaccine and, we hope, a cure can be found. Many of the opportunities presented in Chapter Eight are less likely to transmit the AIDS virus than other sexual interactions, but they are not preventive measures. Only sexual exclusivity is a reasonable approach at this time, making super marital sex even more of a positive health step for self and for society.

Dr. Harold Lief, a pioneer in the study of sex and marriage, describes what he calls FAIDS, or the fear of AIDS. It is certainly to be expected that any of us would fear a deadly disease, but fear will not help us find the exclusive intimacy that would decrease the spread of AIDS. Fear and anxiety actually weaken the immune system and allow even more vulnerability to the AIDS virus. If we want to lessen our chances of falling victim to any virus, I believe we must strengthen our immune system by healthy daily living and loving styles, not weaken it medically or by our living style. The focus on insertion, ejaculation, variety, and adventure that dominated the first three perspectives only makes us more vulnerable to any disease, including AIDS. The editors of a major journal, *The Journal of Sex and Marital Therapy*, state, "Voluntary abstention from sex with infected persons is our best weapon against the spread of AIDS to the general population." Another positive step is to commit intimately, intensely, and over time to one partner, to find super sex in one long-lasting, loving relationship.

Fertility and Sexuality

Eight years ago, couples started coming to me for help with fertility problems. They were referred by doctors who were working on the mechanical and metabolic aspects of fertility, working with drugs and timing and, in some cases, surgery. These doctors knew that emotions played a major role in fertility, but they did not know, and none of us know, how. They did know that the couples were becoming stressed by the constant vigilance, the repeated disappointments, the blaming and self-blame, the anger, the jealousy of those who seemed to get pregnant so easily. "Why is it," asked one of the wives, "that the only people who seem to get a child so easily are those who don't seem to want them or need them as much as we do?"

I cannot discuss the complexities of the fertility issues here. I can tell you, however, that I have now treated thirty-six couples in the last eight years. Three of these couples were in my couples sample. Thirty couples have succeeded in having a baby—sometimes more than one! I don't know, and I am sure that their doctors don't really know, why they succeeded. Was it the drugs, the hope, the timing, chance? I have found that mutual emotional support and reduction of stress can help relationships. I don't really know if it helps cause pregnancy, but I would guess that it does some good, perhaps again by enhancing the immune system, which has much to do with pregnancy. Here are some of the recommendations I give to the couples after consultation with their referring doctor.

1. It is not true that "just when someone adopts, they get pregnant." There are many such stories, but statistics do not bear them out. Nonetheless, a necessary first step in solving a fertility problem is to discuss together what options you will or will not accept. Would you adopt if necessary? What age, gender, race, and health-status child would you consider? Why do *we* want a child anyway? Don't fall for the simplistic "just adopt and you'll get pregnant" or "just relax and take a vacation" ploys. Fertility, all of loving and life, is much more complex than that.

2. Do you want a child or a baby? Babies sound nice and have millions of effective press agents, but they bring with them bundles of problems, too. Talk over the fact that parenting is an approximately seventy-year phase of development during which you will try to help someone become more mature than you are. Do you want to be parents together, or are there individual ambivalences that may need talking out, perhaps with a counselor or clergyperson? Learning to cooperate and share parenting and the continuing development of parenting goals and expectations is one of the

most intimate parts of marriage. It is a form of sharing available only within a relationship committed to nurturing the lives of persons growing within and from that relationship.

3. Don't panic. No matter what you hear, almost half of the couples in the United States have some trouble with fertility. Anxiety and fear won't help, so remember the perspective of your relationship. You have somebody already. You are just trying to add to the group.

4. It's not your fault or his fault or their fault. We just don't know enough about fertility to blame anybody anyway, and there are women getting pregnant every day who were told they were never going to have a child. Think of this issue as a systems issue, not an individual issue.

5. Just as in parenting, you must not personalize the problem. When parents take the credit or diminish their self-worth because of their children, they experience family problems. If you are trying to have a child to prove something, such as your masculinity or femininity, you are probably getting in your own way.

6. Your immortality does not rest in some genetic relay race. What you give to this world will not be measured in amounts of DNA. Remove this "pass it on" motive from your problem and you will have less stress.

7. There are no magic postures for fertility. No matter what you may have heard, there are no secrets about fertility. Mutually pleasing sexuality and intimacy are important, however, and constant focus on fertility can rob your marriage of sexual joy and closeness. Talk with your doctor about the timing issue and make sure he or she is aware that you would also like to have sex as well as have a baby, have fun as well as fertility, to maintain your loving.

8. Imagery helps. It is not just pop psychology to suggest that the mind is a powerful instrument for change. Both of you must enjoy the imagery of a child, not the focus on a problem, on succeeding. Talk "as if," think of "when," not "what will we do if we fail."

9. Speaking of failure, it is important to be realistic. Sometimes, for reasons that are not always understood, couples do not have their own biological children. Planning for a future together, for growth and joy and optional ways of parenting or giving back to the world, is important not as a surrender strategy, but as a viable if not the most desirable option.

10. Sometimes, in the focus on fertility, we forget the holistic approach to general health. While there are no magic vitamins or diets that automatically improve fertility, sound nutrition, exercise, prayer or meditation, balance between working and playing, and a large dose of laughter can help anything. Don't forget these factors in your focus on fertility.

11. Sometimes, rarely, there are underlying marital or individual psychological problems that get in the way of, not prevent, pregnancy. For both the husband and the wife, unresolved marital and personal problems should

be addressed in counseling. I'm not suggesting that personal psychological problems cause infertility. It's just good common sense to look to your own and your partner's own general life philosophy and happiness without blame but with support and interest in personal and relationship development.

12. Some of the steps in Chapter Eight have been very popular with the fertility couples. You may want to open up your own sex clinic and have some fun. You deserve it. Fertility counseling tires you out, angers you, and lets you down. I close this chapter with a report from one of the wives in the fertility program that summarizes the health and sexuality relationship.

Juggling Sex for Health

"We were sitting in your waiting room and got to talking with this older couple who said they were in your super marital sex program. They said they were your oldest couple." The young wife was reviewing the first visit to the clinic and her husband was nodding.

"They told us about the tests and the recommendations. They said something about a posture of the future. You know us. We thought that maybe that would get us pregnant, but they just wouldn't tell us. They laughed and said we would have to find out for ourselves. When your secretary came to get them, they turned to us and the husband said, 'We love it. You'll find it. But first, try these juggling bags. Dr. Pearsall gave them to us. They work like magic.' "

"Well," she continued, "we persons in fertility will try anything. We would stand on our heads if it would work. We took those things home and laughed like crazy. We got so daffy at home that we got carried away. We had sex on the wrong night. We had never—I mean never—done that. Some weeks later, we got pregnant. When we came to your office to see you, we met the same people. I gave him the bags back and told him that they worked. He laughed and took his wife's hand. "Do you think we should juggle tonight? Two seventy-year-olds might just juggle themselves more than they could handle."

Removing the burden of fear, pressure, and misunderstanding that can accompany health problems is the first step to protecting your sexual rights. To review this issue, try the next opportunity.

Super Marital Sex Opportunity Number Eleven

There is no way for persons who have no serious impairment to know what it is like to attempt to return to sexual intimacy following the insult of disease or injury. To help you and your spouse communicate about this issue and to broaden the range of your sexual interaction to include a small degree of imposed interference in sexual behavior, spend one love session with one partner blindfolded. Make sure there is plenty of light for one spouse while the other partner experiences the absence of one sense. Change the opportunity around on a different night. Talk about the experience both from the blind position and the sighted position in making love. Notice how you must accentuate your other senses, learn to love beyond the limits of light, and modify your sexual system and roles within that system. How adaptive were you? How adaptive was your marital system?

Some of the couples in the clinic invented their own opportunities to understand about impairment and sensory compensation and enhancement. One couple taped large wads of cotton under their arms and behind their knees, just enough to restrict movement. They wondered together about a time when their own movements might be restricted by the aging process. Some couples extended the sensory deprivation and compensation opportunity outside of the lovemaking sessions to daily living, with one partner wearing the blindfold or cotton all day while being helped by the spouse. There is a big difference between seeing and perceiving, "knowing" and experiencing, and super marital sex depends on a depth and range of adaptive sensuality, a sex strong enough to survive the most catastrophic of times. If we are able to learn this lesson and teach it to our children, we have provided them with an important love legacy. The next chapter discusses love education for super relationships.

CHAPTER TWELVE

𝕌𝔸𝕌𝔸𝕌

Sexual Inheritance: Leaving Your Children Something to Love By

> I could ask my parents what they wanted me to ask, what they were comfortable enough for me to ask. Never did I ever really tell them anything about my sex life, and they certainly never told me about theirs. In fact, they still haven't.
>
> HUSBAND

The Thirteenth Key: Making Sex A Snap

He would never find it back there. He grappled, searching for the magic snap that would open the bra that was worn more as formality and culture costume than for any real physical necessity. He had seen his mother reach behind her and do something that released it, but could find nothing at all now but a band of elastic. Maybe she puts it on over her head. Maybe there isn't any snap at all, he thought. He had never heard of such a thing in the secret tribal stories related by his peers, but this one could be an exception. After all, he thought, this might be a special therapeutic bra made for small breasts like these. He didn't know that the connection was in the front, and she was offering no help at all, apparently in some form of tolerant trance, a feigned innocence oblivious to his struggle.

As he moved around the steering wheel to get a better angle, she banged her lip on his shoulder. He heard a little groan, the first

323

sound, perhaps an indication that she might be coming out of her
trance. Her orthodontic braces cut against her upper lip. Oh no!
she thought. I taste blood. What if he tastes it? What if I'm bleeding
all over? It's too dark to tell. What if I need stitches? She licked
her lip several times and forced herself to swallow until the blood
taste was gone. His head was around to her back, so she quickly
brushed her wrist across her mouth and tried to hold her hand close
to the windshield where there was some light. Is that blood or not?
she wondered. I can't see what this is on my wrist. She held it up
a little higher, and he straightened up, took her hand, and kissed
it.

She must like her hands kissed, he thought. She's probably been
holding it up there for me and I never saw it. She probably thinks
I don't know about girls liking their hand kissed.

He gave up his search for the magic snap. She must be wearing
a new type of protective bra, one designed to keep boys away from
girls' breasts. It must be a chastity bra. Just my luck that they would
come up with this invention in time for my adolescence. I know I
should start on the breasts, but I guess I'll go for her vagina. His
effort to follow sexual protocol had failed, foiled by a modern world
that teased him constantly with sexual enticements and now had
designed a new obstacle to their attainment. He didn't seem to
notice that his sexual arousal was gone, replaced by a closequarters
wrestling match with another person who seemed almost unconscious. The search had displaced the purpose.

Her skirt was now bunched up around her waist. She couldn't
see and had to make a passage through the material so she could
breathe. What if I get blood from my mouth on the skirt? How will
I ever explain that to my mother? What if she sees sex wrinkles.
She'll know for sure what I've been doing.

And then, panic. He's going to kiss me again, and he'll taste
blood. Blood! Oh no! He's reaching between my legs and I have a
pad on. Oh no! She relaxed after the first flush of panic as she
remembered that she had a built-in genital protector. She had only
to spread her legs and her pantyhose would spread out like a genital
safety net.

"I don't believe this," he said, loudly enough so she could hear
him. I always thought their stockings were sheer and sexy, he
thought. These are industrial strength. They're another trick to stop
me. Why isn't she wearing the nylons and garter belt like in the
magazines I hide under my stereo speaker? Those things even point
the way for you. Maybe over the top will work. I'll never be able
to pull them down. I'll go in over the top, he thought. As he searched

for the top, some seam to slip under, the bunched skirt hid the approach route. Maybe I better kiss her again. It's been a while, and I better keep her hot or she'll stop me. She probably thinks I'm an absolute incompetent already. She probably thinks this is my first time. It is, but I never thought she would find out. What if she tells somebody? I'm going to give her a good, deep kiss. A real plunger, a Roto-Rooter job. That'll get her going again.

I better get him to kiss me. If I can get back to kissing, we can get back to talking, then back to holding, then go home. I'm getting scared, she thought. She lowered her head as he quickly raised, his, and they banged foreheads so hard she saw stars. She thought, My god. I'll end up knocked out instead of up. They'll find us here unconscious, my lip bleeding, my skirt around my neck. Oh God, what a mess. And my forehead and lip hurt so bad I could cry.

Damn, that hurt, he thought, wanting to grab his forehead but noticing that she seemed unfazed, apparently used to sexual head-banging as part of the whole sex act. Maybe she's into that pain stuff. Maybe I've been too gentle. Maybe she thinks I'm a sex wimp. It didn't faze her, and it nearly killed me.

A bright light shone directly in his face. My God, he thought. I must have broken my skull. I'm seeing bright light. "Let's go, kids." said the police officer from behind the flashlight. "Time to head home."

Both young people were startled from any remnant of sexual arousal, relieved that they were not arrested and imprisoned for immature and clumsy sexual conduct. They rode home together silently, heads hurting, lips sore, hoping only that their parents would never detect from their appearance any signs of their sexual struggle.

The thirteenth key to super marital sex is to teach and learn, to teach and learn with each other as husband and wife and as a family. The thirteenth key is the most important of all the keys, and the one that has seldom been discussed from the first three perspectives. The focus has been an individual focus, an adult focus, when in fact sexuality is a lifelong process that begins in the uterus and affects the entire family every day. The thirteenth key is a family sexual orientation, an openness and specificity of sexual discussion to prevent the tragedy of abortion, sexually transmissible disease, sexual problems, even the emotional trauma that results in drug abuse and an alarming rise in adolescent suicide. Our children are, and we have been, looking for love in all the wrong places and in the wrong ways, seldom benefiting from a strong and supportive sexual and loving education from within our family, educational, and religious institutions.

This chapter is about sex education in the United States. In spite of all of the talk and writing about sex education, there are very few programs that are successfully teaching the combination of love, sensuality, morality, and responsibility. With few exceptions, we continue to teach mechanics and the first three perspectives with their genital and energy-release focus. We are not offering love education, not talking about the purpose behind the struggle of the young people in the story you have just read. We are teaching "preventive sexuality," a way of preventing disease and pregnancy rather than an enhancing intimacy that can bring the joy of closeness with another person.

Think about your sex and love education. Where and how did you learn about sexuality? Have you really learned enough to teach it yourself? There will never be a school- or church-based sex-education course that will do the job that needs to be done, the job of telling the whys and hows of making love and not just the mechanics of procreation and contraception. As long as sex remains a dirty joke in our schools and a mystery in our homes, we will continue to suffer in a sexually stagnant society. There has never been a sexual revolution at all, but a sexual involution, a turning in to a mechanical, pleasure-oriented sex rather than a looking forward to loving, fulfilling, long-lasting sexual relationships in a daily living context. We will never really be able to have super marital sex by looking only for super sex. You have read throughout this book that sex and love, and all the learning that each requires, cannot be separated from each other. This is the connection that can be opened with the thirteenth key, the key of lifelong learning.

Teaching sex will never be enough. We have to role-model love and caring, talk about everything sexual with everyone in our home, and continue to learn about sexuality and intimacy throughout life. We cannot leave our children to struggle blindly in parked cars. We will have to talk about the snaps on bras and the zippers on jeans. We will have to help them find a safe place and a safe way to be sexual, and not tease them with the joys of sex, then try to hide sex from them. They will always find it. They have already found it. They were born with it and born doing it. Do we want them to suffer without our help? If that happens, what they find will never be super marital sex. We have to put the love, the real snap of sex, back into sexuality.

The Wrong Lessons of Love: Twelve Erotic Errors

The young couple in the parked car struggled so not only because they didn't have a place for sex or a way to be safely comfortable and communicate sexually, but also because they had learned well the wrong lessons of sex. Ironically, this young couple's struggle was similar in many ways to sexual struggles within marriage. They didn't have their own place, they couldn't find privacy, they didn't talk about sex, they didn't work as a team. They were trying to do sex to each other or for each other, not with each other, and they were victims of the same genital focus I have discussed throughout this book.

Here is a list of the twelve erotic errors that have served as the sexual lesson plan for the first three perspectives of sexuality.

1. Sex is an impulse. It is the strongest, the most difficult to control of all human impulses.

2. If you start touching erotic zones, it is difficult to turn back, to control the "sexual impulse," the gravity of sexual drive pulling us helplessly toward intercourse.

3. "Foreplay" is a preset collection of guaranteed sexual maneuvers that must be learned primarily by boys to get girls ready for sex.

4. Boys are always ready for sex, always want it, will do it with almost any girl if they have the chance. Anything less than constant sexual urgency is less than manly. A quote by Emo Philips illustrates this focus. "My schoolmates would make love to anything that moved, but I never saw any reason to limit myself." So goes the "folk myth" of sex in the school years.

5. Good girls don't want sex. Bad girls may want it, so boys should have it with them and then find a good girl to marry. Good girls need a lot of "foreplay," so boys, who are never bad for wanting sex and are "queer" if they don't, should practice their technique on bad girls.

6. Everything you do sexually is for intercourse. Intercourse is the best, most adult thing in the whole world.

7. "Playing around" with hugging and kissing is fun, but if you don't finally "go all the way," you aren't grown up and you may end up hurting yourself.

8. Sex is natural and simple. Anybody can do it. You don't have to learn how to "make out," you just have to let yourself go.

9. You had better use contraception and always have it ready. It takes away from the "real thing," but you have to have it ready, because once you start "playing around," you will lose control and always want to "go all the way."

10. If you are really deeply in love, you will want to have intercourse. If you are a girl, intercourse means love, so if you have done "it," you are probably in love. If you are a bad girl, and just like sex for fun, feelings, and closeness, you can have a lot of sex and never been in love. Intercourse is something good girls try to save and give later as a marital gift. Bad girls might trade intercourse too soon and for too little.

11. If you are a boy and in love, you will know just what to do to please your girlfriend. You will magically know, through love, every secret turn-on. Love is so strong that it makes sex remarkable.

12. Your parents would never understand about your sexual feelings. They are older, times were different for them, and they just want to tell you about not doing it or contraception, sperm, and eggs. Nobody tells their parents what they really do or would want to do sexually. Old people don't have the same sex feelings as young people, if they have any left at all.

Here are some answers to these misassumptions regarding sexuality. In each of the twelve areas, I have included a quote from sessions with the children of the thousand couples to illustrate their concerns. The parents in the couples program were present for family sexual counseling sessions as a part of their super marital sex program. Such sessions were optional, but 63 percent of the couples elected to have them. Fifty-two percent of those couples requested additional sexual counseling sessions with their children. I have found that dealing with the entire family system, not just the marital couple, is most effective in clinical work. The couples I am now seeing are electing this approach at an almost 75 percent frequency.

1. If you get turned on, you know, you get horny-like, you really don't know what you're doing. You might do anything. You can't control it, so you shouldn't get a boy turned on. You could end up attacked and not even know what happened to you.

TWELVE-YEAR-OLD GIRL

Make sure you understand one thing about sex. You always are in control. It is just a story, a made-up thing, that you get out of control. Unless you do something dumb like take drugs or drink alcohol, you always know what you are doing, even when you are enjoying getting turned on in sex. Boys always know, too, even if they get really turned on. If you or the boy keeps saying that you just might not know what you are doing, then it can be an excuse for doing anything, for fooling yourself and each other. Your parents know that everything in life is a decision, and that applies to sex.

> 2. You should never let a boy touch you down there. If you get it touched, then you will want more touching, and then you just get more and more, like you just have to have it.
>
> THIRTEEN-YEAR-OLD GIRL

That's right. You should never let a boy, or anybody, ever touch your genitals or any part of your body except for two purposes. One is for health, when a doctor or nurse or some professional person is trying to help you. The other is for love, for loving for a long long time. You should decide if you will let someone touch you or whether or not you will touch someone based on whether or not you love that person. It's that simple. When someone wants to touch you, it should be to help or to love, and in both cases the person should have earned your trust so you believe that he or she is giving the real reason for touching. One more important thing to know about this is that even if someone does touch you, it is not like you jumped off a cliff and can't stop. You can stop anytime, and you can, if you want to, just touch and touch without going any further. Touching someone you love, letting that someone touch the one thing that God gave you that you can see, your body, is the most special act in the world.

> 3. I dated this girl for a long time, man. She was a fox and everything. A real fox. But she didn't get it on or like that. I did all the stuff, and she was like nothing', man. She said I didn't know how to do it. I felt like a jerk.
>
> FOURTEEN-YEAR-OLD BOY

There is one magical way to turn a girl on. Only one person in the whole world knows this magical way. I'll let you in on the secret. The person who knows is the person herself. There isn't any one way that is the right way. Everyone is different. Getting turned on is something two people do together. Boys don't turn girls on and girl don't turn boys on. Even though the books and some of the guys or girls might brag that there are certain ways to do it, they are just plain wrong. Remember, anybody except your parents or the boy or girl you love who is telling you about what they do in sex is either lying, bragging, or covering up their own ignorance. Talk to your parents. They have proven they know at least a little bit of what they are doing, because you are sitting here talking very maturely about sex. They must have done something right.

> 4. Boys are always turned on. It's all they ever think about. Just walk down the hall at school, and they are ready to jump you. They say things all the time. Boys are just all sexed up.
>
> FOURTEEN-YEAR-OLD GIRL

You're right that it seems like boys are always all sexed up, because they seem to act that way when they are around each other. When you talk to them alone, face to face and seriously, you will find that they are not different from you. It's just like with girls. There are certain ways you have to act to belong to the right group, to fit in. We all do that, even as adults. Some girls pretend they don't ever think about sex, because that's what other girls say, but everyone has strong sexual feelings sometimes. Remember, God didn't give one set of feelings to boys and another to girls. Everybody got everything when it comes to feelings.

> 5. There are two types of girls in school. Some have a lot of sex and talk about it and everything. The other girls are nice, and they don't do it or talk about it much. If you get to be like a bad one, the boys know it and flock around you like flies, but the good girls will stay away from you and you won't have nice friends.
>
> SIXTEEN-YEAR-OLD GIRL

If there are a thousand girls at your school, then there are a thousand types of girls, because everyone is different. During our school years, and even when you are an adult, it seems easier to classify or put people into categories, especially if someone else is seen as less or worse than we are. That seems to keep us safe from being on the wrong side of things, looking bad ourselves. We are all insecure. Some girls and boys use sex to be popular, to get friends, or to get noticed, even if it is bad notice. Good girls will never draw boys like flies, but you won't want to. You will want to have a lot of friends and sooner or later just one boy. Remember, boys and girls make up a lot of stories about sex because they don't get to talk with their parents. A lot of that is wishful thinking or even fear coming out. And you know what? I have never met a really bad girl or a bad boy, just sometimes troubled, angry, frightened boys and girls who make up stories because they are confused. The more confused they are, the more they have to make things up.

6. My boyfriend and I have done almost everything. Sorry about that,
   Mom and Dad, but you said we should be honest. We have made
   out and all that, but we never did it, the real thing. He wants to, but
   I stop him from having intercourse. It's a real battle sometimes.

   FIFTEEN-YEAR-OLD GIRL

I think the best thing you could have done is be able to talk about
this with your parents, so you shouldn't apologize. I'm sure they
thank you for letting them be a part of this important area of your
development. You made a mistake, though. You said that you
haven't done "it," like touching, kissing, holding, and allowing
each other to touch and be touched was not the real thing. You will
find as you get older that touching, holding, and kissing are the
best, most enjoyable part of sex. Intercourse is for having babies
and is one way to be very close, but there is nothing at all that
makes it more arousing than other closeness. The reason everybody
talks about it so much and makes it sound so much more exciting
is that it seems forbidden, more grown-up. It really is for marriage
only anyway, because it requires planning on being together forever
before you do it. Remember, too, that intercourse is not something
for boys or men, it is for loving people. Talk to your boyfriend
about this. Just because you choose not to have intercourse at this
time does not mean you don't want to have intercourse.

7. Can't you hurt yourself if you just fool around too much? I was told
   that some guy had his testicles permanently enlarged by just playing
   around and not going all the way. He said it was blue balls.

   THIRTEEN-YEAR-OLD BOY

More people have gotten hurt, that is to say, have gotten into problems, by going all the way than not going all the way. There is no
such thing as blue balls, and boys and girls cannot be hurt by not
having intercourse after getting very aroused. As a matter of fact,
feeling blue is more related to intercourse before you are really
ready for it, so fooling around is a great choice if you feel enough
love and respect to trust each other and really share the experience.
Remember, there are ways to relieve the buildup of sexual feelings
other than intercourse. Discuss some of these options with your
parents.

8. I don't need to discuss this stuff. I don't know why my mom and
   dad wanted me to come here. It's just natural stuff. You don't have
   to learn what comes naturally.

   FIFTEEN-YEAR-OLD GIRL

You're half right and half wrong. Being sexual is natural. You inherit that by being human. But making love, relating to another person sexually, must be learned. Even animals have to be taught, have to be helped to be able to copulate, to have sex together. If you see them doing it, they learned it by watching other animals.

What separates us from other animals is how much and how well we can learn things, and that includes sexual things. That means we can learn to do much more than copulate. We can learn to love, to touch, to treat each other with respect. If you ever have a sexual problem, it will really be a learning problem, so you will have to ask your parents or the person you love to help you learn more.

> 9. In school they taught us to always have contraception available. They said you could end up pregnant if you start kissing and stuff and don't have protection.
>
> FIFTEEN-YEAR-OLD BOY

Being old enough to have sex means being old enough to be totally responsible for yourself and your behaviors. That includes not having children if you don't want or can't handle them. If you are not ready for children, you are not ready for intercourse. But don't think that just because you kiss and are feeling romantic that you should automatically think of intercourse and contraception. I tell all of the young people I talk to that they should not have intercourse until they are married. Plain and simple, just don't do it. Touch, hold, kiss, and love, but no intercourse. If you have learned a lot about contraception, you are really far ahead because that's very important knowledge. If you have learned that you must or almost automatically will have intercourse because you are a sexual person, you have learned the wrong lesson. Such sex should not mean intercourse. No matter what you hear, self-control is just as important as birth control, and contraception never replaces self- and partner responsibility. Saying no is an excellent contraceptive.

> 10. I don't plan on letting any guy have it unless he is really special. I might give it to a guy if he shows he loves me, but not just because he wants it. They lie anyway, and they will say they love you. You have to be sure before you give it to them.
>
> SIXTEEN-YEAR-OLD GIRL

You make it sound as though intercourse is a gift. It is really something you do with someone else for joy, closeness, and love in a relationship that you think will last a very long time. It's for you, too, not just your lover. Intercourse is an exchange of feelings emotionally and physically, something for both people to enjoy. It is not a thing you give to someone, it is a process of life you share with someone. Doing it for someone is not intercourse, it's just "course." The "inter" part of intercourse is what is important, and that means together, between. You can't tell you love someone by whether or not you have had intercourse with them and you shouldn't hold intercourse out as something to be earned. You will only end up being hurt, because when the boy thinks he has to earn it, he won't be thinking of you, he'll be thinking of it. He might try to make making love a goal, and then the lies and manipulation start.

> 11. When I find the right girl, I will know it, because it will be special. We will know what to do, I will know just how to please her. It will be like some of the songs, you know. It will make you walk on air.
>
> SIXTEEN-YEAR-OLD BOY

If love and sex were anything like the records say it is, nobody would work or eat because they would be too busy making love. Songs are fantasy. The reason the records are popular is that they sometimes describe a type of romance that nobody else ever has, but wishes they could have and thinks someone else, perhaps the singer, does have. Songs are a way to dream to escape. Listen more carefully to some of the songs and you will hear that intense feelings of love cause some real sadness. You might hear that love hurts. Being in love is something you think about, plan, and work on, too. It doesn't guarantee sexual skill or fulfillment and, even if sexual technique and turn-on with someone are really excitement, it doesn't mean that there is necessarily love. Love does not lead you, you lead love. Both of you will make it. It won't convert you. Love doesn't teach you, you learn to love.

> 12. This is impossible. You want me to just talk about sex and tell my parents about this. Are you crazy? They are from another world. They would die if I really told them what is going on out there.
>
> FIFTEEN-YEAR-OLD BOY

What makes them upset is not being told or not feeling able to talk with you about these things. You know what? Your parents have had more sex than you have. Yes. I know you may find that hard to believe, but your parents have had and do have sex. They love each other. There is nothing absolutely nothing, you cannot tell your parents. It is very, very sad that young people are out there in large numbers fumbling around trying to learn sex on their own, or pretending they've already learned it, when they have parents to talk to and from whom they could learn. And one more thing. You don't have to start out by telling them anything. Ask them things. Ask about their feelings, about their sexuality. Fair is fair. They'll tell you theirs if you'll tell them yours. You don't have to talk about what you do or they do, but talk about feelings and values and beliefs and specifics about what can, cannot, and sometimes should not be done. Go ahead. Make their day. Ask them a good, strong question you think they can't handle.

The couple in the last question braced themselves, looking at me with a "what have you done?" stare. Their son looked down, then shyly looked at me instead of his parents. "Okay. Here it is." He never looked at his parents, but looked at me as if to say "watch them die right here in your office." "Dear Mother and Father. Do you think a sixteen-year-old boy should have sex?" He looked down as if waiting to hear two thuds of falling parental figures.

"Okay. Here goes," said his mother. "We'll see what we have learned from Dr. Pearsall." She meant she was about to see if what she and her husband had learned about super marital sex really worked at this serious time in their marriage, this very sexual time. "Yes and no."

Their son did the adolescent flop. This is a rapid motion of slouching down in a chair while murmuring toward the sky some not quite audible profanity of disbelief at the redundant stupidity of the parent species. This is also known as the "I told you so" slide.

"No, wait," said the father. "I know what she means, I think. Nobody thinks of their own kid of sixteen as much older than eight, really. We sure don't think of you having sex. But we are not as dumb as we look to you. We know everyone is sexual. We know every sixteen-year-old is having some type of sex. So no, we wish you didn't. Yes, we know you do and will. No, we hope it won't be intercourse. Yes, we hope it's necking, even masturbation, because it's just natural. It's as hard for us to think of you having sex as it is for you to believe that we did at your age and still do. I didn't have intercourse then, and neither did your mother. But we necked up a storm. I would go home and masturbate and feel guilty as hell. So there, I said it."

The father did the parental drop. This is a much slower easing into a chair, with lowering of the head as if in prayer for some special parental dispensation, and waiting for the next barrage or challenge. Parents of adolescents can't slouch down too far because they may be to tired or too weak to unslouch. They do it as an appeal for the slightest form of mercy or empathy from their teenager.

"You did it, Dad?" said the son. "Far out. I mean, far out." The mother looked at me as if to ask, "He isn't going to ask me more is he?" The son looked almost startled. He went into the adolescent fidget, cracking his fingers and making noises with his mouth that seemed prerecorded. "Okay," he said, lingering on the *O* and the *kay*. "Let's eat, I'm starved."

As all parents of adolescents know, the eating reflex signals a recuperation, a rallying for the next battle. It also means that, for now, their teen will break bread with them. In this case, it means that a more open and direct discussion about sex could take place.

As the family rose to leave, and the son and father shook my hand, the mother gave me a big, long hug. As she left, she looked back and raised her hand high. Her first two fingers were crossed.

Ten Rules for Talking with Kids About Sex

> "Every time I sit down to talk about sex, to have 'the talk,' my son says, 'Oh Dad, I know all that," and walks way."
>
> FRUSTRATED FATHER

The reason the mother's fingers were crossed is that she knew there were still years of sex education to go. She knew what the peer group exerts profound influence, and she feared for the welfare of her son in a world confused about sexuality. The rules for effective loving and sex education are really simple. Here is the list. Talk it over with your whole family and see if they don't agree.

Rules of Family Sex Education

1. Never have a "sex talk." Sitting down for a formal birds and bees lecture is bound to fail. Sex cannot be separated from life, so deal with any problems of life when they relate to sex. If you look, you will see the relationship everywhere. Phone calls, assertiveness, curfews, discipline, respect, differing treatment of the father, mother, brother or sister, TV programs, movies, and dozens of everyday events relate to sex. Sex mini-lessons should take place then, related to an issue everyone can actually experience.

2. There is no need to do all of the talking. Listen and you will hear. You will hear questions even if they are not put in question form. "Nobody around

here cares about me" is a sex question about self-esteem and acceptance. "I wish our family was taller" is a question about body-image. "Look at that chick" is a question about sexism. "He's a fag" is a question about gender identity. Use of explicit sex words is always a question about what and how to have sex, about values and morals and social appropriateness, even about technique. Good sex education is much more listening than telling.

3. Your children know a lot already, but they think they know a lot more than they do, and a lot of what they know just is not so. What they know something about is the mechanics, but much less about values and right and wrong. They wonder about love, about how and what to do with whom sexually. They want to know what love is, what it means, how you know when you are in love. Start talking about that openly and see how much discussion takes place. Another guideline is that the more they pretend to know, the more mechanical and mythological their knowledge really is. Teens seldom come to you and say, "You know, Mom and Dad, I'm really very vulnerable and immature. Your experience is so much broader than mine. Could you please fill me in?" Such statements may occur only when there is emergency need to use the family car, not when there is real need to know.

There are really four basic areas that need to be addressed. These are what I call the "BARE" facts. B stands for biology. As I have said, many kids have learned something about the basic biology of sex. You may want to make sure all four, not just the first three perspectives of sexuality, are a part of your children's biological knowledge. Most formal sex education emphasizes the same genital/energy approach of the early sex perspectives, not the fourth perspective of this twenty-first-century marriage manual.

A stands for attitudes. They need to know yours, you need to know theirs. What is their attitude toward premarital sex and intercourse, abortion, masturbation, various sexual behaviors and preferences?

R stands for reproduction. They need to know about menstruation, conception and contraception, sexually transmitted diseases, responsibility for sex, children, and family.

E stands for emotion. They need to know about your feelings, be able to clarify and express their own feelings. An important warning here! Your feelings, their feelings, change. Sometimes they may shock you and test you. Give it some time. They may try a feeling out for a while. Teenagers particularly use the "feeling for a day" system of trying out for life. They are less moody than they act, and they do tend to "act" moody. Don't overreact, because overreaction is what they are testing for and afraid of, in you and within themselves. When you overreact, teens go from the more acceptable playacting and testing of parents to acting-out, which almost always signals unexpressed feelings of helplessness.

4. Sex and love education cannot be done "one way." One obvious reason sex education can be a difficult family problem is that the child or teenager

is "on the spot," the student. In my teaching, I have found that I am most effective when I am learning and sharing, not telling. I'm not really sure there is any such thing as teaching if it means telling. Changing behavior and thinking always depends on interaction, on a two-way learning. Ask your children to teach you about their world. Remember, you were *never* their age! They live in their own time, and, as the poet Kahlil Gibran stated, we cannot visit there, not even in our dreams.

5. Sexual education does not have to be same-gender-oriented. The "talk to your father" or "go ask your mother" routine is totally unnecessary if both parents are comfortable with sexuality. Your sexual insignia, your genitals, are not prerequisites for sexual educating. As a matter of fact, both parents together are the best arrangement, because you are discussing sex *and* love education, best illustrated by a model of love and loving.

6. The focus in sexual and love education must be on "do's" and not "don'ts." Presenting a list of fears and sanctions against sexual behaviors can result in a list of "sounds interesting, I should try that." Give them ideas of what to do. "Touch, hold, kiss, and fondle" is much more intriguing than "don't have sex until you're married." There are two exceptions to this focus on the "do." Always teach two "don'ts" along with the "do's." Don't have intercourse until you are married, and don't ever hurt anyone else.

7. Practice your approach together. The biggest danger in sex and love education is what I call "split-parent sex education." This happens when parents' values and ideas are different. Kids are expert at using this difference to collect whatever support they need for whatever it is they want to do or not to do. If the two of you can't get it together, you really can't expect your children to get themselves together.

This is a book about marital sex, but even in a single-parent home, it is a good idea to try to get someone you trust and respect to help with sex and love education. This "unit" approach seems to be a very helpful technique, but one that takes some very open prior communication with the person chosen to help.

8. Sex and love education is not a one-time thing. Sexuality is a lifetime process. Both you and your children will learn forever. We will know we are making some progress when regular sex- and love-education classes are offered in our nursing homes. Sex education is definitely not for children! It's for everyone.

The "inoculation theory" of sex education does not work. You cannot teach children once and render them sexually immune. Repeating over and over never really works for getting their room clean, but they do learn that you value cleanliness. They will also learn through repetition what you value sexually, your marriage-intimacy emphasis.

9. In spite of what children say or how they seem to act, if you have raised them in love, they have and know love. They may try to shock you, but in spite of the fact that the boy your daughter is dating has green hair and honks the horn instead of coming to the door, she still has you in her. In

spite of the fact that your son is dating a girl who looks as if she might have invented the words "surly" and "sultry" and puts her gum on the corner of her plate while she eats your Thanksgiving dinner, he has you in him. Remember that much of your work is already done by how you have loved them and loved each other. That is what will be there in emergency values situations. Another meaning of the term "super marital sex" is that the lesson of your own loving can transcend the moment and provide an infinite lesson of love.

10. Tell me exactly, in no uncertain terms, what you hope they will do sexually. Offer them the use of your home for sex. It's your choice. They will do it somewhere. Where is up to you. Be explicit and direct. "If you're going to make out, make out here in your room. It's safer. Don't do anything but make out. No intercourse. We won't interrupt you if you don't interrupt us when we make out. Of course, *we* can have intercourse. We're married." Don't let the car, motels, or the homes of less caring or absent parents determine the sexual destiny of your children.

Sex in 6-D: The Six Dangers of Flunking Sex Education

When sex education and love education fail, there are clear signs of such failure. They are all very, very important signs of problems for the developing young person.

Drugs: There is no high like the high of intimacy with another person. When that high is not available, it may be sought elsewhere, and that elsewhere might be drugs. Moodiness, changes in eating habits, anger without explanation, pallor, darkened circles beneath the eyes, withdrawal, defensiveness, and marked personality change are some of the signs of drug use. There are others, but I believe that our society's failure to help our young people become sexual people plays a major role in their turning to artificial and deadly ways to get high. The war on drugs must be accompanied by an emphasis on teaching loving and intimacy. We are leaving our children with nothing to do with their developing sexuality. If we don't teach them safe means of sexual self-expression, they may find other, dangerous ways to express themselves.

"Just say no" has been the new major campaign against drug use. It will never work. The issue is, What can our developing young people say yes to? How can they safely say it? Both answers relate as much to sexuality as any other aspect. A society that campaigns against sex, drugs, and violence, but fails to teach sexuality, love, and tenderness, is running a dishonest and ineffective campaign.

Depression: I mentioned earlier that there is a direct relationship between feelings of loneliness and isolation and serious depression. The sexual needs of the developing person cry out for direction and understanding, for discussion and focus. Adolescent suicide is dangerously increasing, in part because sexual feelings in our young people are not tolerated and have few safe avenues for expression.

There are many myths about teen depression and suicide. If they threaten it, they won't do it. If they are active and involved, they won't do it. If they are doing well in school, they won't do it. If they come from a good home, they won't do it. These statements are false. If you are worried, there is reason to worry, so reach out now. It is *not* just depressed people who kill themselves. Agitated, afraid, worried, insecure, hyperactive people kill themselves, too. Healthy sexuality is a key part of making it through the stress of young adulthood. Wrong turns on the love maps of these young people can result in death through sexual experimentation gone wrong. Some adolescents hang themselves to cause a high related to lack of oxygen while masturbating, failing at the last moment to control the lack of oxygen. This cause of death is known to all clinicians, but is not often talked about. The sexual problem, called asphyxiophilia, is one of the so-called paraphilias, problems with relationships and loving sexuality. We might hear the comment, "He never said anything at all to me about being really that upset," after a young person has killed himself, because what he might have said was not something we wanted to hear or were too uncomfortable to allow him to tell us.

Dropping out: Some young people withdraw not only from school or life, but from sex. They feel unaccepted or undesirable, or their parents overtly or covertly convey a message of sex as unimportant or unacceptable. The young person then seeks all fulfillment outside of sexuality. As dangerous as focusing exclusively on sexuality, this type of adjustment is tolerated by schools and society. The person may look for meaning through cultism. He or she may become overinvolved in isolated activities such as working at the computer, watching television, playing video games or the recently popular so-called adventure games that seem to become a substitute reality. Young people may look to a pseudoreligiosity, reborn before they have had their full chance to have been born at all. We often are on the alert for "hypersexuality" and promiscuousness, but we should be equally vigilant as parents for our tendency to keep our children delightfully benign Peter Pans, desexualized, alone, and afraid to reach out to others for pleasure and intimacy.

Deception: When your children seem to be lying more than you might expect (and remember, lying is a natural part of growing up in our society, whether we like it or not), when they avoid open conversations about sex or other topics, even more discussion is necessary. Accusing them of deception will only lead to more deception. Viewing that deception as pain and fear and a need for knowledge about sexuality and living is much more productive. Deception usually means that children are trying in their own way not only to protect themselves, but you as well. They are trying to protect you from discovering a "them" they feel you could not accept.

If your children have not talked to you at all about sex issues, no matter what their age, they are deceiving you. You can be sure the concern is there. There is only one perfect age for sex and love education, and that is the age of your child right now. There is no "when" problem for this type of education. Children are always ready and they always need it. Educational experts agree with child researcher and educational therorist Urie Bronfenbrenner that any child can learn anything at any time. What matters is the teacher and the type of teaching.

Developmental psychologist Jean Piaget called this problem of the right teaching at the right time in the right way the "problem of match." As a flower needs not too much or too little water and sun, but just the right amount, so it is with education, and sex education particularly. Our society is providing plenty of fertilizer, but that will only burn and kill the flower if we don't counterbalance it with the light of knowledge and the nurturance of love.

Deference: A young person who seems to defer not only to parents, but peers and everyone else, is showing the danger sign of low sexual self-esteem. Make no mistake about it. Self-esteem is sexual esteem, and to ignore that dimension of development while trying to provide more education, more experiences, more special training or therapy, will never completely overcome a self-esteem problem. There is no escaping the fact that sex and love education is a fundamental part of self-development, the development of the child's reputation with himself or herself.

Developmental Retardation: Much has been written about learning disabilities and other developmental problems. Unfortunately, little is written about the sexual dimension of such problems. And the impact as well as a cause of some developmental problems is deprivation of sex and love education, on the part of the child and/or the parents. When we begin to "work" on our children, to correct them, therapize them, drug them to slow down or drug them to speed up, to tutor them, test them, and place them, we sometimes forget their needs for sexual education. I have spoken for years throughout North America on the topic of sex and the impaired child. I have learned one important rule: the more the impairment, the more the need for touching, holding, and closeness and for information about sex.

Marriages who raise impaired children have their own unique stresses and joys. It is an extra challenge to remember and find time to provide good sex education when providing life experiences and education itself can demand so much energy. Parents of impaired children sometimes struggle to find enough time, even any time, for their own sexual lives, let alone find time for sex education. It is important to find this time, even at the expense of other opportunities for the child, for his or her sexual life is at the apex of overcoming and/or coping with these special disadvantages.

I have found that the questions asked of me by some of these children are the best, most basic sex-education questions of all. I have included their questions here, with my brief answers, so you may see how important sex is to them, and how important those "BARE" facts really are, and how the most basic of questions can teach us all about sexuality. The questions from teenagers and their parents were different from the following questions only in complexity of expression, not intensity of the need to know. Try to answer each question as a marriage before reading my answer. Try to relate each question to your own life, even if the questions come from children with developmental problems. There is a wisdom and a lesson in the simplicity and honesty of these children's wonderings about sexuality.

Twenty-Five Most Often Asked Children's Questions About Sex

1. "Do girls have balls, too?"

Yes. In boys the balls, where the sperm is made, are called testicles, and they are on the outside of the body's body in a sac called the scrotum. In girls, the balls, where her eggs are made, are inside, in the lower part of her body. They are called ovaries. "Balls" is just a slang word some people use for testicles, but boys and girls both have similar sexual organs. As usual, slang or bad words for sex and sex parts can confuse things.

2. "Why do women bleed between their legs?"

They don't really bleed, as they would from a cut. Every month a nesting place for a baby is made in a part of the woman's body called the uterus. If a sperm and egg get together, a baby grows there. If the nest is not needed, it comes out the way a bird's nest can fall from a tree. What comes out is the nesting material, with some blood and other things that make the nest. This is what is called menstruation. Women catch this unneeded nesting material with various types of pads. This is all part of a very natural process.

3. "How do the boys get their sperm?"

Sperm is made in the testicles and the eggs are made in the ovaries. Boys make millions of sperm every day, but girls are born with several hundred eggs, and only some of them ripen and become eggs that can join with sperm.

4. "How big is an egg, and does it have a shell?"

The egg is about as big as the head of a small pin. It has something like a very, very thin shell, but it is not hard like a chicken egg is hard. Sperm is much, much smaller.

5. "How does sperm get in the egg?"

Hundreds of sperm go up to the egg. It depends on good timing for the sperm and the egg to meet at the right place. Then usually one of the sperm enters into the egg and everything starts to happen to make a little you or a little somebody.

6. "Would you die or have a baby if you ate sperm?"

No, you wouldn't die and the only way a woman can have a baby is by having sperm go in through the vagina when the man puts his penis inside the vagina. Sperm is not dirty and can't hurt you at all, but it joins with eggs to cause babies, so you should never let sperm go in the vagina unless you are ready to have and raise a baby.

7. "How can sperm swim? Do they have fins?"

Well, they have something better. Each one has a little tail that goes very, very fast so they can go up to the egg. Even if the sperm go on the outside of the vagina, some could get into the vagina, so you should never take a chance with sperm near the vagina.

8. "Why do some people take babies out too early and kill them?"

Nobody ever really wants to kill a baby. Sometimes, but not often, a baby does not get made quite right and the nesting place takes the not-finished baby, called a fetus, out of the mother. Sometimes some people who did not want a baby stop it from growing in the nesting place after the sperm and egg met. That is what an abortion is. The not-yet-finished baby, the fetus, really doesn't look like a real baby because it was still getting made, just like a seed starting to grow does not look too much like a flower. Some people feel it is okay to stop the growth early because they don't want a baby, and some people feel it is never right to do that.

9. "Does it hurt bad to have a baby?"

I guess you're asking the wrong person. Men will never know. Women tell me that it's not like a hurt they have had from getting hurt. They say it is a very strong feeling, and that it is a lot of work and very tiring to have a baby, but they say it was a most special experience for them. Doctors and nurses know a lot of ways to make having a baby easier, and a lot of moms and dads think it is important that they are both there while the baby is coming out so they can share that special time.

10. "Why would a woman let a man put his thing in her?"

When you grow up and can take care of yourself and others, there are times when a woman wants to love, to hold, and to kiss and touch a man, and a man wants to do the same thing. Sometimes, but not every time, the man and woman want to join together and have the penis inside the vagina. This is one of the most important things to do in all the world, and a baby can start to grow when the sperm goes with the egg. It is a way of loving, a very special grown-up way of sharing yourself with someone, so it should only happen when you are married and going to be together forever.

11. "How can a baby eat in there?"

The baby is inside something like a space capsule, and food and other things needed to live are brought in from the mother. There is a special capsule filter that only lets in what the baby needs to live. The baby grows in this capsule and gets food through a cord attached at her or his belly button. The mother and baby are a team and are living together making each other healthier.

12. "Why doesn't the baby drown in the water in the sac?"

You are very smart. Yes, there is something like water made by the mother that the baby floats in inside the uterus. It keeps the baby from getting hurt and keeps the baby safe and healthy. The baby can't drown because he or she does not breathe through the mouth until he or she comes out. It's just like a person in space, with all the food and even their oxygen coming in through that special cord.

13. "Can you break your penis off when it is hard?"

No, you can't break it off. The penis does not really get hard like the word "hard" when you think of wood or a rock. It really gets full of blood that makes it firm so it can join with the vagina for intercourse or be touched and held when you make love with someone you want to be with for a long time. The penis gets firm sometimes because you have to pee or when you are excited and sometimes just because it is part of the way your body works, like when you yawn or sneeze. Just because your penis is rigid doesn't mean that you are feeling like making love, and you can feel very loving without your penis being rigid.

14. "Don't girls get all wet when they want a penis in them?"

The vagina sort of sweats sometimes, and that is just like the penis getting firm. It happens for lots of reasons, including being afraid, being happy, and just because girls and women are human and that's how the body works. The vagina getting wet can make joining the penis and vagina easier, but it doesn't mean they want to make love all the time. These are things our bodies do that are part of being human, and they happen to you even when you were in the uterus, in that birth capsule.

15. "How do you know if you love somebody or if they love you?"

There is a special secret about that. You can tell if you love somebody if you want to help them grow and be a better person. You can tell if they love you if they feel the same. If you or the person lies, or just wants to touch and kiss, or sometimes hurts your feelings intentionally, they don't love you. And remember, love is work. You have to try to love, and touching and holding is the easy part that comes with trying to treat someone very, very nicely and letting them treat you nicely, too. That's how you can be sure that your parents love you so, because they work to make you happy and your being happy makes them very, very happy. You can love a person very much and not have sex.

16. "Could you get it stuck in there? Can you get stuck together?"

A vagina and penis can never get stuck together. There are a lot of stories about sex that you will hear, and unless they come from someone you love, or from someone who somebody you love told you to listen to about sex, you really can't believe any of it. These stories are just like ghost stories. Sometimes kids want to scare you or make you think that they know a lot about sex. You know that people who brag don't really know too much or they wouldn't have to brag or tell other people how to live.

17. "Is it right if a grown-up touches you?"

Sure, it's right. Touching is human, but if someone ever touches the private parts of your body, or if they ask you to touch them, you should tell someone you love. They can talk about it with you. If you ever wonder if it's right, you shouldn't let it happen until you talk to someone you love. If someone is doing it and telling you not to tell, that means tell someone right away. Anytime someone tells you not to tell, you know something isn't right. You should never do anything you can't tell to people you love.

18. "How can you tell if a kid is a queer?"

First, "queer" means unusual, so we are all unusual, because none of us are completely alike. Sometimes, kids mean homosexual, the bigger word for what they mean by queer or the words "fag" or "gay" or other words like that. But you see, there is no way at all to tell if anyone is anything until you know that person for a very long time. People who say they are homosexual are not really different from anyone else except in one way. They want to love someone who is their same sex, what we call gender. Nobody knows why this happens because we really don't know all about why we become what we are. It's just too complicated. We just have to love who we are and accept people for who they are. Calling somebody any name is just mean and ends up hurting everyone. If you call someone a name, you can be sure you will end up having someone call you a name, too.

19. "Could you drink pee or eat your own crap?"

It would not be good for you at all to do it. Urine and feces are the names doctors use for pee and crap, and they are what is left when the body is done with whatever you eat and drink. It is what the body is throwing away. I guess we are kind of silly about these things, because even adults will use words for these things when they are mad. They say things like "shit" and "piss" and "asshole," when really these are just bad words for natural parts of us. When we talk like that, we really talk like we are very confused and silly. It's important to be clean, to wash our hands after we go to the bathroom, but there is really no big deal about these parts of us if people just get more comfortable about it. See, all of you are listening and so are the grown-ups. Nobody gets all upset if we talk like we respect everything about our body.

20. "How much milk is in a woman's breasts, and can they shoot it across the room if they want to?"

Women's breasts only have milk for babies just after they have had a baby and while the baby needs it. Other times, what can come out just a little sometimes is not milk like you would buy at the store. It's not like cows who make milk all the time. They do that because farmers make it so they can do it. And no, the milk or the fluid cannot shoot far at all. It just sort of leaks out in small amounts sometimes. We make a big deal about women's breasts, but they are really just bigger than men's breasts. When we get all shy or secret about something, we start to make things that are just natural sort of mysterious.

21. "What happens if you put a stick up yourself?"

You should never put anything in any part of your body that is not very, very clean. Sometimes little girls experiment by putting something in the vagina. They really shouldn't do that, because they could get a sore or cause an infection, like when you don't keep a cut clean. The skin inside the vagina is very, very sensitive, so it should be protected.

22. "Can you suck on somebody's thing?"

When you are able to take care of yourself and somebody else, you may start to be in love with someone. When you love someone and they love you, you may want to kiss them. Some people like to kiss the penis and vagina and some people don't. It's just like anything else. Everybody likes different things. We should never make anyone do something they don't want to do, but if we are very clean and grown-up, we can learn to make our own choices about what we like and don't like to do with other people.

23. "What do the boys look at in the dirty books they have? My daddy has some, too. What's in there?"

Books aren't really dirty or bad. Sometimes people who write the books or take the pictures that go in the books or in the movies put in stuff that they think is interesting or will sell their books or movies. They might put in pictures of breasts, penises, vaginas, naked people, people pretending to make love. They are really very boring, because they don't tell a story or help you learn about life or about yourself. Boys and men and some girls and women look at them to try to see some things they can't see anywhere else or because they are curious. The whole trouble is, the books, movies, and pictures with such things in them are all made up and exaggerated so you can learn all the wrong things. If you are still curious, ask your mom and dad to show you one of the books you wonder about and talk about it with you. You will probably get real bored real quick.

24. "You should never play with yourself. Isn't that right?"

Anything about how you live depends on what you think your parents think, and on what you decide together. Talk with your parents about touching yourself and playing with your penis or vagina or clitoris, that little area on girls' vaginas that feels good when you touch it. A lot of kids do it and a lot of adults do it, and it does not damage your body, but some people believe it is wrong to do it. Just because you can do something and a lot of people do something doesn't make it right. Right depends on you, your parents, and what you think about life, not what most people do or don't do.

25. "Why do Mommy and Daddy make funny noises when they are in bed together?"

Well, kids make funny noises all the time, so we grown-ups should have a chance to make them, too. I don't really know why your mommy and daddy are making their noises. They might be laughing, talking, dreaming, teasing, hugging, kissing, holding—who knows? Everybody enjoys being with someone they love, and they might make enjoyment noises just like you make fun noises when you play or watch television.

The discussion with these children went on for more than one and one half hours. In a room full of kids, some of who were diagnosed as severely retarded, emotionally impaired, and hyperactive, they all sat and listened. They laughed sometimes, but no more than their parents and the staff. They asked, listened, and learned. You can tell by their questions that they had put a lot of thought into this area already. You noticed the kids asked the questions in no particular order or interconnection in most cases. They were just more direct than some of us.

In each of my answers, I used a sex-education principle that has worked well for me. I always overanswer the question. I give more information than is required just so long as I give a specific answer to whatever was asked. I suggest you try the same approach. It's a good chance to make a lot of points you would like to make about living.

I have done this type of teaching with groups of senior citizens. I recently met with over two hundred senior citizens, most of whom were permanently living in nursing homes. I thought you might like to read just a few of their questions and my answers to support my earlier point that sex education is not for children only, and to provide information on the relationship between sexuality and aging.

Senior Citizen Sex Education: Twelve Most Often Asked Senior Sex Questions

1. "I notice that I don't have as much of an erection as I used to. Isn't that just aging?"

The quality of erections changes throughout the life. Usually, good health, good exercise, good diet, low stress, no drugs or alcohol, and an interested and interesting partner are the best guarantee that you will have whatever genital reflex the body can have. Remember, though, the erection of the penis or clitoris is not necessary for a fulfilling sex life. It is not the measure of enjoyment, only blood flow. That changes through life, so erections change.

2. "Don't a lot of these drugs we are taking knock out our sex life?"

Anything we do can affect our sex life, and that certainly includes whatever drugs we take. It's important to ask your doctor at least three questions about drugs. First and foremost: "Is this drug necessary?" Necessary, lifemaintaining drugs make up less than 10 percent of prescriptions written every year. Second, ask "Are these painkillers or sedatives necessary?" These drugs can have real affect on sexuality and usually do not deal with the health problem you are trying to solve. Finally, ask if better health habits such as regulating weight, exercising in moderation, and avoiding junk foods can reduce the need for some drugs prescribed by your doctor. You might also ask about the dosage and time of day you take drugs, because that can affect how the drug works and what the drug might do to your sexuality.

3. "Do men have menopause?"

A very small percentage of men over age sixty experience what some doctors call the male climacteric, and this relatively rare condition is related to a decrease in a certain hormone in the blood. If the doctor tries to provide the hormone and the symptoms don't disappear or reduce, it is probably not the male climacteric that is causing the problem.

The symptoms of male climacteric usually include a combination of loss of appetite, distractability, decrease in sexual urge or interest, edginess, fatigue, and some problems with erection. Of course, these problems happen to everyone sometime, so don't be too quick to jump to conclusions about male climacteric. My experience teaches that this is a very rare condition that is not at all the same thing as menopause in women.

4. "Does menopause mean loss of sex interest?"

No. Menopause is just the reverse of a process that started early in your life as you developed fertility. Menopause is not a thing, but a process of several years, so fertility does not just stop one day. Menopause definitely does not end sexual interest or ability to want to and to be able to enjoy sex.

5. "Doesn't a woman lose her ability, though? She gets old down there."

We get old everywhere. A woman might notice less lubrication in her vagina and some pain when stimulated genitally, so adding lubrication can help. The ability to have orgasm and certainly psychasm is not affected. Some of the genital reflexes and the contraction of the muscles in the pelvic area might feel differently than years ago, but different doesn't mean less. It is just plain myth and ageist attitudes that view sex as decreasing with the aging process.

6. "Same thing for men? Can we keep it going?"

Absolutely. There may be less ejaculate, less pressure at ejaculation, different contraction sensations, less frequent and less firm erections, but psychasms and orgasms continue. All health habits should continue through life, and that includes sex. Not only does aging not stop sex or sex interest and arousal, but some of the changes that come with aging can be slowed by remaining sexually active, either alone or with a partner.

7. "Alone? What are you suggesting? That we old people touch ourselves? That's sick."

It isn't sick and it has nothing to do with mental or physical illness. You might—and many people do—think that it is wrong to masturbate, to stimulate yourself sexually. If you feel it is wrong, then it would not be something enjoyable, and doing things which are not enjoyable is not good for your overall health. But let's not stop being honest here. The older you get, the less easy it may be to find partners to hold, to kiss, to cuddle, to have sex with if you want. One important option is to maintain sexual self-stimulation if you want to. It is something that people do, children and babies do. It is part of sexual living.

8. "I just can't see having intercourse at my age."

Who said anything about having intercourse? That, too, is an option. We should not just equate sex with intercourse. Touching, holding hands, being close, kissing are important sexual behaviors. All life is a cycle. Our teenagers should learn that all sex is not intercourse. They should be able to touch, to hold, and so should you if you want to. I'm just talking about your rights, not a list of sex assignments.

9. "Do you really think any of us are sexually attractive? Who would want to do anything with us?"

First let me say that, yes all of you are sexually attractive. Look around you now. Look at the eyes, the hands, the wrinkles that symbolize living and loving and hurting, the love lines. Feel the warmth of the person next to you. See how you feel if you smile at each other. Don't fall for the same discrimination that others cast upon you. If you don't teach us the beauty of aging, who will? Maybe that's one of the benefits of aging as it relates to sexuality. You can be free of popular notions of what makes a person attractive, and you can relate to people for what they are, how they are, and how they have been, not just how they look. And don't tell me that some of you haven't taken a good look around and seen some people here you wouldn't mind laying a big hug on.

10. "They wouldn't let us if we wanted to."

Now you are talking basic freedoms. You have the right to privacy, to do in private what you will with whom you will. If you feel inhibited by someone else's encroachment on your life, you should act on that or ask for help to act on that. If any group of people deserves and has earned privacy, the dignity of continued personal and sexual development, it certainly is you. You have earned it much more than some thirteen-year-old in a parked car. Stand up for your sexual rights and the sexual rights of everyone in this room. Even if you don't want to exercise those rights, they are yours for the choosing. Protect them.

11. "How can you have sex if you don't feel good?"

How can you feel good if you don't have sex? How can you feel good if you never touch and get touched, hold and get held? We have to stop thinking about aging as meaning not feeling good. Being sick is not automatically related to being older, and feeling active, alert, happy, and energetic depends much on behaving that way, and the same applies to sex. You will feel sexier if you keep on being sexual, and that in turn will help you feel generally better.

12. "Maybe you just don't want to face it. Getting old means getting high blood pressure, losing your memory, your ability to get around and move around. It's just a fact that you are trying to romanticize away."

You're right that there are changes that come with aging. Changes in your skin, your hair, even your eyes, and other general mechanical deterioration are a fact of life over time no matter what we do. Research shows, however, that memory, intelligence, mobility, even such things as high blood pressure and circulatory changes are affected by the oldest principle in the world. Use it or lose it seems to be correct for many aspects of life and aging, and that is certainly true for sex. I think we'll find, if we have the courage to study it, if we have the sensitivity to the needs of our older population to care, that the neurochemical changes that accompany sex are vital for staying healthy. Aging is strongly related to changes in brain chemistry, and I suspect that such changes could in turn be affected by sexual activity. It is not enough just to condone sex in aging, it must be advocated. In studying cultures where sex is not only allowed but expected of their aging populations, scientists have written that continuing to be sexual later into life is one of the major components of longevity.

Super Marital Sex Opportunity Number Twelve

Sit down as a family and play the "Sex Contingencies" game. This exercise will allow you to review the material from all twelve chapters of this book and to share your feelings now that you have read and thought about super marital sex. Each person should take a turn responding to each of the following ten items.

1. WHAT do you consider to be a sexual act? Do you view sex in a different, more inclusive manner after reading this book?

2. WHO would be the best sexual partner for you? What would be the characteristics of someone you could love for life?

3. WHY would you have sex? Has your personal "model" of sexuality changed in the direction of the fourth perspective?

4. WHEN would you prefer to have sex? Do you relate your personal intimate relationship to the systems view that incorporates all phases of daily living, a sex beyond the limits of "nighttime"?

5. WHERE would you prefer to have sex? Have you thought about your own private, intimate place and about providing an intimate place for everyone in the family?

6. HOW do you prefer to have sex? Have you learned that the posture of the future is really a positioning for a new intimacy, a finding of a new perspective for sex in lasting relationships?

7. WHERE DOES SEX FIT IN YOUR LIFE? What priority do you assign to sexuality, and are you making the commitment necessary to match your own priority for sex?

8. HOW SECRET should sex be? Have you learned about making sexuality an open discussion of family life, to be discussed and examined together even as it is protected as the most personal and private of all life experiences?

9. HOW MUCH VARIETY do you feel you require in your sexuality? Have you learned that the comfort of sameness can exceed the challenge and pressures of newness, that super sex is not different sex?

10. SO WHAT? What does sex mean to you, to your family, to your marriage now that you have read about another perspective on sexuality?

I hope that you find in these sample questions and in the material I have shared with you in this book a new challenge for a new sex for a new time. I hope you have made progress toward a super marital sex, a committed, enduring, comfortable intimacy that is "super" because it goes beyond the limits of the body to the potential of the merging of spirits.

After Words

They could hear crying coming from her bedroom, but she would not respond to their repeated attempts to cajole her out of her hideaway. "Come on, honey, we want to help you. We can help you," begged her mother.

"Go away. I don't want to live. Go away," came the response.

She had held on tightly to her moral convictions, the teachings of her parents. Her boyfriend of four years had pressured her to have intercourse, and she had refused. She was accused of teasing, of immaturity, of having hang-ups, of being afraid, of being out of it, behind the times. "Nobody is a virgin anymore," her boyfriend had said. She would not give in, and now he had announced that their romance was over. He had found a more modern girl who was free of these terrible restrictions her parents had put on her.

"It's your fault, it's all both of your fault," she hollered angrily through the closed door. "I should have been a slut. I'm going to be a slut. Maybe that will make you both happy. Or maybe you'd like me just to be a nun, the world's first Jewish nun."

The parents had just struggled through the most trying time of their life together, for this was the same couple who rediscovered their love in the hospital miracle I described in Chapter One. They had found their own super marital intimacy and had taught it vigorously to their daughter. "Touch, hold, enjoy sex, but don't have intercourse. There's a lot you can do to enjoy sex without intercourse." They had taught her the facts, correcting the myths that focused her teen sex world on the same erection, orgasm, mechanical sex that limited their own "pre-crisis" marriage. Her boyfriend remained trapped into the "doing it" focus of sex.

"We love you, we will always love you, and we both suffer with you, Betty. We do, we really do. Your mother and I almost lost each other before we found out what sex could really be," said her father, crying with his wife.

"We just want you to understand, to trust us that it is the right thing, the real thing," said the mother.

"I'll never speak to you, either of you. You've ruined my life. I lost Ron forever. You took him away from me," cried their daughter.

The struggle for super marital sex—the integration of the new perspective of psychasms; the freedom from the emphasis on intercourse; a whole new sexual-response system; a way for men and women to share the same types of response instead of working on each other or trying to live up to each other's or experts' expectations of what should be taking place; the struggle to integrate sex into a full life system—is much more difficult than just "doing it" and trying by timing or effort to "do it right" and "keep it exciting." It is a struggle made more difficult because the couple, the family, is affected by a society that ignores the family concept of unity, of the togetherness of all persons and things. And now this little girl, trying so courageously to grow up sexually, and her parents found themselves alone and desperate. Did this young person really have to sacrifice love for sex or sex for love? Were they really different?

The husband and wife sat on the floor and leaned their backs against their daughter's bedroom door. They held each other and listened to their daughter crying. Maybe they were wrong, they thought. Maybe this sexual system just can't work for their daughter as it had for them. Maybe this society, this time, had irreparably split sex from love. The couple embraced and tried urgently to send loving messages to their daughter, "super" mental and emotional messages beyond words. They tried to use the power of their marriage to break through the door, a door created by a harsh and insensitive, a sexy but not sexual society. They tried to send their super love to their daughter.

After a few minutes, with all three too tired to cry anymore, there was silence. Only the ticking of the clock in the hall could be heard.

"Is Betty sleeping?" said the wife.

"I can't tell," said the husband. "I can't hear a thing."

The phone rang, and the husband groaned as he fought to stand up. Every part of his body seemed to get up reluctantly and separately. His left foot was asleep, and he dragged it to the phone. "Hello, this is Ron. Is Betty there?" came the voice. The father's first reaction was to threaten to seek Ron out and torture him as he felt his daughter had been tortured. How could you do this to my daughter, you animal? was the father's silent thought. Ron's voice was quivering and unsure. He expected to be attacked, and would gladly accept it verbally rather than physically. He had fantasies himself of Betty's father tearing down his family's front door and coming in with a shotgun, demanding, "Marry my daughter or die."

The father hesitated, stomping his sleeping foot several times on the floor to bring it back to life. "Just a moment, Ron," said the father, covering the phone and telling his wife, "The bastard wants to talk to Betty."

The same daughter who seemed to have a hearing deficit for most parental requests opened the door so suddenly that her mother fell backward into the room. Betty ran past her mother, grabbed the phone from her father, and, as calmly as if she were saying grace at the family dinner table, said, "Hi, Ron. What's up?"

The parents looked at one another, stunned. The father incredulously mouthed but did not say out loud the words "What's up?" The mother silently mouthed back "Shhhh."

"Sure, come on over," said Betty. "Yeah, I know. Okay. I'm sorry, too." She hung up and said to both her parents, "Ron is coming over to watch TV, okay?"

"Is that okay with you, Betty?" asked her mother.

"Sure, why not? He apologized. He knows I'm never going to do it with him, but we'll make out like crazy while we watch TV. He'll probably want me to touch him and he'll touch me, but he knows we won't do it. You know it, too, don't you, Mom and Dad?"

"Yes, we do, honey," said the mother trustingly.

"Sure we do," said the father hopefully.

Betty hugged her father, then reached over and helped her mother up. "Super," said Betty. "Super. You know, I never really said this, but you two have a super marriage. I'll bet you have super sex, too. I'll bet I will, too, when I'm married. I hope my marriage is as super as yours.''

Appendix I

The Super Marital Sex Couples' Program

This report is based on the interviews of the first thousand couples to complete the sexual therapy program in the Problems of Daily Living Clinic in the Department of Psychiatry at Sinai Hospital of Detroit. I set out to work with an atypical group, a group that worked consistently and over time for a super marriage with super sex. I made no attempt to select couples other than reporting only on the first thousand to complete the entire program and to be interviewed by myself. This biased, highly atypical and selected group were my teachers, the stars of the adventure in marital sex enhancement.

The first couples began their treatment in 1972 and the last couples of the thousand completed their five-year follow-up session in 1985. The years of initiation of the treatment program were as follows:

YEARS OF INITIATION OF TREATMENT PROGRAM

1972	115
1973	115
1974	110

1975	112
1976	108
1977	110
1978	110
1979	110
1980	110

Couples that dropped out of treatment for any reason were not computed in the thousand. The numbers above reflect only the couples that completed the entire program. I did all interviews myself. Numbers of actual treatment visits varied, but the interviews upon which this report is based followed the schedule listed below.

INTERVIEW SCHEDULE

- Initial interview and evaluation (fifty-minute interview)

- Operationalization (stating sexual problem measurably)

- Husband or wife sexual history (love-map history)

- Wife or husband sexual history (love-map history)

- Physical examination of both spouses.

- Taylor-Johnson Temperament Analysis Test (paper-and-pencil test used to demonstrate systems approach)

- Videotape session (couple assigned communication roles, then communicating spontaneously)

- Feedback session explaining systems nature of sexual problem

- Cognitive-behavioral therapy session—sexual prescriptions (super sexual sigs)

- Debriefing session (review of therapy prior to follow-ups)

- One-month, three-month, one-year, and five-year follow-up sessions

- Eleven interviews minimum per couple, plus therapy sessions

- Total number of interviews for this report—19,464, including therapy visits

- All interviews on audiotape and numerically coded

- Confidentiality of couples protected by number-code system

- All tapes destroyed following analyses

This was not a research project. It was a collection of subjective reports by couples in one type of sexual treatment program who managed to complete all steps of the program to follow-up visit. In a sense, these are "hardy" couples, and this was a study of high-level well people trying to improve their sexual intimacy. Their marriages were strong enough, "super" enough to learn a new form of intimate communication, and this book is based on their experiences. This is not a representative sample and in no way is a test of the therapy program. There are many studies of troubled couples, but this report is based on the attainment of wellness, a study in health. I was interested in learning from a thousand couples who learned about sexuality as marriages over a five-year period in their lives. A simple description of the group follows, but the numbers are not significant. The words of the spouses in the pages of this book are important.

THOUSAND-COUPLE PROFILE

726 first marriages

203 second marriages

69 third marriages

2 fourth marriages

43 couples—one prior therapy experience

26 couples—two prior therapy experiences

10 couples—three or more prior therapy experiences

946 Michigan-resident couples

25 Ohio-resident couples

3 Indiana-resident couples

2 Florida-resident couples

2 West Germany-resident couples

23 Canada-resident couples

3 New York-resident couples

6 Illinois-resident couples

Male age range 21-86, Average age 53.5

Median male age 36

Female age range 19-80, Average age 49.5

Median female age 31

YEARS OF MARRIAGE OF COUPLES INTERVIEWED

YEARS	NUMBER OF COUPLES	YEARS	NUMBER OF COUPLES
1	46	22	10
2	20	23	8
3	6	24	40
4	0	25	2
5	2	26	2
6	80	27	4
7	111	28	4
8	67	29	15
9	0	30	10
10	12	31	5
11	6	32	4
12	10	33	1
13	80	34	3
14	101	35	2
15	116	36	1
16	100	37	2
17	0	40	2
18	40	47	2
19	52	50	1
20	13	52	1
21	28	63	1

DISEASE PROFILE WITHIN 1,000 COUPLES
(Diagnosis per physician report—some multiple diagnoses)

	Male	Female
Forms of heart disease (including mitral-valve prolapse, cardiac arrythmia, ischemic heart disease, etc.)	237	186
Diabetes	87	43
Hypertension	118	46
Alcoholism	81	43
Cancer (various forms)	46	51
Multiple sclerosis	18	23
Arthritis	33	64
Allergy, respiratory disorders	34	23
Visually impaired	6	3
Paraplegia, quadriplegia	27	12
Post-stroke	8	4
Renal disease	11	6

This appendix has presented a sketch of the two thousand people I interviewed. The numbers reported here and throughout this book are presented for illustration, not documentation. The numbers in all of the above tables show clearly how atypical this group of people was in comparison to expected averages and distribution of diseases. They were also atypical in their attainment of the new form of super marital sex described in this book. I hope you, too, will work to make your marriage atypical, ''super.''

Appendix II

VAIVAV

Knowing When and How to Get Professional Help for Sexual Problems

All help is really self-help, for we only hire helpers for a healing process that comes from within ourselves and our relationship. Follow the flowcharts in this appendix if you have doubts about your ability to solve your sexual problems without professional intervention. If you do seek help, be sure you remember that you are making a consumer decision, buying professional time. All of the thousand couples you read about in this book sought help, and I hope they have been helpers to you and your marriage.

The first flowchart will help you decide if you need professional help. The second takes you through steps that prepare you to hire a professional help. The last chart reminds you of what a therapist can and cannot do. If you can talk about these issues with your spouse, you are already ahead of many people who seek marital help.

DO YOU NEED PROFESSIONAL THERAPY?

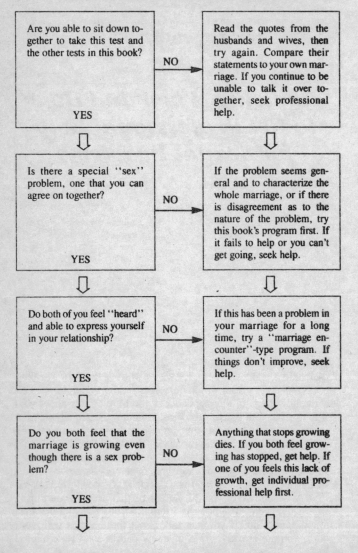

Are you able to sit down together to take this test and the other tests in this book?

YES

NO →

Read the quotes from the husbands and wives, then try again. Compare their statements to your own marriage. If you continue to be unable to talk it over together, seek professional help.

Is there a special "sex" problem, one that you can agree on together?

YES

NO →

If the problem seems general and to characterize the whole marriage, or if there is disagreement as to the nature of the problem, try this book's program first. If it fails to help or you can't get going, seek help.

Do both of you feel "heard" and able to express yourself in your relationship?

YES

NO →

If this has been a problem in your marriage for a long time, try a "marriage encounter"-type program. If things don't improve, seek help.

Do you both feel that the marriage is growing even though there is a sex problem?

YES

NO →

Anything that stops growing dies. If you both feel growing has stopped, get help. If one of you feels this lack of growth, get individual professional help first.

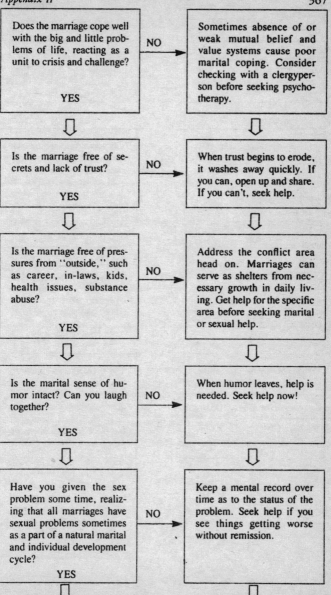

Does the marriage cope well with the big and little problems of life, reacting as a unit to crisis and challenge?

YES

NO →

Sometimes absence of or weak mutual belief and value systems cause poor marital coping. Consider checking with a clergyperson before seeking psychotherapy.

Is the marriage free of secrets and lack of trust?

YES

NO →

When trust begins to erode, it washes away quickly. If you can, open up and share. If you can't, seek help.

Is the marriage free of pressures from "outside," such as career, in-laws, kids, health issues, substance abuse?

YES

NO →

Address the conflict area head on. Marriages can serve as shelters from necessary growth in daily living. Get help for the specific area before seeking marital or sexual help.

Is the marital sense of humor intact? Can you laugh together?

YES

NO →

When humor leaves, help is needed. Seek help now!

Have you given the sex problem some time, realizing that all marriages have sexual problems sometimes as a part of a natural marital and individual development cycle?

YES

NO →

Keep a mental record over time as to the status of the problem. Seek help if you see things getting worse without remission.

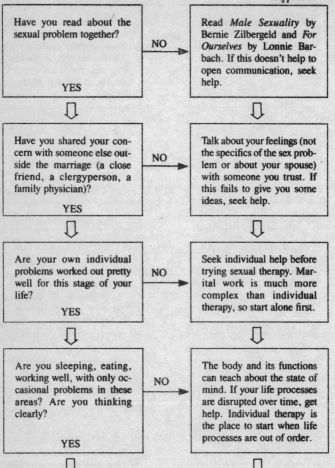

Have you read about the sexual problem together?

YES

NO →

Read *Male Sexuality* by Bernie Zilbergeld and *For Ourselves* by Lonnie Barbach. If this doesn't help to open communication, seek help.

⬇ ⬇

Have you shared your concern with someone else outside the marriage (a close friend, a clergyperson, a family physician)?

YES

NO →

Talk about your feelings (not the specifics of the sex problem or about your spouse) with someone you trust. If this fails to give you some ideas, seek help.

⬇ ⬇

Are your own individual problems worked out pretty well for this stage of your life?

YES

NO →

Seek individual help before trying sexual therapy. Marital work is much more complex than individual therapy, so start alone first.

⬇ ⬇

Are you sleeping, eating, working well, with only occasional problems in these areas? Are you thinking clearly?

YES

NO →

The body and its functions can teach about the state of mind. If your life processes are disrupted over time, get help. Individual therapy is the place to start when life processes are out of order.

⬇ ⬇

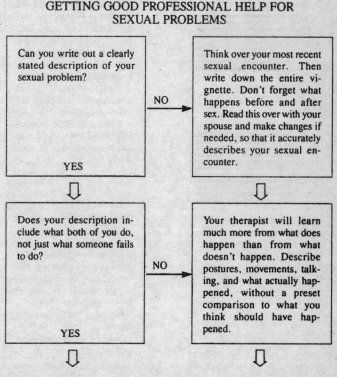

Do other people seem to see your marriage the way it "really is" rather than a distorted public marital image?
YES

NO →

When people are relating to you and your marriage in a way quite different than you feel to be "real," get help.

You are ready to "own and operate" your own sex clinic for super marital sex.

NO →

Read the chart on getting professional help.

GETTING GOOD PROFESSIONAL HELP FOR SEXUAL PROBLEMS

Can you write out a clearly stated description of your sexual problem?

YES

NO →

Think over your most recent sexual encounter. Then write down the entire vignette. Don't forget what happens before and after sex. Read this over with your spouse and make changes if needed, so that it accurately describes your sexual encounter.

Does your description include what both of you do, not just what someone fails to do?

YES

NO →

Your therapist will learn much more from what does happen than from what doesn't happen. Describe postures, movements, talking, and what actually happened, without a preset comparison to what you think should have happened.

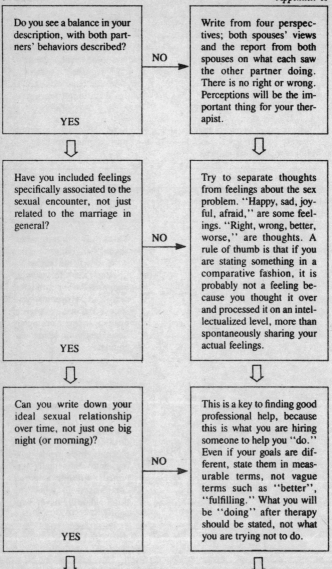

Do you see a balance in your description, with both partners' behaviors described?

YES

NO →

Write from four perspectives; both spouses' views and the report from both spouses on what each saw the other partner doing. There is no right or wrong. Perceptions will be the important thing for your therapist.

Have you included feelings specifically associated to the sexual encounter, not just related to the marriage in general?

YES

NO →

Try to separate thoughts from feelings about the sex problem. "Happy, sad, joyful, afraid," are some feelings. "Right, wrong, better, worse," are thoughts. A rule of thumb is that if you are stating something in a comparative fashion, it is probably not a feeling because you thought it over and processed it on an intellectualized level, more than spontaneously sharing your actual feelings.

Can you write down your ideal sexual relationship over time, not just one big night (or morning)?

YES

NO →

This is a key to finding good professional help, because this is what you are hiring someone to help you "do." Even if your goals are different, state them in measurable terms, not vague terms such as "better", "fulfilling." What you will be "doing" after therapy should be stated, not what you are trying not to do.

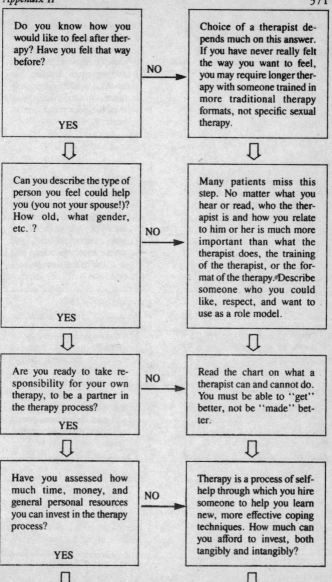

Do you know how you would like to feel after therapy? Have you felt that way before?

YES

NO →

Choice of a therapist depends much on this answer. If you have never really felt the way you want to feel, you may require longer therapy with someone trained in more traditional therapy formats, not specific sexual therapy.

Can you describe the type of person you feel could help you (you not your spouse!)? How old, what gender, etc.?

YES

NO →

Many patients miss this step. No matter what you hear or read, who the therapist is and how you relate to him or her is much more important than what the therapist does, the training of the therapist, or the format of the therapy. Describe someone who you could like, respect, and want to use as a role model.

Are you ready to take responsibility for your own therapy, to be a partner in the therapy process?

YES

NO →

Read the chart on what a therapist can and cannot do. You must be able to "get" better, not be "made" better.

Have you assessed how much time, money, and general personal resources you can invest in the therapy process?

YES

NO →

Therapy is a process of self-help through which you hire someone to help you learn new, more effective coping techniques. How much can you afford to invest, both tangibly and intangibly?

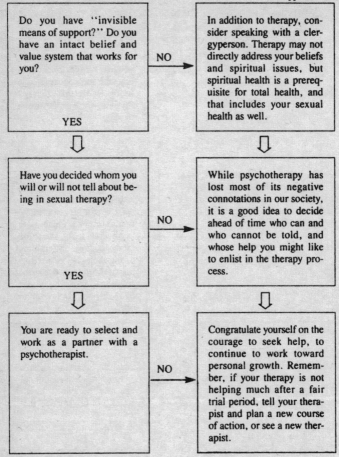

Do you have "invisible means of support?" Do you have an intact belief and value system that works for you?

YES

NO →

In addition to therapy, consider speaking with a clergyperson. Therapy may not directly address your beliefs and spiritual issues, but spiritual health is a prerequisite for total health, and that includes your sexual health as well.

⇩

⇩

Have you decided whom you will or will not tell about being in sexual therapy?

YES

NO →

While psychotherapy has lost most of its negative connotations in our society, it is a good idea to decide ahead of time who can and who cannot be told, and whose help you might like to enlist in the therapy process.

⇩

⇩

You are ready to select and work as a partner with a psychotherapist.

NO →

Congratulate yourself on the courage to seek help, to continue to work toward personal growth. Remember, if your therapy is not helping much after a fair trial period, tell your therapist and plan a new course of action, or see a new therapist.

WHAT A THERAPIST CAN DO AND WHAT A THERAPIST CAN'T DO

WHAT PROFESSIONALS CAN'T DO	WHAT PROFESSIONALS MIGHT BE ABLE TO DO
1. Cure you.	1. Help change your behaviors in the direction of your identified goals.
2. Advise you.	2. Identify options and probable outcomes and consequences of behavioral changes or failure to change.
3. Be your friend.	3. Be a partner and team member in problem-solving. The difference between therapy and friendship is a unilateral benefit and direction of one of the persons (the patient).
4. Be a source of strength.	4. Help you identify your strengths and put them to work in solving problems you confront in daily living.
5. Be a surrogate.	5. Be a role model in terms of his or her interaction with you as a patient, but never replace partners you chose for parenting and for sexual interaction.
6. Change your life.	6. Help you find more control of your own destiny and see your own self-responsibilities within your life system.

7. Redo or correct the past.	7. Accept life as a journey and not a destination (the neutrality rule). One will not predict the present or future based on the past.
8. Help you become a new person.	8. Help you integrate your behavior into a growing person who will develop throughout life and not achieve "health" but work toward wellness.
9. Find your identity.	9. See your behavior more clearly by holding up an objective mirror to you, your life, and your behaviors, and protect your options for change.
10. Make you feel better.	10. Help you take responsibility for yourself and see that in the final analysis you are your own physician, psychotherapist. Your degree of wellness depends upon your assuming responsibility for coping more effectively with day-to-day problems.

CHAPTER ONE

Page 6: Therapist Clark Moustakas writes, "The exquisite nature of love, the unique quality or dimension in its highest peak, is threatened by change and termination. . . . To love is to be lonely. Every love eventually is broken by illness, separation, or death." This book is dedicated to the idea that we do not have to wait until the threat of loss of love before we maximize the joys of love. See Clark Moustakas, *Loneliness* p. 101.

Page 7: Extramarital sex frequency has been researched in several sources. The original Kinsey studies a 50 percent rate of such behavior for men and about a 25 percent rate for women in that same study. Subsequent surveys have shown about the same frequency, with only gradual increase, particularly among women. See Alfred Kinsey, et al., *Sexual Behavior in the Human Male* and *Sexual Behavior in the Human Female*. See also R. Athanasious, et al., "Sex"; Morton Hunt, "Sexual behavior in the 1970s"; and Linda Wolfe, "Sexual profile of that *Cosmopolitan* girl."

Page 7: Varieties of extramarital sex are described in John and Mimi Lobell, *John and Mimi: A Free Marriage*, Jackie and Jeff Herrigan in *Loving Free*, and Richard and Ulla Anobile in *Beyond Open Marriage*.

Page 10: Janet Saltzman Chafetz writes, "The truth of the matter is that we have very little understanding of what it means to be human, divorced from notions of masculinity and femininity. See her book *Masculine/Feminine or Human: An Overview of the Sociology of Sex Roles*.

Page 10: The decline in number of female orgasm after marriage and the finding that the primary source of female orgasm was not intercourse but masturbation was reported in the 1953 sequel to Kinsey's *Sexual Behavior in the Human Male*, entitled *Sexual Behavior in the Human Female*.

Page 10: Donald Symons's work is found in *The Evolution of Human Sexuality*. See also R. Trivers, *Social Evolution*, and M. Daly and M. Wilson, *Sex, Evolution, and Behavior*.

Page 11: The controversial idea of "our genes wearing us" is in E. O. Wilson, *Sociobiology: The New Synthesis*.

Page 11: For information on male/female brain differences, see G. J. De Vries et al., *Sex Differences in the Brain*, and Richard Restaks's *The Brain: The Last Frontier*.

Page 11: Roger Gorski's work is "Sexual Dimorphisms of the Brain." See also his work "Sexual differentiation of the brain: possible mechanisms and implications."

Page 11: Dr. Reinisch's work is "Fetal hormones, the brain, and human sex differences: A heuristic, integrative review of the recent literature." See also her "Prenatal exposure to synthetic progestins increases potential for aggression in humans" and "Prenatal exposure to synthetic progestins, and estrogen: effect on human behavioral development."

Page 11: Dr. Jacklin's work is in Maccoby and Jacklin's work *Psychology of Sex Difference*. See also C. Tavris and C. Wade, *The Longest War*, and J. S. Hyde and B. A. Rosenberg, *Half the Human Experience*.

Page 12: Carol Gilligan's work is *In a Different Voice*.

Page 12: The Blumstein and Schwartz study is in their work *American Couples*.

Page 13: The work of Abraham Maslow focused on the importance of inner sources of stimulation. See his *Toward a Psychology of Being* and *The Further Reaches of Human Nature*.

Pages 14–15: Dr. Sarrel and his wife report on the importance of mutual interaction between sexual partners in *Sexual Unfolding*.

Page 15: Dr. Lief's orientation is found in his *Sexual Problems in Medical Practice*. Dr. Persky and Dr. Lief described their current work on hormonal cyclicity in an address on the development of sexual hormonal cyclicity at the 1986 Kinsey Summer Institute and in his "Reproductive hormone levels and sexual behavior of young couples."

Page 15: For a review of the new field of psychoneuroimmunology, see Pearsall, *Superimmunity: Mastering Your Emotions Improving Your Health*. See also Steven Locke's *The Healer Within*. See also J. Bowlby's work *The Making and Breaking of Affectional Bonds* for documentation of the neuroimmunal impact of bereavement.

Page 22: For research on "hassles" and their impact on emotional and physical health, see A. D. Kanner et al., "Comparison of two modes of stress measurement: daily hassles and uplifts vs. major life events." See also A. De-Longis et al., "Relationship of daily hassles, uplifts and major life events to health status."

Page 23: For more information on adult developmental stages and processes, see R. L. Gould's *Transformations: Growth and Change in Adult Life* and "The phases of adult life: a study of developmental psychology." See also D. J. Levinson's *The Seasons of a Man's Life* and "The mid-life transition: a period in adult psychosocial development."

Page 25: A discussion of the difference between an individual and relationship definition of high-level wellness, see J. Shapiro and D. Shapiro's "Well-being and relationship" in *Beyond Health and Normality*, edited by R. Walsh and D. Shapiro.

Page 27: For a description of John Money's concept of "love maps," see his new book *Lovemaps*. See also his *Love and Love Sickness*.

Chapter Two

Page 35: The concept of a universal system of wellness is discussed by L. Dossey in *Space, Time, and Medicine* and his *Beyond Illness: Discovering the Experience of Health*.

Page 37: A discussion of the concept of the Tao is found in F. Capra *The Tao of Physics* and his *The Turning Point*.

Pages 38–39: The concept of order in systems was discussed originally by L. von Bertalanffy in *General Systems Theory*.

Pages 40–41: The idea of rhythm in systems as this applies to psychology and health is discussed by G. Schwartz in "Psychobiology of health: a new synthesis" and "Behavioral medicine and systems theory: a new synthesis."

Page 42: The word "cybernetics" is from the Greek *kybernan*, meaning to govern, to regulate. The importance of this concept to systems theory is described by H. Brody and D. Sobel in "A Systems View of Health and Disease" in *Ways of Health*, edited by D. Sobel.

Page 43: "Supersensory" communication and the several realms of experience and consciousness are described in L. LeShan and J. Margenau's *Einstein's Space and Van Gogh's Sky*.

Page 44: The quote on the two types of knowledge is found in F. Capra, *The Turning Point*.

Page 45: Balance within systems and relationships and unique ways of achieving this balance are described in a field called Neuro-Linguistic Programming. See L. Cameron-Bandler's *Solutions: Practical and Effective Antidotes for Sexual and Relationship Problems*.

Page 48: The holistic approach to health is described in K. Pelletier's *Holistic Medicine*.

Page 52: The concept of negotiating and contracting for common relationship goals is described in N. S. Jacobson and G. Maragolin's *Marital Therapy*.

Page 55: Communicational and systems approaches toward these "accommodating" marriages are described in R. Stuart's *Helping Couples Change*.

CHAPTER THREE

Page 59: Two studies that examined courtship rituals in the United States are "Dating behaviors in university students" by D. Knox and K. Wilson and *Flirting Behavior in Public Settings* by T. Perper and S. Fox.

Page 56: A discussion of the Morier and Herriot statements is in "Sexual extremes are out; but adult eroticism is in" by N. McWhirter.

Page 62: "Bonding" was discussed by Desmond Morris in his book *Intimate Behavior*. He suggested that a fear of the open expression of emotions related to bonding results in the behaviors described in this chapter and the evolution of certain disguises for touching needs, such as clapping hands for performers instead of patting them on the back, waving instead of embracing, and tickling instead of holding.

Page 64: "Proception" as a term for the first phase in pairing was first used by F. Beach in *Hormones and Behavior: A Survey of Interrelationships Between Endocrine Secretion and Patterns of Overt Response*. See also his "Cross-species comparisons and the human heritage" and "Sexual attractivity, proceptivity, and receptivity in female mammals." The term "proception" was also used by S. Rosenzweig in "Human sexual autonomy as an evolutionary attainment, anticipating proceptive sex choice and idiodynamic bisexuality." J. Money, in his *Love and Love Sickness*, discusses three phases of sexual eroticism, proception, acception, and conception. I used these concepts as a starting point in developing the categories I used in interviewing the couples regarding their courtship patterns.

Page 64: Desmond Morris discusses the universality of body "conversations" and somatic ways of acknowledging sexual messages in *Man Watching: A Field Guide to Human Behavior*. Our "love language" often includes descriptions of "getting closer," "falling in and out of love," and "merging," a movement vocabulary signaled by our increasing emotional and physical "inclination" toward one another. It seems easier to describe the geography of our loving to others than to actually demonstrate to love object.

Page 70: Whether or not sexual encounters are more directed by the male or female, it appears that sexual pleasure from the intimacy of touching and bonding is crucial to healthy psychological and physical development. J. W. Prescott has shown that the absence of nurturance, closeness, and touch results in actual physical changes in the human brain and a resultant tendency toward more violent behavior. See his work in ''Body pleasure and the origin of violence.''

Page 70: While these differences in sexual behavior during courtship emerged in my interviews, research indicates that men and women are not as different in their response to erotic stimuli as once assumed. See J. Heiman in ''The physiology of erotica.''

Page 74: Patterns of behavior during courtship and the process of decision-making that goes into the bonding process are discussed in R. Libby et al., ''Social scripts for sexual relations.''

Pages 74–75: There are many theories for the way in which men and women interact and for how they make their decisions regarding bonding vs. friendship. See I. L. Reiss, ''Toward a sociology of the heterosexual love relationship''; A. C. Kerckoff, et al., ''Value consensus in mate selection''; and B. Murstein, *Exploring Intimate Life Styles: Love, Sex, and Marriage Through the Ages*; ''Mate selection in the 1970s''; ''Stimulus-value-role: A theory of marital choice''; *Who Will Marry Whom? Theories and Research in Marital Choice;* and ''A theory and investigation of the effect of exchange-orientation on marriage and friendship.''

CHAPTER FOUR

Page 78: Freud became disillusioned with the concept of love, eventually emphasizing the concept of death as the aim of living. See S. Freud, *Psychoanalysis and Faith*. He did, however, continue to study the importance of loving to living, and the struggle for healthy loving. He wrote, ''the history of the world which our children learn at school is essentially a series of murders of people.'' In S. Freud, *The Standard Edition of the Complete Psychological Works of Sigmund Freud*, vol. 14, p. 292. On the other hand, one researcher counted 133 discussions of love in Freud's works. See E. Hitschmann, ''Freud's Conception of Love'' in the *International Journal of Psychoanalysis*. Freud was always writing about love from many different perspectives. One of his favorite quotes was a quatrain from Shakespeare's *Hamlet*:

> Doubt thou the stars are fire;
> Doubt that the sun doth move;
> Doubt truth to be a liar;
> But never doubt I love.
> *Act II, Scene 2, Lines 116-119*

Page 79: Limerence is discussed by D. Tennov in *Love and Limerence—The Experience of Being in Love*. The mini-quiz is my adaptation of some of Tennov's points with additions for my interviews.

Page 80: Dr. Sol Gordon is one of the leading sex educators who speaks directly and sensitively to children and adolescents. See S. Gordon and R. Libby, editors, *Sexuality Today and Tomorrow*.

Page 81: R. Fine states, "Love cannot be divorced from sexuality; sex without love is possible, though not the most gratifying of all human experiences." See R. Fine in *The Meaning of Love in Human Experience*. Scott Peck, in his book *The Road Less Traveled*, writes, "Love is as love does" (p. 120). He stresses that true love is an act of will, intentional, and that we deceive ourselves when we attempt to separate sex from love, when we make subjective what is objective, real, and related to everything we do, our loving behavior. My patients have found Peck's book a source of support and enlightenment and I used his concepts in developing my treatment program. He writes, "The feeling of love is the emotion that accompanies the experience of cathecting [bonding]" (p. 117).

Page 83: The material on "falling in love vs. being in love" is in S. Peck, *The Road Less Traveled*, p. 84.

Page 84: "Love cultures" are described in R. Fine, *Meaning of Love*, pp. 1-40.

Page 78: A. Montagu describes his view of love aggression in *Touching* and *Learning Non-Aggression*.

Page 84: K. Lorenz wrote about aggression as a basic drive state in *On Aggression* and *The Foundations of Ethology*.

Page 87: S. Campbell's work *The Couple's Journey* is noted in M. Ferguson's *The Aquarian Conspiracy*, p. 394.

Page 87: The role of "process" over "product" in loving and the related quote about the artist and his or her craft is in M. C. Richards, *Centering in Pottery, Poetry, and the Person*, p. 143.

Pages 87–88: The material on endings and separations is in Z. Rubin, *Liking and Loving: An Invitation to Social Psychology*.

Page 88: The Shirley Luthman quote on the pain of ending a relationship is in her *Intimacy: The Essence of Male and Female*, pp. 151-52.

Page 90: "Love-mapping" is described in J. Money's *Love and Love Sickness* and *Lovemaps*.

Page 90: The biology/sociological connection in the development of sexual orientation or sexual status was recently described by J. Money at the August 1986 meeting of the American Psychological Association.

Page 92: The W. Farrell material is in his *Why Men Are How They Are*, and the C. Gilligan book is priorly cited.

Page 105: Information on "locus of control" is in J. B. Rotter, "Generalized expectancies for internal versus external control of reinforcement."

Page 106: The Shapiro and Shapiro quote is in "Well-being and relationship," p. 211.

CHAPTER FIVE

Page 112: The Robinson quote is in P. Robinson, *The Modernization of Sex*, p. 3. Robinson traces the romantic/hedonistic orientations of the work of Ellis, Kinsey, and Masters and Johnson, and discusses the sociocultural orientation of each sexual theorist.

Page 112: For more information on Ellis, see E. Haeberle, *The Sex Atlas*. Ellis's original work is in his *Studies in the Psychology of Sex*.

Page 113: The material on female sexuality is in Ellis, *Psychology of Sex*, "The Sexual Impulses of Women." His views on marriage and love are found throughout his *Studies in the Psychology of Sex*. P. Robinson offers a clear and concise outline of the work of Ellis in his book *Modernization of Sex*.

Page 114: The Robinson quote on Ellis as a Romantic is on p. 194 of *Modernization of Sex*.

Page 114: The information on Graham and Kellogg is in G. B. Leonard, *The Transformation: A Guide to the Inevitable Changes in Humankind*.

Page 115: The material on Kinsey in this chapter is from A. C. Kinsey et al., *Sexual Behavior in the Human Male* and A. C. Kinsey et al., *Sexual Behavior in the Human Female*.

Page 115: The Kinsey quote on not being prescriptive is on p. 7 in *Sexual Behavior in the Human Male*.

Pages 117–18: The Masters and Johnson material is in their *Human Sexual Response* and *Human Sexual Inadequacy*. See also *The Pleasure Bond* and *On Sex and Human Loving*.

Page 119: For clarification of the difference between the HTLV-III virus associated with AIDS and the disease of AIDS itself, see D. B. Carter, "AIDS and the sex therapist: just the facts, please ma'am." I believe that progress in solving the AIDS problems rests with understanding that the virus is *not* the disease and that all diseases happen with systems, not "to people" because of viruses.

CHAPTER SIX

Page 133: Material on the male sexual experience is in B. Zilbergeld, *Male Sexuality*. This is a good self-help reference. I suggest this book to husbands and wives and ask them to discuss their reactions.

Page 137: The Shere Hite data is in S. Hite, *The Hite Report* and *The Hite Report on Male Sexuality*.

Page 138: The "inductor theory" is described by M. J. Sherfey in *The Nature and Evolution of Female Sexuality*.

Page 138: The example about the female as the source of "the rib" was used in a lecture by Dr. June Reinisch, director of the Kinsey Institute for Research in Sex, Gender, and Reproduction at the University of Cincinnati Medical School in February 1983.

Page 141: Information on the "hot" and "cold" styles of daily living and related neurohormonal patterns is in P. Pearsall, *Superimmunity*.

Page 141: The yin/yang material is described in F. Capra, *The Turning Point*, pp. 35-39.

Page 145: The Masters and Johnson quote on orgasm is in W. Masters et al., *Human Sexuality*, p. 67.

Page 145: The Masters and Johnson quote on the ejaculation/orgasm relationship is in W. Masters et al., ibid., p. 67.

Page 147: Information on sexuality and physical disabilities is in A. Comfort, *Sexual Consequences of Disability*. See also T. Cole and S. Cole, "The Handicapped and Sexual Health," in A. Comfort, *Sexual Consequences*.

Page 147: The quote on multiple orgasms and men is in W. Masters, *Human Sexuality*. p. 71.

Pages 148-49: Masters and Johnson's definition of premature ejaculation is in their *Human Sexual Inadequacy*. H. Kaplan suggested that premature ejaculation applied to men who lacked voluntary control of their ejaculation. See H. Kaplan, *The New Sex Therapy*. J. LoPiccolo defined premature ejaculation as a condition in which one or the other sexual partner is affected by concerns for ejaculatory timing. See J. LoPiccolo, "Direct treatment of sexual dysfunction in the couple," in J. Money and H. Musaph editors, *Handbook of Sexology*.

Page 150: Hormonal patterns and the effect on sexual behavior are described in C. Ford and F. Beach, *Patterns of Sexual Behavior*.

Page 156: Gay Talese, in his book *Thy Neighbor's Wife*, describes the forms of liberal sexuality that have been dominate since the 1960s. He quotes from one of his interviews, "Marriage is a form of arms control over the penis" (p. 532). His quote about feeling more love after having sex outside of marriage is on p. 201.

CHAPTER SEVEN

Page 164: The quote on witchcraft and its relationship to sexism is in H. Kramer and J. Sprenger's *The Malleus Maleficarum*. See also J. Achterberg in *Imagery in Healing*, pp. 67-72, where, in summary of the fear of women that resulted in the witch-hunts, she states, "The fury against women became self-perpetuating . . . and women were attacked wholesale for the sole crime of not being born male" (p. 68).

Page 164: For pioneering work with orgasmic problems in women, see L. Barbach, "Group treatment of preorgasmic women." See also her *For Your-*

self: The Fulfillment of Female Sexuality; and *Women Discover Orgasm: A Therapist's Guide to a New Treatment Approach*, and *Shared Intimacies*.

Page 165: For information on the G spot and female emission of fluid during sexual response, see B. Whipple et al., "The varieties of female orgasm and female ejaculation"; "Vaginal myography, and multiple components of female orgasm," in B. Graber, editor, *The Circumvaginal Musculature and Sexual Function*; "Female 'ejaculation,' " and "Pelvic muscle strength of female ejaculators: evidence in support of a new theory of orgasm." For a recent update on research findings about this controversial topic, see H. Alzate and Z. Hoch, "The 'G Spot' and 'Female Ejaculation': A Current Appraisal."

Page 171: For information on urinary problems in men and women as related to sexual function, see R. Kolodny, et al., *Textbook of Sexual Medicine*, pp. 205-232.

Page 172: For a clear description of the A-frame and tenting responses, see R. Francoeur, *Becoming a Sexual Person*, pp. 155-160.

Page 172: The Kaplan quote on the absence of orgasm during coitus is in H. Kaplan, *The New Sex Therapy*, p. 374.

Page 172: The quote on the mind turning inward during orgasm is in W. Masters and V. Johnson, *Human Sexuality*, p. 65.

Pages 172-73: The quote on the clitoral origins of orgasm is in W. Masters and V. Johnson, ibid., p. 66.

Page 173: The quote about the absence of the "brink" phenomenon in women is in W. Masters and V. Johnson, ibid, p. 66.

Page 175: The mind/body relationship during orgasm is documented by distinct brain-wave changes accompanying pelvic contractions. See H. Cohen et al., "Electroencephalographic Laterality Changes During Human Sexual Orgasm."

Page 175: For research on "types" of female orgasm, see J. Singer and I. Singer, "Types of female orgasm"; C. Fox and B. Fox, "Blood pressure and respiratory patterns during human coitus"; and L. Clark, "Is there a difference between a clitoral and a vaginal orgasm?" See also S. Fisher, *The Female Orgasm.* The research on female orgasm is abundant, illustrating my point that the male response has been assumed, as Masters and Johnson state in *Human Sexuality*, "to be more uniform than women's" (p. 67). I hope the material in Chapters Six and Seven has offered new questions about the male response and illustrated similarities and the equal complexity of male and female sexual responses.

Page 180: The quote on male and female response after orgasm is in W. Masters and V. Johnson, *Human Sexuality*, p. 68.

Page 180: The Eric Berne quote is in *Sex in Human Loving*, p. 3.

Page 180: The quote on unlimited orgasmic potential in women is in W. Masters and V. Johnson, *Human Sexuality*, p. 67.

Page 181: A key book in focusing attention on the issue of rape is S. Brownmiller's *Against Our Will*. See also A. N. Groth, *Men Who Rape*.

Page 188: Two books on the dichotomies of the evil and the pure in human sexuality and the evolution and impact of these concepts are J. Money's *The Destroying Angel* and *Venuses Pensuses*.

CHAPTER EIGHT

Page 192: Information on broad-spectrum natural lighting is in J. N. Ott, *Health and Light*.

Page 193: Kay Gardner's music is on *A Rainbow Path: An Album of Healing Music*.

Page 194: Information on ions and healthy air is in A. P. Krueger and D. Sobel, "Air ions and health," in D. Sobel, editor, *Ways of Health*.

Page 196: An easy-to-read source of information on diet and psychological health, including special diets and testing for food allergies, is in W. Crook, *Tracking Down Hidden Food Allergy*. A more technical and research-oriented source of information on nutrition and psychological wellness is in J. Bland, editor, *Medical Applications of Clinical Nutrition*.

Page 198: The M. Gross statement about the misuse of labels for psychological problems is in M. Gross, *The Psychological Society*, p. 7. See also B. Zilbergeld, *The Shrinking of America*.

Page 215: For more information on the ideas of Buckminster Fuller and his views on creativity, see his *Critical Path*, p. 26.

Page 217: The categories of belief systems are in T. DeAngelis, "What's it all mean?"

Page 219: The quote by R. Targ and K. Harary is in their *The Mind Race: Understanding and Using Psychic Abilities*, p. 8.

Page 223: For a clear pictorial guide to sexual posturing that is not limited to more traditional erection/penetration model, see W. J. Janson, *Sexual Pleasure Sharing*. Dr. Janson also includes drawings of the frenulum and clitoral areas and sexual self-exploration exercises. He also includes drawings by P. Lisieski, which show postures that allow positioning of the genitals to maximize F- and R-area contact with the C area. I have recommended this book to my patients who require a visual guide to learning postures, but the couple's development of their own postures has been the most effective approach. I have not found the use of explicit films, videotapes, or pictures to be consistently helpful. Sometimes such aids restrict the couple's creativity, communication, and mutual learning.

CHAPTER NINE

Page 243: A sensitive accounting of the impact of loss on relationships is in R. Anderson, *I Never Sang for My Father*, in O. L. Guernsey, Jr., editor, *The Best Plays of 1967-1968*. Anderson writes, "Death ends a life, but it does not end a relationship, which struggles on in the survivor's mind towards some resolution which it never finds" (p. 277).

Page 245: The Lodge quote is from R. Byrne, editor, *The Other 637 Best Things Anybody Ever Said*, p. 115.

Page 249: The Darrow quote is in ibid., p. 114.

Page 249: The Bette Davis quote is in ibid., p. 116.

Page 250: The Kobasa "three C's" are in S. C. Kobasa et al., "Health under stress."

Page 253: Examples of couples' coping with issues related to money is in C. Colman, *Love and Money*.

Page 254: The Jackie Mason quote is in *637 Best Things*, p. 218.

Page 262: Levinson's work is in his "The mid-life transition: A period in adult psychosocial development." See also D. J. Levinson et al., *The Seasons of a Man's Life*. See also R. Gould, *Transformations: Growth and Change in Adult Life*, and R. L. Gould, "The phases of adult life: a study in developmental psychology." See also E. Erikson, *Childhood and Society*. See also C. Jung, *Collected Works*, H. Read et al., editors.

CHAPTER TEN

Page 274: The idea of behavioral change preceding feeling change is developed by the cognitive behaviorists. See D. Burns, *Feeling Good: The New Mood Therapy*. See also A. Ellis and R. A. Harper, *A New Guide to Rational Living*; and A. Beck, *Cognitive Therapy and Emotional Disorders* and *Depression: Causes and Treatment*.

Page 275: For information on give-and-take within marital systems, see B. I. Murstein et al., "A Theory and Investigation of the Effect of Exchange-Orientation on Marriage and Friendship," in *Love, Sex, and Marriage Through the Ages*.

Page 276: Information on male and female response to pornography is in V. Sigusch et al., "Psychosexual stimulation: sex differences."

Page 279: An old but important study by E. Hooker points out the heterogeneity of "homosexual" life-style and sexual orientation. See her *Final Report of the Task Force on Homosexuality*. See also A. Bell and M. Weinberg, *Homosexualities: A Study of Diversities Among Men and Women*.

Page 282: K. Dalton has conducted extensive studies of premenstrual and menstrual mood states. See her *The Premenstrual Syndrome*. See also her "Cyclical Criminal Acts in Premenstrual Syndrome." For more information on the effect of hormonal cycles on couples, see H. Persky et al., "Plasma testosterone level and sexual behavior of couples." See also his "Reproductive hormones, moods, and the menstrual cycle," in R. C. Friedman et al., editors, *Sex Difference in Behavior*.

CHAPTER ELEVEN

Page 290: My own work in the field of sexual medicine can be found in *Sex Education for the Health Professional: A Curriculum Guide*, co-edited with N. Rosenzweig. See also my "Roles for the physician in the prevention and treatment of sexual problems."

Page 298: Statistics on the relationship between sexual health and heart disease may be found in R. F. Klein et al., "The physician and postmyocardial infarction invalidism." See also W. B. Tuttle et al., "Sexual behavior in postmyocardial infarction patients." Also L. A. Abramov, "Sexual life and sexual frigidity among women developing acute myocardial infarction." Also A. W. Green, "Sexual activity and the postmyocardial infarction patient."

Page 299: Data on heart rate and blood pressure during sexual activity is in H. K. Hellerstein and E. H. Friedman, "Sexual activity and the postcoronary patient." See also R. A. Stein, "The effect of exercise training on heart rate during coitus in the post-myocardial infarction patient." A good source of direct information about sex after heart attack is in N. S. Puksta, "All about sex after a coronary."

Page 301: Information on sex and cell disease is in my "Sexual wellness and cell disease: Counseling for the maintenance of intimacy."

Page 301: Cell-surveillance theory is described in K. Pelletier, *Longevity*, and A. de la Pena, *The Psychobiology of Cancer*.

Page 301: The statistics on sex and mastectomy are in L. Leiber et al., "The communication of affection between cancer patients and their spouses." See also D. Frank et al., "Mastectomy and sexual behavior: a pilot study." See also D. G. Bullard et al., "Sexual health care and cancer: A needs assessment." Documentation of the correlation between frequency of patients' questions about sex and physician comfort with this topic is in D. Burnap and J. S. Golden, "Sexual problems in medical practice." See also H. Lief, "Sexual concerns of the mastectomy patient," See also P. Boyd, *The Silent World: A Startling Report on Breast Cancer and Sexuality*.

Page 303: For data on sexual behavior and testicular tumors, see R. B. Braken and D. E. Johnson, "Sexual function and fecundity after treatment for testicular tumors."

Page 304: Data on the effect of chemotherapy and sexuality are in W. M. Fosdick et al., "Preliminary report: Long-term cyclophosphamide therapy in rheumatoid arthritis." See also S. M. Watkins and J. P. Griffin, "High incidence of vincristine-induced neuropathy in lymphomas."

Page 305: For information on sex and chronic illness, see A. Comfort, *Sexual Consequences of Disability*. See also E. A. Steinbock and A. M. Zeiss, "Sexual counseling for cerebral palsied adults: Case report and further suggestions." See also T. O. Mooney et al., *Sexual Options for Paraplegics and Quadriplegics*.

Page 309: Information on diabetes on sexuality is in R. C. Kolodny et al., "Sexual dysfunction in diabetic men." See also A. Rubin, "Impotence and diabetes mellitus." Also M. Brooks, "Effects of diabetes on female sexual response."

Page 311: Diabetes and vaginal infection are discussed in R. C. Kolodny, *Textbook of Sexual Medicine*.

Page 311: Information on ostomy and sexuality is in B. M. Dlin et al., "Psychosexual response to ileostomy and colostomy." See also L. H. Stahlgren and L. K. Ferguson, "Influence on sexual function of abdomino-perineal resection for ulcerative colitis." See also W. R. Burnham et al., "Sexual problems among married ileostomists."

Page 315: Data on alcoholism and sex are in F. Lemere and J. W. Smith, "Alcohol-induced sexual impotence." See also A. N. Browne-Mayers et al., "Psychosocial study of hospitalized middle-class alcoholic women." Also M. Bowen, "Alcoholism as viewed through family systems theory and family psychotherapy."

Page 316: The suggestions for sexual rehabilitation of paraplegics and quadriplegics are in T. P. Anderson and T. M. Cole, "Sexual counseling for the sexually disabled," and in T. O. Mooney et al., *Sexual Options*.

Page 317: A clear and accurate review of the status of findings on AIDS is "AIDS: Deadly but hard to catch," in *Consumer Reports*, November 1986, pp. 724-28.

Page 318: H. Lief's discussion of the fear of AIDS (FAIDS) is in his letter to the editor of *The Journal of Sex and Marital Therapy*, Fall 1986, vol. 12, no. 3, pp. 159-60. This same issue contains recommendations for the prevention of the spread of AIDS. See also H. Kaplan et al., "AIDS and the Sex Therapist."

Page 318: My reasons for optimism about the power of our immune system to protect us from AIDS and speculation that the puzzle of AIDS will be solved by strengthening, not weakening, our immune system, are in my chapter "The Supersystem versus the Disease of the Century" in *Superimmunity*. Recent work by Dr. Jay Levy at the University of California at San Francisco on suppressor T-cells indicates that we may have within us a means of controlling the HTLV-III virus. This work is to be published in *Science*, 1986. The answers to our sexual and health problems rest within us and between us, not outside us.

CHAPTER TWELVE

Page 325: A source for understanding how children learn about sex is E. Roberts, *Childhood Sexual Learning*.

Page 339: Asphyxiophilla, or self-strangulation, and other paraphilias are reviewed and their origins explained in J. Money, *Love and Love Sickness*.

Page 340: The theory that what children can learn depends on how something is taught, more than how old the child is, was initially developed by Jerome S. Bruner in *The Process of Education*. For a clear discussion of Piaget's views of learning, see J. L. Phillips, *Piaget's Theory: A Primer*.

Page 349: The issue of medications and use of drugs with an aging population is described in D. M. Vickery and J. F. Fries, *Take Care of Yourself: A Consumer's Guide to Medical Care*.

Pages 349–50: The male climacteric and its neurohormonal factors is described in A. Vermeulen et al., "Testosterone secretion and metabolism in male senescence." See also R. C. Kolodny et al., *Textbook of Sexual Medicine*, pp. 107-8.

Page 350: A summary of findings on menopause is in P. A. Van Keep, *Consensus on Menopause Research*.

Page 352: Data on the effects of sexuality on aging and longevity is in K. Pelletier, *Longevity*. A 132-year-old male Vilcabamban is reported to have shown strong sexual interest in author Grace Haisell. She reports this in her *Los Viejos—Secrets of Long Life from the Sacred Valley*.

Bibliography

Abramov, L. A. "Sexual life and sexual frigidity among women developing acute myocardial infarction." *Psychosomatic Medicine* 38 (1976):418-25.

Achterberg, Jeanne. *Imagery in Healing*. Boston and London: Shambhala Press, 1985.

Alzate, H., and Z. Hoch. "The 'G Spot' and 'Female Ejaculation': A Current Appraisal," *Journal of Sex and Marital Therapy* 12 (1986):211-20.

Anderson, B. G. *The Aging Game: Success, Sanity, and Sex After Sixty*. New York: McGraw-Hill, 1979.

Anderson, R. *I Never Sang for My Father*. In Guernsey, O. L., Jr., *The Best Plays of 1967-1968*. New York: Dodd, Mead, 1968.

Anderson, T. P., and T. M. Cole. "Sexual Counseling of the Physically Disabled." *Postgraduate Medicine* 58 (1975):117-23.

Anobile, U., and R. J. Anobile. *Beyond Open Marriage*. New York: A and W Publishers, 1979.

Arafat, I., and B. Yorburg. "On living together without marriage." *Journal of Sex Research* 9 (1973):97-106.

Athanasiou, R., P. Shaver, and C. Tavris. "Sex." *Psychology Today* 4 (1970):37-52.

Barbach, L. *For Yourself: The Fulfillment of Female Sexuality*. New York: Anchor/Doubleday, 1976.

——. "Group treatment for preorgasmic women." *Journal of Sex and Marital Therapy* 1 (1974):139-45.

——. *Women Discover Orgasm: A Therapist's Guide to a New Treatment Approach*. New York: Free Press/Macmillan, 1980.

——, and L. Levine. *Shared Intimacies*. Garden City, New York: Anchor/Doubleday, 1980.

Beach, F. (ed.). *Sex and Behavior*. New York: John Wiley & Sons, 1965.

——. *Hormones and Behavior: A Survey of Interrelationships Between Endocrine Secretion and Patterns of Overt Response*. New York: Hoeber, 1948.

——. "Sexual attractivity, proceptivity, and receptivity in female mammals." *Hormones and Behavior* 7 (1976):105-38.

——. *Human Sexuality in Four Perspectives*. Baltimore: Johns Hopkins University Press, 1977.

Beck, A. T. *Cognitive Therapy and Emotional Disorders*. New York: New American Library, 1979.

——. *Depression: Causes and Treatment*. Philadelphia: University of Pennsylvania Press, 1972.

Bell, A. P., and M. S. Weinberg. *Homosexualities: A Study of Diversities Among Men and Women*. New York: Simon & Schuster, 1978.

Bell, R., and P. Bell. "Sexual Satisfaction Among Married Women." *Medical Aspects of Human Sexuality* 6 (1972):136-44.

Berne, E. *Sex in Human Loving*. New York: Pocket Books, 1971.

Bland, J. (ed.) *Medical Applications of Clinical Nutrition*. New Canaan, Conn.: Keats Publishing, 1983.

Blumstein, P., and P. Schwartz. *American Couples*. New York: Pocket Books, 1985.

Bowen, M. "Alcoholism as viewed through family systems theory and family psychotherapy." *Annals of the New York Academy of Sciences* 233 (1974):115-22.

Bowlby, J. *Attachment and Loss*, vol 1. New York: Basic Books, 1969.

——. *The Making and Breaking of Affectional Bonds*. London: Tavistock Publications, 1979.

Boyd, P. *The Silent Wound: A Startling Report on Breast Cancer and Sexuality*. New York: Addison-Wesley, 1985.

Bracken, R. B., and D. E. Johnson. "Sexual function after high retroperitoneal lymphadenectomy" *Urology* 7 (1976):35-38.

——. "Sexual function and fecundity after treatment for testicular tumors." *Urology* 7 (1976):35-38.

Brody, H., and D. S. Sobel. "A Systems View of Health and Disease." In David S. Sobel (ed.). *Ways of Health.* New York and London: Harcourt Brace Jovanovich, 1979.

Brooks, M. H. "Effects of diabetes on female sexual response." *Medical Aspects of Human Sexuality* 11 (1977):63-64.

Browne-Mayers, A. N., E. E. Seelye, and L. Sillman. "Psychosocial study of hospitalized middle-class alcoholic women." *Annals of the New York Academy of Sciences* 273 (1976):593-604.

Brownmiller, S. *Against Our Will.* New York: Simon & Schuster, 1975.

Bruner, J. S. *The Process of Education.* Cambridge, Mass.: Harvard University Press, 1963.

Bullard, D. G., G. G. Causay, A. B. Newman, R. Orloff, K. Schanche, and D. H. Wallace. "Sexual health care and cancer: a needs assessment." *Frontiers of Radiation Therapy and Onocology* 14 (1980):55-58.

Burnap, D. W., and J. S. Golden. "Sexual problems in medical practice." *Journal of Medical Education* 7 (1977):7-14.

Burnham, W. R., J. E. Lennard-Jones, and B. N. Brooke. "Sexual problems among married ileostomists." *Gut* 18 (1977):673-77.

Burns, D. *Feeling Good: The New Mood Therapy.* New York: Signet Books, 1980.

Byrne, R. (ed.) *The Other 637 Best Things Anybody Ever Said.* New York: Atheneum, 1985.

Cameron-Bandler, L. *Solutions: Practical and Effective Antidotes for Sexual and Relationship Problems.* San Rafael, Cal.: FuturePace, Inc. 1985.

Capra, F. "Can Science Explain Pyschic Phenomena?" *Re-Vision.* Winter/Spring, 1979.

——. *The Tao of Physics.* Berkeley, Cal.: Shambhala Press, 1975.

——. *The Turning Point.* Toronto and New York: Bantam Books, 1983.

Carter, D. B. "AIDS and the sex therapist: just the facts, please, ma'am." *Journal of Sex Research* 22 (1986):403-8.

Chafetz, J. S. *Masculine/Feminine or Human: An Overview of the Sociology of Sex Roles,* 2d edition. Itasca, Ill.: Peacock, 1978.

Clark, L. "Is there a difference between a clitoral and a vaginal orgasm?" *Journal of Sex Research* 6 (1970):25-28.

Cohen, H., R. C. Rosen, and L. Goldstein. "Electroencephalo-

graphic Laterality Changes During Human Sexual Orgasm."
    Archives of Sexual Behavior 5 (1976):189-99.

Cole, T. M., and S. C. Cole. "The Handicapped and Sexual
    Health." In A. Comfort (ed.). *Sexual Consequences of Dis-
    ability*. Philadelphia: George F. Stickley Co., 1978.

Colman, C. *Love and Money*. New York: Coward-McCann, Inc.,
    1983.

Comfort, A. (ed.). *Sexual Consequences of Disability*. Philadel-
    phia: George F. Stickley Co., 1978.

Consumer Reports, "AIDS: Deadly but hard to catch." 51
    (1986):724-48.

Crook, W. *Tracking Down Hidden Food Allergy*. Jackson, Tenn.:
    Professional Books, 1980.

Dalton K. "Cyclical Criminal Acts in Premenstrual Syndrome."
    Lancet 2 (1980) 70-71.

———. *The Premenstrual Syndrome*. Springfield, Ill.: Thomas,
    1964.

Daly, M., and M. Wilson. *Sex, Evolution, and Behavior*, 2nd edi-
    tion. Boston: Willard Grant Press, 1983.

DeAngelis, T. "What's it all mean? We never stop asking." *Amer-
    ican Psychological Association Monitor* 11 (1986):20.

de la Pena, A. M. *The Psychobiology of Cancer*. South Hadley,
    Mass.: J. Bergin, Publishers, 1983.

DeLongis, A., J. C. Coyne, G. Dakof, S. Folkman, and R. S.
    Lazarus. "Relationship of daily hassles, uplifts, and major
    life events to health status." *Health Psychology* 1 (1982):119-
    36.

Derogatis, L. R., M. D. Abaeloff, and C. D. McBeth. "Cancer
    Patients and their physicians in the perception of psychologi-
    cal symptoms." *Psychosomatics* 17 (1976):197-201.

De Vries, G. J., J. P. C. DeBruin, H. B. M. Uylings, and M. A.
    Corner, (eds.). *Sex Differences in the Brain*. New York: El-
    sevier, 1984.

Dlin, B. M., A. Perlman, and E. Ringold. "Psychosexual response
    to ileostomy and colostomy." *American Journal of Psychiatry*
    126 (1969):374-81.

Dossey, L. *Beyond Illness: Discovering the Experience of Health*.
    Boulder and London: Shambhala, 1984.

———. *Space, Time and Medicine*. Boulder and London: Shamb-
    hala, 1982.

Ellis, A. *Reason and Emotion in Psychotherapy*. New York: Lyle
    Stuart, 1970.

———. *Sex Without Guilt*. New York: Lyle Stuart, 1958.

———, and R. A. Harper. *A New Guide to Rational Living*. North Hollywood, Cal.: Wilshire Book Co., 1975.

Ellis, H. *Studies in the Psychology of Sex*. 2 vols. New York: Random House, 1942.

Erikson, E. H. *Childhood and Society*. New York: W. W. Norton, 1953

Farrell, W. *Why Men Are How They Are*. New York: McGraw-Hill, 1986.

Ferguson, M. *The Aquarian Conspiracy*. Los Angeles: J. P. Tarcher, Houghton Mifflin, 1980.

Fine, R. *The Meaning of Love in Human Experience*. New York: John Wiley & Sons, 1985.

Fisher, S. *The Female Orgasm*. New York: Basic Books, 1973.

Ford, C. S., and F. A. Beach. *Patterns of Sexual Behavior*. New York: Harper & Row, 1951.

Fosdick, W. M., J. L. Parson, and D. F. Hill. "Preliminary report: Long-term cyclophosphamide therapy in rheumatoid arthritis." *Arthritis and Rheumatism* 11 (1968):151-61.

Fox, C. A. "Recent studies in human coital physiology." *Clinics in Endrocrinology and Metabolism* 2 (1973):527-44.

———, and B. Fox. "Blood pressure and respiratory patterns during human coitus." *Journal of Reproduction and Fertility* 19 (1969):405-15.

Francoeur, R. T. *Becoming a Sexual Person*. New York: John Wiley & Sons, 1982.

Frank, D., R. L. Dornbush, S. K. Webster, and R. C. Kolodny. "Mastectomy and sexual behavior: a pilot study." *Sexuality and Disability* 1 (1978):16-26.

Freud, S. *The Standard Edition of the Complete Psychological Works of Sigmund Freud*. (24 vols.) London: Hogarth Press and the Institute of Psychoanalysis, 1953-1974.

Fuller, R. B. *Critical Path*. New York: St. Martin's Press, 1981.

Gardner, K. *A Rainbow Path: An Album of Healing Music*. Ladyslipper Records. Ladyslipper Inc., Durham, N.C. 27705.

Gilligan, C. *In a Different Voice*. Cambridge, Mass.: Harvard University Press, 1982.

Gordon, S., and R. W. Libby (eds.). *Sexuality Today and Tomorrow*. Belmont, Cal.: Wadsworth Publishers, 1980.

Gorski, R. A. "Sexual differentiation of the brain: possible mechanisms and implications." *Canadian Journal of Physiology and Pharmacology* 63 (1985):577-594.

———. "Sexual Dimorphisms of the Brain." *Journal of Animal Science* 6 (1985):38-61.

Gould, R. L. "The phases of adult life: a study in developmental psychology." *American Journal of Psychiatry* 129 (1972):521-31.

——. *Transformation: Growth and Change in Adult Life*. New York: Simon & Schuster, 1978.

Graber, B. (ed.). *Circumvaginal Musculature and Sexual Function*. Basel, Munchen, Paris, and London: Karger, 1982.

Green, A. W. "Sexual activity and the postmyocardial infarction patient." *American Heart Journal* 89 (1975):246-52.

Gross, M. *The Psychological Society*. New York: Random House, 1978.

Groth, A. N. *Men Who Rape*. New York: Plenum Press, 1979.

Haeberle, E. J. *The Sex Atlas: A New Illustrated Guide*. New York: Seabury Press, 1978.

Halsell, G. *Los Viejos—Secrets of Long Life from the Sacred Valley*. Emmaus, Pa.: Rodale Press, 1976.

Heiman, J. "Female sexual response patterns." *Archives of General Psychiatry* 37 (1980):1311-16.

——. "A psychophysiological exploration of sexual arousal patterns in females and males." *Psychophysiology* 14 (1977):266-74.

——. "The physiology of erotica." *Psychology Today* 9 (1975):91-94.

Hellerstein, H. K., and E. H. Friedman. "Sexual activity and the postcoronary patient." *Archives of Internal Medicine* 125 (1970):987-99.

Herrigan, J., and J. Herrigan. *Loving Free*. New York: Grosset & Dunlap, 1973.

Hite, S. *The Hite Report*. New York: Macmillan, 1976.

——. *The Hite Report on Male Sexuality*. New York: Alfred Knopf, 1981.

Hitschmann, E. "Freud's conception of love." *International Journal of Psychoanalysis* 33 (1952):421-28.

Hooker, E. *Final Report of the Task Force on Homosexuality*. Bethesda, Md.: National Institutes of Mental Health (NIMH), 1969.

Hunt, M. "Sexual behavior in the 1970s." *Playboy*, Oct., Nov., Dec. 1973.

——. *Sexual Behavior in the 1970s*. Chicago: Playboy Press, 1974.

Hyde, J. S. *Understanding Human Sexuality*. New York: McGraw-Hill, 1979.

——, and B. A. Rosenberg. *Half the Human Experience*. Lexington, Mass.: D. C. Heath, 1976.

Jacobson, N. S., and G. Margolin. *Marital Therapy: Strategies Based on Social Learning and Behavior Exchange Principles*. New York: Bruner/Mazel, 1979.

Janson, W. J. *Sexual Pleasure Sharing*. Jaffrey, N. H.: Human Development Publication, 1983.

Jung, C. *Collected Works*. In Read, H., M. Fordham, and G. Adler (eds.). New York: Bollingen Series/Pantheon Books, 1953.

——. *Man and His Symbols* Garden City, N.Y.: Doubleday & Company, 1964.

——. "Psychological Types." In *Collected Works*, vol. 6. Princeton: Princeton University Press, 1921.

——. *The Undiscovered Self*. New York: Mentor, 1958.

Kanner, A. D., J. C. Cloyne, C. Schaffer, and R. S. Lazarus. "Comparison of two modes of stress measurement: Daily hassles and uplifts vs. major life events." *Journal of Behavioral Medicine* 4 (1971):1-39.

Kaplan, H. S. *Disorders of Sexual Desire*. New York: Bruner/Mazel, 1979.

——. *The Illustrated Manual of Sex Therapy*. New York: Quadrangle/New York Times, 1975.

——. *The New Sex Therapy*. New York: Bruner/Mazel, 1974.

——, C. T. Sager, and R. C. Schiavi. "Editor's Reply" (and follow-up to) "AIDS and the Sex Therapist." *Journal of Sex and Marital Therapy* 12 (1986):163-64.

Kerckoff, A. C., and K. E. Davis. "Value consensus and need complementarity in mate selection." *American Sociological Review* 27 (1962):295-303.

Kinsey, A. C., W. B. Pomeroy, and C. E. Martin. *Sexual Behavior in the Human Male*. Philadelphia: Saunders, 1948.

——, W. B. Pomeroy, C. E. Martin, and Ph. H. Gebhard. *Sexual Behavior in the Human Female*. Philadelphia: Saunders, 1953.

Klein, R. F., A. Dean, L. M. Willson, and M. D. Bogdonoff. "The physician and postmyocardial infarction invalidism." *Journal of the American Medical Association* 194 (1965):123-28.

Knox, D., and K. L. Wilson. "Dating behaviors of university student." *Family Relations* 30 (1981):255-58.

Kobasa, S. C., R. R. Hilker, and S. R. Maddi. "Health and stress." *Journal of Occupational Medicine* 21 (1979):595-98.

Kolodny, R. C. "Sexual dysfunction in diabetic females." *Diabetes 20* (1971):557-59.

——, C. B. Kahn, H. H. Goldstein, and D. M. Barnett. "Sexual dysfunction in diabetic men." *Diabetes* 23 (1974):306-9.

———, W. H. Masters, and V. E. Johnson. _Textbook of Sexual Medicine_. Boston: Little, Brown, 1979.

Kramer, H., and J. Sprenger. _The Malleus Maleficarum_. Translated by Rev. Montague Summer. London: Pushkin Press, 1928. Original writing, 1486.

Krueger, A. P., and D. S. Sobel. "Air ions and health." In D. Sobel (ed.), _Ways of Health_. New York and London: Harcourt Brace Jovanovich, 1979.

Leiber, L., M. M. Plumb, M. L. Gerstenzang, and J. Holland. "The communication of affection between cancer patients and their spouses." _Psychosomatic Medicine_ 38 (1976):379-89.

Leiblum, S. R., and L. A. Pervin. _Principles and Practice of Sex Therapy_. New York: The Guilford Press, 1980.

Lemere, F., and J. W. Smith. "Alcohol-induced sexual impotence." _American Journal of Psychiatry_ 130 (1973):212-13.

Leonard, G. B. _The Transformation: A Guide to the Inevitable Changes in Humankind_. New York: Delacorte, 1972.

LeShan, L., and H. Margenau. _Einstein's Space and Van Gogh's Sky_. New York: Macmillan, 1982.

Levinson, D. J. "The mid-life transition: a period in adult psychosocial development." _Psychiatry_ 40 (1977):21-27.

———, D. Darrow, B. E. Klein, M. H. Levinson, and B. McKee. _The Seasons of a Man's Life_. New York: Alfred Knopf, 1978.

Levy, J. "Research on T- suppressor cells and AIDS" in press. _Science_, 1986.

Libby, R. W. "Social scripts for sexual relationships" in S. Gordon and R. W. Libby (eds.), _Sexuality Today and Tomorrow_. North Scituate, Mass.: Duxbury Press, 1976.

———, and R. N. Whitehurst (eds.), _Marriage and Alternatives: Exploring Intimate Relationships_. Glenview, Ill.: Scott, Foresman, 1977.

Lief, H. "Sexual concerns of mastectomy patients." _Medical Aspects of Human Sexuality_ 12 (1978):17.

———. Letter in response to "AIDS and the sex therapist." _Journal of Sex Therapy_ 12 (1986):159-61.

——— (ed.). _Sexual Problems in Medical Practice_. Monroe, Wis.: American Medical Association, 1981.

Lobell, J., and M. Lobell. _John and Mimi: A Free Marriage_. New York: St. Martin's, 1972.

Locke, S. _The Healer Within_. New York: E. P. Dutton, 1986.

LoPiccolo, J. "Direct treatment of sexual dysfunction in the couple." In J. Money and H. Musaph (eds.), _Handbook of Sexology_. Amsterdam: Elsevier/North Holland, 1977.

Lorenz, K. *King Solomon's Ring*. New York: New American Library, 1952.

——. *The Foundations of Ethology*. New York: Simon & Schuster, 1981.

——. *On Aggression*. New York: Harcourt, 1963.

Luthman, S. G. *Intimacy: The Essence of Male and Female*. Los Angeles: Nash, 1972.

Maccoby, E. E., and C. N. Jacklin. *Psychology of Sex Differences*. Stanford, Cal.: Stanford University Press, 1974.

McWhirter, N. "Sexual extremes are out; but adult eroticism is in." *The Detroit Free Press*, Monday, November 17, 1986, p. 1D.

Maslow, A. H. *The Further Reaches of Human Nature*. New York: Viking, 1971.

——. *Motivation and Personality*, 2nd edition. New York: Harper & Row, 1970.

——. *Toward a Psychology of Being*. New York: Van Nostrand Reinhold, 1968.

——. *Homosexuality in Perspective*. Boston: Little, Brown, 1979.

——. *Human Sexual Inadequacy*. Boston: Little, Brown, 1970.

Masters, W., and V. Johnson. *Human Sexual Response*. Boston: Little, Brown, 1966.

——. *On Sex and Human Loving*. Boston: Little, Brown, 1986.

——. *The Pleasure Bond*. New York: Bantam Books, 1976.

——, and R. C. Kolodny. *Human Sexuality*. Boston: Little, Brown, 1982.

May R. "Mood shifts and the menstrual cycle." *Journal of Psychosomatic Research* 20 (1976):125-30.

Money, J. *The Destroying Angel*. Buffalo, N.Y.: Prometheus Books, 1985.

——. *Love and Love Sickness*. Baltimore and London: Johns Hopkins University Press, 1980.

——. *Lovemaps*. New York: Irvinton Publishers, 1986.

——. *Venuses Penuses*. Buffalo, N. Y.: Prometheus Books, 1986.

——, and H. Muspah. *Handbook of Sexology*, vols. I-V. New York: Oxford University Press, 1978.

Mooney, T. O., T. M. Cole, and R. A. Chilgren. *Sexual Options for Paraplegics and Quadriplegics*. Boston: Little, Brown, 1975.

Montagu, A. *Learning Non-Agression*. New York: Oxford University Press, 1978.

——. *Touching*. New York: Columbia University Press, 1979.

Morris, D. *Intimate Behavior*. New York: Bantam, 1973.

———. *Loneliness*. Englewood Cliffs, N. J.: Prentice-Hall, 1961.

———. *Man Watching: A Field Guide to Human Behavior*. New York: Harry Abrams, 1977.

Murstein, B. *Exploring Intimate Lifestyles: Love, Sex, and Marriage Through the Ages*. New York: Springer, 1978.

———. *Love, Sex, and Marriage Through the Ages*. New York: Springer, 1974.

———. "Mate selection in the 1970s." *Journal of Marriage and the Family* 42 (1980):777-92.

———. "Stimulus-value-role: A theory of marital choice." *Journal of Marriage and the Family* 32 (1970):465-81.

———. *Who Will Marry Whom? Theories and Research in Marital Choice*. New York: Springer, 1976.

———, M. Cerreto, and M. G. MacDonald. "A theory and investigation of the effect of exchange-orientation on marriage and friendship." *Journal of Marriage and the Family* 39 (1977):543-48.

Ott, J. N. *Health and Light*. New York: Pocket Books, 1976.

Pearsall, F. P. "Roles for the physician in the prevention and treatment of sexual problems." *Michigan Journal of Osteopathic Medicine* 45 (1980):19-26.

———. "Sexual wellness and cell disease: counseling for the maintenance of intimacy." *Proceedings of the Fourth National Conference on Cancer Nursing—1983*. New York: American Cancer Society, Inc., 1983.

———. *Superimmunity: Mastering Your Emotions/Improving Your Health*. New York: McGraw-Hill, 1987.

Peck. S. *The Road Less Traveled*. New York: Simon & Schuster, 1978.

Pelletier, K. *Holistic Medicine: From Stress to Optimum Health*. New York: Delacorte Press/Seymour Lawrence, 1979.

———. *Longevity: Fulfilling Our Biological Potential*. New York: Delacorte Press/Seymour Lawrence, 1981.

Perper, T., and S. V. Fox. *Flirting Behavior in Public Settings*. A final report to the Harry Frank Guggenheim Foundation, 1981.

———, and N. Rosenzweig. *Sex Education for the Health Professional: A Curriculum Guide*. New York: Grune & Stratton, 1978.

Perksy, H. "Plasma testosterone level and sexual behavior of couples." *Archives of Sexual Behavior* 7 (1978):157-73.

———. "Reproductive hormones, moods, and the menstrual cycle." In R. C. Friedman, R. M. Richar, and R. L. Vande

Weiele (eds.), *Sex Difference in Behavior*. New York: John Wiley & Sons, 1974.

——, H. I. Lief, C. P. O'Brien, D. Strauss, and W. Miller. "Reproductive hormone levels and sexual behavior of young couples." In R. Gemme and C. C. Sheeler (eds.), *Progress in Sexology: Selected Papers from the Proceedings of the 1976 International Congress of Sexology*. New York: Plenum, 1977.

Phillips, J. L. *Piaget's Theory: A Primer*. San Francisco: W. H. Freeman, 1981.

Prescott, J. W. "Body pleasure and the origins of violence." *The Futurist* 9 (1975):64-74.

——, and D. Wallace. *The Role of Pain and Pleasure in the Development of Destructive Behaviors: A Psychometric Study of Parenting, Sexuality, Substance Abuse, and Criminality*. Colloquium on the correlates of crime and the determinants of criminal behavior. The National Institute of Law Enforcement and Criminal Justice, 1978.

Puksta, N. S. "All about sex after a coronary." *American Journal of Nursing* 77 (1977):602-5.

Reinisch, J. M. "Fetal hormones, the brain, and human sex differences: A heuristic, integrative review of the recent literature." *Archives of Sexual Behavior* 3 (1974):51-90.

——. "Prenatal exposure to synthetic progestins increases potential for aggression in humans." *Science* 211 (1981):1171-73.

——, and W. G. Karaow. "Prenatal exposure to synthetic progestins, and estrogen: effect on human behavioral development." *Archives of Sexual Behavior* 6 (1977):257-88.

Reiss, I. L. "The sexual renaissance: A summary and analysis." *Journal of Social Issues* 22 (1966):123-37.

——. "Toward a sociology of the heterosexual love relationship." *Marriage and Family Living* 22 (1960):139-45.

Restak, R. *The Brain: The Last Frontier*. Toronto and New York: Bantam, 1984.

Richards, M. C. *Centering in Pottery, Poetry, and the Person*. Middletown, Conn.: Wesleyan University Press, 1964.

Roberts, E. *Childhood Sexual Learning: The Unwritten Curriculum*. Cambridge, Mass.: Ballinger Publishing Company, 1980.

Robinson, P. *The Modernization of Sex*. New York: Harper Colophon Books, 1976.

Rosenzweig, N., and P. Pearsall (eds.), *Sex Education for the Health Professional: A Curriculum Guide*. New York: Grune & Stratton, 1978.

Rosenzweig, S. "Human sexual autonomony as an evolutionary

attainment, anticipating proceptive sex choice and idiodynamic bisexuality." In J. Zubin and J. Money (eds.), *Contemporary Sexual Behavior: Critical Issues in the 1970s*. Baltimore: Johns Hopkins University Press, 1973.

Rotter, J. B. "Generalized expectancies for internal versus external control of reinforcement." *Psychological Monographs* 81 (1966):36-47.

Rubin, A., and D. Babbott. "Impotence and diabetes mellitus." *Journal of the American Medical Association* 168 (1958):498-500.

Rubin, Z. *Liking and Loving: An Invitation to Social Psychology*. New York: Holt, Rinehart and Winston, 1973.

———. "The love research." *Human Behavior*. Feb. 1977, 27-30.

———. "Measurement of romantic love." *Journal of Personality and Social Psychology* 16 (1970): 265-273.

Sarrel, L. J., and P. M. Sarrel. *Sexual Unfolding: Sexual Development and Sex Therapists in Late Adolescence*. Boston: Little, Brown, 1979.

Schwartz, G. "Behavioral medicine and systems theory: a new synthesis." *National forum*. Winter 1980, 25-30.

———. "Psychobiology of health: a new synthesis." *Master Lecture Series; Psychology and Health*. Washington, D. C.: American Psychology Association (1983):149-93.

Shapiro, J., and D. H. Shapiro. "Well-being and relationship." In R. Walsh and D. H. Shapiro (eds.), *Beyond Health and Normality: Explorations of Exceptional Psychological Well Being*. New York: Van Nostrand Reinhold Company, 1983.

Sherfey, M. J. *The Nature and Evolution of Female Sexuality*. New York: Random House, 1966.

Sherman, A. *The Rape of the APE: The Official History of the Sex Revolution 1945-1973*. Chicago: Playboy Press, 1973.

Sigusch, V., G. Schmidt, A. Reinfeld, and I. Wiedemann-Sutor. "Psychosexual stimulation: sex differences." *Journal of Sex Research* 6 (1970):10-24.

Singer, J., and I. Singer. "Types of female orgasm." *Journal of Sex Research* 8 (1972):255-67.

Stahlgren, L. H., and L. K. Fergusson. "Influence on sexual function of abdominoperineal resection for ulcerative colitis." *New England Journal of Medicine* 259 (1958):873-75.

Stein, R. A. "The effect of exercise training on heart rate during coitus in the postmyocardial infarction patient." *Circulation* 55 (1977):738-40.

Steinbock, E. A., and A. M. Zeiss. "Sexual counseling for cerebral palsied adults: Case report and further suggestions." *Archives of Sexual Behavior* 6 (1977):77-83.

Stuart, R. *Helping Couples Change*. New York: The Guilford Press, 1980.

Symons, D. *The Evolution of Human Sexuality*. New York: Oxford University Press, 1979.

Talese, G. *Thy Neighbor's Wife*. New York: Doubleday & Company, 1980.

Targ, R., and K. Harary. *The Mind Race: Understanding and Using Psychic Abilities*. New York: Ballantine Books, 1984.

Tavris, C., and C. Wade. *The Longest War*. Chicago: Harcourt Brace, 1984.

Tennov, D. *Love and Limerence—The Experience of Being in Love*. New York: Stein & Day, 1979.

Trivers, R. *Social Evolution*. Menlo Park, Cal.: Benjamin/ Cummings, 1985.

Turkington, C. "Political 'pseudo-science' defines sexual pathology." Washington, D.C.: *American Psychological Association Monitor*, 1986, p. 18.

Tuttle, W. B., W. L. Cook, and E. Fitch, "Sexual behavior in postmyocardial infarction patients." *American Journal of Cardiology* 13 (1964):140-53.

Van Keep, P. A., R. B. Greenblatt, and M. Albeaux-Fernet. *Concensus on Menopause Research*. Baltimore: University Park Press, 1976.

Vermeulen, A., R. Ruben, and L. Verdonck. "Testosterone secretion and metabolism in male senescence." *Journal of Clinical Endocrinology and Metabolism* 34 (1972):730-35.

Vickery, D. M., and J. F. Fries. *Take Care of Yourself: A Consumer's Guide to Medical Care*. Reading, Mass.: Addison-Wesley Publishing Company, 1981.

von Bertalanffy, L. *General Systems Theory*. New York: Braziller, 1968.

Watkins, S. M., and J. P. Griffin. "High incidence of vincristine-induced neuropathy in lymphomas." *British Medical Journal* 1 (1978):610-12.

Whipple, B., F. Addiego, E. Belzer, J. Comolli, W. Moger, and J. Perry. "Female 'ejaculation.' " *Medical Aspects of Human Sexuality* 14 (1980):99.

——, and J. D. Perry. "Pelvic muscle strength of female ejaculators: evidence in support of a new theory of orgasm." *Journal of Sex Research* 17 (1981):22-39.

——, and J. D. Perry. "Vaginal myography, and multiple components of female orgasm." In B. Graber (ed.), *The Circum-vaginal Musculature and Sexual Function*. Philadelphia: Saunders, 1982.

——, and J. D. Perry. "The varieties of female orgasm and female ejaculation." *The SIECUS Report*, May 1981.

Wilson, E. O. *Sociobiology: A New Synthesis*, abridged edition. Cambridge, Mass.: Belknap Press, 1980.

Wolfe, L. "Sexual profile of that Cosmopolitan girl." *Cosmoplitan* 189 (1980):254-57.

Zilbergeld, B. *Male Sexuality*. New York: Bantam Books, 1968.

——. *The Shrinking of America: Myths of Psychological Change*. Boston and Toronto: Little, Brown, 1983.

Index

All Futura Books are available at your bookshop or newsagent, or can be ordered from the following address:
Futura Books, Cash Sales Department,
P.O. Box 11, Falmouth, Cornwall TR10 9EN.

Please send cheque or postal order (no currency), and allow 60p for postage and packing for the first book plus 25p for the second book and 15p for each additional book ordered up to a maximum charge of £1.90 in U.K.

B.F.P.O. customers please allow 60p for the first book, 25p for the second book plus 15p per copy for the next 7 books, thereafter 9p per book.

Overseas customers including Eire please allow £1.25 for postage and packing for the first book, 75p for the second book and 28p for each subsequent title ordered.